ReFocus: The Films of Paul Schrader

ReFocus: The American Directors Series

Series Editors: Robert Singer, Frances Smith, and Gary D. Rhodes

Editorial Board: Kelly Basilio, Donna Campbell, Claire Perkins, Christopher Sharrett, and Yannis Tzioumakis

ReFocus is a series of contemporary methodological and theoretical approaches to the interdisciplinary analyses and interpretations of neglected American directors, from the once-famous to the ignored, in direct relationship to American culture—its myths, values, and historical precepts. The series ignores no director who created a historical space—either in or out of the studio system—beginning from the origins of American cinema and up to the present. These directors produced film titles that appear in university film history and genre courses across international boundaries, and their work is often seen on television or available to download or purchase, but each suffers from a form of "canon envy"; directors such as these, among other important figures in the general history of American cinema, are underrepresented in the critical dialogue, yet each has created American narratives, works of film art, that warrant attention. *ReFocus* brings these American film directors to a new audience of scholars and general readers of both American and Film Studies.

Titles in the series include:

ReFocus: The Films of Preston Sturges
Edited by Jeff Jaeckle and Sarah Kozloff

ReFocus: The Films of Delmer Daves
Edited by Matthew Carter and Andrew Nelson

ReFocus: The Films of Amy Heckerling
Edited by Frances Smith and Timothy Shary

ReFocus: The Films of Budd Boetticher
Edited by Gary D. Rhodes and Robert Singer

ReFocus: The Films of Kelly Reichardt
E. Dawn Hall

ReFocus: The Films of William Castle
Edited by Murray Leeder

ReFocus: The Films of Barbara Kopple
Edited by Jeff Jaeckle and Susan Ryan

ReFocus: The Films of Elaine May
Edited by Alexandra Heller-Nicholas and Dean Brandum

ReFocus: The Films of Spike Jonze
Edited by Kim Wilkins and Wyatt Moss-Wellington

ReFocus: The Films of Paul Schrader
Edited by Michelle E. Moore and Brian Brems

edinburghuniversitypress.com/series/refoc

ReFocus:
The Films of Paul Schrader

Edited by Michelle E. Moore and
Brian Brems

EDINBURGH
University Press

Edinburgh University Press is one of the leading university presses in the UK. We publish academic books and journals in our selected subject areas across the humanities and social sciences, combining cutting-edge scholarship with high editorial and production values to produce academic works of lasting importance. For more information visit our website: edinburghuniversitypress.com

© editorial matter and organization Michelle E. Moore and Brian Brems, 2020
© the chapters their several authors, 2020

Edinburgh University Press Ltd
The Tun—Holyrood Road
12 (2f) Jackson's Entry
Edinburgh EH8 8PJ

Typeset in 11/13 Ehrhardt MT by
IDSUK (DataConnection) Ltd

A CIP record for this book is available from the British Library

ISBN 978 1 4744 6203 7 (hardback)
ISBN 978 1 4744 6205 1 (webready PDF)
ISBN 978 1 4744 6206 8 (epub)

The right of the contributors to be identified as authors of this work has been asserted in accordance with the Copyright, Designs and Patents Act 1988 and the Copyright and Related Rights Regulations 2003 (SI No. 2498).

Contents

List of Figures	vii
Acknowledgments	ix
Notes on Contributors	x
Introduction: *Taxi Driver* Forward Brian Brems and Michelle E. Moore	1

Part I: Ideas, Influences, and Intellect

1. Schrader and Style — 17
   Erik M. Bachman
2. Movement and Meaning: The "Unmotivated" Camera in Four Films by Paul Schrader — 33
   Deborah Allison
3. Late Schrader: From the Canon to the Canyons — 51
   Billy Stevenson

Part II: Instincts, Investigation, and Innovation

4. "Thinking White": Performing Racial Tension in *Blue Collar* — 71
   Scott Balcerzak
5. Prophets and Zealots: Paul Schrader's Adaptations of *The Mosquito Coast* and *The Last Temptation of Christ* — 87
   Erica Moulton
6. "So I Found Another Form of Expression": Art and Life/Art in Life in Paul Schrader's *Mishima: A Life in Four Chapters* — 105
   Thomas Prasch
7. Schrader's Women: *Cat People* and *Patty Hearst* — 122
   Brian Brems

8   Paul Schrader's Experiment in Italian Neo-decadence:
    The Comfort of Strangers and the Sadean System   139
    Robert Dassanowsky
9   "Just Being Transparent Baby": Surveillance Culture, Digitization,
    and Self-regulation in Paul Schrader's *The Canyons*   155
    James Slaymaker
10 "Every Act of Preservation is an Act of Creation": Paul Schrader's
    Eco-theology in *First Reformed*   171
    Tatiana Prorokova
11 Leaning on the Everlasting Arms: Love and Silence
    in *First Reformed*   189
    Robert Ribera

Part III: Interview
12 Interview with Paul Schrader conducted by Michelle E. Moore
    and Brian Brems on 9/27/2018 at the Rail Line Diner, NYC   209

Filmography   231
Criticism and Selected Interviews   233
Bibliography   236
Index   248

Figures

1.1	Final shot of *Light Sleeper*	29
1.2	Final shot of *First Reformed*	30
2.1	*American Gigolo*: in the record store	37
2.2	*The Comfort of Strangers*: in Robert's bar	41
3.1	The decline and desuetude of cinematic infrastructure	57
3.2	The post-cinematic space of Westfield Century City	59
4.1	Richard Pryor and Harvey Keitel in *Blue Collar*	71
4.2	Harvey Keitel and Richard Pryor in *Blue Collar*	84
5.1	Jesus shows his bloody heart in *The Last Temptation of Christ*	94
5.2	Allie Fox holds out a bloody finger to his son in *The Mosquito Coast*	97
6.1	Scene from the Kyoko's House segment	112
6.2	Mishima's *seppuku* (ritual suicide)	115
7.1	At the conclusion of *Cat People*, Schrader restages the end of Bresson's *Pickpocket*	133
7.2	Schrader's *Patty Hearst* also ends with a gloss on *Pickpocket*	136
8.1	*The Comfort of Strangers*: Robert entertains a lost Colin and Mary at his bar	142
8.2	*The Comfort of Strangers*: Colin and Mary enter Caroline's timeless world	148
9.1	*The Canyons*: Christian is obscured behind a pane of glass in his Malibu mansion	160
9.2	*The Canyons*: Christian and Tara enclosed in their prison-like living space	164
10.1	*First Reformed*: at Michael's funeral, the viewer is forced to face the death of the environment	177

10.2	*First Reformed*: the mass grave: Michael's ashes are scattered over nature's grave	178
11.1	*First Reformed*: Reverend Toller's bedside reading: the mystical theologians as well as Schrader's own childhood bible	194
11.2	*First Reformed*: "this journal is a form of speaking . . ."	195
12.1	Interview with Paul Schrader	210
12.2	Interview with Paul Schrader	213

Acknowledgments

We would first like to thank the series editors, Gary D. Rhodes, Robert Singer, and Frances Smith, for their unflagging enthusiasm for this book and "all things Schrader." Their comments, editing, and advice provided insights that made this book much stronger. We would also like to thank Gillian Leslie at Edinburgh University Press for her support with this project, as well as our Dean, Sandra Martins, who approved financial support at a pivotal moment.

We would also like to express our appreciation for the contributors to this volume. Each produced insightful and important work that went far beyond what we had imagined for the volume and did so while meeting tight deadlines.

We would also like to thank our partners, Genna Brems and Mark Weissburg, who are always supportive, encouraging, and enthusiastic.

Finally, we would like to express our gratitude to Paul Schrader, without whom this volume would not exist. His films have provided the source for a lifetime of curiosity about filmmaking techniques, screenwriting, and film criticism for film students, scholars, and us. His career is unparalleled as the blueprint for making one's own art and being true to a vision over a lifetime. He is the consummate auteur, the director's director, and an expert screenwriter and film critic. He was kind and generous during our interview with him, and we are forever grateful for his time and insights that afternoon.

Notes on Contributors

Deborah Allison is based in the UK where she is a senior programmer for Picturehouse Cinemas and an associate research fellow at De Montfort University's Cinema and Television History Research Institute. She is the author of *The Cinema of Michael Winterbottom* (2013) and co-author of *The Phoenix Picturehouse: 100 Years of Oxford Cinema Memories* (2013). She also edited the short anthology *The Enchanted Screen* (2017) to accompany an award-winning cinema season of fairy-tale films for which she was lead curator. Her writings appear in more than twenty books and journals, including *Film International, Quarterly Review of Film and Video, Senses of Cinema, Screen,* and *The Schirmer Encyclopedia of Film*. She recently contributed the lead article "On the Other Side of the Mirror" and a career profile of Paul Schrader to the DVD/Blu-ray booklet for *The Comfort of Strangers* (2018).

Erik M. Bachman is a lecturer in the Department of Literature and Porter College at the University of California at Santa Cruz. He is the author of *Literary Obscenities: U.S. Case Law and Naturalism after Modernism* (2018) and series co-editor of the *Lukács Library*, for which he has translated both volumes of *The Specificity of the Aesthetic* (Brill Publishers, forthcoming).

Scott Balcerzak is Associate Professor of film and media in the Department of English at Northern Illinois University. He is the author of *Buffoon Men: Classic Hollywood Comedians and Queered Masculinity* (2013) and *Beyond Method: Stella Adler and the Male Actor* (2018). He has also written about film and performance for such publications as *The Quarterly Review of Film and Video, The Journal of Film and Video,* and *Camera Obscura*.

Brian Brems is Associate Professor of English at the College of DuPage. His academic work has focused on genre, with pieces on horror and westerns appearing in book-length edited collections. This collection is his first as editor. In addition, he publishes regularly in online film magazines and websites, including *Bright Wall/Dark Room*, *Vague Visages*, and *Film Inquiry*. He has also contributed to *Film School Rejects*, *Little White Lies*, and *Senses of Cinema*. He teaches film courses in the English department.

Robert Dassanowsky is Professor of German Studies and Visual and Performing Arts, and Director of the Film Studies Program at the University of Colorado, Colorado Springs. He also works as an independent film producer and is a delegate of the European Academy of Sciences and Arts, and a voting member of the European Film Academy (EFA). His books include *Austrian Cinema: A History* (2007), *New Austrian Film* (ed.) (2011), *The Nameable and the Unnameable: Hofmannsthal's 'Der Schwierige' Revisited* (ed.) (2011), *Tarantino's 'Inglorious Basterds': A Manipulation of Metafilm* (ed.) (2012), and *Screening Transcendence: Film under Austrofascism and the Hollywood Hope 1933-1938* (2018).

Michelle E. Moore is Professor of English at the College of DuPage. She is the author of *Chicago and the Making of American Modernism: Cather, Hemingway, Fitzgerald, and Faulkner in Conflict* (2019). Her work also appears in the collection *Rape in Art Cinema*, as well as the journals *Literature/Film Quarterly*, *Faulkner Studies*, and *Cather Studies 9 and 11*.

Erica Moulton is a PhD candidate in Film Studies at the University of Wisconsin–Madison, where she earned an MA in Film Studies. She also holds a Masters in Shakespeare Studies from King's College London, where she wrote a thesis on discourses of intoxication and military service in the *Henriad*. Her research is primarily in the field of screenwriting and adaptation, focusing on the evolution of the Story Department as an institution during Hollywood's studio era. Her article, "Crafting an 'authentic' monster: Dialogue, genre, and ethical questions in *Mindhunter* (2007)," was published by the *Journal of Screenwriting* in July 2019.

Thomas Prasch is Professor and Chair of History at Washburn University. Recent publications include essays on Robin Williams's performance as the genie in Disney's *Aladdin*, Alfred Hitchcock's *The Lodger*, F. W. Murnau's *Faust*, Robert Eggers's *The Witch*, noir-screwball fusions of the mid-1980s, Alfred Russel Wallace's Spiritualism and evolutionary thought, and ethnicities in Henry Mayhew's *London Labour and the London Poor*.

Tatiana Prorokova is a postdoctoral researcher at the Department of English and American Studies, University of Vienna, Austria. She holds a PhD in American Studies from the University of Marburg, Germany. She was a Visiting Researcher at the Forest History Society (2019), an Ebeling Fellow at the American Antiquarian Society (2018), and a Visiting Scholar at the University of South Alabama, USA (2016). She is the author of *Docu-Fictions of War: US Interventionism in Film and Literature* (2019) and a co-editor of *Cultures of War in Graphic Novels: Violence, Trauma, and Memory* (2018).

Robert Ribera is an instructor of Film Studies at Portland State University. He edited the collection, *Martin Scorsese: Interviews, Revised and Updated*. His current projects include a book on Walt Disney's propaganda during the Second World War, and a book of interviews with authors and directors on contemporary film adaptations.

James Slaymaker is a PhD student in Film Studies at the University of Southampton, UK, whose thesis is entitled "No Comment: Jean-Luc Godard and the Digital Audiovisual Essay." He earned an MA in Film Studies from that institution in 2018. Selected publications include: "Cinema Never Dies: Abbas Kiarostami's 24 Frames and The Ontology of the Digital Image," appearing in *Senses of Cinema*; "Modernity, Melancholia and Cultural Heritage in Johnnie To's *Sparrow*," appearing in *Bright Lights Film Journal*; and "To Think With Hands: The Films of Josephine Decker," appearing in *MUBI Notebook*.

Billy Stevenson received his degree from the University of Sydney with a dissertation entitled "The Cinepheur, Post-Cinematic Passage, Post-Perceptual Passage." Selected publications and presentations include: "From Los Angeles to La La Land: Mapping Whiteness in the Wake of Cinema," appearing in *Senses of Cinema*; "The Post-Cinematic Venue: Towards an Infrastructuralist Poetics," in *Post-Cinema: Theorizing 21st Century Film*; and "*Showgirls*, Promiscuity and Post-Cinematic Media," presented at *Showgirls* 1995–2015: A Symposium, September 2015 (University of Sydney). He is currently working on a book that focuses on *Twin Peaks: The Returned* as exemplary post-quality television, along with book chapters on *Crazy Ex-Girlfriend, Showgirls, The Kettering Incident* and the Hallmark Channel.

Introduction: *Taxi Driver* Forward

Brian Brems and Michelle E. Moore

Paul Schrader was late. We called and texted, and when we finally got in touch with him, he apologized, explaining that he was stuck in a car, not moving, on the West Side Highway. All southbound lanes were shut down because there had been a shootout between a fleeing drug dealer and the NYPD and the cops were hunting for the shell casings. When Schrader arrived, we began the interview and asked him what his plans were in the wake of *First Reformed*. He told us: "There was something I was going to do in April that I wrote but that fell apart half an hour ago on the West Side Highway." This was a fitting introduction to the writer of *Taxi Driver*; some latter-day Travis Bickle was holding up traffic and preventing the interview from happening as planned. Bickle is American cinema's quintessential angry young man, sexually frustrated, alienated by a city he despises, fascinated by pornography, and eventually obsessed with guns. As written by Schrader, Travis is a landmine waiting to go off and a template against which the rest of his career would react.

He would continue to explore the themes Travis personified, albeit with a different visual approach than *Taxi Driver*'s director Martin Scorsese, a frequent collaborator. Elsewhere, Schrader seems eager to leave Travis behind altogether, traveling as far afield from his iconic creation as possible. Schrader would remark later in the interview: "Well, you don't have that many stories to tell. I think it was [Jean] Renoir who said, 'Every director has one movie to make, and he just makes it in different ways.' And for me, the defining moment is when I realized I needed to get out of an insular community, one which was not only trying to dictate what you did but also what you thought. And you'll have to do that with a certain amount of propulsion and a certain amount of cruelty. And so when you take that urge and then you mix it with the Christian dogma which is a lot about the dark night of the soul and the need for redemptive blood, and you start mixing those two together, and in an adolescent way, it comes out as *Taxi Driver* and in an old man's way it comes out in *First Reformed*. It's not really that different. Now, clearly, a film that has such a strong signature as those films, you can't do every single time. And so I have made other kinds of films. They are united. I see the linkages."

His fascination with theological themes—a product of his strict Calvinist background that restricted his access to cinema[1]—has long been manifest in his critical work, such as his 1972 book *Transcendental Style in Film: Ozu, Bresson, Dreyer*, which he updated in 2018. Therein, Schrader examines what he calls "Transcendental Style" in the films of Jasujirō Ozu, Robert Bresson, and Carl Theodor Dreyer, exploring their use of formal and thematic elements to craft films inspired by religious art, analyzing the films' narrative and stylistic design schematically.[2] This work of criticism has led a number of scholars to argue for a connection between the "transcendental style" he described in the book and his own cinema.[3] Schrader has resisted this comparison, but nonetheless encouraged them through his work's continued derivations from those filmmakers, but especially Bresson, whose work has provided scaffolding for his own films for many years.

This collection is the first serious treatment of Schrader's own film criticism and analytical writing in addition to later films which respond to the oft-studied *Taxi Driver*. Schrader's work as a critic makes him quite different from other filmmakers—in American cinema circles, he stands virtually alone in this respect, certainly in the modern era. He began as a reviewer, a disciple of the influential Pauline Kael. Early criticism of Sam Peckinpah[4] and Robert Bresson's *Pickpocket* (1959)[5] would linger into his writing and directing work. Schrader's negative review of *Easy Rider* (Hopper, 1969), which he has since regarded with good humor, demonstrates that he has long been both a part of New Hollywood and apart from it.[6] He has been less reliant on Classic Hollywood genres than his contemporaries like De Palma, Scorsese, Bogdanovich, and Spielberg, finding more inspiration in the work of international art cinema, which influenced his criticism and film work. In particular, Schrader's writing on Robert Bresson and other "transcendental" filmmakers provides a basis for understanding many of Schrader's films, as does his 1969 essay "Notes on Film Noir."[7] Schrader's long career writing for sundry publications includes a series of essays on cinematic formal technique for *Film Comment* magazine published in 2015. The essays show how Schrader watches films and may yield insight into how he makes them. Though many other filmmakers are willing to sit for interviews about their processes and decision-making and influences, Schrader is one of the only members of the American cinema community with a foot in both the filmmaking and critical camps.

Schrader's screenwriting career began with *The Yakuza* (Pollack, 1974), inaugurating a long interest in Japanese cinema, but also establishing consistent

Schrader themes, especially vigilante justice. Schrader's true breakout is the screenplay for *Taxi Driver*, which appeared the same year as his ill-fated collaboration with Brian De Palma on *Obsession* (1976), a source of frustration for Schrader that appears to have lingered; creative differences over De Palma's elimination of the screenplay's third act might have colored Schrader's opinions about his one-time collaborator's other work, which he recently voiced on social media.[8] He was also furious over director John Flynn's handling of his screenplay for *Rolling Thunder* (1977), in which a Vietnam veteran seeks vengeance against the criminals who murdered his family.[9] *Old Boyfriends* (1979), for which Schrader provided the screenplay, was directed by Joan Tewkesbury, the writer of Robert Altman's *Thieves Like Us* (1973) and *Nashville* (1975).[10] The screenwriter's contributions have long been minimized in Hollywood cinema—one is reminded of an aggravated producer in the Coen Brothers' Hollywood satire *Barton Fink* (1991) telling the titular scenarist over lunch in a crowded restaurant, "A writer? Throw a rock in here and you'll hit one. And do me a favor, Fink—throw it hard."[11] The auteur theorists successfully reoriented the default assumption about cinema, making it into a director's medium, with the resulting effect that screenwriters, especially those who do not become directors, often remain frustratingly anonymous. Schrader's collaborations with other directors, especially those with strong visual signatures, demonstrate that even a screenwriter of his stature is a second-class citizen. De Palma notoriously excised the third act of Schrader's screenplay for *Obsession*, the pair's reworking of Alfred Hitchcock's *Vertigo* (1957).[12] Similarly, Scorsese and Robert De Niro flew to the island of St. Martin's to rewrite his screenplay for *Raging Bull* (1980), jettisoning a number of Schrader's ideas; the disregard for Schrader's words extends into the finished film's freewheeling improvisations between De Niro and Joe Pesci.[13] Examining what remains of Schrader's work in these films alongside his directorial efforts raises fascinating questions about the complex, ever-shifting understanding of cinematic authorship.

Creative challenges extended into his directorial debut, *Blue Collar* (1978), when his stars, Richard Pryor, Harvey Keitel, and Yaphet Kotto, spent much of the production embroiled in a series of clashes over performance styles and male ego.[14] Despite the challenges behind the scenes, Schrader's debut carried forward *Taxi Driver*'s thematic concerns, focusing on alienated men in desperate conflict with their surroundings, trapped in existential quandaries that threaten to destroy them physically and spiritually. Though he maintained this thematic focus, Schrader fared little better on the set of his next film, *Hardcore* (1979), a reworking of John Ford's *The Searchers* (1956) starring George C. Scott as a Calvinist Michigander drawn from Schrader's own upbringing, searching for his missing daughter among California pornographers. Schrader has often dismissed *Hardcore* as immaturely written and overly colorful in its visual style. Schrader's working relationship with Scott was difficult; in order to coax the recalcitrant Scott out of his trailer to shoot on location, he had to promise that he would never direct again.[15]

He lied. Schrader has said his first visually mature film was 1980's *American Gigolo*, starring Richard Gere as a sex worker wrongly accused of committing a murder. Schrader has consistently shared credit for the film's neon-drenched plasticity with visual consultant Ferdinando Scarfiotti, but the story and characterization are entirely Schrader's, aided by some of the higher-minded literary and cinematic references that always drive his work.[16] Schrader's foundational metaphor—the gigolo who can't experience love—is a contradiction furthered by Schrader's lifting of the ending of Bresson's *Pickpocket* for his own film; in prison, Julian Kay (a gloss on Kafka's Joseph K. in *The Trial*) finally feels the love that has thus far eluded him when he accepts a lover's gesture of good faith and sacrifice. In Schrader's estimation, *American Gigolo* is the film where he became a director, not just a writer directing his own work. Though this perception shows remarkable self-criticism, it also belies the visual invention of *Blue Collar* and *Hardcore*, despite Schrader's dismissals.

Schrader's concern with alienation, personified in Travis Bickle, the auto workers, Jake Van Dorn, and Julian Kay, continued to shape his films ranging from low genre works to high art. He attempted to fuse the two in his remake of Jacques Tourneur's 1942 low-budget horror thriller *Cat People*, produced by Val Lewton's horror unit at RKO Studios; Lewton's films are well known for their effectively crafted moodiness and their B-picture budgets hiding behind shadows and implication. Schrader's remake, freed from the restrictions of the Hollywood Motion Picture Production Code, is about a woman, Irena, who becomes a panther when sexually aroused and must kill in order to become human again. As he did in *Hardcore* and *American Gigolo*, Schrader again explores carnality through the lens of his theological perspective, clashing the erotic journey of his heroine with the existential quandary in which she finds herself. He litters the exploitation-lite film, replete with sexuality and nudity, with references to high art—a bust of Dante's Beatrice adorns a dresser, and the male zookeeper who falls in love with Irena (both the woman and the panther) has a biography of Japanese artist Yukio Mishima on his bedside table. Schrader's kaleidoscopic take on the artist's life would be his next film, *Mishima: A Life in Four Chapters* (1985), one of the most visually adventurous of his career. Spoken entirely in Japanese and expressionistic in design, the film is no conventional biopic; it is a wonder that more filmmakers have not attempted to tackle the lives of notable subjects in such experimental fashion. Todd Haynes's wildly impressionistic Bob Dylan film, *I'm Not There* (2007), comes close in its audacious inventiveness, matching the structural form to its subject's endless predilection for reinvention. In it, Haynes creates "a narrative and cinematic parallel to what Dylan did to popular music in his era."[17] Schrader's film does the same with the artist Mishima.

Schrader continued to work on screenplays for other directors, drawn to projects that speak to his fascination with characters caught in existential despair. His screenplay for Peter Weir's *The Mosquito Coast* (1985) makes use of one of his favorite devices, voiceover narration, to tell the story of a teenage boy (River Phoenix) coming to realize that his father (Harrison Ford) is a narcissistic tyrant, not a hero, as the patriarch takes the family on a quixotic dropout journey to South America, far away from traditional society's materialist trappings. Schrader's parental focus continues into his next film behind the camera, 1987's *Light of Day*, from his own script originally titled "Born in the USA," until intended collaborator Bruce Springsteen lifted it for his 1984 record; as recompense, Springsteen contributed a song, "Light of Day," to Schrader's retitled film, and its lyrics adorn the poster.[18] This Cleveland rock and roll story returns Schrader to autobiographical territory; as the protagonist of *Hardcore* was modeled on his father, the maternal figure of *Light of Day* is based on his mother. Schrader, his typical self-flagellation on display, ranks *Light of Day* alongside *Hardcore* at the bottom of his filmography, perhaps because each project is so close to his own personal life.[19] Schrader would also feature a female protagonist in his 1988 biopic *Patty Hearst*, about the heiress's 1975 kidnapping at the hands of the Symbionese Liberation Army. The visual invention of *Mishima: A Life in Four Chapters* returns throughout *Patty Hearst*; the heiress's time in captivity, represented in the film's first thirty minutes, take place almost entirely inside a theorized, abstract closet. The elliptical editing collapses the heroine's sense of time and continues Schrader's approach to *Mishima*, but for an American subject and in English. This middle portion of Schrader's career shows a desire to expand his repertoire of characters; his protagonists are women, children, and international in origin. Despite these surface differences, Schrader's preoccupations with alienation and spiritual bankruptcy in the face of modernity remain; as they perplexed Travis, they continue to bedevil his creator.

A series of projects beginning in the late 1980s and continuing through the 1990s challenges Schrader's authorship during several high-stakes collaborations, which eventually pave the way for the writer/director to return to more familiar territory. During this period, Schrader oscillates between personal projects generated from his familiar cinematic influences and adaptations of works by other authors both as screenwriter and director. Schrader collaborated with Scorsese once again on 1988's *The Last Temptation of Christ*, the latter's long-gestating passion project which had originally been set to go before the cameras in 1983, but lost financing at the last minute. Though the script was revised by Jay Cocks and Scorsese himself, the film boasts Schrader's fascination with theology.[20] The complicated authorship of 1990's *The Comfort of Strangers*, with Schrader behind the camera as director, and legendary playwright Harold Pinter writing the screenplay, based on Ian McEwan's novel, renders the Venice-set drama a meditation on excess; the four characters, played by Christopher Walken, Helen Mirren, Natasha Richardson, and Rupert Everett, play bizarre games of sexual one-upmanship and power amid the splendor of one of the world's most beautiful cities. Schrader withdraws into more personal territory with *Light Sleeper* (1992), a film that begins his fruitful director-actor collaboration with Willem Dafoe, who played Christ in *Last Temptation* and impressed Schrader greatly.[21] Dafoe's Manhattan drug dealer wanders through middle age as Schrader borrows heavily from Bresson's *Diary of A Country Priest* (1949), giving his protagonist a journal. Once again, he repurposes the ending of *Pickpocket*, as Dafoe's character, incarcerated, finds grace with a woman across the divide between imprisonment and freedom. After directing the deeply strange *Witch Hunt* for HBO in 1994 from a script by Joseph Dougherty, Schrader provided the script for Harold Becker's 1996 drama about corruption in New York, *City Hall*, starring Al Pacino as its fictional mayor. Though Schrader has expressed ambivalence over the changes to his script, the finished film bears his signature in its treatment of the central character, the deputy mayor played by John Cusack.[22] In 1997, Schrader wrote and directed an adaptation of Elmore Leonard's novel *Touch*, coming in the context of a number of big-screen versions of the author's work, including *Get Shorty* (1995, Sonnenfeld), *Jackie Brown* (1997, Tarantino), and *Out of Sight* (1998, Soderbergh). Schrader's Leonard adaptation is about religious hucksters—of course—negotiating their own levels of hypocrisy, a theme that places his take on the crime novelist's work firmly in line with his own cinematic fascinations.

In 1998, Schrader gained critical praise for his adaptation of Russell Banks's novel *Affliction*, about a small-town police officer (Nick Nolte) slowly unravelling as he attempts to solve a possible murder while fighting against the legacy of male violence inherited from his abusive father. The New Hampshire-set film returns to the snowy settings of *Hardcore*; the opening sequences of both films are nearly identical, as Schrader depicts the residents of both masking their pain beneath middle-American stoicism that eventually explodes into fury. A year later, Schrader collaborated once again with Scorsese on 1999's *Bringing Out The Dead*, which echoes *Taxi Driver*. Nicolas Cage plays the De Niro stand-in, a paramedic mitigating his despair with alcohol. The final image of Bickle erratically adjusting the mirror of his cab ominously suggests his cycle of violence is fated to begin again, with no redemption coming; Cage's Frank Pierce earns it in the arms of a woman in the film's closing moments, an image filled with the religious significance that has so captured both Scorsese and Schrader throughout their collaborations. The film's alternately brazen and sensitive return to the emotional minefield of *Taxi Driver* bears the weight of time, as both Schrader and Scorsese, nearly twenty-five years after their landmark pairing, appear to have mellowed out.

In interviews, Schrader has been eager to comment on the changing cinematic landscape since the turn of the century.²³ His transition has not always been easy and has occasionally threatened to exile him into obscurity, but he has remained interested in the same themes, content to explore the overlap among spirituality, sexuality, violence, and self-destructive male behavior. His 1999 melodrama *Forever Mine*, about a man's passionate love for a woman that runs him afoul of a belligerent gangster, was met with shrugs. He received a number of strong notices for 2002's *Auto Focus*, another biopic about *Hogan's Heroes* star Bob Crane (Greg Kinnear), who was murdered in 1978, that continues the filmmaker's fascination with pornography and its impact on male ego. In Schrader's film, Crane's friendship with video technician John Carpenter (Willem Dafoe) explores strange sexual territory that indicates the director's twisted sense of humor. In the director's commentary available on the DVD, he refers to the wide shot of the two men masturbating together on a couch while watching porn as his "Norman Rockwell moment."²⁴ Its hyper-reflexive approach to the cinematic apparatus demonstrates Schrader's burgeoning interest in the intersection between film and technology, a dynamic that would come to define his work in the 2010s, mostly out of financial necessity as budgets shrank and producers recoiled from his uncompromising vision.

Schrader's creative work has occasionally been marked by behind-the-scenes conflict and creative differences with his collaborators, but *Dominion: A Prequel to the Exorcist* (2005) surely has one of the strangest journeys to the screen in Hollywood history. Hired to direct a prequel to *The Exorcist* (Friedkin, 1973) after original director John Frankenheimer died before production could commence, Schrader delivered a philosophical film, like *Cat People* before it, that was light on scares and heavy on theological dilemma for its central character, Father Merrin (Stellan Skarsgard). Warner Brothers, unhappy with Schrader's take on the material, commissioned action director Renny Harlin to reshoot the film from a reworked script, retaining Skarsgard and the setting, but adding sequences more deliberately designed to invoke the famous possession scenes of the original film. It was released, with Harlin's name as director, as *Exorcist: The Beginning* (2004). When it failed financially and critically, the studio gambled and released Schrader's version. Schrader's film is characteristically melancholy and contemplative, making him an unlikely match for the studio's patently crass play for horror audiences. It was Schrader's first and only interaction with Hollywood's newly dominant franchise machine; his vision of genre as a vehicle to express larger ideas rather than deliver on audience expectations was out of step with the shifting cinematic landscape.²⁵

After his foray into big-budget filmmaking resulted in such a high-profile clash with a feckless studio, Schrader went small, returning to safer, more personal ground with *The Walker* (2007), about a gay companion for politicians' wives in Washington, DC. As played by Woody Harrelson, the central character walks in the footsteps of Travis Bickle, Julian Kay, and John LeTour, a superficial man who has lived a superficial life bereft of real emotional connection, now left hauntingly alone.[26] Isolation also drives Schrader's 2008 feature *Adam Resurrected*, starring Jeff Goldblum as a Holocaust survivor who suffered trauma and humiliation at the hands of a brutal Nazi officer (Willem Dafoe). Based on a novel by Yoram Kaniuk, the film is set in an Israeli asylum, where Goldblum's Adam Stein attempts to recover from his shattering experience in the camps.

An extended break from filmmaking followed, with Schrader returning to direct *The Canyons* (2013), from a script by *American Psycho* novelist Bret Easton Ellis and starring Lindsay Lohan, desperately seeking career reinvention after troubles with substance abuse and the law. The film, financed through Kickstarter, became infamous even before its release thanks to a magazine profile that focused on Schrader's increasingly outlandish attempts to get his actress to honor the clause in her contract that required her to appear nude on screen.[27] The much-maligned movie, shot on digital video and co-starring adult film actor James Deen, opens with a montage of dilapidated movie theatres, its director's lament for a bygone era emphasized by his own feelings of drift in a changing cinematic landscape. Schrader would next write and direct the feature *The Dying of The Light* (2014), which, as was the case with his *Exorcist* prequel, similarly ran afoul of the producers who secured the financing. Before the film was released, Schrader, along with the film's stars, Nicolas Cage and the late Anton Yelchin, posted images on social media of themselves wearing t-shirts bearing non-disparagement contract clauses to protest the producers' re-editing of the film without Schrader's permission.[28] Schrader has bucked the system by using DVD capture software to take back as much of the film as he could, re-editing the co-opted footage into a wildly experimental work, titled *Dark*, which he has made available in his archives at the Harry Ransom Center at the University of Texas at Austin and through torrent download.[29] In these two works, he has embraced technology's redefinition of the distribution model more rapidly than a number of filmmakers of his generation.

Schrader likewise attempted to reassert some authorial control over the supremely low-budget crime movie *Dog Eat Dog* (2016), an off-the-wall remix of contemporary gangster movies indebted to the pop-culture mishmash approach of filmmakers like Tarantino and his imitators.[30] The result is a ludicrous pastiche, mixing bawdy humor with outrageous violence, complete with Nicolas Cage's Humphrey Bogart impression. The film presents a welcome opportunity for Schrader to engage in playful reflexivity. *Taxi Driver* made him one of the fathers of the modern crime film; in *Dog Eat Dog*, Schrader turns the camera back on those he influenced by mimicking their anything-goes approach to narrative and stylistic incoherence. After the heavy themes of *The Walker* and *Adam Resurrected*, the critical drubbing earned by *The Canyons*, and the contested authorship of both *Dominion* and

The Dying of The Light, *Dog Eat Dog* finds Schrader throwing caution to the wind and, above all, having fun.

It may all have been leading to 2017's *First Reformed*. A supremely realized work of intense pain, the film draws upon Schrader's work throughout his career as a screenwriter, director, and critic. Though he has consistently denied stylistic relationship between his theory of transcendental style and his films, *First Reformed* deliberately makes use of its signifiers, which Schrader discussed in numerous interviews around the film's release.[31] Starring Ethan Hawke as Reverend Ernst Toller, a tormented country priest in the Bressonian mold, the film traces his journey from quiet despair to passionate fury as he takes up the environmental cause of a parishioner who sought his advice before committing suicide, leaving behind a pregnant wife. Laced with visual references to Bresson and borrowing a premise from Ingmar Bergman's *Winter Light* (1963), Schrader reflectively uses numerous cinematic devices that have populated his films, including voiceover narration, a character's journal, and vigilante violence. He makes overt references to *Taxi Driver*, most prominently in a dread-inducing close-up of a purple cloud of liquid stomach medicine gurgling in a glass of whiskey, recalling Scorsese's Alka-Seltzer in a glass of water close-up from Travis's point of view, itself a lift from Jean-Luc Godard's *2 or 3 Things I Know About Her* (1967). In *Taxi Driver* and *First Reformed*, the bubbling glass reflects the protagonist's inner rage, which will eventually explode into violent catharsis.

The film is a triumph, earning the prolific Schrader the first Academy Award nomination of his career, a surprising oversight for the writer of so many landmark films. The cultural impact of *Taxi Driver* and its central character cannot be overstated; *First Reformed* will unlikely reach the same heights, given the changes in the cinematic landscape that have intervened to relegate films of its stature to the margins of American moviegoing. *Taxi Driver* was a major release by Columbia Pictures, a top-line studio. *First Reformed* was admirably released and championed by small distributor A24, but its footprint was a fraction of *Taxi Driver*'s in 1976. Cultural impact notwithstanding, *First Reformed* is an essential bookend to the career of an American artist that directly responds to his most famous film and enacts his critical obsessions through its striking themes and images. As Schrader has repeatedly said, he hopes that *First Reformed* is not his last film, but if it is, it is "a pretty good last film."[32] He may have more films to make, but even if he does, they will likely be codas to *First Reformed*'s powerful conclusion.

Schrader's wry observation to us about *Taxi Driver* dominating his career speaks to his self-awareness, but also effectively summarizes the bulk of critical discourse about his work. Though he is the director of twenty-three films and the credited writer of twenty-four, Schrader's career has consistently been regarded as adjunct to Scorsese's; the latter filmmaker has unquestionably cemented his status as an essential American master, while the same honorific has eluded Schrader, who has often earned derision instead of accolades. In *Hollywood From Vietnam to Reagan*, critic Robin Wood calls Schrader's work "quasi-fascist."[33] Wood goes on to argue that Schrader's films (though he lets *Taxi Driver* off the hook because of Scorsese's counterbalancing influence) represent the "glorification of the dehumanized hero as efficient killing machine."[34] When Wood is not criticizing Schrader, he discusses him not at all, while Scorsese receives extended attention. The historical record has likewise been unkind to Schrader, with Peter Biskind writing in *Easy Riders, Raging Bulls* that after his 1985 film *Mishima: A Life in Four Chapters*, Schrader "was rarely heard from again, and he never approached, either as a writer or a director, his films of the 1970s."[35]

In sum, Schrader is "less important" than Scorsese and, by extension, other members of the New Hollywood generation, not least because he has had difficulty escaping the shadow of his frequent collaborator. Scorsese's cinematic legacy looms so large that Schrader's own work with and without him has often been eclipsed by the more famous and celebrated director. Though much has been written about Schrader's contribution to cinema through his screenplay for *Taxi Driver* in the numerous volumes about Scorsese, few authors have explored Schrader's work in much depth beyond it. Analysis of Scorsese's career has left him canonized within cinema discourse, while Schrader stands on the outside looking in.

This collection makes an argument for Schrader as an auteur in three ways. First, the collected essays examine Schrader's directing career from an auteur perspective, granting him the same stylistic and thematic analyses that have been afforded to many of his contemporaries. Second, because Schrader has often written scripts directed by other filmmakers, the resulting films function as artifacts against which his own films can be compared in an effort to distinguish his authorial voice. Finally, the book argues that Schrader's criticism yields insights into the films he has written and directed. The structure of the book intends to mimic the general trajectory of Schrader's career, but in an unconventional way. Rather than include each essay on the scholars' chosen films in chronological order of their release date, this volume will be split into three sections: "Ideas, Influences, and Intellect;" "Instincts, Investigation, and Innovation;" and finally, our "Interview of Paul Schrader Conducted at the Rail Line Diner."

In the first section, the essays focus on the numerous sources that provide the ideas for Schrader's work, including establishing many of the important stylistic and thematic concerns that define Schrader as an auteur. In "Schrader and Style," Erik M. Bachman asks, "What do we mean by 'style' when we talk about the films of Paul Schrader?" This question gains special emphasis in light of Schrader's critical work, including *Transcendental Style in Film: Ozu, Bresson, Dreyer*. Deborah Allison continues the focus on

Schrader's stylistic approach in "Movement and Meaning: The Unmotivated Camera in Four Films by Paul Schrader," examining his visual efforts in *American Gigolo, The Comfort of Strangers, Auto Focus,* and *First Reformed*. In "Late Schrader: From the Canon to *The Canyons*," Billy Stevenson analyzes the much-maligned *The Canyons* against Schrader's series of 2006 articles for *Film Comment*, entitled "Canon Fodder," wherein he established criteria for a cinematic canon while also investigating the theoretical difficulty of such an exercise. Together, these three chapters place Schrader's film work in conversation with his criticism.

The second section of the book is called "Instinct, Investigation, and Innovation," and contains chapters devoted to individual films representing different periods of Schrader's career. Scott Balcerzak begins with "'Thinking White': The Actor, the Comedian, and Tension in *Blue Collar*," examining the racial dynamics at play both in front of and behind the camera in Schrader's directorial debut. Erica Moulton follows up with "Zealots and Prophets: Paul Schrader's Adaptations of *The Mosquito Coast* and *The Last Temptation of Christ*," in which she focuses on two of Schrader's screenplays for Weir and Scorsese to uncover Schrader's authorial stamp. Thomas Prasch's subject is also writing, as he examines Schrader's most unconventional film in his chapter, "'So I find another form of expression': Art and Life/Art in Life in Paul Schrader's *Mishima: A Life in Four Chapters* (1985)." In it, Prasch explores what he calls "the tension between word and world" in Schrader's visually stunning biopic of the Japanese artist.

In the next chapter, Brian Brems examines Schrader's female characters in "Schrader's Women in Prison: *Cat People* and *Patty Hearst*," by offering the influence of Bresson as a model for his women. Robert Dassanowsky's subsequent chapter, "Paul Schrader's Experiment in European Neo-Decadence: *The Comfort of Strangers* and the Sadean System," places Schrader's 1990 adaptation of the Ian McEwan novel in the context of Italian neo-decadent cinema like Luchino Visconti's *The Damned* (1969) and *Death in Venice* (1971). Next, James Slaymaker, in "Surveillance Culture, Digitization and Self-Regulation in Paul Schrader's *The Canyons*," reads Schrader's pseudo-pornographic film in light of the modern world's inexorable slide towards ubiquitous, often self-administered surveillance. The final two essays of the collection focus on Schrader's most recent film, the near-universally celebrated *First Reformed*. The first of these two essays, "'Every Act of Preservation is an Act of Creation': Paul Schrader's Eco-Theology in *First Reformed*," written by Tatiana Prorokova, studies the film's fusion of transcendence and environmentalism. Finally, in "Culmination: Silence, Redemption, and Love in *First Reformed*," Rob Ribera sees the film, in his words, "as an embodiment and fulfillment of Schrader's career, a capstone that serves as a meditation on our responsibilities toward each other, our earth, and god." The collection of essays in this second section of the book tie together several threads relevant to Schrader's career, but make no claim to study its totality. The included chapters offer the illumination that Schrader's work has badly needed for some time, as the depth of these authors' analyses ably demonstrate.

The third and final section is devoted to the interview the editors conducted with Paul Schrader at the *Rail Line Diner* in New York City on September 27, 2018. The substantive discussion sheds additional light on the subjects covered in each of the book's preceding chapters, and allows Schrader himself the opportunity to comment on many of the same areas of focus chosen by the chapters' authors. Its organizational placement gives Schrader the final word on his own career and serves as a valuable complement to the work done in the other two sections.

A challenging case study for the auteur approach, Schrader's flexibility—as a director, screenwriter, and critic—makes him unique among filmmakers of his generation, but also places him in conversation with the originators of the auteur theory, those French critics writing for *Cahiers du Cinema* in the 1950s, who later became the filmmakers of the French New Wave. While Schrader's long career deserves more attention than we have together devoted in these pages, it is our hope that these collected chapters are not the final word on this important filmmaker. While Schrader's assessment about *Taxi Driver*'s prominent place in his career arc is accurate, the work contained here demonstrates that Travis Bickle was just the beginning.

NOTES

1. George Kouvaros, *Paul Schrader* (Urbana: University of Illinois Press, 2008), 11–15.
2. Paul Schrader, *Transcendental Style in Film: Ozu, Bresson, Dreyer*, Revised Edition (Oakland, CA: University of California Press, 2018).
3. See Bill Nichols, "'American Gigolo': Transcendental Style and Narrative Form," *Film Quarterly* (Vol. 34, No. 4, Summer 1981), 8–13, for a representative example.
4. Paul Schrader, "Sam Peckinpah Going to Mexico," in *Schrader on Schrader*, Revised Edition, edited by Kevin Jackson (New York: Faber and Faber, 2004), begins page 67.
5. Paul Schrader, "Pickpocket I," in *Schrader on Schrader*, Revised Edition, edited by Kevin Jackson (New York: Faber and Faber, 2004), begins page 38.
6. Paul Schrader, "Easy Rider," in *Schrader on Schrader*, Revised Edition, edited by Kevin Jackson (New York: Faber and Faber, 2004), begins page 34.
7. Paul Schrader, "Notes on Film Noir," in *Schrader on Schrader*, Revised Edition, edited by Kevin Jackson (New York: Faber and Faber, 2004), begins page 80.
8. Zack Sharf, "Paul Schrader Criticizes Brian De Palma as 'Trite' and Artistically Weak," *IndieWire*, June 29, 2019, https://www.indiewire.com/2019/06/paul-schrader-brian-de-palma-trite-artistically-weak-1202154370/.
9. In *Schrader on Schrader*, the filmmaker says *Rolling Thunder* typifies a common problem: "films about fascism become fascist films," 121.
10. Maya Montanez Smukler, *Liberating Hollywood: Women Directors & The Feminist Reform of 1970s American Cinema* (New Brunswick, NJ: Rutgers University Press, 2019), 183. According to the author, Schrader and Tewkesbury differed over the film's tone.

11. *Barton Fink*, directed by Joel Coen (1991: Los Angeles, CA: Kino Lorber, 2019), Blu-ray.
12. *Schrader on Schrader*, Revised Edition, edited by Kevin Jackson (New York: Faber and Faber, 2004), 115.
13. *Scorsese on Scorsese*, Revised Edition, edited by Ian Christie and David Thompson (New York: Faber and Faber, 2003), 77.
14. *Schrader on Schrader*, 144–5.
15. Ibid., 157.
16. Ibid., 158.
17. Todd Haynes, "Bob Dylan Times Six: An Interview With 'I'm Not There' Director Todd Haynes," interview by Greil Marcus, *Rolling Stone*, November 29, 2007, https://www.rollingstone.com/movies/movie-news/bob-dylan-times-six-an-interview-with-im-not-there-director-todd-haynes-67251/.
18. *Schrader on Schrader*, 184.
19. Kouvaros, 63.
20. *Scorsese on Scorsese*, 121.
21. *Schrader on Schrader*, 233.
22. Ibid., 217.
23. Paul Schrader, "'First Reformed' Director Paul Schrader on Why The Film Industry is Dying," interview by Sarah Foulkes, *Slashfilm*, October 25, 2018, https://www.slashfilm.com/paul-schrader-interview-film-industry/.
24. Paul Schrader, "Audio Commentary," *Auto Focus*, DVD, directed by Paul Schrader (Culver City, CA: Columbia Tristar Home Entertainment), 2002.
25. Scott Tobias, "Dominion: Prequel to the Exorcist," *The AV Club*, May 24, 2005, https://film.avclub.com/dominion-prequel-to-the-exorcist-1798200762.
26. *Schrader on Schrader*, 242.
27. Stephen Rodrick, "Here Is What Happens When You Cast Lindsay Lohan in Your Movie," *The New York Times*, January 10, 2013, https://www.nytimes.com/2013/01/13/magazine/here-is-what-happens-when-you-cast-lindsay-lohan-in-your-movie.html.
28. Jen Yamato, "Paul Schrader Wages Silent Protest Over Re-Edited 'Dying of the Light,'" *Deadline*, October 16, 2014, https://deadline.com/2014/10/paul-schrader-dying-of-the-light-nicolas-cage-protest-853521/.
29. Eric Kohn, "Paul Schrader's Secret New Movie: How The Director Resurrected a Wild Nicolas Cage Performance Without Permission," *IndieWire*, December 11, 2017, https://www.indiewire.com/2017/12/paul-schrader-dying-of-the-light-nicolas-cage-dark-new-cut-1201905124/.
30. Paul Schrader, "Interview: Paul Schrader on Making *Dog Eat Dog* His Own Way," interview by Magdalena Maksimiuk, *Slant Magazine*, October 31, 2016, https://www.slantmagazine.com/film/interview-paul-schrader-on-making-dog-eat-dog-on-his-own-terms/.
31. Paul Schrader, "Paul Schrader," *The Film Comment Podcast*, June 21, 2018, https://www.filmcomment.com/blog/film-comment-podcast-paul-schrader/.
32. Paul Schrader, "Paul Schrader Tells Nicolas Cage Why *First Reformed* is His Masterpiece," interview by Nicolas Cage, *Interview Magazine*, April 6, 2018, https://www.interviewmagazine.com/film/paul-schrader-nicolas-cage-april-issue-2018-interview.
33. Robin Wood, *Hollywood From Vietnam to Reagan* (New York: Columbia University Press, 1986), 51.
34. Ibid., 51.
35. Peter Biskind, *Easy Riders, Raging Bulls* (New York: Touchstone Books, 1998), 427.

PART I

Ideas, Influences, and Intellect

CHAPTER 1

Schrader and Style

Erik M. Bachman

> In its simplest manifestation, style is ingratiation. It is an attempt to gain favor by the hypnotic or suggestive process of "saying the right thing."
> —Kenneth Burke, *Permanence and Change* (1935)

What do we mean by "style" when we talk about the films of Paul Schrader, and in what ways has a focus on style availed or thwarted our understanding of them? A supremely influential interpreter of style in film noir and the works of Yasujirō Ozu, Robert Bresson, and Carl Theodor Dreyer, Schrader has nevertheless put together a filmography that evades the stylistic salience or coherence customarily ascribed to other notable filmmakers of his generation, especially those directors with whom he has notably collaborated as a screenwriter. If we take style to be a filmmaker's "systematic and significant use of techniques of the medium," then Schrader's directorial efforts often seem too labile and disparate to engage with a favored set of techniques on enough of a recurring basis to invest any patterns or changes in his use of them with much significance.[1] For instance, there is no obsessive use of split-focus diopters and split screens, as in the films of Brian De Palma; no editing rhythms dependably in sync with the soundtrack's (often diegetic) pop music from the 1960s and 1970s, as in those of Martin Scorsese. At most, one could say there is a notable reliance on the use of freeze frames at the end of many of his films up until the late 1980s—*Blue Collar* (1978), *American Gigolo* (1980), *Cat People* (1982), and *Light of Day* (1987)—but Schrader has tended to avoid this as a stop button in his work since then.[2] Alternatively, if we characterize style "by its stylistic elements, by its stylistic systems [that is, by narrative logic, cinematic time, and cinematic space], and, most abstractly, by the relations it sets up among those systems," then there simply is not enough consistency at any of these levels from film-to-film to make such a threefold analysis of style all that useful.[3] How far, for instance, would an inventory of such elements in *The Canyons* (2013), *Dog Eat Dog* (2016), and *First Reformed* (2017) take us when they are in the service of incongruent narrative logics and inconsistent conceptions of cinematic space and time that, when comparatively assessed across these three particular films, appear to be pursued without regard for each other at all?

Schrader's critics have therefore had a hard time coming to a consensus about how to describe (much less interpret and evaluate) his films in terms of style. For some, hazy imprecision has been the result, as when Kevin Jackson notes that Schrader's cinematic styles include "documentary, theatrical, painterly, operatic," notwithstanding the fact that these adjectives have more to do with genres and modalities than with style as such.[4] For others, a functionally motivated heterogeneity seems to be the best way to account for Schrader as a film stylist, as when George Kouvaros notes, "How do I tell this story? What approach could do justice to the issues and characters involved? [Schrader's] eclectic style—its mixing of traditional formulas and more overtly experimental tendencies—was formed in response to these questions."[5] In this view, narrative, representation, and character are dispositive in a Schrader film, and so all decisions made by him connected to style are to be decoded by way of them rather than the other way round.[6] In short, a focus on style in and of itself will not get you very far when it comes to an understanding of Schrader's movies, because style always serves something else in them. For still others, *Transcendental Style in Film: Ozu, Bresson, Dreyer* (1972) and "Notes on *Film Noir*" (1972) perennially tempt one to read style in his films quite reductively (*They're just an occulted expression of transcendental style and/or film noir!*), despite Schrader's contentions since *American Gigolo* that "my current work as a writer and director and my previous work as a critic have nothing in common."[7] Thus, Roy Scranton finds that "the viewer can only nod and agree: Yes, I see, *First Reformed* is a film in the transcendental style."[8] Yet the grounds Scranton provides for this agreement more or less disregard the fact that the "sparse" technical means stipulated by transcendental style are conspicuously absent in *First Reformed*, whereas the customary popular ones of expressive professional acting, continuity editing, character development, psychological depth, suspense, and dramatic tension—all of which are among the "abundant" devices that are to be abolished or progressively undermined and removed as much as possible in a film exhibiting transcendental style—persist throughout.[9]

Bill Nichols's review of *American Gigolo* in the early 1980s offers a more generative model for how to apply transcendental style to Schrader's films, insofar as it eschews reductionism altogether. Neither materialist nor transcendental, Schrader's style as a filmmaker is said to confound the technical resources of the one with those of the other to such a degree that the ideas and problems explored in a given film remain as rooted in mundane everyday life as they do in the disjunction between that mundane everyday life and a putative world beyond the senses: "what is most intriguing is not the possibility of placing Schrader squarely in either camp, but of teasing out the (contradictory) tension between material conditions and transcendental resolutions to which he gives compelling expression."[10] Contradiction, particularly between the physical and the metaphysical, is what Nichols ultimately understands to be the animating attribute of Schrader's style as a filmmaker, and some critics have credibly taken Nichols's cue without necessarily following his lead. Kouvaros, for instance, frames Schrader's career around a number of dialectical contradictions—independent and mainstream filmmaking, transcendental austerity and psychological realism, intellect and commerce, spirituality and iconoclasm, self-realization and self-destruction, escape and imprisonment—but these contradictions are primarily a way of accounting for the institutional, thematic, and conceptual issues, rather than the essentially stylistic ones, raised by that career.[11] For Nichols, however, contradiction in Schrader's filmography is singular and is indeed a matter of style, in that he presents the foundational contradiction in Schrader's early film style as being that between Marxism and Christianity, between the necessity for political commitment and the conditions of possibility for religious faith:

> For either a Marxist or a transcendentalist, a satisfying resolution in the face of irresolvable contradiction is extremely problematic . . . To allow tensions to be resolved is to provide false contentment, artificial satisfaction. The narrative needs to point beyond—for a Marxist, to those contradictions which, since they are real, remain, and require change in the real world; for a Christian, like Bresson, or perhaps Schrader, to those contradictions which, since they defy logic and commonsense, we must embrace with faith.[12]

Synonym for genre or mode, an instance of eclecticism in the service of character and narrative, an example of transcendental style and/or film noir, contradiction: it seems as though critics have used *style* to refer to a disparate range of things in the films of Paul Schrader, and whatever understanding has come from these speculations has likewise come at the expense of like-mindedness. That is to say, we are not any closer to having a shared understanding of what the significance of style is in Schrader's filmography, which I take not so much to be the fault of Schrader's critics but rather an indicator both of the vexed nature of style as a category of analysis in the first place and of the complications raised by *this* particular filmmaker when one tries to make use of it to interpret his work to date. To begin with the category itself: for some twentieth-century art critics and aestheticians, the word *style* has tended to be invoked for those constant formal elements or choices that persist across a number of works. Talking of style is thus a way of addressing forms that are not to be treated as merely superficial or inessential. For others, style is primarily a matter of the distinctive, that is, of whatever makes a given work or set of works stand out from others. Still other critics and aestheticians use the word as a way of taxonomically linking works together. None of these approaches is necessarily inconsistent with the others, and each is further complicated by whether or not one applies it to individuals or groups. Are we talking about the persistent formal elements that characterize a given artist's work or those of a period? About what is distinctive of a particular artist's work or of the movement of which she happened to have been a part for a few years in her career? Are we taking a singular artist as our measuring stick for the works that are worth drawing together, or is the place (city, nation, empire, continent, hemisphere) in which these works were produced taken to be more germane? If we opt to make style a matter of discrete individuals rather than of groups (however we happen to define them), how do we avoid presumptuously ascribing an implausible level of consciousness and freedom to each of these individuals when it comes to their art-making? That is to say, just how free from environmental influences can the styles of artists actually be? Alternatively, if individual style is in fact not something that is subject to artistic intention, then why individuate style in the first place? Likewise, if we view style in general (rather than individual) terms, then how can we be sure not to take for granted a level of social and/or cultural determinism we might be apt to reject outright, or at the very least fret over, in the works of other critics?[13]

These and other questions could be multiplied at length. I merely pose them in this abrupt and telegraphic fashion to underscore the degree to which much follows from (and a lot, in turn, gets pre-emptively foreclosed by) how we decide to apply style as a category of analysis to a given set of works, though each of the approaches outlined above (both at the individual and general levels) presupposes that context-analysis is essential to adequately dealing with matters of style, even if the respective ways of formulating that context (biographical, psychological, historical, institutional, geographical, socio-economic, etc.) hence vary qualitatively. What is remarkable about Schrader's book on transcendental style is that context (howsoever defined) is said ultimately not to matter at all when it comes to style. To be sure, in *Transcendental Style in Film*, he offers the following stipulative definitions of *style*: (1) "'a contemporary view of the world' expressed by a particular geographic-historical culture" (style as codeword for ideology); (2) "the 'creation of a personal, a subjective, a "non-objective" world'"(style-as-signature); and (3) "what Heinrich Wölfflin called a 'general representative form,'" which for Schrader entails "the expression of similar ideas in similar forms by divergent cultures" (style as universal means of expression).[14] Schrader rejects the first two options, which we might respectively characterize as general and individual notions of style, as ill-suited to his book's focus on "man-made, man-organized, or man-selected works which are more expressive of the Wholly Other than of their individual creators."[15] Style-as-ideology and style-as-authorial-signature are accordingly far too immanent and assumptively materialist in the limits they place on what works of art are capable of expressing, and if the word *style* means anything in *Transcendental Style in Film*, then it must refer to a coalescence of form and content that is prospectively available to all filmmakers, irrespective of their immediate historical, cultural, personal, or developmental horizons, because this coalescent form-content necessarily expresses something beyond what immediate sensory or collective experience can disclose to us on its own:

> By delaying edits, not moving the camera, forswearing music cues, not employing coverage, and heightening the mundane, transcendental style creates a sense of unease the viewer must resolve. The film-maker assists the viewer's impulse for resolution by the use of a Decisive Moment, an unexpected image or act, which then results in a stasis, an acceptance of parallel reality—transcendence.[16]

Yet there are some obvious inconsistencies with choosing between the options presented here in this way. For one thing, Schrader's first two stipulative definitions do not drop out of the picture entirely. He has no choice but to admit that Ozu, Bresson, and Dreyer do indeed make films that express their situatedness in their respective social structures (their films hail viewers and bear the marks of having been hailed in turn by the filmmaking institutions and national cultures in which they were produced); likewise, Ozu, Bresson, and Dreyer do indeed make films that express their own subjectivities (their personal identifying marks are all over the films they respectively make). In a dexterous sleight of hand, however, Schrader recasts these two ways of addressing style as ultimately having nothing to do with style:

> The differences between Ozu and Bresson are personal and cultural, their similarities are stylistic, but until the moment of transcendental stasis, the personal and cultural differences are all-important. [. . .] Without stasis, there is no expression of the Transcendent, and without expression of the Transcendent, there can be no fundamental interrelation between cultures, and without interrelation there can be no "universal form of representation."[17]

No style without the Transcendent, then, which makes the adjective *transcendental* in Schrader's account of transcendental style in film something more than just a mere modifier or inflection of the noun *style*. It does not just indicate a demotion of interest in ideology and authorship (of the general and individual approaches) when it comes to style; in the end, it remarkably signifies the effacement of both from a consideration of style worthy of the name.

Understandably, resolving the untenable disparities within everyday life (emblematized here as the limitations that arise when reducing style to matters of ideology or authorship) by referring to a plane of existence inaccessible to the senses is not something that all critics have been able to take on faith. Steven Shaviro, for instance, reclaims the films of Bresson for an immanent interpretation that remains rooted in the mundane world and an understanding of style as primarily an attribute of auteurs (style-as-signature) by overtly rejecting the negative theology implied by *Transcendental Style in Film*. Schrader, Shaviro writes,

> argues that [Bresson's] films express the ineffable, the totally Other and Transcendent, by emptying out the everyday to the point where a "disparity" emerges, where the experience of privation leads to a radical rupture with phenomenal existence . . . [However, e]verything turns on the allegorical discontinuity between the deliberate banality of concrete expression (gestures, movements, words) and the ineffability of what is being expressed. There is no participatory movement, no direct and ready passage, linking one realm to the other. In Bresson's peculiar version of Roman Catholicism, the very logic of salvation demands that it be infinitely deferred. Everything is thrown back upon the everyday and upon the body.[18]

In short, what is distinctive about Bresson is certainly a matter of style, and this style has everything to do with calling into question or endlessly putting off the possibility of interacting with a world we cannot perceive by focusing instead on our sensory access to the unsatisfying one we indeed already indisputably do. For Shaviro, transcendental style in film is thus really just a mystification of Deleuze's time-image and slow cinema.[19]

We do not need to have deep and abiding skepticism about metaphysics to discern the limits of Schrader's claims being made on behalf of transcendental style, however; after all, *Transcendental Style in Film* itself already implicitly shares them. For example, Schrader's reliance on Heinrich Wölfflin for his preferred definition of *style* altogether undermines the barrier he at times purports to build between style proper (transcendental style) and style *manqué* (style-as-ideology and style-as-signature), both of which are reduced to inessential cultural and personal differences in the face of transcendental style. After all, the passage cited in Schrader's third stipulative definition of the word *style* comes from *Principles of Art History* (1915), in which Wölfflin expressly conceptualizes style in terms of the changing schema of visual perception that qualitatively distinguish historical periods of art (for instance, Early Renaissance, High Renaissance, baroque) from each other:

> Our investigation deals with these most general forms of representation. It does not analyze the beauty of Leonardo or Dürer so much as the element in which that beauty found form. It does not analyze the representation of nature in terms of its imitative content or how the naturalism of the sixteenth century differs from that of the seventeenth so much as the type of perception that underlies the representational arts in these different centuries.[20]

Style, in this view, refers to the artistic expression of a way of seeing shared among artists in a distinct period, which means that Schrader's preferred definition is more akin to style-as-ideology than his book otherwise tends to let on.

Moreover, Wölfflin's "most general forms of representation" are not universal in the way that Schrader would have us understand transcendental style to be. In a preface to a later edition of the book that responds to contemporary criticisms of it, Wölfflin notes,

> All development in this world is tied up with certain conditions and proceeds within certain limits. Not everything is possible at all times. Thinking has its own development and we distinguish between different stages of thinking—why should art be an exception in its perceptual relationship to the world? And is it really so impossible to find a rough formula for these developments, which have already recurred numerous times in ever-new combinations? . . . "New world content is crystallized in every new form of seeing."[21]

Remarkably, Schrader takes one of the foundational conceptualizations of period style and tries to pass it off as a way of understanding style beyond the limits of time, place, author, and context as such. Alternatively, Schrader uses Wölfflin to mix up all three styles: style-as-ideology, style-as-authorship, and period style persist in *Transcendental Style in Film* insofar as Schrader ascribes authorship and its attendant ways of seeing to a Wholly Other source of expression. In this sense, transcendental style would be the signature of a Transcendent-Something-or-Other that is able to express its otherwise impalpable bare presence by ruthlessly and ritualistically voiding a film of its contemporary routinized appeals to experience, reality, and convention: "Transcendental style *stylizes* reality by eliminating (or nearly eliminating) those elements which are primarily expressive of human experience, thereby robbing the conventional interpretations of reality of their relevance and power. Transcendental style, like the mass, transforms experience into a repeatable ritual which can be repeatedly transcended."[22]

So, despite Schrader's best efforts in *Transcendental Style in Film* to make the concept of style coincide exactly with transcendental style as such, the continuing legitimacy of his other definitions in a stylistic analysis of film cannot be made to vanish into thin air, even in the case of films putatively expressive of the Transcendent. To be clear, I do not understand this to be an oversight or failure on his part as a critic but instead consider it a pretty incisive expression of the sorts of opportunity costs that are an essential part of any responsible discussions of style. In effect, Schrader's three stipulative definitions consciously foreground the interpretive scope, stakes, and commitments of the choices we otherwise tend to assumptively or intuitively make when discussing style in art. These definitions are thus perhaps better grasped as levels of stylistic analysis available to any interested critic rather than mutually exclusive classifications. None cancels out the others, nor can we always credibly talk about one without momentarily disregarding those same others. Instead, each level is better suited to certain analytical procedures or rhetorical goals than others, which would appear to make the use of style in the interpretation of art akin to the role Hayden White says literary tropes play in the writing of history: it "*pre*figures the historical [or, in this case, the artistic] field and constitutes it as a domain upon which to bring to bear the specific theories he will use to explain 'what was really happening' in it."[23]

What do we mean by "style" when we talk about the films of Paul Schrader? This answer would seem to suggest that, whatever we may happen to mean by it, discussions of style ultimately say more about us and our interpretive commitments than they do about Schrader's films themselves and thus cannot help but inform our understanding of them. We may have doubts as to whether or not meaning is ultimately even what is at stake in a given work of art. The past century in particular has been rife with examples of works that test the limits of comprehensibility or even undermine its very conditions of possibility. For instance, does a credible interpretation of Gertrude Stein's *Tender Buttons* (1914) really come down to providing us with a decoder ring that discloses once and for all what's really happening in that text? Or should we jettison content or meaning as such and attune ourselves instead to the sorts of experiences that works such as this make possible for their readers?[24] In any case, the work of art itself has to be taken as a significant unit of relevance (even if its possible meanings remain optative or only shine forth in relation to all sorts of other things), which in turn necessitates that our discussions of it cannot only be about ourselves alone.

Schrader, both as a critic and as a filmmaker, makes style a problem that *films* pose for their receivers, and not the other way around. It is thus not something we should take for granted, either in terms of what it is in itself or how it happens to get expressed in a given film by a particular filmmaker (Schrader included). For instance, though one may very well have reservations about metaphysics and the Transcendent, if a film's style plausibly serves the expression of such things, then we fail to reckon with that style itself by denying their existence and only succeed in gearing it to our own preferred ideological frameworks when we in turn throw everything back on to a level—like that of the material world—in which we do happen to believe or have faith. Hence the irreducibility of the word *style* in *Transcendental Style in Film* to any one of the stipulative definitions he offers: *style* refers to all of them, *is* all of them, lest one risk making style all about oneself rather than about the film by focusing on one of them to the exclusion of the others. And hence the uncertainty among Schrader's many critics as to how to account for style in his films.

To date, Nichols provides perhaps the best attempt to manage this uncertainty constructively by framing Schrader's film style in terms of the contradiction between Marxism and Christianity, but even this solution fails to completely convince, in no small part because Nichols reduces this contradiction to a choice between dialectical materialism and illogical faith. Again, as quoted earlier, he observes that "The narrative needs to point beyond—for a Marxist, to those contradictions which, since they are real, remain, and require change in the real world; for a Christian, like Bresson, or perhaps Schrader, to those contradictions which, since they defy logic and commonsense, we must embrace with faith."[25] However, the very language of contradiction itself carries with it the implication that we do in fact have to choose between the competing models of dialectical thinking offered by the two contradictory poles here (Christianity and Marxism) in order to resolve it. That is to say, adopting the procedures of dialectical materialism would seem to rig the game in advance in one way, just as using Kierkegaard's inverted dialectic or dialectical theology would in the other. In either case, the foundational contradiction identified by Nichols would necessarily be wiped out, rather than adequately processed or justifiably addressed, by the very dialectical means or methodology one chooses to utilize in responding to this state of contradiction in the first place.

I would like to propose one way of dealing with this dilemma first by situating Schrader's understanding of style in relation to an influential philosophical account of it that is consistent with his own and then by putting forward an alternative way of approaching what looks to be the pivotal role of contradiction in his filmmaking style. Nelson Goodman's roughly contemporaneous reflections on style in art provide a useful summation of the sorts of convolutions raised for Schrader by style, albeit in clear propositional statements rather than through critical prose that tends to rely on insinuation and suggestive discrepancies. In "The Status of Style" (1975), Goodman argues that style is not simply a matter of form, nor is it subject to conscious artistic intent, nor, in turn, is it comprised of everything that is distinctive about a given work of art. "Style," for Goodman

> has to do exclusively with the symbolic functioning of a work as such . . . Basically, the style consists of those features of the symbolic functioning of a work that are characteristic of author, period, place, or school. If this definition does not seem notably novel, still its divergence from some prevalent views must not be overlooked. According to this definition, style is not exclusively a matter of how as contrasted with what, does not depend either upon synonymous alternatives or upon conscious choice among alternatives, and comprises only but not all aspects of how and what a work symbolizes.[26]

Style is whatever is distinctive about the properties of a work of art connected with the meanings that it does make, and the word *distinctive* here operates at the individual, group, geographical, and historical levels all at once. It thus refers to the ways in which the significant parts of a work can be seen to act as a metaphorical signature (both personal and collective), GPS tracker, and time stamp all rolled into one, and much like Schrader himself does, though with a good deal more forthrightness, Goodman is insistent here that any artistic style worthy of the name does all of these things, not just some of them. Just as reducing the word *style* to form distorts the ways in which it actually refers to the meaningful confluence of form with content and sentiment, using it to speak exclusively of a filmmaker's particular style omits all of the other ways in which style also necessarily articulates linkages with groups (arranged into schools, times, and locations at a minimum). For both Schrader and Goodman, none of these levels of stylistic analysis can be made to go away, because each is an essential component of style as such.

Given the strict space constraints for the essays in this collection, this is regrettably not the place to build on these affinities between the conceptualizations of style in the writings of Schrader and Goodman with detailed multi-level analyses of style in representative scenes and movies from Schrader's filmography. These constraints necessitate that we instead approach these issues at a certain level of abstraction and generalization, and with this in mind, I would like to conclude with some speculations as to how any such analyses ought to be framed. As we have seen, speaking of Schrader's filmmaking style as the embodiment of the contradiction between dialectical materialism and Christian spirituality (between Marx and God) presents that style as a problem that can never be satisfactorily resolved. As noted earlier, the very means between which one would have to choose in the course of venturing a solution to this contradiction would necessarily prefigure the answer arrived at. Perhaps just as notably, however, it is indeed a stretch to present either Marxism or Christianity as opposing articles of faith in Schrader's films. To be fair, when Nichols posited this as the foundational contradiction in his style as a filmmaker, Schrader's directorial output up to that point consisted solely of *Blue Collar*, *Hardcore* (1979), and *American Gigolo*, which certainly present a much more coherent representation of materialism and spirituality than Schrader has been able to maintain ever since. In fact, Schrader's subsequent filmography has focused much more obsessively on the representation of interpersonal relationships—either through the spectacular failure of friendships and families on which one cannot hope to depend or through their climactic salvaging by means of improbably reciprocated demonstrations of love—which shape much of the meaningful content, form, feeling, and symbolic investment on offer, whereas the competing collectivities, institutions, and commitments at issue in Marxism and Christianity tend to occur in much more scattershot and ambiguous fashion. Indeed, whether an expression of love or fidelity for another person gets unexpectedly affirmed—*American Gigolo*, *Light of Day*, *Light Sleeper* (1992), *Witch Hunt* (1994), *Touch* (1997), *Forever Mine* (1999)— or violently spurned—*Blue Collar*, *Hardcore*, *The Comfort of Strangers* (1990), *Affliction* (1997), *Auto Focus* (2002), *The Walker* (2007), *The Canyons*—has proven to be favored by Schrader throughout his career as a means of giving his feature-length films a sense of an ending.

What is needed, therefore, is a way of talking about these indeterminacies of style in Schrader—not just between Marxism and Christianity but also between a skepticism toward and a faith in the redemptive power of friendship, family, and love—that does justice to the contradictions involved here without reducing itself to those particular contradictions or to contradiction as such. I believe Kenneth Burke's secular and rhetorical reconceptualization of piety and impiety provides us with just such a way. In *Permanence and Change: An Anatomy of Purpose* (1935), Burke defines *piety* not as a matter of reverence or faithful devotion but rather as

> a system-builder, a desire to round things out, to fit experiences tougher into a unified whole. Piety is *the sense of what properly goes with what*. And it leads to construction in this way: If there is an altar, it is pious of a man to perform some ritual act whereby he may approach this altar with clean hands. A kind of symbolic cleanliness goes with altars, a technique of symbolic cleansing goes with cleanliness, a preparation or initiation goes with the technique of cleansing, the need of cleansing was based upon some feeling of taboo—and so on, until pious linkages may have brought all the significant details of the day into coordination, relating them integrally with one another by a complex interpretative network.[27]

Piety is thus the level at which a given cultural, social, or historical framework for interpreting the world is lived and acted upon in a way that is meant to give a sense of identity and coherence to a person's life. Notwithstanding the religious subject matter in Burke's example of the pious man faced with an altar, this account of piety likewise encompasses all sorts of secular identities, like those of gang member and drug addict, so long as they "act to prove themselves, every minute of the day, true members of their cult."[28] In the case of the gang member, this would involve acting upon what they understand to be "the proper oaths, the correct way of commenting upon passing women, the etiquette of spitting"; in the case of the drug addict, this would necessitate that he "gradually organize his character around this outstanding 'altar' of his experience—and since the altar in this case is generally accepted as unclean, he will be disciplined enough to approach it with appropriately unclean hands, until he is derelict."[29]

Conversely, impiety is associated by Burke with evangelism, but again, the customary religious resonances of that word are demoted. For Burke, the evangelism of piety has merely to do with the "attempt to *reorganize* one's orientations from the past," and in modernity this attempt has increasingly become the remit of scientific (not Christian) doctrine.[30] In particular, though, Burke associates this impiety with the attempt either to "invent new terms, or apply our old vocabulary in new ways, attempting to socialize our position by so manipulating the linguistic commitment of our group that our particular additions or alterations can be shown to fit into the old texture."[31] In short, impiety is not a faulty or ignorant sense of what goes with what (that is, impiety is not a failure to be pious). It is, instead, an attempt to invent new ways of being, acting, and identifying as a socialized self that are not just in conflict with existing ways of being, acting, and identifying but, more importantly, are shown to be more desirable or persuasive than those already existing ways. As Ann George has noted in her book-length commentary on *Permanence and Change*, Burke's

> point here—one particularly aimed at Marxist activists—is that persuading Americans to reject capitalism will be far messier and more difficult than they have imagined because Americans have tremendous psychic and physical as well as financial investments in the system . . . Indeed Burke argues, via piety, that most Americans do not experience capitalism primarily as an economic system; rather it is a way of life, deeply embedded in their identities and behaviors.[32]

The usefulness of this framework for approaching Schrader's stylistic contradictions extends well beyond the fact that Schrader has explicitly signposted his evangelical impulse as a filmmaker.[33] More importantly, it allows us to deal with the contradictions posed by his style without favoring one set of terms in this contradiction over the others. Though Burke uses the language of piety and impiety, he strips them of their religious denotations and presents them as a secular and ultimately rhetorical way of dealing with how ideological outlooks and assumptions get embodied. For Schrader, these outlooks and assumptions primarily revolve around the conditions of possibility for love, friendship, and family. What thus matters when it comes to parsing style in Schrader's films is not the fact that one of these outlooks sometimes gets favored over the other or that each is confounded with the other, but rather *the ways* in which they get favored and confounded. The sudden appearance of the decisive moment and stasis identified by Nichols in *American Gigolo*—but also notably present at the end of *Blue Collar*, *Cat People*, *Mishima: A Life in Four Chapters* (1985), *Light of Day*, and *Light Sleeper*—ought not cue us to be on the lookout for the presence of transcendental style in Schrader's films but for the ways in which he is applying these elements incorrectly: they do not belong with the abundant stylistic elements on display throughout the preceding film, and the point is not that Schrader has failed to combine them in the way he describes in Ozu and Bresson in particular (after all, he knows very well what goes with what in transcendental style) but simply that another way of being or behaving entirely is potentially being offered in the incongruous styles and perspectives that are expressed by that given film.

What the contours of this new way of being or behaving might prospectively be is not something that can be rigorously demonstrated here, but I would note that the recurrence in *First Reformed* of many of the stylistic preoccupations just detailed gives us some grounds for articulating one of them: the ways in which that film depicts the tense interrelation of the Transcendent

Figure 1.1 Final shot of *Light Sleeper*.

and the material world, the uncertain conditions of possibility for the forging of meaningful friendships and family ties, and the decisive moment that leads ambiguously either to the final delusional fantasies of a suicide victim or his improbable redemption through an unexpected dizzying embrace, all serve to scramble the customary associations that have tended to form between such things in Schrader's other films. For what this film ultimately does is refuse to choose for us whether an avowal of love or fidelity for another person gets improbably reciprocated or violently spurned, and it pointedly stages this for us not in a static image (either a literal freeze frame or a shot in which movement is minimal), as happens so often at the end of Schrader's films throughout his career, but rather in a *Vertigo*-like swirl that abruptly cuts to black. This should not be construed as a failure of transcendental style in film but rather its impious reorientation, for what is prospectively speaking here is not some Transcendent-Something-or-Other but a very tangible world we have made in which the pursuit of friendship, family, and love can no longer provide us with a satisfactory sense of an ending, because the felicities and devastations of such a pursuit matter not one jot in the face of the sublime catastrophes impending over all higher organized life forms on this planet now as we write, speak, film, watch, read, and hold on to each other.

Figure 1.2 Final shot of *First Reformed*.

Paul Schrader's impiety as a film stylist is thus addressed not to film history or other filmmakers, nor is it aimed at Marxists and Christians. Instead, his films frame for us all of the ways in which we as inhabitants of this world do not tend to experience the forces—be they mundane or transcendent—that shape it and us, because our attentions are too wrapped up in ourselves and the friends, lovers, and family members that surround us. What makes Schrader's cinematic depictions of this impious, and thus ultimately a matter of style, is that they consistently remind us that friendship, love, and family are all that we have and nonetheless remain beside the point.

NOTES

1. David Bordwell, *On the History of Film Style* (Cambridge, MA: Harvard University Press, 1997), 4.
2. Compare George Kouvaros, *Paul Schrader* (Urbana and Chicago: University of Illinois Press, 2008), 53: "Schrader's use of the freeze frame suggests something irreconcilable about the drama that has just concluded. It is not an ending to the story as such but a literal fixing in place of a dilemma—a final moment of fetishization and disavowal prior to the lights coming back on." Kouvaros's list of Schrader films that end in freeze frames includes *Mishima: A Life in Four Chapters* and *Light Sleeper* as well. However, *Mishima*'s final shot, which plays out behind the end credits, is not actually a freeze frame, as evidenced by the fact that the shipping vessel beneath the rising sun on the horizon traverses the screen from left to right as the credits roll. Likewise, the last shot of *Light Sleeper* is in fact a close-up tableau vivant of John LeTour's (Willem Defoe) embrace of Ann's (Susan Sarandon) hand, not a freeze frame as such.
3. David Bordwell, Janet Staiger, and Kristin Thompson, *The Classical Hollywood Cinema: Film Style & Mode of Production to 1960* (London: Routledge, 1994), 6.
4. Kevin Jackson, "Introduction," in Paul Schrader, *Schrader on Schrader*, edited by Kevin Jackson (London and Boston: Faber and Faber, 1990), xvii.
5. Kouvaros, *Paul Schrader*, 13.
6. Compare John Howard Wilson, "Sources for a Neglected Masterpiece: Paul Schrader's *Mishima*," *Biography* 20, No. 3 (Summer 1997), 265–83.
7. Paul Schrader, "A Postscript from Paul Schrader," *Film Quarterly* 34, No. 4 (Summer 1981), 13.
8. Roy Scranton, "Film in Review," *The Yale Review* 107, No. 1 (January 2019), 190–1.
9. For more on the relationship between "sparse" and "abundant" means in transcendental style, see Paul Schrader, *Transcendental Style in Film: Ozu, Bresson, Dreyer* (Berkeley: University of California Press, 2018), 177–80.
10. Bill Nichols, "*American Gigolo*: Transcendental Style and Narrative Form," *Film Quarterly* 34, No. 4 (Summer 1981), 13.
11. Kouvaros, *Paul Schrader*, 2, 4, 14–15, 54, 70.
12. Nichols, "*American Gigolo*," 12.
13. A useful summary of these issues and their attendant questions can be found in Stephanie Ross, "Style in Art," in *The Oxford Handbook of Aesthetics*, edited by Jerrold Levinson (Oxford and New York: Oxford University Press, 2003), 228–44.
14. Schrader, *Transcendental Style in Film*, 40. Schrader's first stipulative definition of *style* derives from Wylie Sypher, *Rococo to Cubism in Art and Literature* (New York: Vintage Books,

1963), xix: "During my discussion I have assumed that a genuine style is an expression of a prevailing, dominant, or authentically contemporary view of the world by those artists who have most successfully intuited the quality of human experience peculiar to their day and who are able to phrase this experience in forms deeply congenial to the thought, science, and technology which are part of that experience." Style for Sypher (if not for Schrader, given his sparingly selective quotation from this passage) is thus not merely ideological but also typical and conformist: the word *style* is to be used for those artists who themselves best typify the ways of perceiving indicative of their time and place *and* who can in turn express these ways of perceiving in ways that are likely to be acceptable to their contemporaries. Schrader's second stipulative definition of *style* comes from Raymond Durgnat, *Films and Feelings* (Cambridge, MA: MIT Press, 1967), 30: "'Style'—or rather, *nuance*—is conventionally associated with the creation of a personal, a subjective, a 'non-objective' world—a world that is *this* artist's (or *this* character's, or both)."
15. Schrader, *Transcendental Style in Film*, 38.
16. Ibid., 3.
17. Ibid., 81.
18. Steven Shaviro, *The Cinematic Body* (Minneapolis and London: University of Minnesota Press, 1993), 250.
19. Schrader has recently noted that there are indeed affinities between Deleuze's time-image and films that have been made in transcendental style, but he insists that the former is not reducible to the latter. See Paul Schrader, "Rethinking Transcendental Style," in *Transcendental Style in Film*, 1–33. Compare Gilles Deleuze, *Cinema 2: The Time-Image*, translated by Hugh Tomlinson and Robert Galeta (Minneapolis: University of Minnesota Press, 1989).
20. Heinrich Wölfflin, *Principles of Art History: The Problem of the Development of Style in Modern Art*, translated by Jonathan Blower (Los Angeles: Getty Research Institute, 2015), 95.
21. Ibid., 77.
22. Ibid., 42.
23. Hayden White, *Metahistory: The Historical Imagination in Nineteenth-Century Europe* (Baltimore and London: Johns Hopkins University Press, 1975), x.
24. Compare Nicholas Gaskill, *Chromographia: American Literature and the Modernization of Color* (Minneapolis: University of Minnesota Press, 2018), 191–201.
25. Nichols, "*American Gigolo*," 12.
26. Nelson Goodman, *Ways of Worldmaking* (Indianapolis: Hackett Publishing Company, 1978), 35.
27. Kenneth Burke, *Permanence and Change: An Anatomy of Purpose* (New York: New Republic, 1935), 100.
28. Ibid., 104.
29. Ibid., 103, 104.
30. Ibid., 106.
31. Ibid., 53.
32. Ann George, *Kenneth Burke's "Permanence and Change": A Critical Companion* (Columbia: University of South Carolina Press, 2018), 35.
33. See Jackson (ed.), *Schrader on Schrader*, 29: "I have the evangelical impulse, which is the need to go out and preach to as many people as possible and to reach all of them. I also know that the true way to reach them is via a method that is uncommercial. But when you are working in a mass medium you have to accept the restrictions of a mass audience, which means millions of people, because to make a movie you need to deal with a minimum of two or three million units."

CHAPTER 2

Movement and Meaning: The "Unmotivated" Camera in Four Films by Paul Schrader

Deborah Allison

You don't want a cinematographer just to make pretty pictures. You want him to somehow be involved in the storytelling process and have a sense of what is right for these characters now.

—Paul Schrader[1]

Paul Schrader has worked in many genres. Although his films vary greatly in both subject and style, his hand is rarely mistakable. His ethos that "style determines the theme in *every* film,"[2] that "unity of form and subject matter"[3] is paramount, and that for a film to succeed artistically its unique style must deliver "the right solution to the right problem"[4] runs through them all. Consequently, while the visual schemes of, say, *The Comfort of Strangers* (1990) and *First Reformed* (2017) could hardly be further apart, the strategy is constant though the stylistic solutions bespoke.

This essay centers on Schrader's use of camera movement (or absence of movement) as a means of articulating themes within his films and, furthermore, as a tool with which he expresses himself prominently as an author.

In many films he makes regular use of "unmotivated" camera movement. He describes this as "when the storyteller imposes himself on the story, when the camera calls attention to itself."[5] It encourages us to participate actively in the process of viewing and the construction of meanings. "The unmotivated camera is *wonderful*,"[6] he has said, observing elsewhere that a great film "not only comes at the viewer, it draws the viewer toward it."[7]

To illustrate and elucidate these points, I focus on four films from different stages of Schrader's career: *American Gigolo* (1979), *The Comfort of Strangers*, *Auto Focus* (2002), and *First Reformed*, each of which features very different styles and camera techniques. In all these films, style is paramount. Every aspect of production design, performance, cinematography, editing, and music combines to create a distinctive milieu and to draw out the themes of the story at hand. Camerawork cannot exist or function in isolation from these other aspects; to attempt to extricate it fully from them would be folly. Nevertheless, my primary focus is the extent to which in certain scenes or sequences particular camera movements are brought to the fore. In the most extreme examples, they jolt the viewer. Schrader intends that these movements are noticed and they clamor to be interpreted. By this I mean they are not just there to be picked apart by scholars, but to be thought about (however briefly, and perhaps even subconsciously) there and then by the general viewer.

Through such "unmotivated" movements we are granted an especially clear sense of Schrader as narrator, proffering a particular perspective on the stories and characters he brings to the screen. "Unmotivated," he explains, "simply means that the camera frame reflects the director's point of view first and the characters and narrative second. Camera movement is motivated by the storyteller, not the story."[8] It is through this narration that latent themes crystallize and exteriorize, the act of expressing meaning being also the act of its creation.

Despite their superficial differences, the films discussed in this essay share certain core themes. They all feature lead characters that struggle to forge meaningful connections with other people. In each case this failure is associated (be it in terms of cause and/or effect) with narcissism, with a focus on self-image, even if the protagonists' degree of introspection varies greatly. In keeping with this aspect, each film assigns a central place to the act of looking and being looked at (although in *First Reformed* this is expressed through other means than the film's exceptionally sparse camera movements). In the absence of intimate interpersonal relationships, ritualistic behaviors and infatuation with external paraphernalia are also strongly marked. Moreover, in each film the narratives and characters develop and their associated themes unfold in ways that are at once linear and circular.

Each of these elements is inscribed within the film style and they are often pointed to through "unmotivated" camera movements. In the following short studies, I take a handful of examples from each film with the aim of showing Schrader's motivations for "unmotivated" movements and how those moments contribute to the films' thematic architecture.

AMERICAN GIGOLO

Schrader has described *American Gigolo* as the first film for which he started to think in a visual rather than a literary way.[9] Heavily influenced by the "high style" of *The Conformist* (Bertolucci, 1970), it was, like its immediate successor,

Cat People (1982), photographed by John Bailey with *The Conformist*'s Ferdinando Scarfiotti serving as visual consultant.[10]

This tale of a well-heeled, emotionally self-sufficient gigolo whose life unravels after he becomes the prime suspect in the murder of a client is not simply stylish (though it certainly is that) so much as saturated by style. It is a film that, before the eighties, seemed to define the eighties—the look, the feel, the aspiration of the eighties, the shiny garish surfaces of the eighties, the colors of the eighties.

Its protagonist Julian Kay (Richard Gere) is a superficial man who lives off his image. His strongest connections are not with people but with things—with their style and their lustrous veneers. This is why, as the duplicitous pimp Leon (Bill Duke) ultimately explains, he is such a suitable candidate to frame for murder: a beautiful but near-empty vessel whom nobody except his new girlfriend Michelle (Lauren Hutton) really likes or cares for. The formal aspects of the film are designed to bring out these qualities as, through the course of the narrative, Julian's meticulously structured life is systematically dismantled.

This aspirational superficiality, and the concomitant desire to look and be looked at, explodes onto the screen in the film's very first moments. "One of the things an audience wants in the opening moments of a film," Schrader argues, "is the sense that someone is in control."[11] Here, he leaves no doubt about the presence of a guiding directorial hand. After a handful of initial credits and the main title, the image track bursts into motion as Julian zips along a sun-drenched coastal freeway in his open-top Mercedes, the images accompanied by Giorgio Moroder's pulsating score: "Call Me" performed by Blondie. The first images are low-angle shots of the car: a whirring tire, a gleaming bumper as the blacktop whizzes past. The camera then drops down from a high angle to show Julian at the wheel, before moving lower and round to the side of the car to show him in profile.

What is notable as this sequence proceeds is that the camerawork traces the contours of the vehicle as intently as it does those of its driver. It fetishistically caresses its shining surfaces much as Kenneth Anger had done in his odes to the erotic symbiosis of man and machine: *Scorpio Rising* (1963) and *Kustom Kar Kommandos* (1965). In these first shots, Schrader already employs the "unmotivated" camera to impose his perspective on Julian's relationship with his surroundings—as he will continue to do through the remainder of the sequence.

As the credits continue, the camera remains highly mobile, following disconnected scenes of Julian as he is fitted for a suit, drops a woman off at her home and then enters the beach house of his high-class pimp Anne (Nina Van Pallandt). Although Julian is never off the screen for long, the camerawork does not track his movements in a conventional or "classical" style. Instead, it swoops down to discover him from high angles: in the store, or outside the beach house as he pulls up and runs his hand through his hair. Other shots trace the imposing designer storefront, its opulent interior, the bonnet of the Mercedes, the coastal view with its "slide area" warning sign (a portentous nod to Gavin Lambert's classic 1959 novel *The Slide Area: Scenes of Hollywood Life*, about LA's affluent lost souls, perhaps?), before discovering Julian within those spaces. As the credits end, a series of quite lengthy Steadicam shots follows him into Anne's house. There he briefly disappears from view behind an enormous painting that adorns a partition wall before re-emerging as the camera follows his confident strutting around the modishly decorated room.

This sequence dexterously and economically establishes one of the ideas that drive the film: that Julian is defined, and indeed defines himself, by the fashionable accoutrements of the materialistic culture he celebrates. Much later in the film, this opening is mirrored darkly in a sequence shot in a very different style. Under the low but harsh lighting of his apartment-block garage at night, he savagely slashes and strips his car's lush interiors as he searches for some stolen jewelry he suspects has been concealed there as another nail in the murder frame. Rapid editing, closer angles and short, jerky camera movements contrast with the sinuous style of the opening sequence. Here, Schrader's "unmotivated" camera movements help to accentuate an important reversal whereby Julian's relinquishment of long-cherished values and the possessions that embodied them will eventually unlatch the door to his spiritual salvation.

Two further meticulously paired scenes center on Julian's interactions with other people. Both take place in or outside a retail arcade and involve furtive pursuits and encounters. One is a clandestine meeting between Julian and Michelle; the other is the confrontation between Julian and the inept amateur sleuth her suspicious husband has sent after him. In each case, the non-classical camera style contributes significantly to our experience of the scene at hand, but it is through the clinical replication of "unmotivated" movements across these parallel scenes that Schrader makes his points most forcefully.

In the first scene, the camera picks up Julian as he walks along the boulevard, following and keeping pace behind him from a distance of several meters. A slight jerkiness to its movement suggests the point of view of an unknown pursuer. As Julian stops and turns, we cut briefly to his point of view as he scans the cluster of pedestrians, affording the viewer a fleeting, almost imperceptible glimpse of a woman's rapid sidestep into the cover of a shop doorway. In the next shot the camera has moved to Julian's front, pulling backwards to hold him in medium close-up as he carries on along the street, pausing behind a pillar to sneak another look at his pursuer. In another point-of-view shot we see more clearly that it is Michelle who follows him. The sequence proceeds in similar vein until, smiling and casually smoothing his hair, he enters a music store. As he does so, he passes a prominent advertisement for the latest record by The Police, one of several moments in the film in which a roguish placement of the written word presages a downturn in his fortunes.

Once inside, an unbroken Steadicam shot follows Julian up a flight of stairs, around the balcony of a mezzanine level and thence up one further flight. A cut to a frontal view reframes him as he walks across to a record rack and turns his back to the camera while he flicks through discs at the far left of the frame. Schrader holds the shot as Michelle emerges from the staircase in the center background, the camera then following her as she circles the store to a rack behind Julian's from which she picks up an album. A cut to an opposite angle shows Julian's face in the left foreground with Michelle in the background to screen right. The camera tracks right with Julian as he walks to the end of the aisle, where he disappears briefly from shot before reappearing in the frame, whereupon the camera tracks left to follow him as he approaches Michelle and makes a show of "accidentally" colliding with her.

This scene is memorable for the playfulness and wit with which it is assembled. Its eloquent portrayal of the flirtatious but covert relationship that is beginning to emerge between Julian and Michelle humorously unfolds through the camera's teasing participation in their game of cat and mouse. A little over twenty minutes later, this scene will be recalled in a blackly droll pastiche of their assignation.

The parallel sequence opens as Julian, seen from the rear, runs across the road toward a similar but slightly shabbier row of shops. As he slows to walking pace, the camera follows him at closer proximity than in the first sequence.

Figure 2.1 *American Gigolo* (1980): in the record store.

Here, again, he pauses and turns to look over his shoulder. Again, we cut to his point of view. This time, a young man follows behind, ineffectually lowering his head instead of darting away from his quarry's gaze. In contrast to the first sequence, when the camera returns to Julian it resumes its rear perspective.

A further cut frames Julian in profile, moving laterally with him as he continues along the street, pausing when he pauses to look behind him once more. Then, as Julian presses ahead, the camera suddenly doubles back in the opposite direction, tracking laterally along the line of the curb until it comes to rest upon the pursuer, whose turn it has come to pause. When he moves forward, the camera reverses direction once again to track with him as he strides purposefully toward the off-screen Julian—all this in one unbroken take. The next shot frames the man's face as he approaches the camera, his progress brusquely curtailed when Julian suddenly breaks into the frame and slams him against the wall in a moment that blindsides the viewer as much as it does the hapless stalker. At this point, the shots become shorter and jerkier as the men's confrontation plays out in front of a large movie poster advertising, appropriately enough, *The Warriors* (1979, Hill).

Neither the similarities nor the contrasts between these pickup sequences are easy to miss as we shift gear from whimsical anticipation of romance to a choreography more redolent of a cruise for rough trade. Julian's failure to observe the boundary between sex and violence was, after all, one of the errors of judgment that led him to be framed for murder in the first place. Yet, despite strong similarities between the behavior of the characters in these sequences, it is the dazzlingly elaborate "unmotivated" camera movements that serve most effectively to bind them together and to assign them meanings that far exceed their narrative content.

THE COMFORT OF STRANGERS

Adapted by Harold Pinter from a short novel by Ian McEwan, this story follows an English couple, Mary and Colin (Natasha Richardson and Rupert Everett), vacationing in Venice as they seek a new direction for their staling relationship. There they meet Robert (Christopher Walken) and, soon after, his wife Caroline (Helen Mirren). What seems, at first, a chance encounter slowly reveals itself as something far more sinister.

For this film, Schrader adopted a more opulent style of camerawork than he had used in any previous film. "I just felt that if I'm going to tell a story this dark and this bitter I have to polish the exterior of the apple to a fine shine so that it looks so delicious that you cannot resist the temptation to bite in," he has explained. "Only then does the viewer realise that this delicious apple is full of worms and maggots."[12]

This is not the only motive for, nor effect of, the complex and striking camerawork of *The Comfort of Strangers*. The Venice setting is crucial to the film, its geography a powerful metaphor for the protagonists' psychological journeys. The view of the city with which Schrader presents us is a touristic, outsider's view that frames it as an insoluble puzzle: a city articulating a sense of destiny that frustrates goals or purpose. Throughout the film, cinematographer Dante Spinotti's serpentine camerawork loops and coils like the narrow, twisting alleys and waterways of Venice. Its surprising turns externalize the psychosexual labyrinth the four lead characters traverse while simultaneously encouraging and frustrating audience attempts to untangle its mystery.

Like *American Gigolo*, *The Comfort of Strangers* opens boldly and confidently, but this time to very different effect. A discomfiting air of strangeness pervades the film from the start. This arises, in large part, from a concurrent sense of portentousness and of holding back. The feeling, as a viewer, is that one is being toyed with; that everything will unfold with an unwavering inevitability, but that to reach the dark heart of the labyrinth we must fumble our way forward, following the clues while unsure if the destination is one we'll truly be pleased to reach.

During the opening titles we are taken on a mysterious and tantalizing tour that has no direct equivalent in McEwan's book. It begins as the camera creeps slowly across an elaborate ceiling hung with magnificent middle-eastern lamps, the framing perfectly symmetrical and the imagery almost abstract in its beauty. In subsequent shots it roves sinuously around a sumptuous apartment, picking out details of its décor through a haze of gauzy screens, pausing and tilting to observe pictures on the walls (paintings of women, an antique map of Venice). It winds through doorways, passing through a kitchen to a bedroom where it lingers over the bed. In the living area it passes a desk where a photograph album and an assortment of other mementos are fastidiously laid out in frozen display. A door opens and a woman crosses the frame, her face unseen as she moves slowly through the shadows, almost as one who walks in sleep. At this moment, a voiceover begins—not hers, but a man's. As he describes his father, a fearsome figure, the camera does not follow her. Instead it pursues its winding course past a mirror that reflects her distant silhouette as she approaches a Byzantine window where the sequence ends on a panorama of church towers in the dusk.

Where are we? Who is speaking? This sequence betokens a riddle to be solved: one the filmmakers will disclose in their own good time, but in which we are challenged to participate actively. Lasting for almost three-and-a-half minutes and containing only the barest of action, it epitomizes Schrader's definition of "unmotivated" camera movement: "motivated by the storyteller, not the story." It is, perhaps, needless to say that we will return to this apartment later in the film. Following McEwan's example, Schrader makes extensive use of foreshadowing, each tiny detail piling up in subtle variations until we reach the climax in which every element has been augured by a murmuration of pointers.

A similar sense of mystery permeates the other sequences discussed here, the first of which follows on almost immediately from the opening sequence. Two establishing shots of the city (the famed Grand Canal and the iconic domes of the Basilica di San Marco) are succeeded by a static long-shot of Colin idling on his hotel balcony. Schrader cuts to a shot of a passing vaporetto (the angle too low and close to represent Colin's point of view) before returning to a shot of the balcony. This time, we see Colin from a closer angle, the camera moving unsteadily from a side-angle until it pauses as he is center-frame.

Is this simply a curiously framed establishing shot, or could it, perhaps, represent a point of view? This suspicion will be borne out some minutes later when Mary and Colin are out and about in the city. There, a prowling camera pursues them in what is unquestionably a series of point-of-view shots, which, to negate any possibility of doubt, is punctuated by several freeze-frames accompanied by the distinctive sound of a camera shutter. The voyeuristic quality of the opening scene spills over into the first episodes of narrative action where, as in *American Gigolo*, the double-edged act of seeing and being seen is a cardinal quality. Moreover, while the camera movements of the two scenes are differently motivated, in each case they are clearly marked as arising from an agency other than that which might best serve the viewer's own instincts.

The final scene I consider is one of the film's most celebrated. It occurs slightly under half an hour in, taking place shortly after Mary and Colin, who have become lost in a tenebrous maze of eerily deserted blind alleys while searching for a restaurant, first meet Robert. He conducts them to a bar where he circuitously answers Mary's question about how he met his wife by relating an extremely long childhood anecdote.

Much of the time it takes for Robert to tell his tale is occupied by classical conventions of scene dissection and continuity editing as Schrader cuts between shots of the speaker and the reactions of his listeners. Yet there is also a period of more than a minute during which we do not see Robert, Colin or Mary at all. When a young man passes their table, Robert glances up momentarily and makes a small gesture of acknowledgment. At this juncture, the camera takes an unexpected turn. Instead of staying with the group, it follows the newcomer across the room, passing other tables until it comes to rest on a cluster of men at the main bar. Pausing on one as he lights a cigarette, it then flips direction, backtracking to study his companion as he applies a lipstick.

During the next four shots, the camera continues to roam around the room, studying its other occupants. First, it tilts up from a spinning jukebox record to the chiseled face of a spruce young man hunched intently over the machine. It then peers over the shoulder of another man as he flirtatiously primps his hair

Figure 2.2 *The Comfort of Strangers* (1990): in Robert's bar.

while chatting with a coquettish transvestite, circling around him to see her better. Next it slowly approaches a woman who sits alone at a table, quietly watching. The fourth shot is a bird's-eye view of a card game, the camera moving in closer as it pauses to note the fleeting caress of fingers as hands come together to swipe away the discarded cards. At last, it returns to Robert's table, peering down at the protagonists through a high-arched doorway before settling back into classical framing and editing conventions for the remainder of the scene.

One very practical motivation for this "travelogue," as Schrader dubs it, is that it provides visual interest and intrigue during Robert's lengthy monologue, which, he reports, Walken had insisted on shooting in a single ten-minute take.[13] It also serves to alert the viewer to something Robert's guests have failed to note—that he has brought them to a gay bar. The significance of this will be clarified as the story unfolds.

Each camera movement, as purposefully inquisitive as it is meandering, is suggestive of a point of view. Yet, as in the opening scene, it does not correlate with the perspective of any character within the film. Instead, it is another striking example of "unmotivated" movement, which "reflects the director's point of view first and the characters and narrative second." Just as Pinter's dialogue demands to be carefully weighed, interrogated, and read between the lines, so Schrader adds countless layers of nuance through the "high style" of the camerawork and mise-en-scène. As baffling and disorientating as La Serenissima itself, the camera twists and turns, repeating, backtracking, roving restlessly but seldom penetrating the lush but deceitful surfaces until they are finally ripped asunder as the film crescendos in one of its devastating final scenes.

AUTO FOCUS

This biopic of actor Bob Crane (Greg Kinnear) follows a similar narrative and stylistic trajectory to *American Gigolo*, but with the formal development ramped up to the nth degree. Here again, the disintegration of a superficially stable and satisfactory life is articulated through the visible moldering of its once alluring veneer.

As we move through *Auto Focus*, the formal techniques Schrader employs change dramatically. A relatively static camera technique, not dissimilar from that employed in *Hogan's Heroes* (1965–71), the long-running television sitcom in which Crane starred, gives way to handheld camera as he becomes increasingly obsessed with shooting home video pornography and his personal and professional lives founder. The changes in camera style partake of a broader formal shift as set design, lighting, color palettes, film stock, music, and performance style also mutate. The goal, says Schrader, was "that, at some point, the viewer would realize he or she is now watching a film extremely different from what they were watching an hour ago."[14]

Auto Focus synthesizes the voyeurism of *The Comfort of Strangers* with the narcissistic display of *American Gigolo*. This is, of course, part and parcel of the fact that the main character is an actor, staging a performance for the television cameras and for the audiences of the strip clubs in which he plays drums as an extracurricular hobby. He is also mounting an off-camera show of being a certain kind of guy for the press, his fans, and (in the early stages of the film) his family. This changes after electronics whiz John Carpenter (Willem Dafoe) introduces him to an early form of home video recording and he gets hooked on creating amateur sex films. Despite being captivated by his own appearance within these films, which he repeatedly re-views, his self-awareness and the care with which he had previously tended his public image diminish exponentially.

This change is powerfully expressed through the film style. Like *American Gigolo* and *The Comfort of Strangers*, *Auto Focus* simultaneously moves forward while also folding back on itself in a loop. All three films have a circularity whereby key early scenes are mirrored later on but with pointedly different emphases.

After an animated opening title sequence that riffs on the mid-century modern style and the movie-star glamour and materialism of the 1950s and early 1960s, the action begins with a scene of Bob at work as a radio show host. This is followed by a scene in the office of his agent Lenny (Ron Leibman) and then by a family mealtime scene. In each case, Kinnear's performance style is cheery and superficial. Bob's manner and mode of speech at home are as shallow and inauthentic as when he is performing professionally; he talks like a television sitcom character. The film style echoes this; the colors are light and bright and the editing and camera movements discrete. Later, performance style and dialogue become rawer and the camerawork begins to undermine, rather than support, the initial sense of order and decorum. Two later scenes in Lenny's office highlight this contrast.

The very first scene in Lenny's office opens with Bob in long-shot near the center of the frame, idly tapping the windowsill with his drumsticks before approaching his agent's desk. As he sits down, Schrader moves to a sequence of shot/reverse shot at progressively closer angles as the men converse. The camera is relatively static bar slight reframing movements and it remains, for the most part, at their seated head height. By Bob's next visit to Lenny's office, around fifty-three minutes in, the film has already become darker and the camera movements jerkier and more erratic. Schrader adopts a primarily shot/reverse structure again but, this time, the camera is never still. Although, as before, its major movements follow those of the characters, now it joggles incessantly in "shaky cam."

A further twenty minutes into the film, after behaving deplorably on a television cookery show, Bob finds himself in Lenny's office once again. This time (as in the scene that directly precedes it) the camera wavers wildly, much as it does in Bob and John's home videos. Yet, whereas in scenes I discussed from *American Gigolo* and *The Comfort of Strangers* a slight jerkiness of camera movement had been used to indicate point-of-view shots, here the camera position rarely approximates the eyeline of either character. Its behavior is as agitated and seemingly uncontrolled as Bob's, with sudden changes in height, direction and shot scale. At one point it pans rapidly from Lenny's face to Bob's, aping the style of an amateur moviemaker endeavoring to keep pace with intensifying action.

By now, the film's dominant style is notably disjointed; establishing shots and conventional scene dissections have been all but abandoned. "The reason I was doing that," Schrader says, "was to create the sense that all the days are swimming together now and the boat is unanchored."[15] The technique is effective and highly disconcerting. Although these "unmotivated" camera movements are, of course, every bit as controlled as the velvety cinematography of *The Comfort of Strangers*, the effect is to implicate the storyteller and the viewer in what comes across as a mushrooming instability. It is almost as though the toxicity of Bob's voyeuristic obsessions has projected its poisoned spores beyond the screen, infecting his audience with the same disease.

The other scene I wish to consider serves as a key indicator of Bob's irreversible slide from a functional addict to a man whose life has skidded out of control. This is a fantasy sequence that occurs around three-quarters of an hour through the film. Exhausted by his attempts to balance the rigors of late-night sex parties with early-morning set calls, and obligations to his wife and family with the demands of his new girlfriend, co-actor Patti Olsen (Maria Bello), he slips into a daydream while shooting *Hogan's Heroes*.

The scene opens with a long-shot of the set as the clapperboard snaps shut and the action begins, after which two closer shots of the actors mimic the angles of the television cameras. After Bob makes a Freudian slip with one of his lines, the camera holds on a close-up of his face as a whirling spiral appears in superimposition, an intentionally old-fashioned movie gimmick that signals the transition into a subjective sequence. Accompanied by a piercing, discordant score, the camera cranes rapidly up from his face to a bird's-eye view, twisting as it does so in imitation of the animated spiral, while the lighting shifts to a bilious green. In the blink of an eye, Bob has transformed from man to manikin, standing trapped within the diminutive three-sided box of the set.

For the next shots, Schrader drops back down to the level of the actors. Now the camera circles around Bob as, in fear and confusion, he seeks an exit from the claustrophobic cage in which he is imprisoned with characters that have overstepped their diegetic roles and begun to comment on his personal life. In this waking nightmare, a laughing Colonel Klink (Kurt Fuller) and another German officer interrogate him from leering, low-angle shots while he tests the doors and windows, closing and bolting the only open one to barricade himself from a neon-lit glamour girl who gyrates with a feather boa just outside.

Patti now enters this giddy phantasmagoria in her *Hogan's Heroes* character of Hilda. Stripping down to racy red lingerie, she splays herself provocatively on Klink's desk where she entreats a stupefied Bob to fuck her as she devours the sexual attentions of both officers. By now, the camera has ceased its spinning; instead, as Bob watches her lascivious display, it shifts to a shakier, more disjointed style. The skittish handheld camerawork continues as John enters the room with his video camera and starts to film the debauchery with a palpable enthusiasm.

As Bob looks on aghast, a door opens to reveal his wife Anne (Rita Wilson), a child clutched under each of her arms as she surveys the carousal and incongruously enjoins him to fuck his mistress. The camera then follows Bob as he steps toward the doorway, from which his young son stares dispassionately at the intensifying orgy, before it follows him back to the desk. Here Klink tears himself away from Patti/Hilda for just long enough to tell Bob he has no answers to his problems before tipping him an ironic salute. The scene fades out and Schrader cuts back to a long-shot of the set, the lighting now cold and even and the restless camera stilled as Bob emerges from his reverie.

In this short sequence of barely more than two minutes' duration all the separate pieces of Bob's carefully compartmentalized life crash into unwelcome contact. At the same time, the rapidly evolving camera style succinctly prefigures what will become the film's dominant stylistic trajectory. By the time the final scenes of *Auto Focus* play out in an unstable montage of temporal and spatial fragments, we have re-entered the ghastly, disquieting realm of subjectivity from which the true facts of Bob Crane's savage murder may never fully emerge.

FIRST REFORMED

The first thing to strike the viewer of *First Reformed* is the singularity and power of its style. This is rammed home at the very outset by the proclamation: "The following film was shot in an aspect ratio of 1.33 per the artistic request of the director and will be shown exclusively in this format across all media." Further infractions of contemporary filmmaking norms become apparent from the moment the first photographic image fades in behind the opening titles.

A chronicle of spiritual despair, *First Reformed* follows Reverend Ernst Toller (Ethan Hawke), the minister of a sparsely attended Protestant church, as he wrestles his own demons beneath the oppressive canopy of looming ecological apocalypse. Schrader's most austere film to date, it evokes the films and filmmakers that first drew him to write about cinema, most notably in his 1972 book *Transcendental Style in Film: Ozu, Bresson, Dreyer*. The inspirations he draws from Robert Bresson's *Diary of a Country Priest* (1951) and *Pickpocket* (1959), and from Carl Theodor Dreyer's *Ordet* (1955), as well as Ingmar Bergman's *Winter Light* (1963), are unmistakable.

Writing about *Pickpocket*, Schrader astutely observed that "the convergence of spirituality and cinema would occur in style, not content. In the How, not the What",[16] which he demonstrates with *First Reformed*. "By delaying edits, not moving the camera, forswearing music cues, not employing coverage, and heightening the mundane, transcendental style creates a sense of unease the viewer must resolve."[17]

In this ultra-ascetic film, Schrader moves the camera very rarely, abjuring classical conventions of editing and camerawork. Especially striking throughout the greater part of the film is the extent to which his almost entirely static camera set-ups fail to follow the movement of characters through, or beyond the limits of, the frame. Consequently, the rare occasions on which he chooses to move the camera are very noticeable. Small movements that might seem utterly inconsequential in other films assume enormous weight. Tiny though they may be, their rarity begs the question: what motivates this movement?

In the course of this 113-minute film, the camera moves in just twelve scenes. In several cases, the movement is restricted to a single shot. In fact, nearly a full hour goes by before a scene occurs that contains more extensive movement than this. Up to that point, the camera only moves three times. In each of these cases, it draws us toward something important.

The film's first photographic image is spartan in the extreme: a sixty-second shot comprised of a slow movement toward the exterior of the titular church. Framed perfectly symmetrically amid an unpeopled winter landscape of leafless trees and immaculate topiary, First Reformed presents a somber and forbidding aspect, its pallid spire a feeble shaft of light in the heavy, crepuscular sky. The washed-out gray-blue color palette, the low angle of the camera, and the obdurately slow movement toward the church's firmly closed doors all combine to intensify this impression. This will not be a cheery film, nor one that proffers easy pleasures.

Thirteen minutes elapse before Schrader moves the camera again. He does so during a scene in which Toller endeavors to counsel parishioner Michael (Philip Ettinger), a deeply troubled environmental activist. Occupying the first fourteen seconds of a twenty-two-second shot, the movement is small but emphatic. Shifting from medium close-up to a close-up of Toller's face, it draws nearer to him as he listens to Michael. The move is accompanied by the verbal account of this exchange he will later record in his diary: "I felt like I was Jacob wrestling all night with the angel. [. . .] It was exhilarating." When the interior monologue ceases, so does the camera movement. In a more conventional film this movement would be unexceptional. Here it marks a pivotal moment: the problematic convergence of Toller's ecological radicalization and his Christian faith.

The third camera movement takes place thirty-three minutes into the film and lasts for around thirteen seconds of a forty-two-second shot. Michael's wife Mary (Amanda Seyfried) wishes to show Toller something that worries her. This time, Schrader sandwiches the movement between two static camera set-ups. The shot starts outside Mary's home, holding still on the front door while she exits the house. As she follows the sidewalk round to the adjacent garage, Toller behind her, the camera tracks laterally to the right, holding both characters in profile until they turn away into the drive, at which point it holds briefly on their receding figures.

Here is a conspicuously "unmotivated" camera movement that pushes Schrader, the storyteller, to the fore. It serves no clear narrative purpose; the scene could have been shot just as lucidly without it. Its significance is as the marker of another decisive moment; a small hint of coming change is encoded within the very act of moving the camera. It immediately precedes the scene in which Mary reveals her discovery of Michael's explosive-laden suicide vest, which Toller takes away with him.

It is not until fifty-eight minutes into the film that camera movements occur consecutively in the five middle shots of a seven-shot sequence. It is a lyrical interlude in which Toller takes a woodland bicycle ride with Mary. Though the tree branches remain as barren as in the opening shot, this scene has a more relaxed and carefree tone than any other, an air to which the camera movements contribute substantively. It introduces a rare moment of connection between Toller and the positive aspects of social interaction and the natural world alike. There is a rare flash of joy as he speeds along the leaf-littered path and, in one moment, even laughs. But this idyll will not last long. Immediately afterwards, we are back in Mary's dingy garage from which, loosely inverting their previous entry into that space, a leftward camera movement follows their return to her house.

Schrader uses the next movement, seventy-three minutes in, to ramp up the burgeoning sense of dread. Accompanied by a nerve-jangling, discordant rumbling, the camera draws in close to Toller's whiskey glass as he adds a generous dash of Pepto-Bismol to his drink, the viscous pink fluid swirling and bubbling forebodingly in anticipation of the more toxic cocktail he will later prepare for himself. The final act approaches. From here on in, camera movement occurs at more frequent intervals and over more extended periods as the action builds to a climax.

During the last half-hour of the film, camera movement is found in six more scenes. The third and fourth are driving scenes. In the first of these, Toller journeys under overcast skies to the BALQ Industries energy plant for a behind-the-scenes tour of an organization he has pegged as a particularly heinous environmental polluter. In the second, he makes a nocturnal vigil to the contaminated estuary flats where the suicidal Michael's ashes had been scattered and where, as dawn finds him still pacing this fetid Gethsemane, the ragged cruciform mast of a keeling ship looms prominently in the background.

These scenes in which Toller seeks to validate the extreme course of action he intends are enclosed within two briefer camera movements, both of which occur in scenes directly related to his drastic plan. A couple of minutes prior to his factory visit we witness a scene between Toller and Mary in which she embraces him. Holding her warmly by both hands, he tells her not to come to First Reformed's upcoming reconsecration ceremony. As he does so, the camera moves in toward them. Both their pose and its framing clearly imply their intensifying emotional connection with one another, while the movement also underscores the import of his interdiction.

The other brief movement occurs as the reconsecration gets under way. A shot of Reverend Joel Jeffers (Cedric Antonio Kyles) entering the church is framed as through the viewfinder of a video camera, complete with superimposed digital readouts of battery and recording status. Here again is a shot that in a less formally austere film would not seem out of place in such a context but which, in this instance, jars. Its incongruity invites interpretation. Might it suggest, perhaps, that Toller's intended act will be meaningless unless media recording can bear permanent witness?

Important though all six camera movements are in this final half-hour, the first and last occurrences, which work together as a pair, are by far the most extensive and powerful. These are the scenes where, in Schrader's words, the story will "transcend the material world, and touch the world of the spirit."[18]

First comes Toller and Mary's "magical mystery tour" where, lying on top of one another in deep but chaste physical and mental connection, they begin to levitate. As the room spins away, they rise into a computer-generated galaxy. An unbroken two-minute shot holds the pair in frame almost to its end, while a series of dissolves in the background floats them above the natural wonders of snowy mountain peaks, majestic canyons, crashing waves and forest canopies. Alas, this beatitude is only fleeting. The moment Toller turns his head and breaks their connection, the paradise gives way to an ecological abyss; now they float above a congested superhighway, slipping out of frame above a wasteland of abandoned car tires. Five more aerial panoramas complete the sequence: infernal vistas of smoking factories, deforestation, and rivers of trash that occupy the full frame, neither mediated nor motivated by characters or plot.

It is the levitation sequence that makes *First Reformed*'s final scene possible. When Mary propitiously interrupts Toller at his moment of suicide, grace is expressed less in the sublime carnality of their osculation than in the vertiginous orbit of the camera as it spins round and round them. In this bold and breathtaking movement, style and meaning become one. When the shot abruptly ends with a cut to black, the brusqueness with which Schrader hurls his viewers off the carousel pulls us sharply out of the diegesis. It is an audacious move and it ensures that with this film, more than any of his others, our final thoughts will dwell not on the story so much as on the motivations of its teller.

CONCLUSION

Through a career as director, screenwriter, critic, and historian that now spans more than fifty years, Schrader is long-established as one of the most distinctive voices in American cinema. While, as a director and screenwriter, he regularly pursues favored themes and narrative structures, such as the psychological journeys of lost or damaged characters to a defining moment in their lives, the distinctiveness of his voice goes beyond that. He not only describes; he also questions and challenges.

Schrader's personal perspective, both as critic and filmmaker, is invariably loud and clear. In his filmmaking, his frequent use of "unmotivated" camerawork to put the director's point of view first accords with his broader intellectual approach to film culture. The prominence of his authorial voice encourages active reading on the part of his viewers; he harnesses the potential of camera movement to deliver a rhetoric that encourages a similar kind of dialogue with his audiences to that found in his critical works.

Often characterised as one of the "movie brat" generation—film school educated and steeped in the history of Hollywood classicism and European modernism alike—Schrader undoubtedly shares many qualities with his contemporaries, who emerged from a milieu characterized by changing industrial structures and technologies as well as cross-pollination of ideas. One is his unabashed willingness to employ bold stylistic devices to accentuate his authorial voice; another is intertextual referencing of his other films alongside those of venerated predecessors.

Yet Schrader also stands apart in his detailed knowledge and application of wider traditions of art and design theory and practice, from the early lesson he took from American designer Charles Eames that "images are ideas"[19] to his own superbly thought-out and wide-ranging essay, "Canon Fodder" (2006).[20] With such a rigorous intellectual underpinning to his creative work it is little wonder to find him dubbed "the philosopher's 'movie brat' director."[21]

Schrader's relentless search to find the "right solution to the right problem" in every undertaking has also prevented his style from ossifying in the ways sometimes observable among his peers. Consider, for instance, his use of the Steadicam, which would become a celebrated trademark of Brian De Palma and Martin Scorsese. After pipping these directors to the post in using this newly available technology for *American Gigolo*, Schrader would tailor other styles of camerawork to specific projects. Moreover, while many filmmakers had seized on the Steadicam as a tool with which to follow the actions to which viewers might instinctively incline ("motivated" movements), Schrader more often does the opposite. In many scenes, his approach is more akin to an innovation he credits to Jean-Luc Godard: "to make the camera's perspective just as valid as that of its subjects. [To say . . .] I'm part of the story."[22]

Here lies the crux of Schrader's penchant for "unmotivated" camera movement. This is the device through which he most insistently articulates his presence as narrator, using it to promote a diegetic, rather than mimetic, approach to storytelling, and debarring intellectual passivity on the part of his audiences. While always keeping within the framework of commercial narrative cinema, Schrader's camera sometimes leads us toward the boundary line where narrative immersion collides with philosophical speculation, reminding us time and again that he makes his films because he has something to say.

NOTES

1. Paul Schrader, "Director Commentary," *Auto Focus*, DVD (Sony Pictures Classics, 2002).
2. Kevin Jackson (ed.), *Schrader on Schrader & Other Writings* (London: Faber and Faber, 1990), 91.
3. Paul Schrader, "Canon Fodder," *Film Comment*, September/October 2016, 44.
4. Alex Simon, "Paul Schrader: The Hollywood Interview," January 8, 2013, http://thehollywoodinterview.blogspot.co.uk/2008/01/paul-schrader-hollywood-interview.html (last accessed April 24, 2019).

5. Paul Schrader, "Game Changers: Camera Movement," *Film Comment*, March/April 2015, https://www.filmcomment.com/article/game-changers-camera-movement (last accessed April 24, 2019).
6. Ibid.
7. Paul Schrader, "Canon Fodder," *Film Comment*, September/October 2016, 46.
8. Schrader, "Game Changers."
9. Simon, "Paul Schrader."
10. Jackson, 160.
11. Jackson, 147.
12. Paul Schrader, "Director Commentary," *The Comfort of Strangers*, DVD/Blu-ray (British Film Institute, 2018).
13. Ibid.
14. Schrader, "Director Commentary," *Auto Focus*.
15. Ibid.
16. Schrader, "Rethinking Transcendental Style," 2.
17. Ibid., 3.
18. Hunter Harris, "How Paul Schrader Made Ethan Hawke Float in *First Reformed*," *Vulture*, 8 February 2019, www.vulture.com/2019/02/paul-schrader-first-reformed-script-ethan-hawke-levitation-scene.html (last accessed April 24, 2019).
19. Jackson, 27.
20. Schrader, "Canon Fodder."
21. John R. Hamilton, "Paul Schrader," *Senses of Cinema*, 56, October 2010, http://sensesofcinema.com/2010/great-directors/paul-schrader (last accessed April 24, 2019).
22. Schrader, "Game Changers."

CHAPTER 3

Late Schrader: From the Canon to the Canyons

Billy Stevenson

THE CANON

While many directors are considered to be part of the canon of American cinema, few directors have been so preoccupied *with* that canon, and with the idea of film canons, as Paul Schrader. In an interview conducted with George Kouvaros, Schrader notes that "film itself, in fact, is one of the things that destroyed the notion of the canon. When people talk about a film canon, it's kind of a contradictory phrase."[1] Schrader later explains that this is because the canon is a high cultural concept, whereas film is typically seen as a low cultural medium. However, Schrader argues, this does not mean that the idea of a film canon is untenable. Instead, he advocates for a selective film canon, akin to the academic canon of literature:

> There's a de facto canon in populist literature, and there's a de facto canon in the academy. So, if you have a de facto canon, why not try to find a way to justify it and raise the bar so fucking high that only a few films get over it?[2]

Schrader recommends starting with the "de facto" canon of film and then refining it into an "academic" canon of film. However, his use of the expletive "fucking" conveys an inherent contradiction to this project. By aligning a vernacular expletive with the idea of the film canon, Schrader suggests that the cultural capital of a film canon denies the demotic address of film.

Schrader's main published work, *Transcendental Style in Film: Ozu, Bresson, Dreyer*, provides a possible resolution of this situation. Here, Schrader advocates a rigorous criterion for what constitutes transcendental film. He also uses openly canonical language, observing that "directors are represented by the films discussed rather than by their body of work. Not every slow director is included. Transcendental style occupies a bit of a space just inside the ring."[3] Within Schrader's account, canonicity is defined by director, but even canonical directors do not consistently live up to their directorial vision. This assertion draws upon the language of auteur theory, as formulated in English by Andrew Sarris, who insisted upon the "technical competence" and "distinguishable personality" of the director as a key "criterion of value."[4]

Schrader does not explicitly use the term *auteur* in *Transcendental Style*. However, he does consistently connect the act of directing a film, and the act of composing a piece of literature, which is the figurative basis of the auteur theory, and its rationale for a film canon. The problems of establishing a canon are resolved by recourse to writerly films—not necessarily films that are wordy, or script-driven, but films that use the metaphor of writing to problematize cinema itself. For Schrader, this "doubling technique," in which directorial and literary labor mirror each other, is embodied in narration. Narration forms a point of contact between the visual field of the film and the verbal field of the screenplay. As such, it is a contested zone where the canonical potentiality of film is most vividly articulated, and where Schrader makes some of his most pointed reflections on canonicity in his own film practice.

While this cinematic-literary space might provide a point of departure for canonical reflection, it is less applicable to an American context. Drawing upon Gilles Deleuze, Schrader notes early in *Transcendental Style* that "World War II dates the rough demarcation of a shift, more in Europe than America, from movement-image to time-image."[5] In Schrader's gloss, this means that "a film edit is determined not by action on screen but by the creative desire to associate images over time." Schrader understands this predisposition to "associated images" as a predisposition to transcendental style. However, he also understands it as a predisposition to European style. Whereas Deleuze finds American counterparts in directors like John Cassavetes, Martin Scorsese and Francis Ford Coppola—Schrader's own contemporaries—Schrader only alludes to Orson Welles as an exponent of the time-image, and even then as a harbinger, or trailblazer, rather than as an American actively working at its aesthetic peak.

Schrader therefore poses the cinematic canon as a quasi-literary entity with transcendental cinema at its core. His next critical work was planned as an account of this cinematic canon. Like Harold Bloom's *The Western Canon*, this would feature discussions of key canonical periods in film history, along with an actual list of films deemed to be part of the canon.[6] However, this project never eventuated. Instead, Schrader published an article, titled "Canon Fodder," about his inability to write the book, and the key problems that it posed.[7] These problems are encapsulated in an anecdote he includes about his motivations for writing the book. In this anecdote, Schrader asked an assistant to look up information about actor Montgomery Clift to help with his research. The assistant confused the actor for a place and asked Schrader where it was. In turn, Schrader replied that "I thought it was in the Hollywood Hills." Meanwhile, the assistant "returned to his search engine," none the wiser for the talk.[8]

In this anecdote, three distinct challenges are posed to constructing a cinematic canon. First, the lack of general knowledge about Hollywood history means that Schrader's assistant does not have the cinematic vocabulary required to help Schrader with his canonical enterprise, or to form an appropriate audience for that canonical enterprise. Second, the anecdote suggests that Hollywood as a signifier of cinematic history has been absorbed by Hollywood as a signifier of place. More generally, the anecdote conjures up a world in which spatiality, locality, and geography have reasserted themselves against the cinematic industry that once contained and mediated them. When Schrader responds that Clift is somewhere in the Hollywood Hills, he is telling the truth, since the residues of Clift's existence are most tangible in the photographs, plaques, and paraphernalia present in Hollywood, despite the fact that he was buried in Quaker Cemetery, New York, following his death in New York City in mid-1966. By situating Clift "in" Hollywood in this way, Schrader implies that the materiality of the Los Angeles cityscape has exceeded the capacity of cinema to act as its primary media signifier.

LOS ANGELES AFTER CINEMA

Both of these challenges converge upon a third challenge to the film canon. In Schrader's anecdote, the assistant's oblivion to cinema is associated with his position in front of a computer and his reliance upon a search engine. Both these qualities suggest that the rise of digital technology, and the omniscience of computers, have eroded the cinematic sensibility necessary for a cinematic canon to properly ramify. Alternatively, it could be argued that the requirement for a film canon arises precisely because cinema is now on the verge of medial history. In either case, Schrader suggests that digital technology and cinematic canonicity exist in a vexed relationship with one another. Moreover, the prospect of Los Angeles after cinema, or a post-cinematic Los Angeles, is presented as the figurative crux of this challenge to the film canon. If the most canonical city in the history of cinema no longer ramifies cinematically, how can a cinematic canon be expected to ramify? Establishing a cinematic canon thus becomes a way to establish dialogue between the cinematic and post-cinematic components of the Los Angeles cityscape as much as elaborating a specific body of releases.

In Schrader's account, the challenge of forming a film canon is thus equated with the challenge of conceptualizing Los Angeles after cinema. Conceptualizing Los Angeles after cinema means considering how its traditionally cinematic ecology responds in the face of a media regime in which, as Steven Shaviro puts it, "all activity is under surveillance from video cameras and microphones, and in return video screens and speakers, moving images and synthesized sounds, are dispersed pretty much everywhere."[9] This challenge is exacerbated by the fact that post-cinematic technology often focuses on imaging devices that are "radically discorrelated from human perception and perceptual technologies," removing the audiovisual field further from the realm of traditional mapping.[10] This question of post-cinematic Los Angeles informs the model of the canon that Schrader outlines over the article. Initially, he argues that the canon is a transcendent concept in and of itself, asserting that "it is, by definition, based on criteria that transcend taste, personal and popular."[11] This demonstrates his initial affinity with Harold Bloom's model of the canon, which he cites frequently. Like Bloom, Schrader starts by dismissing any non-transcendent criteria for the canon as mere "resentment," consigning cultural critique of the canon to academic pedantry.

However, Schrader's account grows more original as it proceeds, starting with his account of cinema. Schrader argues that the demise of cinema coincides with the end of the Anthropocene, forming the first stage in a properly post-human future. This transforms cinema into the last properly human art, and the cinematic canon into a way of recording the last properly human art. However, Schrader also understands the cinematic canon as a way of preparing for a post-cinematic and post-human future, a new "subset of . . . planet life."[12] In the process, he enjoins a very different vision of art from Bloom's static model of universal applicability, instead suggesting that "Art looks to the future; it is society's harbinger. The demise of Art's human narrative is not a sign of creative bankruptcy."[13] While the capitalization of "Art" suggests a transcendent imperative, Schrader's vision of art here is immanent, positing artistic endeavor as a way of articulating what remains inchoate in the world around us. Schrader extends this philosophy to his own work, observing that he is prepared to use film for the remainder of his career, which he estimates to last about a decade, but also conceding that if he was starting his career at this point he wouldn't use film.

"Canon Fodder" was written in 2006, meaning that Schrader's later work has exceeded this window of cinematic production, instead entering a post-cinematic phase that has simultaneously played as a reflection on the canonicity and legacy of cinema itself. This does not necessarily mean, however, that Schrader has entered a post-cinematic period as a conscious experimental choice. Instead, "Canon Fodder" insists that cinema cannot be clearly delineated from post-cinema, and that cinema is already incipient post-cinema, since cinema's position at the cusp of the Anthropocene makes it a transitory medium. This means that a cinematic canon must record cinema as a transition between cinema and what succeeds it, and between the idea of the canon as a culturally stabilizing concept, and a world in which canons may no longer be possible as a culturally stabilizing concept. Schrader's canon is therefore torn between the transcendent imperatives of a regular canon, and his prescience that the cinematic canon must be an anti-canon, or elegy for the canon, as much as a regular canon. In addition, it must be a canon that is enacted by and within film, rather than criticism.

These competing imperatives mean that Schrader's film canon remains both written and unwritten, never completed as a work of film criticism, but also present within his later body of work. In this body of work, Schrader draws upon a radically intermedial conception of cinema that is first formalized in "Canon Fodder," where reconceptualizing the canon also induces him to reconceptualize artistic media more generally. Since a film canon can only be justified by "evaluating cinema [as] a transitional moment" and by "embracing a multiplicity of aesthetic criteria," cinema itself can only be understood in relation to other media, meaning that artistic media can only be understood intermedially.[14] Diverging from auteur theory and canonical discourse in cinematic criticism, which tends to focus on the unique or defining features of film, Schrader instead argues that "cinema is not so much a new art form as a reformulation of existing art forms . . . the twinkling of changes to come."[15] Provocatively, Schrader frames these changes as occurring within a cinematic space, but also ushering the audience beyond a human space, observing wistfully and plangently that "such thoughts fill me not with despair but with envy. I wish I could be there to see the curtain rise."[16]

Schrader's cinematic canon is therefore not a body of works first and foremost, but a heightened attention to the ways in which spaces once associated with cinema, or considered to be specific to cinema, can be refashioned and reconceptualized as spaces of post-cinematic apprehension. In order to broker this idea of the canon, Schrader follows Bloom by listing a series of conservative aesthetic criteria for canonical inclusion, only to radically reformulate—and remediate—what these criteria mean in the context of his own refurbished canon.

The first of these criteria is beauty. Schrader defines beauty, unusually, as medial versatility, suggesting that a text is beautiful if it has the capacity to remediate other texts, and to be remediated in turn: "Beauty is not defined by rules and attributes . . . but by its ability to qualitatively transform reality."[17] The second criteria is strangeness, which Schrader understands as a text's ability to defamiliarize the world by remediating it in an unusual way. The third criteria is unity of form, which Schrader transforms to mean intermediality of form, or unity within intermediality, suggesting that the canonical potential of a film text inheres in its ability to occupy the inherently intermedial situation of film in a poised and profound manner. As a result, film does not have a "significant form" that needs to be canonized, but "a significant juxtaposition of form," meaning that "form follows friction," and these frictions between film and other forms of media need to be accounted for when thinking canonically.[18]

The fourth criterion that Schrader invokes is tradition. This is the most pervasive criteria when it comes to creating canons, which tend to be based on the assumption that texts that pass into tradition have a greater canonical potential than those that are discarded or ignored. In Bloom's account of the canon, tradition is defined by the anxiety of influence that enjoins writers to rework and reinterpret the texts that have come before them. In Schrader's account, this process is more simultaneous than sequential. Rather than tradition signifying a cumulative accretion of canonical texts, each of which is in dialogue with those that came before it, Schrader uses tradition to designate the receptivity of the original film text to being repurposed, remediated, and reappropriated from the moment it is released. Since "it's not unusual for major filmmakers, shunted aside, to watch . . . as their life's work is remade and redefined," enduring films must be alive from the outset to this process of reinvention, and to court the tradition of simultaneous reinvention that distinguishes cinematic production.[19]

All four of these criteria culminate with the fifth, which Schrader describes as repeatability. This is his version of the criterion of universality that underpins Bloom's model of the canon, where it complements the criteria of tradition by suggesting that a canonical text must speak to audiences in vastly different contexts and situations from that of the text's original production. Most provocatively, Schrader transforms universality into repeatability, or remediability, as he suggests that the most canonical films are—paradoxically—those that are able to survive the medium of film itself, and speak to a post-cinematic landscape. While he calls this process repeatability, the examples he draws from the other plastic arts—a Van Gogh painting remade as a poster, an Eames chair remade as a replica—make it clear that this criterion depends on the capacity of the original art work to take a different material form. This criterion thus doesn't simply involve the capacity of a film to endure across multiple screenings, but throughout its remediation as "videotape, DVDs and downloadable digital files," all of which changes, Schrader suggests, fundamentally alter its meaning and nature.[20]

Between these five criteria, and despite the trappings of Bloom's more conservative canon, Schrader thus outlines the situation of post-cinematic media four years before Steven Shaviro's iconic account of it in *Post Cinematic Affect*. Rather than theorize this media ecology further, however, Schrader proceeded to deflect and expand the import of "Canon Fodder" into his subsequent films, most of which contemplate these five aesthetic criteria, and the transition from a cinematic to a post-cinematic environment, in different ways. Most of these films also reflect upon the cinematic canon as a figure for this transition, rather than a static or viable entity in itself, while *The Canyons*—the most fully formed of these medial reflections—grounds it in the post-cinematic iteration of Los Angeles that commences "Canon Fodder."

THE CANYONS

Released in 2013, *The Canyons* quickly became notorious for its difficult and unconventional production.[21] The script is written by Bret Easton Ellis and revolves around three characters. Christian, played by James Deen, is a wealthy producer living in Malibu. He is currently financing a slasher film. Tara, played by Lindsay Lohan, is his girlfriend. She lives with him in his house. Ryan, played by Nolan Funk, is an actor who used to date Tara, and who is appearing in Christian's upcoming film. *The Canyons* opens with these three characters in conversation, and follows their love triangle as it develops, along with the implications for Christian's slasher film. Ostensibly, the focus is on whether or not this film will be made, and the power that Christian holds as its producer. However, this focus is gradually displaced as all three characters realize that the buying power of cinema in Hollywood has waned. Schrader foreshadows this situation in the credit sequence, which features images of old multiplexes, shot in an ugly sepia tint that looks like a deliberately unsuccessful attempt to capture the '70s graininess that became so fetishized in American cinema in the early 2010s. At the same time, this style recalls the grittier appearance of Schrader's early films, as if considering the role that his own cinematic legacy plays in a post-cinematic media ecology.

Figure 3.1 The decline and desuetude of cinematic infrastructure.

This opening sequence shows interiors and exteriors, but continually falls short of cinematic framing, or an elegiac register. The multiplexes of the past simply look ugly, removing Los Angeles's cinematic heritage as a stable signifier from the outset, and impoverishing the noir register typically used in elegies for Los Angeles. The cinematic viability of the city and the noir viability of the city thereby become intertwined as the narrative proceeds. Neither is especially convincing in these opening images, which are too cursory and peremptory to allow the viewer to even immerse themselves in their decayed grandeur. Nor do these multiplexes intrude into the action in any immediate way, despite forming the backdrop to the recurring intertitles that announce the day of the week (the action taking place over a couple of days).

The first scene between the three main characters also signals an impoverished cinematic lexicon. All three members of the cast existed on the fringes of cinematic legitimacy in 2012. While Lohan had the most conventional cinematic career, her activities off-screen had removed her from the upper echelon of Hollywood casting. Nolan Funk was primarily known for his work on the high school musical television show *Glee* (2009–15) and has done very little big-budget cinematic work since. Finally, James Deen was and is an adult performer, rather than a cinematic actor. The parodic twist of James Deen's name encapsulates this awry relation to the cinematic heritage of Hollywood. In the first scene between these three actors, Schrader adopts a 180-degree style of conversational editing and cuts away from characters when they are speaking or participating in conversation. This displaces the focus of the scene and orients the space toward the distracting presence of digital technology. Midway through, Tara yawns as Christian shows her a shirtless man on his phone, while Christian talks to Ryan about the pleasures of making movies on an iPhone.

During these opening sequences, Schrader shoots the film as if prescient that most viewers will be immediately distracted from the film by their own digital devices. This removes the cinematic sheen, or cinematic substrate, from the image, which is doubly disorienting because Schrader also adopts a heightened style of cinematic framing at key moments, as in a stylized shot of a lemon being placed in a glass of lemonade. This odd combination of cinematic style and cinematic indifference is encapsulated in Christian's interest in hookup culture. Unlike Ryan and his girlfriend Gina, played by Amanda Brooks, Christian and Tara engage extensively in threesomes and orgies. While these provide Christian with sexual pleasure, they also form his main creative outlet. He records and compiles footage of himself and Tara with other men, and is scrupulous about chatting online with prospective hookups to get a clear image of them. These hookup scenes are also where Deen's performance in the film is most powerful and unusual. Like many adult movie stars, he is used to being in front of the camera, but doesn't have a cinematic presence, or a charismatic presence, per se. That odd combination drives the film, perhaps explaining why Schrader chooses to be quite coy about Deen's naked body, in a film that is otherwise replete with nudity and frank sexual scenes.

This post-cinematic presence informs the odd spatiality of *The Canyons*. For a film named after Los Angeles, and set in Los Angeles, many of the scenes feel as if they could be shot anywhere. Two of these scenes are especially striking in terms of Schrader's project. In the first, Schrader uses a tracking-shot to follow Tara as she walks through Westfield Century City. This sequence mirrors the tracking-shot in Brian De Palma's *Body Double* (1984) in which Jake Scully (Craig Wasson) tracks Holly Body (Melanie Griffith) through the shopping complex at 421 Rodeo Drive.[22] Like De Palma, Schrader's camera is torn between the sensuality of the actress's body and the consumer objects and spaces on display. However, in De Palma's version, the allure of Griffith results in a similar allure for the lush fixtures and décor of 421 Rodeo Drive. In Schrader's version, Westfield Century City seems to repel this allure, displacing Lohan from the focus of the shot, and disturbing its sensuous organization.

In part, this is due to the way in which Schrader shoots this scene. The camera is alternately too fluid and not fluid enough, never sufficiently sinking into the rhythm of Tara's walk to situate the audience in the scene, but too mobile to allow for any kind of distance or detachment either. Similarly, the camera looks a little too fluid to feel properly handheld, but a little too handheld to play as a bravura tracking-shot either. At times, it feels like a drone shot at ground level, too removed from the hand of a director, or of a guiding artistic agent, to be immersive, atmospheric, or even aesthetic in a conventional sense. Accordingly, when Tara arrives at the end of her trajectory, the scene that ensues is atonal, awkward, and anticlimactic. This is when we first learn that she used to date Ryan. However, the revelation is swallowed up by the diffuse and half-formed nature of the space where she articulates it.

Figure 3.2 The post-cinematic space of Westfield Century City.

The sensuous disruption of this scene is also due to the space where it takes place. Before 2002, Westfield Century City was the Century Square Shopping Mall. This is one of the most consistently refurbished malls in Los Angeles, and each refurbishment represents a new stage in the evolution of the mall. In 1976, the mall was extended into the parking lot, and expanded to accommodate a greater variety of chain stores. In 1987, the mall was refitted with a multiplex and a food court. In 1996, the original flagship stores were replaced by a new generation of tenants, and integrated more into a globalized mall structure, with Bloomingdale's and Macy's replacing The Broadway and Bullock's respectively. Westfield then acquired the mall in 2002, and renovated the food court and multiplex to add more screens and impose the Westfield brand and look onto the décor. Finally, in 2009, plans for a high-end residential tower further eroded the original demotic address of the mall, with Nordstrom and then Eataly arriving to mark the acceleration of real estate prices in the area.[23]

Westfield Century City therefore evokes the erosion of public space in Los Angeles in a particularly emphatic manner, especially in the wake of its acquisition by Westfield. That change is all the more dramatic when compared to 421 Rodeo Drive, and to Rodeo Drive as a whole, which has been preserved in much the same state of architectural luxury as when De Palma filmed there, in a similar manner to a historic district. By invoking De Palma's vision of 421 Rodeo Drive as Tara moves through Westfield Century City, Schrader evokes the transition from a studied postmodern placelessness to a more banal post-cinematic placelessness. Part of the appeal of postmodern architecture lay in the challenges that it posed to media to map it. While Fredric Jameson posits the Bonaventure Hotel as an incitement to hyperspatial discourse, most treatments of its unique contours came from films that saw it as a provocation to narrative, spatial, and stylistic ingenuity.[24] Conversely, the post-cinematic placelessness of Schrader's Westfield is, by definition, indifferent to cinematic "completion."

Both of these factors divest Los Angeles of the figurative potential that it typically exudes in cinematic treatments. This process is explicitly tied to the demise of cinematic enjoyment in a scene that takes place at Café Med at Sunset Plaza, at the junction of Sunset Boulevard and Sunset Plaza Drive. This marks the metaphorical juncture between the traditional cinematic ecology evoked by the film, symbolized by Sunset Boulevard, and the incipient post-cinematic ecology evoked by the film, symbolized by the transitional space of the canyons, since Sunset Plaza Drive is the most direct point of access between this part of Sunset Boulevard and the canyons in the surrounding area. Sunset Plaza also forms the epicenter of the Sunset Strip, the most iconically cinematic segment of Sunset Boulevard. By positioning his scene at this threshold, Schrader already suggests that even the most resilient cinematic signifiers in the film, and in Los Angeles, have waned in the face of a new transitional media regime. Accordingly, the establishing shot of Café Med, and

Sunset Plaza, features no cinematic infrastructure, but is instead dominated by fashion billboards and boutique luxury housing.

The framing of this shot also reiterates this situation. Schrader shoots the conversation between Tara and Gina at Café Med from an unusual angle that dissolves the threshold between their table and the street outside. From where the camera is located, it is impossible to fully articulate the coordinates of Sunset Plaza, or how they relate to the situation of the restaurant. At times, the streetscape feels remote, like a back-projection. However, at times it feels uncomfortably close, since the two women are sitting right on the curve, which often makes it look as if oncoming traffic is about to careen right into their table. Rather than aligning the audience with a traditional point of view, the shot instead reflects Vivian Sobchack's notion of "electronic presence" as being "ungrounded and nonhierarchical," with "neither a point of view nor a visual situation" in the traditional sense. Instead, "electronic presence randomly disperses its being *across* a network," much as Tara and Gina's shared position in a network drives the scene, rather than any genuinely or exclusively interpersonal relationship.[25] None of the buildings or spaces here presuppose a cinematic camera, meaning that Schrader is unable to frame the scene in a stable manner. Against this backdrop, Tara confesses that movies do not really mean all that much to her anymore. She does not dislike them, exactly, but she's grown indifferent to them. When Gina seems surprised, Tara asks "Do you really like movies?" and then follows up with "No, I mean, like, really *really* like movies. When's the last time you went to see a movie in a theatre, a movie that really meant something to you?" Tara goes on to qualify her question by insisting premieres "don't count."

THE CANONS

This dissociation between cinematic pleasure and the Los Angeles cityscape dovetails with Schrader's canonical reflections in a pair of scenes later in the film. In the first of these, Schrader provides the audience with the first sustained depiction of driving in the film. As Anne Friedberg has argued, driving has conventionally been used as a metaphor for the inextricability of cinema from Los Angeles, reflecting a cityscape in which "cinema spectatorship [is] a radical metaphor for the windshield" and "the private mobility of driving transforms the windshield into a synoptic vista."[26] Just as cinema screens suffuse Los Angeles, so windscreens are also omnipresent. Cinematic infrastructure, and the infrastructure of highways and automobile culture, are therefore often what constitute the hyper-cinematic, or hyper-real, reception and remediation of Los Angeles within Hollywood. By contrast, *The Canyons* initially refrains from any imagery of highways, or any sustained scenes involving driving. While characters are often shot walking to or from cars, most of the outdoor action either occurs on foot, or while characters are dining at cafes and restaurants, removing the city even more vividly from the expansive Los Angeles of the American popular imagination. At the same time, driving plays a key figurative role in the film, as evinced in Schrader's symbolic gesture of offering up "the inscribed money clip that DeNiro gave to him on the set of *Taxi Driver*" as a way to incentivize the crowd-funding that largely financed production.[27]

The first driving scene occurs about halfway through the film, and follows Tara as she drives through the streets, late at night, after an argument with Christian. She is frustrated, drunk, and a little high, but the windscreen does not do anything to stabilize her mood and outlook. Instead, Schrader dissociates the camera from the windscreen, resulting in a series of blurry, messy, ugly shots that continue the impoverished noir lexicon of the opening credits. The palette also grows more muted and sepia-toned at this point, initially suggesting a recourse to a classically cinematic optic, only for Schrader to undercut that promise by refusing to differentiate between the world outside the car and the events taking place inside the car, thereby collapsing the windscreen as a point of cinematic containment. During this sequence, Tara's consciousness appears to be loosely drifting in and out of the car, untethering itself from the experience of driving until the drive ends up leaching the streets outside of any distinctive urban ambience, rather than reaffirming the unique spatiality of Los Angeles as typically occurs in driving scenes set in this particular city. Whereas driving is normally used to bring Los Angeles into focus in cinematic representation, driving here removes whatever residues of the city remain, jettisoning the audience in a diffuse and anonymous murkiness. This murkiness is associated with the text messages Tara has received on her phone, as Schrader aligns his camera with the "mutability of digital data" that, for Lev Manovich, "impairs the value of cinematic recordings as documents of reality," and as mapping tools.[28]

This scene therefore exemplifies the three key challenges posed to Schrader's canonical project. First, this scene divests the Los Angeles cityscape, and those living and driving within it, of any cinematic memory or knowledge. Second, the granularity of Schrader's images, the jerkiness of his hand-held camera, and the documentary-style footage, all combine to reassert the materiality of the Los Angeles cityscape, and Hollywood in particular (which is where Tara typically drives to when she needs personal space and a reprieve from Christian) in contrast to the cinematic signification that was once foisted upon it. Finally, the dissolution of the windscreen as a point of cinematic mediation signals the decline of cinematic media itself, along with the particular ramifications that this has for Los Angeles, the city most embedded within cinema.

All three of these challenges crystallize around the impoverished noir register that connects this scene to the opening credits. This impoverished quality stems, in part, from the ugliness of the images and the fractured quality of Schrader's shooting. However, ugliness was not uncommon in noir, while fractured images were also a feature of noir, especially in flashback sequences. However, as James Naremore has argued, these two noir features were dependent upon a third—the voiceover, or "familiar voice of American pulp fiction"—that is absent here, subordinated to the blasts of sound that percolate throughout the scene.[29] Narration, as noir understood it, was a provisional strategy for containing an inherently unruly visual field, but it also plays a key role in Schrader's canonical typology. For Schrader, the presence of narration, and the dialogue it brokers between visual and literary texts, stands for the possibility of conventional canonical commemoration in the first place. By divesting this scene of the narration that might ground both a noir register and a bid for canonicity, Schrader thus enacts the post-cinematic coordinates of Los Angeles as a query about whether cinema is even medially relevant enough, any more, to be capable of canonical aspirations.

Schrader provides a provisional answer to this question in a scene following this depiction of driving, which takes place at the house of Cynthia, an ex-girlfriend of Christian's played by Tenille Houston. During this scene, Cynthia tells Tara that Christian assaulted her and urges her to leave the relationship as soon as possible. However, the dialogue of this scene is quickly subsumed into the classical Los Angeles vista that emerges in the background. From where Cynthia and Tara are sitting on Cynthia's porch, four distinct planes of space can be seen. The first is the foliage and fence of Cynthia's backyard, which suggests a sprawling suburban lot. The second is a line of palm trees in the streets behind her house. The third is an elevated highway that can be seen in the middle distance. Finally, above the highway, the sunset and foothills are visible. The scene is shot in the evening, meaning that the glow of the sun and the glow of emergent neon bleed into each other, creating a synergy between these features.

This spatial scheme corresponds to Jerome Monnet's spatial scheme for understanding Los Angeles. In "The Everyday Imagery of Space in Los Angeles," Monnet argues that Los Angeles can be divided into three zones: the microcosm, which corresponds to the individual house; the macrocosm, which corresponds to the entire city; and the mesocosm, which corresponds to the intermediate zone between the microcosm and the macrocosm.[30] Since the totality of Los Angeles is difficult to discern, and the city has few clear boundaries, Monnet also uses the macrocosm to refer to the world beyond the city, and the threshold at which the individual moves from the city to whatever lies beyond it. Given the challenges that Los Angeles's urban design poses to the coordination of microcosmic and macrocosmic spatial cues, the mesocosm thus becomes the key spatial register for mapping and negotiating its coordinates. Rather than merely acting as a transitional zone, the mesocosm is the perceptual horizon that any individual has to negotiate in order to orient their trajectory within the city as a whole.

Monnet situates the mesocosm vertically, sandwiching it between the backyard (in the foreground) and the mountains (in the background). This results in an approach to mapping Los Angeles that is primarily vertical, and that is anchored in the view from individual backyards. Within Monnet's scheme, the highways don't ramify horizontally, as a point of lateral access between neighborhoods, but vertically, as the mesocosmic strip between suburbs and the wider horizon, and as the mechanism that allows the horizon to remain open as a point of vertical orientation. Whereas David Brodsly canonized the horizontality of the highways, Monnet sees the vertical situation of the highways within the spatial scheme of the city as a way of compensating for this horizontal sprawl.[31] The relation between the horizontal and vertical situation of the highways thus corresponds to the relation between cinema and post-cinematic media within Schrader's canonical scheme. Just as a cinematic canon brokers a transition from cinematic to post-cinematic media, so Monnet's situation of the freeways brokers a connection between the perceptibility and the imperceptibility of the city's spaces.

This mesocosmic space, and the vertical mapping that accompanies it, is the subject matter of this climactic scene in Cynthia's backyard. Retrospectively, it clarifies that the disorientation of the earlier location scenes in Los Angeles—especially those at Café Med and Westfield Century City—stemmed from Schrader's inability, or unwillingness, to resort to the mesocosmic orientation that keeps Los Angeles open as a perceptually and cinematically available spatial entity. By including that spatial scheme here for the first time, Schrader connects the viability of his canonical project, and the viability of dialogue between cinema and post-cinema, to Cynthia's insistence to Tara that she escape from her relationship with Christian. In part, Cynthia is recommending personal escape, since Christian has been a controlling and abusive figure in both their relationships. However, she is also recommending professional escape, suggesting—somewhat paradoxically—that cinema can only engage with post-cinema by discarding the figure of the director, and the tropes of directorial labor, that are embodied both by Christian, and by the storied production history of *The Canyons* itself.

There is thus a deeply self-reflexive and self-effacing quality to Schrader's negotiation with his own directorial labor during this scene. This intensifies as the implications of this scene play out over the rest of the film, producing two aborted gestures of directorial labor from Christian and Ryan. First, it emerges that Ryan has staged this scene in order to convince Tara to leave Christian and resume her relationship with him.

Then, Christian responds by murdering Cynthia in this same house, and staging the crime so that it looks like a scene from the slasher film that he is trying to get off the ground. In both cases, directorial labor is dissociated from the actual film that is being made *within* the film, and instead used by Christian and Ryan as a device for mapping the Los Angeles cityscape as a cinematically viable entity, or as amenable to a cinematic mode of perception and cognition.

In both cases, that attempt to frame Los Angeles via cinema occurs at the expense of one of the women in the film. In fact, all three women—Tara, Cynthia, and Gina—are increasingly disempowered by these directorial gestures, although Tara is the main target in each case. In classical noir, the femme fatale signified an anxiety around the end of cinema, or at least the end of cinematic representation as it was then understood, since her autonomy reflected the rise of a professional female workforce that was inimical to the modes of heroic masculine individualism that sustained the noir impulse. In *The Canyons*, Lohan's performance taps into this dimension of the femme fatale. Tara is distinct from the other two characters in exuding the body language and haptics of the "dangerous women" of classical Hollywood. However, she is also the character most disenfranchised by these two diffuse directorial gestures from Christian and Ryan. In order to find a line of flight from them, and from the cinematic optic they represent, both she and Lohan take refuge in the parts of the film that seem the least directed, the least controlled, and the least cinematic, such as the driving scene discussed.

More specifically, Tara takes refuge in the parts of the film where post-cinematic media is presented as messy and unruly, especially in the moments where Schrader resists the idea of post-cinema as an avant-garde choice, and presents it more as an inextricable *situation*. The most flamboyant of these moments initially takes place as another directorial gesture from Christian, who invites a couple upstairs for a hookup that he scores to pop music and a rotating light ball. This is the most elaborately staged hookup that we have seen from Christian so far, and the only hookup that has taken place upstairs, in the privacy of the couple's bedroom. However, Tara's consciousness drifts away from the spectacle as the scene proceeds, much as Schrader's direction lapses into the messiness of the driving scene, never quite aligning itself with the spectacle as it has been conceived by Christian. The scene thus forms one of the "transformation-images" that Mark B. N. Hansen identifies as a hallmark of post-cinematic aesthetics, exuding an "extra-perceptual status" that renders it visionary and anticlimactic at the same time, and thereby "wrenches [it] out of any cinematic function."[32] Rather than offering Tara as harbinger of a post-cinematic world, and affirming the masculinity of directorial mapping, Schrader presents the femme fatale as involuting the gendered division of artistic labor that is performed around her.

This is partly evident in Schrader's relative disinterest in Christian's spectacle—or, rather, the camera's relative disinterest. At times, it feels as if Schrader is trying to align himself with Christian's directorial vision, only for the camera to exude an inherent disinterest, and an inherent skepticism in why this spectacle, in particular, should command its attention. It is as if the camera has simply become another smartphone camera, untethered from any obligation to align itself with specifically cinematic tableaux, or to endow what it films with a specifically cinematic sheen in turn. However, the masculinity of Christian's directorial optic is also undercut by the events of the hookup itself, as Tara demands, for the first time, that he allow himself to be the passive partner with the man involved. This is also the first and only time in the film where Schrader depicts Christian in a state of full-frontal nudity, prompting a homoerotic crisis that he tries to assuage with his therapist. Yet his therapist is played by Gus Van Sant, a homosexual director, further removing Christian from the fantasy of directorial control over the Los Angeles cityscape.

While this sequence in the bedroom might not fulfill Christian's artistic vision, it does form the aesthetic pinnacle of *The Canyons* itself. On the face of it, this is one of the messiest and cheapest scenes in Schrader's career. Yet it also fulfills the canonical criteria that he sets out in "Canon Fodder"—or, rather, Tara rearranges the scene to fit these criteria. In her hands, these scenes where the film takes refuge from cinematic aspiration are indeed beautiful (medially versatile) and strange (capable of remediating the world in an unusual way). They also exhibit unity of form (intermediality of form), an awareness of tradition (an openness to simultaneous as much as sequential media) and repeatability (remediability). Rather than contain the femme fatale and continue cinema, Schrader instead uses the femme fatale to suggest a threshold between cinema and what lies beyond it. The canonicity of his vision ultimately discards the directorial voices of its male leads and instead depends on the femme fatale as a space of messy post-cinematic potentiality.

This messiness situates *The Canyons* in an ambivalent position within Schrader's filmography as a whole. It is the film that draws most heavily upon his reflections upon the cinematic canon in "Canon Fodder," establishing his work of the 2010s as a sustained meditation about the process and implications of compiling a film canon. However, it is also his least canonical film, insofar as this messy post-cinematic potentiality resulted in it being derided more volubly than any other film in his career. While many of his films have flown under the radar of critical and popular acclaim, none have been so dramatically disparaged, and even disavowed, as *The Canyons*. Beyond a certain point, it became a badge of pride for critics to dislike the film, as if disliking the film, and ensuring the longevity of film as a medium, were two sides of the same coin. In his review of the film, Wesley Morris compared it, unfavorably, to both David Lynch and Elizabeth Taylor, framing it as a negative cinematic space that only ramifies when set against figures of hyper-cinematic status.[33]

Yet this negative cinematic space is the point of Schrader's vision, which courts canonical signification only to collapse it as it proceeds. In his article, Morris states that the film "believes it's taking risks it actually has no interest in taking."[34] However, taking the kinds of calculated risks that pass for canonical accomplishment and artistic originality are what ultimately constitute the idiosyncrasy of Schrader's directorial vision. Instead of opting for canonical stasis, Schrader uses the trope and expectations of the canon to gesture toward a more incipient and intermedial understanding of cinema. In doing so, he creates a film that is both anti-canonical and engaged with a new understanding of what the cinematic canon can be—an elegant and evocative complement to the insights articulated in "Canon Fodder."

NOTES

1. George Kouvaros, *Paul Schrader* (Champaign: University of Illinois Press), 123.
2. Ibid., 124.
3. Paul Schrader, *Transcendental Style in Film: Ozu, Bresson, Dreyer* (Burbank: University of California Press, 2018). Accessed on Google Books. Available at https://books.google.com.au/books/about/Transcendental_Style_in_Film.html?id=TUVVDwAAQBAJ&redir_esc=y (last accessed May 30, 2019).
4. Andrew Sarris, *The American Cinema: Directors and Directions 1929-1968*. Accessed on Google Books. Available at https://books.google.com.au/books?id=_NGzswEACAAJ&dq=the+american+cinema+directions+and+directors&hl=en&sa=X&ved=oahUKEwiy7Mvo34PjAhWx4nMBHRNYCqoQ6AEIKTAA (last accessed May 30, 2019).
5. Schrader, *Transcendental Style in Film*.
6. Harold Bloom, *The Western Canon: The Books and School of the Ages* (New York: Riverhead, 1995).
7. Paul Schrader, "Canon Fodder," *Film Comment*, September–October 2006, 33–49.
8. Ibid., 34.
9. Steven Shaviro, *Post Cinematic Affect* (London: Zero Books, 2010), 6.
10. Shane Denson, "Crazy Cameras, Discorrelated Images and the Post-Perceptual Mediation of Post-Cinematic Affect," in *Post-Cinema*, edited by Shane Denson and Julia Leyda (Falmer: Reframe, 2016). Digital publication. Available at http://reframe.sussex.ac.uk/post-cinema/ (last accessed May 30, 2019).
11. Schrader, "Canon Fodder," 34.
12. Ibid.
13. Ibid.
14. Ibid., 42.
15. Ibid.
16. Ibid., 34.
17. Ibid., 44.
18. Ibid.
19. Ibid.

20. Ibid., 46.
21. Paul Schrader, *The Canyons* (New York: IFC Films, 2013).
22. Brian De Palma, *Body Double* (Los Angeles: Delphi II Productions, 1984).
23. This information is taken from the Wikipedia article on Westfield Century City. Available at https://en.wikipedia.org/wiki/Westfield_Century_City (last accessed May 29, 2019).
24. Fredric Jameson, *Postmodernism, or the Cultural Logic of Late Capitalism* (Durham: Duke University Press, 1992), 44.
25. Vivian Sobchack, "The Scene of the Screen: Envisioning Photographic, Cinematic and Electronic 'Presence'," in *Post-Cinema*.
26. Anne Friedberg, *Window Shopping: Cinema and the Postmodern* (Burbank: University of California Press, 1992), xi–xii.
27. Braxton Pope, "In Lindsay's Stardust Orbit," *Vanity Fair*, August 2, 2013. Available at https://www.vanityfair.com/hollywood/2013/08/the-canyons-lindsay-lohan-producer (last accessed May 29, 2019).
28. Lev Manovich, "What is Digital Cinema?," in *Post-Cinema*.
29. James Naremore, *More Than Night: Film Noir in Its Contexts* (Burbank: University of California Press, 1998), 24.
30. Jerome Monnet, "The Everyday Image of Space in Los Angeles," in *Looking for Los Angeles: Architecture, Film, Photography and the Urban Landscape,* edited by Charles Salas and Michael Roth (Los Angeles: Getty Research Institute, 2001), 299.
31. David Brodsly, *L.A. Freeway: An Appreciative Essay* (Burbank: University of California Press), 25–6.
32. Mark B. N. Hansen, "Algorithmic Sensibility: Reflections on the Post-Perceptual Image," in *Post-Cinema*.
33. Wesley Morris, "Future Imperfect," *Grantland,* August 8, 2013. Available at https://grantland.com/features/the-disappointing-elysium-terrible-canyons/ (last accessed May 27, 2019).
34. Ibid.

PART II

Instincts, Investigation, and Innovation

CHAPTER 4

"Thinking White": Performing Racial Tension in *Blue Collar*

Scott Balcerzak

Figure 4.1 Richard Pryor and Harvey Keitel in *Blue Collar* (1978).

The final image of Paul Schrader's directorial debut, *Blue Collar* (1978), is a freeze-frame that bookends a series of freeze-frames that opens the film. Set to "Hard Working Man," a blues song with the growling vocals of Captain Beefheart, the opening credits explore a Detroit factory floor, periodically freezing to stress the pulsating sound of the machinery and focus on different individual images of workers during their laborious daily routine. It is a series of shots of both white and black bodies, moving along with the machinery pace of the score, exploited yet functioning together as a working class. In contrast, the freeze-frame of the ending accentuates chaos as a disordered racial mix of bodies surround the film's interracial pair of protagonists, Zeke Brown (Richard Pryor) and Jerry Bartowski (Harvey Keitel), as they lunge toward each other. The shouting that precedes the freeze conveys that the once friends have now crossed a line where their racial identities can no longer peacefully coexist. Zeke screams, "You don't care about nothing but your own dumb Pollack ass!" Jerry rejoins, "I ain't the one that sold out, nigger-shit. You are!" When the frame freezes now, the rhythmic machinery is not heard and there is only silence. Then we hear the words of the murdered Smokey James (Yaphet Kotto), who warns, "They pit the lifers against the new boys, the young against the old, the black against the white. Everything they do is to keep us in our place."

In terms of what constitutes the "they" in Smokey's words, the film focuses on the Detroit chapter of the United Automobile Workers (UAW) as its chief antagonist, showing the union in league with the exploitive practices of capitalism. This negative depiction of union politics appears less as a pro-capitalist critique than a commentary, generally, on the nature of corruptible institutions on the individual. An enthusiastic write-up upon the film's release in *Human Behavior*, a short-lived social science publication, recognizes this larger social critique, stating, "Every scene is a piece of a jig-saw puzzle that reveals a frightening picture: all our respected institutions—unions, companies, police, the government—are corrupt and in collusion to keep the working stiff 'on the line.'"[1] Even the progressive, pro-union publication *The New Republic*, after bemoaning the depiction of corrupt union leadership, had to admit "only the extremely nervous will see *Blue Collar* as anti-unionist."[2] These two responses mirror Schrader's words on the politics of the film, where he does admit to general suspicion toward organized labor leadership since "all organizations of that sort end up being undemocratic, they end up being clubs." But, on the other hand, Schrader certainly does not appear supportive of capitalist class systems, suggesting the story explores "how that kind of dead-end mentality is fostered and engendered by the ruling class in order to keep the working class at odds with itself."[3]

More than just an expression of economic oppression, the final freeze-frame finds its true power as an image of racial conflict. Having class serve as the primary demarcation in the film can be read as, problematically, positioning deeply entrenched racial injustices as, at best, side effects of the economic oppression of all races, ignoring a long history of racism within the working class itself.[4] This viewpoint suggests racial tensions among the lower classes exist as simply a false consciousness, an idealized and white view of race in America. This reading of the film was established by Michael Omi in 1981, when he criticized "Schrader's inability to really deal with the subject [race], in a coherent fashion," contending:

Firstly, the movie leads us to believe that the material basis of racism (as reflected in people's location in the productive process of an auto assembly plant) has been obliterated; second, that cultural contradictions have been accommodated; and last, that black/white relations within the working class are harmonious. Within this context, the ending didactically conveys a popular perspective on racism within liberal arid left circles. It reveals that racism is a form of false consciousness—a form which in fact the working class itself knows to be false.[5]

In response to the above criticism, Derek Nystrom writes, "Although Omi is not incorrect in his diagnosis of Hollywood's less than perspicacious grasp of working-class life, I would argue that it is precisely the film's depiction of a seemingly natural interracial solidarity that is its most noteworthy element."[6] With his view, the working class as "a space of natural interracial solidarity" exists "as the film's utopian fantasy," therefore the final freeze-frame and Smokey's words exist not "as the film's 'real' political message."[7]

There remains one crucial aspect of the final freeze-frame that requires analysis. These are not just any black and white bodies coming to blows. Positioned in the frame are the wiry figure of Richard Pryor and the stocky build of Harvey Keitel. On a narrative level, the film's depiction of race in the working class can be read as, until the conclusion, relatively harmonious on a surface level. Yet when viewing Schrader's film, one cannot help but notice cracks in this interracial solidarity long before the explosive final moments. And these tensions emerge through what constitutes the film's primary selling point as late 1970s social realist cinema, which was its appeal as an actor showcase. *Blue Collar* exists as a performance vehicle for two different manners of star performers with different extratextual codes, techniques of performance tied to distinct racial identities. The performances themselves accentuate a tension Omi proclaims is missing from the film's narrative, a storyline he suggests provides a "superficial vision of race relations which portrays the working class as objectively integrated," since when racism "rears its ugly head" in the conclusion, it "is the expression of truly false consciousness."[8] While this critique corresponds with Smokey's voiceover message in the conclusion, it overlooks the racial tensions evoked by Schrader in his unique casting decisions and choices in directing the actors.

By all accounts, as Schrader's first film as director, *Blue Collar* was a tense production, with the leading actors clashing on multiple occasions. The reason for this conflict can be attributed to the considerably different performing styles of its leads, in particular, the casting of comedian Pryor, whose improvisations clashed with the formally trained Keitel and Yaphet Kotto. In this chapter, I will demonstrate how Schrader employed these conflicting styles and personalities to heighten the film's racial tensions. Focusing primarily on the performance styles of Keitel and Pryor—narratively speaking, the film's protagonists—this chapter particularly focuses on the latter's identity as a transgressive comedian during the mid- to late 1970s. Through casting Pryor and giving him the space to improvise, Schrader does not fundamentally alter his comic persona but rather captures a dramatic variation of it, employing it as a defying signifier against the mid-century "Method" acting style and image of Keitel. Schrader produces a tension between his performers that utilizes the comedian's territorialized black identity as well as his ability to challenge racial boundaries through his humor. He fosters the contrasting styles of Pryor and Keitel to build an anxiety on-screen attuned to the complicated racial tensions of the working class.

After his success screenwriting *Taxi Driver* (1976), Schrader wanted to move into directing, explaining that a "screenwriter is not really a writer; his words do not appear on the screen. What he does is to draft out blueprints that are executed by a team." As a young filmmaker, Schrader took a strategic approach in planning his directorial debut, suggesting, "I went about *Blue Collar* in a very methodical way. I wrote it as an ensemble piece so I could get three hot young actors who would work for minimum, and with whom I could make deals independently, and I followed the Don Siegel maxim of taking the plots from three movies and putting them into one."[9] This comment suggests Schrader's collaboration with Martin Scorsese on *Taxi Driver* might have illustrated to him the power of the director as well as the significance of the actor in creating effective cinema. As R. Colin Tait writes, actor Robert De Niro's archived script for that film shows Schrader's "screenplay was in constant revision once De Niro and Scorsese got involved," creating a type of "triangular authorship" for the film.[10] In deciding his first directorial film to be an ensemble piece, narratively crafted in a screenplay co-written by his brother Leonard, Schrader embraced the New Hollywood approach of presenting on-screen drama as showcases for modern acting styles.

While Schrader suggests the casting and narrative of *Blue Collar* in threes—three lead actors with Pryor, Keitel, and Kotto and, as such, three corresponding plots—the finished film feels more unified in its narrative. Pryor as Zeke is an angry auto plant worker routinely getting into conflicts with the foreman and union leadership over indignities, such as a broken locker and casual racism on the floor. Keitel's Jerry is a less volatile employee yet also embittered over conditions and having to work a second job at a gas station. Both men have home lives shown as strained, exasperated by financial woes and each man's restlessness, which leads to philandering. Each eagerly await sneaking out for hedonistic evenings with the single ex-con Smokey, where they can indulge in drugs and heterosexual sex. With the two married men facing increasing financial hardships, the three friends decide to rob their local union office, only to find little money in the safe. Among the safe's papers, though, Zeke locates a notebook listing illegal loans. Persuaded by Smokey, Zeke and Jerry agree to blackmail the union, a plan that goes awry when the union targets the men. After confronting thugs going after Jerry's family, Smokey is killed in a suspicious workplace accident, which results in a frightened Zeke, originally the most vocal against union management, taking the job of union steward as a payoff. Despite Zeke's offer to secure him the position of foreman, Jerry continues to go at it alone and, after narrowly escaping union thugs, goes to the FBI. Culminating in the above-discussed freeze-frame, the final scene finds Jerry returning to the factory with FBI agents, only to have his former co-workers turn on him as an anti-union "rat." While all three actors receive star credit, the narrative privileges Pryor's Zeke and Keitel's Jerry as clear foils, an interracial friendship of two men with similar financial and family problems but contrasting viewpoints.

It is difficult to read the interracial friendships in the film without asking what the men signify as social representations, especially racial representations. Schrader suggests the casting posed issues because "I knew it would have to have black characters, and I wanted to do something about the petty struggles and the physical need that make up day-to day life and not simplify my black characters or on the other hand be too soft or affectionate toward them." This meant striking a balance that would avoid past movie clichés of interracial male casting: "Now you couldn't have two white and one black, because he would have to assume the Sidney Poitier role, the decent black guy; otherwise it would be two whites and a black villain."[11] The casting of two black actors in central roles also allowed Schrader to sidestep another cliché in that the death of Smokey does not exist as simply a catalyst for a white character. By having Zeke "sell out" to the union and Jerry "rat" to the FBI, an institution largely presented in the film as condescending and manipulative to the working class, both characters end up as cogs in different machines. Both the narrative resolutions for Zeke and Jerry speak to what Schrader contends are the film's overall politics: "Its politics are the politics of resentment and claustrophobia, the feeling of being manipulated and not in control of your life."[12]

If the character arcs explore themes of "resentment and claustrophobia," the casting of the three actors only accentuated these feelings during the shoot. As Schrader contends, "I had approached Richard and Harvey Keitel and Yaphet Kotto separately and led each of them to believe they were the star of the movie, because that's what it took to get them involved." This mischaracterization meant Schrader had to handle "three bulls in a china shop," with, early on, Kotto being convinced "they [Pryor and Keitel] were trying to ace him out."[13] Watching the film, you can see Kotto's fears were not exactly unfounded. While his performance is effective, it often feels overshadowed by Keitel's quiet brooding and Pryor's hyper energy. Kotto had spent a career developing a reputation as a multi-faceted actor, studying at the Actors

Studio and moving between acclaimed film, television, and stage work. The mid-1970s found him portraying a variety of roles, balancing Blaxploitation, such as *Truck Turner* (1974, Kaplan) and *Friday Foster* (1975, Marks) with bigger-budget mainstream films like *Live and Let Die* (1973, Hamilton) and *Alien* (1979, Scott) and dramatic roles in high-profile television projects like *Raid on Entebbe* (1976, Kershner) and *Roots* (1977).[14] The role of Smokey, an ex-con depicted as sexually voracious, physically imposing, and more comfortable with criminal pursuits than his friends, understandably could give the actor pause, especially as the character exists in contrast to the more morally conflicted Zeke and Jerry.

Schrader's descriptions of the conflicts between Pryor and Keitel prove telling in characterizing the cultural significance of each actor as 1970s icons. As he suggests, "Very early on, by the second or third day of production, Richard became convinced he was playing the black sidekick to Harvey's Terry Malloy and Harvey became convinced that he was playing Ed McMahon to Richard's Johnny Carson."[15] In referencing Marlon Brando's iconic performance in *On the Waterfront* (Kazan, 1954) and the unscripted comic patter of *The Tonight Show Starring Johnny Carson* (1962–92), Schrader acknowledges the oddity of pairing these particular performers as each represents different realms of entertainment—dramatic modern acting, often labeled in the 1970s as "Method," and stand-up comedy, as Pryor revolutionized that form of entertainment. Unlike the casting of Pryor, Keitel was an obvious choice for the director considering both of their working relationships with Martin Scorsese. In a sense, Keitel is a quintessential New York-trained mid-century actor, who fostered a reputation as meticulous in his preparation. When asked about his approach to the "Method" in a 1978 interview with *Film Comment*, he states, "Well, I do my homework," then outlines how detailed script analysis and rehearsal time to find the character is "part of the way acting is taught now in New York by such people as Lee Strasberg and Stella Adler, based on the [Constantin] Stanislavski system. It's part of their teaching to 'fill the part.'"[16] His training by both Strasberg and Adler corresponds with Schrader's characterization of Keitel's approach to scenes: "Harvey, with his theatrical training, very self-analytical, would work on the meaning of the scene in the early takes and then after ten takes he'd be terrific."[17] Here, the director suggests Keitel using early takes as a type of exploratory rehearsal focused on finding the meaning behind the script's given situation, similar to the kind of work regularly performed at acting studios promoting variations of the Stanislavski system.[18] During the shoot, this history meant the formally trained Keitel and Kotto largely got along, speaking a similar language of performance, with the latter stating about the experience, "Harvey comes in character, ready to go . . . You can depend on the fact that, when you do something, he'll give you something back."[19]

In contrast, Pryor proved a different manner of performer, a comedian best when keeping a scene fresh and improvisational. This approach developed from his stand-up routines where he adopted various voices as an array of characters and skillfully improvised as he moved between them. This was different from the simple "anything for a laugh" improvisations of previous generations of stand-ups. As James Alvin McPherson writes in his 1975 profile of the comedian for *New York Times Magazine*, "Pryor improvises, but his improvisations are structured, usually springing from within his characters. He seldom throws out one-liners just to haul in laughter, unless it is social commentary leading to a depiction of a character."[20] With such an approach, as Schrader remembers, in contrast to Keitel's multiple takes, "Being primarily versed in stand-up comedy he [Pryor] had a creative life of between three and four takes." Also, more problematic to the trained actors respecting a communicative process when improvising, the comedian would change dialogue without warning to his co-stars or director "just like he would have done in front of a live audience." With these conflicting styles, "there's virtually no way you can film these two men [Pryor and Keitel] together, so you'd have to rehearse Harvey with a stand-in and then bring Richard in without any rehearsal."[21]

The tensions were only intensified by the Michigan heatwave while they were filming at auto plants in Detroit and Kalamazoo, which meant the first-time director dealt with rising tensions leading to daily fights.[22] With managing the performers a primary concern, the film very much became an actors' vehicle as opposed to a chance for the young director to experiment with visual style, since Schrader let "the locations themselves indicate visual style to a large degree."[23] Instead of developing a unique mise-en-scène, the first-time director was trying simply to keep peace on the set and create coherency: "On that film, I very quickly learned to confine myself to talent management, to making sure the actors stayed in character and the storyline remained coherent. I handed over the shot selection and lighting and blocking essentially to my crew. I didn't have time to explore those areas."[24]

Outside of conflicting styles (and egos), the casting of Keitel and Pryor contains clear extratextual connotations related to race. While eventually overshadowed by De Niro as Scorsese's "go-to" actor, Keitel's reputation to mid-1970s cinephiles was as a white ethnic "Method" masculinity from his early work with that director. This reputation corresponds with what Cynthia Baron calls the view of "Method" stars in the popular imagination as "flamboyant (white) male 'solos,'" actors playing "tough, moody, sexually potent male characters."[25] By the 1970s, this kind of figure would often be a type of white urban ethnicity, often Italian-American. More moody and introspective than De Niro's volatile lead performances in *Taxi Driver* and *Raging Bull* (1980), Keitel's lead roles with the director were essentially brooding Italian-American characters conflicted over their Catholic faith in *Who's That Knocking on My Door* (1967) and *Mean Streets*

(1973). The late 1970s saw him cast in more high-profile roles, such as Speed in the titular trio of Peter Yates's *Mother, Jugs, and Speed* (1976) and the co-lead in Ridley Scott's British historical drama *The Duellists* (1977), as well as receiving press for losing the lead in Frances Ford Coppola's *Apocalypse Now* (1979), in the early days of that film's difficult production. The year 1978 returned him to conflicted characterizations of white urban maleness in *Blue Collar*, now shifting the ethnic identity to Polish-American, followed by a performance in James Toback's *Fingers* (1978) playing the conflicted Italian-American Jimmy "Fingers" Angelelli, torn between his passion as a brilliant pianist and his loyalty to his loan shark father. While expanding his roles throughout the decade, the arts magazine *Horizon* would still title a February 1978 piece on the actor "Urban Brooder," opening it by introducing Keitel as "the young character actor best known for his portrayals of contemporary urban brooders."[26]

While known to cinephiles, and receiving profiles in art magazines, Keitel's cultural significance comes nowhere near the impact of Pryor at the time. After years of growing in popularity through his well-received stand-up albums, by 1978 the comedian was being recognized as revolutionizing American comedy through his improvisational approach, frank discussions of race and sex, and a psychological complexity and vulnerability never seen before on the comedy stage. After years of taking supporting parts in both black dramatic fair, such as *Lady Sings the Blues* (Furie, 1972), and comedies, such as *Uptown Saturday Night* (Poitier, 1974), white audiences started to take more notice after he provided a much-needed jolt of subversive energy to the otherwise routine comedy thriller *Silver Streak* (Hiller, 1976), starring Gene Wilder. Nobody as overtly subversive as Pryor had ever broken through to mainstream white success as he resituated racial discourses through comedy in ways his mainstream predecessors, like Bill Cosby and Nipsey Russell, never had. As described by Audrey Thomas McCluskey, Pryor's humor "was both multifaceted and egalitarian in its targets and scope. It traversed racial and class boundaries yet remained 'territorialized' within a black milieu."[27] By embracing and deconstructing his blackness onstage, through a confessional autobiographical approach, "his gutsy public posture did not seek to ease white fears nor conform to white expectation." Pryor's persona was not one just based in black empowerment but appeals to empathy as well as his "topical observations and critiques of racism and police brutality were meshed into his routines along with candid revelations about his sex life and drug use," creating a "simultaneity of rage and vulnerability."[28] In this sense, the comedian is proper casting for Zeke, since, as Pryor biographer Scott Saul writes, "Schrader created a dark-tinted working-class world in which the contradictions of Richard's stage persona—his vulnerability and his aggression, his likability and his rascality, his seriousness and his refusal to take anything seriously—made perfect sense."[29]

By early 1978, when *Blue Collar* was released, Pryor's reputation as a subversive black performer was at its height, as it was two years before he would transition to a series of audience-friendly comedian comedies, starting with his reteaming with Gene Wilder in *Stir Crazy* (Poitier) in 1980. It was also after a series of headline-grabbing controversies that would prove both challenging and intriguing to white audiences. A March 13, 1978 *People* cover, roughly a month after *Blue Collar*'s release, shows him shooting a skeptical eye toward the camera and gives a rundown of multiple public conflicts, stating, "Richard Pryor's Ordeal. He's picking up the pieces after battles with NBC, gays, his 5th wife, and the law."[30] His volatile personal life, fueled by his cocaine addiction, resulted in public displays of disorder—including riddling his wife's abandoned car with bullets, which he later joked about in the acclaimed concert film *Richard Pryor: Live in Concert* (1979, Margolis), and veering into a confrontational routine that horrified a large crowd attending a gay rights benefit at the Hollywood Bowl on September 18, 1977, when, angry by the lack of black representation, he asked, "How can faggots be racists?"[31] More problematic for the industry was Pryor's conflicts with NBC over the short-lived *The Richard Pryor Show* (1977), which featured the comedian pushing the envelope in terms of racial, sexual, and political content in sketches. This conflict showed Pryor to be truly a subversive figure, changing the direction of American comedy in ways that challenged corporate white interests. As Pryor would joke to *People*, "They [NBC] retained about 6,000 people to do nothing but mess with my material."[32] The cancellation of his show did nothing to deter his rising stardom and only solidified his reputation as marketable on film screens, as this period saw him securing multi-picture deals with multiple studios. Schrader plays up Pryor's potential as a draw in the *People* article, stating, "We fought sometimes like crazy [on location], . . . but I feel quite strongly that Richard will be the biggest black actor ever."[33] Also, likely to the dismay of his co-stars, Universal Pictures centralized Pryor in its promotion, including a poster showing two images of Pryor, sans co-stars, with a blurb from Vincent Canby's *New York Times* review, "Richard Pryor has a role that makes use of the wit and fury that distinguish his straight comedy routines."[34]

Many moments in *Blue Collar* utilize Pryor's abilities as a unique comic voice and his reputation as an instigator. Early on, when the workers go to the union hall, a large portrait of Martin Luther King and John F. Kennedy hangs on the wall, promoting the union's public narrative of racial unity. Upon being asked to pass out pamphlets, an agitated Jerry tells Smokey, "Hell. I've got two jobs and they think I'm going to hand out some pamphlets on my day off." True to Pryor's persona, Zeke expresses his disfavor in a more expressive and public manner, standing and proclaiming, "I ain't handing out that shit." Pryor shifts his skinny frame with an excited energy as he speaks, holding his pinkie up to show an injury from his broken locker door. He grabs his crotch to show disgust, yelling, "Everybody knows what the plant is. The plant is just short for plantation," a statement that gains vocal support from primarily the black workers in the room. When the steward attempts to shut him down, Zeke threatens to take his job, joking once he gets it he plans to jet out to Palm Springs to "hang out with Eddie Knuckles and hit a few golf balls with President Ford and Nixon and them motherfuckers," statements that get both laughs and affirmative cheers from the interracial crowd. The film presents Zeke as the comic provocateur of the plant, a reputation enjoyed by all the workers. True to Pryor's comedic persona, his disruptions demonstrate a black masculine bravado (holding his crotch, referencing slavery) that, despite its transgressive blackness, manages to use humor to win over his white co-workers.

Zeke's personality differs from how the film frames the blue-collar restlessness of Jerry. While Zeke and Jerry's families are shown socializing during a night out bowling, there are divides in the depictions of their domestic lives as racial spaces. Zeke's family is introduced through them watching *The Jeffersons* (1975–85), a television sitcom about a black family "moving on up" to the upper class. Zeke's wife (Chip Fields) laughs at the show while he criticizes, "This shit is pitiful. I don't know how a nigger like that gets some money anyway." Eventually, an IRS agent (Leonard Gaines) arrives to investigate Zeke's falsifying his returns, primarily his listing of six children as opposed to his actual three. The scene veers into a comical situation, with his wife rushing to get the neighbor's kids to pass off as their own. Humorously, Zeke has listed his children's names as black celebrities, something the white agent does not recognize, "Sugar Ray Brown, Gloria Brown, O. J. Brown, Gayle Sayers Brown, Jim Brown, and Stevie Wonder Brown." While humor permeates the scene, it is balanced with desperation, as, after learning he owes well over two thousand dollars, Zeke pleads and finally yells, in defiance of the government, "If I had the Navy and Marines behind me, I'd be a motherfucker too!"

In contrast, the depiction of Jerry's home life does not highlight any humor nor a direct vocal defiance of authority. For example, an early scene is simply a quiet one-sided conversation with his wife Arlene (Lucy Saroyan), who stresses that their daughter must get braces. Later, when Jerry discovers his daughter Debbie (Stacey Baldwin) made braces out of wire, the scene is played for dramatic realism. Upon processing the shocking sight of his daughter's bloody gums, Keitel performs the internal struggle of the character through a series of looks and unfinished statements before finally saying, "Let's get them goddamn braces. You get them tomorrow," a decision that confirms his character's involvement in the robbery.

The racial significations of Pryor and Keitel are complicated in scenes exploring their relationship with Kotto's Smokey. Early on, at their after-work drinking hole, Zeke joins Jerry and a young white newbie, Bobby Joe (Ed Begley Jr.), and proceeds to tell them tales of Smokey's exploits. To Zeke, while Smokey is admirable in his sexual freedom, as he is shown in a nearby booth with two women, he also serves as a way to shock his friends with stories from outside their white experience. In a manner typical of Pryor's comedy, he tells of Smokey's past with a note of humor to offset the tragedy, informing Bobby Joe, "My man was the president of Jackson Penitentiary. Wasn't even elected and was the president." To accentuate the interracial space as not truly free from tensions, Zeke turns to a co-worker at the jukebox and asks, "Say, Hank, my man, give me a little break on the hillbilly music, partner?" When Hank responds with an awkward joke about loving the south, Pryor turns to the table and says, "I can't stand that motherfucker." Zeke proceeds to tell a sex-filled and violent story about Smokey, who comes over to the table to give his version. The interactions are largely between Pryor and Kotto, who both laugh when Bobby Joe naively asks why Smokey did not explain the situation to a policeman who figures into the story. Notably, Schrader frames the scene to highlight the racial divide at the table, Pryor and Kotto as black storytellers on one side and Keitel and Begley Jr. as white audience on the other, on a smaller scale reflecting a similar dynamic to Pryor's growing popularity among white audiences as a storyteller of the black experience. The tone, though, becomes uncomfortable when Zeke tells his white friends "this motherfucker killed somebody." Smokey gravely states, "I never killed nobody," to which Zeke sarcastically responds, winking across the table to the white listeners, "OK, brother." As this scene shows, to Zeke, Smokey can serve as a signifier of blackness to both accentuate his own identity among his white friends and push boundaries. Whether Smokey truly murdered somebody or not, the suggestion obviously is not a part of the narrative he feels is appropriate for white ears. But Zeke, ever the Pryor-like transgressor, gleefully crosses that line.

Smokey's criminal past as well as his access to drugs and women serve as an escape for Zeke and Jerry, seen when they sneak away from their wives to visit his apartment for a drug-fueled orgy. The space counters the married men's domestic homes as it is exoticized with candles, black velvet paintings, and brightly colored furniture. Schrader presents the evening as an escapist spectacle of cocaine and sexual pleasure, where racial divides are crossed through heterosexual acts (Jerry performing oral sex on a black woman) and homosocial play (Jerry and Zeke playing like children, crossing dildos like swords). The evening ends with a three-shot of Kotto, Keitel, and Pryor, on the sofa, coming down from their high, with the latter two lamenting their fates. In nearly a single long-take, except for a cut to a clock, Schrader frames the scene to contrast their bodies—a slumped shoulder, bodily defeat in Keitel and Pryor, who sit right of screen, contrasted with a more awake and upright Kotto. As Keitel looks despondently off-camera and bemoans his economic situation, Pryor rubs his eyes, then admits, in a quiet and emotional tone unheard until this point, "Sometimes I get so depressed," admitting, "I think maybe if Smokey wasn't around, we wouldn't have no motherfucking fun." Finally, Smokey has enough of their self-pity and suggests, "Then hit that safe you all the time talking about." The emotional moment is a turning point as Zeke and then Jerry agree to the robbery in the next scenes, meaning the racially integrated fantasy space of Smokey's apartment appears to facilitate the anti-establishment dreams of the two characters.

Schrader depicts the build-up to and the robbery itself as comedic, with the three wearing comical dime store disguises bought by Zeke. During the break-in, Smokey knocks out a guard, whose later description of the robbers earns them the comical nickname "the Oreo gang" in the press, a label that highlights the abnormality of their interracial grouping in the society of the film. The tone shifts after the three begin their blackmailing plan in a somber scene outside the bar when Smokey informs Zeke and Jerry they cannot be seen together because their unique racial make-up targets them for investigation. As this shows, once outside Smokey's apartment, racial difference exists in the narrative as a potentially destabilizing force, threatening to expose their crimes and putting them in further danger. Once Smokey is removed from the picture, in a union-staged industrial accident in the paint room, the once seemingly harmonious interracial friendship of Zeke and Jerry destabilizes. For the final part of the film, the reactions of the two men to the loss of Smokey and the impending danger show once unspoken racial tensions boiling to the surface. These moments constitute some of the most powerful scenes in the film and are the direct result of Schrader's collaborations with his actors, in particular, Pryor.

While the shoot was tense, Schrader's openness to actor input led to a reconsideration of Zeke's motivations in the last act of the film. As Saul writes, "He [Pryor] thought that his character flipped too easily from trickster to sellout—that Zeke risked being seen as a mere weasel rather than a black man in a bind." At first, Schrader "wasn't sympathetic; he thought Richard worried too much about being likable, that he confused being an actor with being a public figure."[35] In their discussions, Pryor stressed he wanted the audience to feel empathy for Zeke, to see him struggle with the difficult choices, telling Schrader, "If you're going to imply that I've done something, . . . then the audience should see me do it so they aren't left to imagine it for themselves."[36] This suggestion led Schrader to add an effective scene after Smokey's death where Zeke stands on an overpass, framed by rushing cars and a sign counting down the number of cars produced by the factory. He jumps as union boss Eddie Johnson (Harry Bellaver) enters the scene and shifts his eyes to anxiously look at another man, who seems present to offer Johnson security. While Zeke has been confident and defiant in the past, Pryor performs this scene with a nervous fear, shifting his body and looking off to the side. He does still confront the white ruling class, stating, "You motherfuckers lied to me." When Johnson suggests Smokey's death was "the result of negligence and improper safety precautions," Zeke proclaims, "Fuck that, man! You had him murdered." In response, Johnson warns him not to make that charge and explains, "When I was your age, there were no blacks working in the auto plants . . . Blacks got jobs because guys like me knew when to stand up and when to look the other way." Throughout this speech, Pryor plays intense anxiety and dismay, attempting but failing to interrupt Bellaver, turning his back to look at the traffic, and placing his hands over his face in a tired and defeatist manner. Finally, Schrader cuts to the busy traffic below, not giving the usually verbose Zeke the final word. By setting the scene amid the diegetic sound of rushing automobiles, the director accentuates Zeke's minuscule position in the machinery of American production and consumption. This setting, along with the nervous energy of Pryor's performance choices, suggests Zeke as a man without any options as a member of the African-American working class, as Johnson reminds him his presence as a black man in the plant remains a recent and, potentially, still contested part of the social order.

Pryor's desire to explore his character's motivations also helped to create one of the most powerful scenes late in the film. On Jerry's porch, Zeke walks out sipping a beer, looking onto the street, while Jerry places his hands on his hips and angrily declares, "Listen, Zeke, we both know Smokey was murdered. It wasn't no fucking accident like the company says. What are we going to do about it?" As if expecting this conversation, Pryor remains calm and looks out to the street, then turns and says, "Nothing. Nothing can help Smokey now." Keitel responds with surprise and a restlessness, swaying his arm, as he pushes to "expose the union." Pryor remains comparatively still and calm, a different body language than the hyper energy often associated with the comedian. As Jerry presses on, suggesting going to the FBI with the evidence against the union, he sits down as Schrader cuts to Pryor in a close medium shot, calmly but forcefully stating, "Things have gotten complicated. It's not that simple anymore." When Zeke finally says he will be the next union steward, Keitel stands with a look of disbelief on his face and runs his hands through his hair. After Zeke tries to explain he wants to make changes from the inside, Jerry angrily states, "They just bought you off with a promotion." As they continue to argue, Zeke states his case, finally bringing in their racial difference as a factor: "You're my friend, Jerry. But you're thinking white." In response, Keitel turns to look directly at Pryor, off-camera, and states, "What the fuck does that mean?"

His calm façade cracking, Pryor impressively performs the next lines with an emotional directness:

> It means that you got more chances than I got, Jerry, and you're always gonna have more chances than me. I got one chance and I'm gonna take it. I'm black, Jerry. The police ain't gonna protect me. Six months after this fucking thing is over, I'll end up right back where I started from, living in some ghetto, up to my black ass in bills, wondering what night they're gonna come in and kill the kids, Caroline, and myself. If I gotta kiss ass, I'm gonna pick the ass I wanna kiss. And it ain't gonna be the motherfucking police, because they ain't going to do nothing but shit in my face.

In response, Keitel matches Pryor's intensity by asking about Smokey's death and, then, eventually asking, "Why is your family more important than my family?" Zeke then offers to secure Jerry a job as foreman, a proposition Jerry briefly considers, which Keitel performs as looking out onto the street and then proclaiming, as he mimes a knife into his back, "I get screwed. That's all I know." After Zeke suggests, "You ought to think about it, man," the scene ends with the two awkwardly standing in silence.

As Saul relates, this scene was scripted as a simpler conversation of about three minutes of screen time, but the two actors improvised elaborations that pushed it to five.[37] The moment proves effective as the two performers' interpretations and improvisations, despite coming from the different backgrounds of stand-up and theatrical training, correspond well. At one point, Pryor interrupts the conversation to tell his son to "get his ass out of the street," a realistic

Figure 4.2 Harvey Keitel and Richard Pryor in *Blue Collar*.

touch that reminds the viewer of his character's commitment to the safety of his family. Keitel's expressive gestures correspond with his character's boiling rage over Smokey and his sense of helplessness, while Pryor plays the scene mostly with slower movements showing his emotional defeat. While his dialogue conveys he wants to change the union from the inside, his defeated body language suggests he is skeptical of this plan and recognizes he might be lying to himself. Ultimately, there is no way for him to explain his reasoning for taking the job without having to tell Jerry that his worldview is different due to his whiteness. This powerful moment is expressed in a line of dialogue that feels related to Pryor's groundbreaking comedy, the suggestion that Jerry is "thinking white," reflecting a fundamental divide in social standing. This description confuses and angers Jerry, but Zeke's speech outlines how the fantasy of working-class racial harmony depicted earlier was fleeting as a black man has fewer opportunities and a more volatile history with social institutions, especially law enforcement. While Jerry wants to expose the union through a sense of righteous anger, Zeke must deal with the reality of his black identity. Even though he is "selling out," he is right that, unlike Jerry, he might never get other chances for social advancement. The scene proves remarkable in how Schrader employs both the performing styles and extratextual significance of Keitel and Pryor to stress the simmering racial tensions underneath the surface of the plot. Jerry's anger is typical of the white male ethnic persona of the "Method" actors of the era as it highlights an overall restlessness, a need to act out against institutions. In contrast, Zeke's emotional words are something more complex, an honest discussion of racial inequalities and an empathetic plea for understanding, a pathos also found in Pryor's stand-up comedy. Through Schrader's lens, the comedian deconstructs the deeper racial tensions in the working class while the "Method" actor is "thinking white."

NOTES

1. Silvia Feldman, "Blue-collar villainy," *Human Behavior*, No. 7.5, May 1978, 75.
2. Stanley Kaufman, "Stanley Kaufman on Films," *The New Republic*, No. 178.6, February 11, 1978, 25.
3. Kevin Jackson, ed., *Schrader on Schrader & Other Writings* (London: Faber and Faber, 1990), 142.
4. For more on this history, see Steven A. Reich, *A Working People: A History of African American Workers Since Emancipation*, (Lanham, MD: Rowman and Littlefield Publishers, 2014).
5. Michael Omi, "Race Relations in *Blue Collar*," *Jump Cut: A Review of Contemporary Media*, No. 26, December 1981, http://www.ejumpcut.org/archive/onlinessays/JC26folder/BlueCollar.html.
6. Derek Nystrom, *Hard Hats, Rednecks, and Macho Men: Class in 1970s American Cinema*, (New York: Oxford University Press, 2009), 164.
7. Ibid., 165.

8. Omi, "Race Relations in *Blue Collar.*"
9. Jackson, 141.
10. R. Colin Tait, "When Marty Met Bobby: Collaborative Authorship in *Mean Streets* and *Taxi Driver*," in *A Companion to Martin Scorsese*, edited by Aaron Baker (Malden, MA: Wiley-Blackwell, 2015), 303.
11. Jackson, 144.
12. Ibid., 148.
13. Ibid., 144.
14. Paul Gaita, "Yaphet Kotto," *TCM: Turner Classic Movies*, http://www.tcm.com/tcmdb/person/104926%7C158298/Yaphet-Kotto/biography.html.
15. Jackson, 144.
16. Stuart Byron, "The Keitel Method," *Film Comment*, No. 14.1, January/February 1978, 37.
17. Jackson, 145.
18. Keitel's meticulous preparation, in particular his script analysis, can be credited to his training with Adler more than Strasberg. As he states, "Stella Adler, who's a great teacher, remarked that the analysis of the text is the education of the actor." Marshall Fine, *Harvey Keitel: The Art of Darkness* (New York: Fromm International, 1998), 56.
19. Ibid., 108.
20. James Alan McPherson, "The New Comic Style of Richard Pryor (1975)," in *Richard Pryor: The Life and Legacy of a "Crazy" Black Man*, edited by Aubrey Thomas McCluskey, (Bloomington: Indiana University Press, 2008), 203.
21. Jackson, 145.
22. The on-location conflicts were also due to Pryor's well-documented cocaine addiction and a resulting paranoia toward his co-stars. See Fine, 107–8.
23. Jackson, 145.
24. Ibid., 147.
25. Cynthia Baron, *Modern Acting: The Lost Chapter of American Film and Theatre* (London: Palgrave Macmillan, 2016), 61. In chapter four, Baron demonstrates how "Method," which comes directly from Strasberg, does not truly define the approaches of many actors given this label. As such, labeling Keitel as "Method" is more about a popular labeling of American actors than assessing the intricacies of his actual training, which also reflects Adler's influence.
26. "Urban Brooder," *Horizon*, No. 21.2, February 1978, 64.
27. Audrey Thomas McCluskey, "Richard Pryor: Comic Genius, Tortured Soul," in *Richard Pryor: The Life and Legacy of a "Crazy" Black Man*, edited by Aubrey Thomas McCluskey (Bloomington: Indiana University Press, 2008), 2.
28. Ibid., 3.
29. Scott Saul, *Becoming Richard Pryor* (New York: Harper, 2014), 423.
30. Sue Reilly, "Richard Pryor's Ordeal," *People*, No. 9.10, March 13, 1978, https://people.com/archive/cover-story-richard-pryors-ordeal-vol-9-no-10/.
31. Saul, 443. Pryor's homophobic rhetoric proves complex here as the comedian spoke openly on-stage about same-sex sexual experiences.
32. Reilly.
33. Ibid.
34. Vincent Canby, "Film: On the Auto Front: The Assembly Line," *New York Times*, February 10, 1978, https://www.nytimes.com/1978/02/10/archives/film-on-the-auto-frontthe-assembly-line.html.
35. Saul, 422.
36. Ibid., 423.
37. Ibid.

CHAPTER 5

Prophets and Zealots: Paul Schrader's Adaptations of *The Mosquito Coast* and *The Last Temptation of Christ*

Erica Moulton

As Paul Schrader neared the end of his interview with Martin Scorsese for a 1982 edition of *Cahiers du Cinéma*, he shifted the conversation from their past collaborations to more heady material:

    PS: That leads me to my last question. This internal battle—
    MS: This "eternal bowel"?
    PS: No, this *internal battle*—
    MS: I'm sorry.
    PS: This internal battle which expresses itself in your films—does it evolve or repeat?[1]

Scorsese's humorous misunderstanding of Schrader's question in fact highlights a duality that would come to define their next collaboration: an adaptation of Nikos Kazantzakis's novel *The Last Temptation of Christ* (1955, first English edition 1960). The concept of an internal battle was already familiar territory for both Schrader and Scorsese, whose depictions of Travis Bickle and Jake LaMotta's disordered psyches in *Taxi Driver* (1976, Scorsese) and *Raging Bull* (1980, Scorsese) were praised for their aesthetic and verbal intensity. Nevertheless, their choice to grapple with the Christ figure, and specifically Kazantzakis's troubled, human version of Christ, pushed their brand of psychological torment to new and profound physical and spiritual limits. However, *The Last Temptation of Christ* (1988, Scorsese) was not Schrader's only Bildungsroman portraying the metaphysical struggle between a father and son in the 1980s, nor was it his only adaptation of a popular novel. During the summer of 1982, after Schrader delivered the second draft of his script for *Last Temptation* to Scorsese, he made a deal with producer Jerome Hellman to adapt Paul Theroux's recently published work, *The Mosquito Coast* (US edition 1982). The novel recounts events involving Allie Fox, an ingenious and increasingly unhinged inventor, through the eyes of his teenage son Charlie as the family journeys to the jungles of Honduras to pursue Allie's dreams of Edenic independence from American society.

Schrader may not have set out to write two adaptations back to back, but when he reflected on the process of adaptation years later, he spoke about the difficulties he faced condensing the lengthy books into two-hour films, stating, "it's actually easier to write original scripts than to adapt books, because when you write an adaptation you have two employers, the person who's paying you and the author of the book, both of whom militate against your own creativity and make writing a slower and more difficult process."[2] This chapter explores the practical challenges that Schrader faced in translating Kazantzakis and Theroux's prose from the page to the screen, but more broadly, it articulates Schrader's contributions to these texts as they evolved from the outline stage, through multiple drafts, including when the drafts passed out of Schrader's hands to the directors. The wealth of archival material in the Paul Schrader Papers at the Harry Ransom Center offers a unique opportunity for adaptation scholars to consider both the practical and theoretical questions raised during the screenwriting process.

ADAPTATION THEORY AND SCHRADER AS SCREENWRITER/ADAPTOR

While much of the last thirty years of adaptation scholarship has been justifiably skeptical toward the concept of "fidelity," Schrader's admiration for his sources, in both cases, led him to write scripts that adhered very closely to the events and characters depicted on the page.[3] This instance of close adherence to the source texts offers a potential alternative view of adaptation from the field's current focus on intertextuality. Robert Stam and Linda Hutcheon's early 2000s output on adaptation helped to crystallize this view, which displaces the source text from its place of authority and instead considers adaptation within a broader context of intertextual influences. Stam's book *Literature Through Film* (2005) conducts comparative analyses of novels and films, but his motivation behind exploring aesthetic questions is to unearth "social questions concerning social stratification and the distribution of power."[4] Hutcheon's *A Theory of Adaptation* (2006) sought to expand adaptation beyond the two-pronged novel–film divide into a matrix of production and reception networks. In her view, adaptation should be accepted as a trans-historical phenomenon, with stories "evolv[ing] and mutat[ing] to fit new times and different places."[5] Her global perspective, however, also takes into account some of the medium-specific issues raised by adaptation, and she offers her own schema to account for shifts between printed texts and other media, from film and television to video games and theme parks. These "modes of engagement" determine how an audience will be exposed to a story, whether through telling, showing, or interacting. By framing the novel to film adaptation process as a shift from telling to showing, Hutcheon begins to delve into the formal decision-making process.[6]

Hutcheon's exploration of the limitations and affordances of shifting from print to screen media was also the subject of Brian McFarlane's 1996 project *Novel to Film*, which took a case-study approach to demonstrating how the Barthesian concepts of *cardinal functions* and *indices* could be applied to the process of adaptation. McFarlane's study breaks stories down into narrative elements like plot events and characters, which may be translated with relative ease from one medium to another, and the *indices*, or the enunciative elements of the story, which have to do with expressive properties of the medium itself. The tension between narrative and formal expression creates a situation in which "the film version of a novel may retain all the major cardinal functions of a novel, all its chief character functions, its most important psychological patterns, and yet, at both the micro- and macro- levels of articulation, set up in the viewer acquainted with the novel quite different responses."[7] The phenomenon described by McFarlane certainly occurs in both *The Last Temptation* and *The Mosquito Coast*, and yet in McFarlane's view, these differing responses are a product of "how far the film-maker has sought to create his own work in those areas where transfer is not possible."[8] McFarlane, Hutcheon, and Stam's writing on adaptation all stakes a place for the creative agency of the filmmaker in adaptation, but it is notable that none of their book-length works devote significant space to the screenwriting stage of the adaptation process. This chapter seeks to rectify this oversight in the case of Schrader by identifying his distinct voice among the other authorial voices that competed while developing *The Last Temptation* and *The Mosquito Coast*.[9]

Schrader's specific voice was already well cultivated by the early 1980s, as was his preoccupation with "the quest-driven obsessive whose attempt to make things right inevitably brings with it a violent outcome."[10] Travis Bickle is Schrader's archetypal loner protagonist, but Jake Van Dorn in *Hardcore* (1979), Julian Kaye in *American Gigolo* (1980), Yukio Mishima in *Mishima: A Life in Four Chapters* (1985), and both Jesus and Allie Fox also exhibit the kind of "terrifically self-destructive" behavior that energized Schrader's writing.[11] Their violence manifests in Schrader's screenplays on two planes. There is the violence inflicted on the bodies of his protagonists (and the violence they sometimes inflict on others) and the violence of their thoughts, which Schrader expresses through his use of voiceover. This style of narration is employed in bringing the struggles of both Jesus and Charlie Fox to film, as their voices float throughout their respective films articulating thematic elements and also revealing their tumultuous internal battle with their fathers. Having a vehicle for pure thematic expression like voiceover is crucial to Schrader's unique style. Speaking about his early outlining and drafting process to *American Film*, he professed, "All movies have themes . . . The *four* most important elements [of screenwriting] are *theme*, story, characterization and structure. You have to know in some way what you are about to do. Even if that theme gets rerouted or ends up in subtext."[12] In the case of his adaptations, the themes of self-destruction and paternal conflict helped to guide his selection of prose passages and dialogue, many of which are lifted directly from the novels.

What Schrader chooses to include from the source texts and how he shapes that material as either voiceover, dialogue, or images, becomes the lens through which to view his contribution. Moreover, by investigating Schrader's own underlined copies of the novels, his outlines and the multiple drafts, we may arrive at a more complete understanding of the micro-adaptations that take place as the stories pass through multiple scripting formats. In both cases, the latter drafts of the scripts were revised by the directors, and in the case of *Last Temptation*, by the screenwriter Jay Cocks. Through a comparative analysis of these drafts, the following two sections bring Schrader's contributions into sharper focus. For *Last Temptation*, Scorsese and Cocks's revisions were frequently rewording and reordering dialogue and short scenes, but ultimately the profound mental and physical anguish that Schrader infuses into Jesus's character through the voiceover and the addition of a graphic scene of self-harm are still identifiably Schrader's voice in the final film. *The Mosquito Coast*, by contrast, maintains some of Schrader's voice in Charlie's narration, but director Peter Weir's revisions move away from the theme of paternal conflict and thereby undermine the function of the voiceover. For both of these film projects, the struggle that ensued between Schrader and the directors over sole writing credit, leading to Writers Guild of America (WGA) arbitration in both cases, will be explored in the final section. Schrader's scripts for *The Last Temptation of Christ* and *The Mosquito Coast* may essentially function as an intermedial step between the novels and the finished films, but this chapter adopts scholar Jack Boozer's view of adapted screenplays as sites of "personal and cultural struggle and perhaps revelation."[13] For both adapted screenplays, Schrader places his identifying and indelible mark on the protagonists, as recognizable zealots and prophets within his canon of characters.

THE PROPHET AWAKES: *THE LAST TEMPTATION OF CHRIST*

The Last Temptation of Christ had a long journey to the screen, beginning in 1972 when Barbara Hershey gave Martin Scorsese a copy of the novel during the filming of *Boxcar Bertha* (1972, Scorsese). Kazantzakis's controversial novel was translated from Greek to English in 1960, causing a stir among religious critics for its gritty depiction of Jesus undergoing the transformation from man to God and the temptations that threatened to derail him on his journey. As opposed to always being divinely ordained, the novel presented "Jesus as a man who discovers his divinity after a mortal struggle . . . [and] Judas as Jesus' strongest, most loyal and loving apostle who . . . prove[s] his love by betraying both his master and his ideals of a revolution that would cleanse both church and state."[14] The three central characters of Jesus, Judas, and Mary Magdalene were shown to be in the thrall of sin and vice, with Judas consumed by hate, Mary by lust, and Jesus by fear and a whole host of other sinful urges. Kazantzakis's stated intention in dramatizing the life of Christ, then, was to shed light on "the dual substance of Christ," who was part flesh and part spirit, in order to provide a model for man's earthly struggle with temptation.[15]

Religious scholars continue to grapple with this radically human and flawed version of Christ, which was condemned by the Orthodox Church of America and perceived "as a blasphemous and sacrilegious assault on traditional Christianity" in 1960.[16] Scholar Graham Holderness attributes this uproar to a "partial reading of the novel," arguing that the dreams and visions that Kazantzakis wove through the text function as subconscious harbingers of Jesus's divine fate.[17] Nevertheless, the "religious intensity" of this conflict between body and mind attracted Scorsese and Schrader to the project, so in early 1982 Schrader began to outline the proposed film based on the thirty-three chapters that comprised the book (the same number of chapters as years that Christ supposedly lived).[18] Although his background in the Dutch Calvinist Church and Scorsese's Catholic upbringing are frequently cited as inspiring the film's interpretation of the Christ tale, Schrader saw Jesus's conflict as "more psychological" than spiritual, and essentially "about a common man possessed by God and fighting it," even going so far as to call God a "demon" in the film.[19] Schrader's first draft of the script takes these psychological struggles and injects them into Jesus's voiceovers, distributing them throughout the forty-six narrative events that he isolates from the novel.

At the outline stage, Schrader listed the forty-six events numerically on a single side of yellow legal paper, effectively placing the viewer on the road with Jesus, like Kazantzakis does, as he journeys from Nazareth to Jerusalem, and at last, to his crucifixion at Golgotha. Next to each of the numbers, Schrader estimates how long the scenes will be by page-length, ranging anywhere from half a page up to four and a half pages long.[20] The outlines serve the purpose of articulating structural elements while giving Schrader the freedom to experiment with how to pace and order each event. Throughout the brief document, there are small notes next to the main events indicating important details as well as the word "narr." scrawled in the margins, which is the abbreviation Schrader uses for voiceover narration. Even at the earliest stages of his planning process, Schrader not only saw the voiceover as integral to the film's structure, but was planning what emotions or ideas each narration would encompass, including "dreaming," "footsteps," "amazed," "doubt," and "despair."[21] In an interview with *New York Times* cultural critic David Itzkoff, Schrader linked this process of outlining to oral traditions, insisting that each time he tells the story of a film aloud, he rewrites and hones his outlines.[22]

Schrader's annotated copy of the book contains no indications about how he plans to order or reorder the narrative events; instead there are many passages that Schrader underlines, including dialogue and images that make their way into his script. The novel narrates in a third-person omniscient voice that drifts freely into and out of multiple characters' consciousness, not just Jesus's. The reader learns of his mother Mary's feelings about her son's struggle and we spend time with the Abbot, with the cantankerous Zebedee (made a minor character in Schrader's screenplay) and his wife, Old Salome (who is eliminated entirely). Schrader's screenplay, by contrast, only allows the viewer access to Jesus's thoughts through his voiceover. This dynamic between what Schrader underlines and his focusing the film on Jesus is especially evident in events nine and ten on his outline, which are taken from Chapter Eleven of the novel. Both scenes concern Jesus's flight to a monastery where he and an Abbot are visited by two serpents that coil together on the floor of Jesus's cell. The action in the novel is perceived first by a young monk named Jeroboam and then by the wizened Abbot, who momentarily succumbs to the sensuous imagery, while Jesus lies curled on the floor. Kazantzakis writes that the Abbot shudders at his sudden weakness and reflects, "everything has two meanings, one manifest, one hidden."[23]

When the scene is shifted to screenplay format in Schrader's initial draft, dated March 25, 1982, the external action plays out in much the same way, but Jesus replaces the Abbot and Jeroboam as the point-of-view character in the scene. The script reads that a snake "emerges from a hole in the wall and slithers across the earthen floor. Another snake follows it. The snakes coil around each other and copulate."[24] Schrader describes Jesus watching the action and in voiceover he utters lines that originally belonged to Jeroboam and the Abbot in the novel:

> Jesus (V.O.):
> Why now after all this time? So
> this is sex. Men and women coupling . . .
> (watches the snakes)
> But everything is of God. And
> everything has two meanings, one
> obvious, one hidden. What are
> they telling me?[25]

Schrader heightens the connection between the serpents' copulation and Jesus's sexual frustration by having a snake speak in Mary Magdalene's voice. Almost as if to clarify that the snakes' behavior is not the source of frustration for Jesus, but rather the emotions their presence stirs up, he writes, "The snakes change color as they coil. Is this real – or a vision? The question doesn't occur to Jesus. Nor would it to his contemporaries. They lived in a time which accepted healings, miracles, stigmata and visions as extensions of the natural world."[26] By reinforcing the illusory nature of this scene in the script's descriptive prose and keeping the dialogue inside Jesus's mind, Schrader draws the audience closer into his psyche.

Scholars writing on the film have noted this exaggerated focus on Jesus's psychological experience. The effect of this narrative strategy is to cast doubt on whether certain mystical occurrences are holy or just a by-product of a troubled young man's disordered mind. Indeed, film scholars Bruce Babington and Peter W. Evans consider Schrader and Scorsese's portrayal "a fragmented, almost schizophrenic Jesus," adding that, "even the signs of his possession by God are ambiguous, something like epilepsy, that could be madness or repressed sexual desire . . . He wavers between . . . the sensual world and the unseen, between the spiritual and the carnal, and between opposed ways of overcoming injustice."[27] Madness and desire are both present in this first scene with the snake, but as Scorsese and Cocks found during their revisions, Schrader's reassignment of the Abbot's words to Jesus's narration is the key to conveying his ongoing struggle and futile search for meaning.

Jay Cocks and Scorsese's August 12, 1983 revision of Schrader's draft begins the monastery sequence by dispensing with the Abbot character and focusing on Jeroboam in the cell. They add an exchange between Jesus and Jeroboam before the snakes' action where Jesus frankly expresses his internal dilemma to the monk, admitting, "I'm a liar. A hypocrite. I'm afraid of everything . . ."[28] He goes on to recount his many sins with language that is lifted from Chapter Ten of Kazantzakis's novel and Jeroboam attempts to console him by offering to hear his blasphemous thoughts.[29] When Jesus calls the voice inside of him 'Lucifer' and says the voice tells him he is God, Scorsese and Cocks write that Jeroboam is left "speechless."[30] In the following scene, they continue to build the relationship between the emerging prophet and this young monk by having Jeroboam witness the snakes' bizarre behavior and tell Jesus, "God has just blessed you," adding, "Everything has two meanings, one obvious, the other hidden."[31] Externalizing this sentiment displaces Jesus as the site of psychological struggle, a fact that Scorsese and Cocks seemed to have arrived at some years later when they were putting the final touches on the shooting script. Their seventh revision, dated August 5, 1987, restores the dual meaning line to Jesus's voiceover narration.[32] In the final filmed version, Willem Dafoe as Jesus does not say the second part of the line—that one meaning is obvious and the other is hidden—but he emphatically beats his chest on the line "Leave me" (spoken aloud in Scorsese and Cocks's draft, but in voiceover in Schrader's), indicating he feels the serpents' presence inside his body, a gesture which was cued in Schrader's original draft which suggested that "Jesus grabs his chest;

the snakes hiss inside his breast."³³ While Kazantzakis's book establishes that Jesus feels the snakes inside his heart, Schrader recasts the scene as an invasion of his mind and body by God.

The impact of this bodily invasion is most strongly felt in the scenes and visual details that Schrader adds during and following Jesus's trials in the desert. Another serpent with Magdalene's voice visits Jesus both in the book and in Schrader's script. The narrative economy mandated by adaptation is apparent in this scene, which plays out over ten pages in the book and only four pages of his script. Schrader carefully selects and juxtaposes salient details from Chapter Seventeen and puts his own spin on them to bring out his intended theme of God and Satan as invading forces. The circle that Jesus draws around himself on page 37 of his draft is accompanied by another voiceover narration in which Jesus demands clarity from God. The gesture of drawing the circle is taken from Kazantzakis,³⁴ but Schrader stages each of Jesus's encounters with the serpent, the lion, and the Archangel at the edge of the circle, an invention entirely his own. Scorsese and Cocks maintain this staging in their drafts and in the final film, also keeping the image that Schrader writes where "Jesus bites into the [Archangel's] apple" and "it turns to blood in his mouth."³⁵

This grisly image prefigures the scene where Jesus returns to confront his disciples, and Schrader uses this occasion to show him finally possessed with the righteous zeal of a prophet. Having just undergone the apex of his internal battle, Jesus releases this anguish in an act of self-destruction by removing his heart from his chest. Schrader's Jesus proclaims to the disciples, "John [the Baptist] baptized with water and they killed him. Now I will baptize with fire," before he "reaches into his chest and pulls out his own bloody heart" and preaches about the coming war.³⁶

Figure 5.1 Jesus (Willem Dafoe) shows his bloody heart to the disciples in *The Last Temptation of Christ* (1988)

Again, Scorsese and Cocks's subsequent drafts make few changes to this scene apart from rewording some of the lines and making Jesus's speech even more militant, as they add this line: "We'll pick up an ax and cut the devil's throat."[37] Ultimately, Scorsese and Cocks's thematic intentions are largely in line with Schrader's. Mark Conrad, a scholar of film philosophy, observes that Schrader and Scorsese's Jesus is a kind of Nietzschean mad god figure, whose trials in the desert allow him to "see reality in flux and values as unstable . . . through wild, made visions," which was an unwelcome and disturbing interpretation of Christ for many viewers at the time of the film's release.[38] Schrader, however, did see the film on these psychological terms—not as a religious film, but as an extension of his interest in self-destructive, dogmatic men. In the next section, I turn my attention to Schrader's script drafts for *The Mosquito Coast* to show how friction between Schrader and director Peter Weir over theme and character was played out in the scripting stage, with voiceover narration serving as the primary battleground.

A ZEALOT'S DESCENT: *THE MOSQUITO COAST*

In both Paul Theroux's 1982 novel and Schrader's draft of the screenplay (dated August 29, 1983), Allie Fox is a God-like figure, dominating the lives of his wife (known only as Mother) and children, and seemingly all-powerful in his manipulation of the earthly matter that surrounds him. Like *Last Temptation*, Schrader translates the main events directly from the novel, as the journey-structure of Theroux's narrative serves Schrader well in depicting Allie's son, Charlie's slow shift away from his father's oppressive influence. The book, Schrader's initial draft, and the final film, which is based on a revised script by director Peter Weir, all follow the family as they leave a quiet New England town for a village on the coast of Honduras, where Allie builds and later destroys his gargantuan ice-machine invention called Fat Boy.

Allie's domination of Charlie's psyche is evident from the first pages of the novel, especially in a sentence that Schrader underlines in his copy and uses in one of Charlie's first voiceovers. The line, lifted nearly verbatim from Theroux, has Charlie declaring, "I grew up with the belief that the world belonged to him [Allie] and everything he said was true."[39] Schrader's scene description above this voiceover characterizes Charlie as sounding at times like "mature man, remembering these events" and at other times like he was "still thirteen, remembering what he felt at that moment."[40] The tension between remembered versus experienced trauma becomes Schrader's organizing thematic principle and guides his use of voiceover and imagery throughout his draft of *Mosquito Coast*.

The conflict between Allie and Charlie plays out both internally, but also, like Jesus within his protective circle in the desert, as a battle over territory and boundaries. Allie purchases the small village of Jeronimo and sets about transforming it and its townsfolk through sheer force of will, giving little heed to the needs of anyone outside himself. Meanwhile, Charlie and his siblings establish their own small shadow town called Acre, which they obsessively hide from their father. Film scholar Jonathan Rayner describes Allie's "ascendancy to the position of absolute power" as part of his subconscious drive to prove himself superior to American society, organized religion, and even God, all of whom are symbolized in the character of Reverend Spellgood.[41] While Allie's role in the book and Schrader's script is the zealot, it is Charlie who must deal with his feelings toward his father, as he comes to see him as a tyrant and a hypocrite. As in *The Last Temptation*, Schrader portrays these internal conflicts as simmering within Charlie's narration before they bubble over and become visible on the body's surface.

One such instance of this bubbling over is in the scene that Schrader writes between Allie and Charlie when they sneak up to Fat Boy in the middle of the night to trap some men who have invaded Jeronimo. After luring them into the ice-machine, Allie summons his teenage son under cover of night to climb onto the roof of the structure and rig it to freeze the men to death. Before Charlie carries out this act on his father's behalf, Allie attempts to justify his actions to his son, but also offers a chilling warning. Schrader begins the exchange by writing that "Allie squashes a mosquito with his finger, shows the blood to Charlie," before saying:

> Allie:
> Don't pity those men, Charlie. Don't
> pity insects. This is not the insect's
> blood; it's my blood . . . .[42]

This line is translated from Chapter 20 of Theroux's novel, but Schrader's decision to include this scene, in particular the moment Allie shows Charlie the blood on his hand and links it to the absolute loyalty he demands from his blood-relatives, reinforces Charlie's dilemma. It also builds Charlie's realization that he is complicit in his father's manic and destructive behavior, as a few lines later, Schrader has him quietly object, saying "The men . . . ?" while Allie tells him to count to three hundred.[43] Schrader builds these moments of mental and physical conflict between Allie and Charlie throughout his script, pieced together by faithfully condensing Theroux's four-hundred-page novel into sixty-six narrative events on his outline.[44]

The film's director, Peter Weir, however, decided to move the thematic needle in an opposing direction, making the film more about Charlie learning to accept and forgive his father's flaws. This shift could be attributed to casting popular

Figure 5.2 Allie Fox (Harrison Ford) holds out a bloody finger to his son, Charlie (River Phoenix) in *The Mosquito Coast* (1986)

action star Harrison Ford as Allie and the decision to emphasize his obsession with controlling his environment rather than controlling his son. Schrader identified this thematic shift in the notes he sent back for Weir's revised draft (dated November 27, 1985), in which he warns that "Theroux wrote a '"bildingsroman [sic],' a coming-of-age novel, in an ethnological setting" whereas Weir's script was "an ethnological movie with a coming-of-age subplot."[45] Schrader felt that Allie needed to be darkly charming in the early scenes of the film and only slowly reveal his manic tendencies for the film to work, suggesting Jack Nicholson for the role.[46] Ford was hot off a successful collaboration with Weir in *Witness* (1985) and hoped to replicate that success, but in this case, his movie-star persona proved an ill fit for the megalomaniacal role. While his loquacious performance was generally regarded as effective, many reviewers identified the diminished importance of Charlie and his narration, which Weir only uses intermittently in his revised screenplay, as a major weakness of the film.[47]

Weir's changes in general skew toward making the film more overtly sentimental; his revised script adds an opening scene of Charlie as an older man returning to his childhood bedroom and reminiscing while looking at photos of his father. Instead of opening with voiceover, Weir writes that Charlie "speaks softly to himself" in an imagined conversation with his father, telling him:

> Charlie:
> You were the best and worst of
> fathers. You could be a bully,

but you could also make us laugh.
You took us on the adventure of
our lives, but it cost you, yours.[48]

In Schrader's copy of Weir's revised script, he scrawled in the margins next to this speech an emphatic "NO." It is clear why Schrader would have objected to this line in particular since it diffuses any tension that could be built between Allie and Charlie by effectively pre-exculpating Allie for his actions. Weir's saccharine opening, in the end, was not used for the final film, which still hews close to the structure of Schrader's second draft. The other changes that Weir makes include deleting a second scene at Acre, in which Charlie expresses his growing restlessness with his father's restrictive lifestyle, as well as rewriting many of Charlie's voiceover reflections to be more awestruck than critical of his father.

These rewordings are often small alterations or insertions of phrases, but unlike Scorsese and Cocks's changes, which generally retained the idea behind the lines, Weir frequently alters Schrader's meaning entirely. Nowhere is this more evident than in the final scenes of the film when the family visits Spellgood's mission at Guampu and Allie lights the church on fire, forcing a confrontation between him and his family. Charlie and his younger brother Jerry want to leave Allie behind and escape. Schrader has Charlie confront his father directly, telling him, "We're not going with you. Not after those lies. Not after you made us suffer for nothing."[49] Charlie pointedly uses the word "suffer," linking Allie's actions to the physical and mental toll that the forced journey has enacted on the family. It is after this accusation that Schrader has Allie raise his hand to strike Mother for the first time (one of the few changes that Schrader makes from the scene in the book), making Allie's violence toward his family physically manifest.

The tables, however, are quickly turned on Allie, who is shot by Spellgood, forcing the family back onto the raft where they drift for several days before Allie dies on Brewer's Lagoon beach surrounded by vultures. The scene that Schrader writes again closely follows Theroux's penultimate chapter depicting Allie's final descent, and Schrader ends his script in the same place as Theroux's novel—with Charlie reflecting in a taxicab on the way back to America. His final voiceover narration declares, "Once I had believed in Father and the world seemed very small. Now he was gone and I hardly believed in myself and the world was limitless . . ."[50] Allie's gruesome fate in Theroux and Schrader's versions did not align with Weir's interpretation of the character, so his revised script excises the moment when Allie threatens to hit Mother and dispenses with the vultures who pick at Allie's corpse. Weir initially leaves out the final narration that Schrader took from Theroux, instead writing his own voiceover speech for Charlie to deliver while kneeling next to his father on the boat:

Charlie (V.O.)
I don't think we ever loved him
more than on that downstream
voyage. The ardor of our mutiny
had cooled, and our feelings
toward him had changed . . .[51]

In Weir's version, Allie is presented as more of an archetypal western hero than the single-minded narcissist he is in Schrader's. Not only does Weir often film the stand-offs between Spellgood and Allie like they are "shoot-outs,"[52] and frame Allie as a pioneer figure, but his death is treated as a stoic and mournful goodbye rather than the traumatic experience that Schrader and Theroux depict it as for the family. The final film mediates between Weir and Schrader's drafts, restoring some of Schrader's voiceover narration, including Charlie's final speech with one slight alteration. In the film, as Allie (Harrison Ford) leans his head back and closes his eyes, a tearful Charlie (River Phoenix) and Mother (Helen Mirren) look down at him. Weir cuts to their boat heading toward an expanse of ocean while Charlie says in voiceover: "Once I had believed in Father and the world had seemed small and old. Now he was gone and I wasn't afraid to love him anymore and the world seemed limitless."[53] Again, Schrader's meaning is changed by softening Charlie's attitude toward his father, a tonal shift that was completely anathema to Schrader's vision of Allie. *The Mosquito Coast* was, therefore, a case where discordant voices during the scripting stage of the adaptation led to a final film with a very loose hold on the all-important element for Schrader—theme.

WHOSE SCRIPT IS IT ANYWAY? DUELING VOICES

Schrader's disappointment reading Weir's revised draft is documented in the twelve pages of notes and marginal comments that he made to the script sent to him by Jerome Hellman on April 3, 1985. Schrader wrote back to Hellman and Weir some months later and cautioned against trying to make the film both a man vs. nature and man vs. son story, joking that "the result is familiar to any drunk (i.e. Artist) trying to straddle two bar stools, you fall between."[54] Weir and Hellman seem to have taken some of this criticism, as the final film reverts to Schrader's 1983 draft in several places. This made Weir's decision to file for co-writing credit particularly offensive to Schrader, who received notification in a letter on August 4, 1986 from Jerome Hellman's assistant. Schrader had already been informed of this plan by Jeff Berg, his agent at ICM, and filed a suit with the Arbitration Committee at the Writers Guild for sole authorship. His letter to the committee, dated July 31, 1986, insists that he was surprised by Weir's filing since he felt the changes did not amount to the 50 per cent contribution required to claim credit, calling Weir's changes "additional condensation" of the novel.[55]

Schrader found himself in the same position two years later when Martin Scorsese and Jack Cocks filed for co-screenwriting credits, leading Schrader once again to file a claim with WGA arbitration for sole writing credit. During the promotional cycle for the film (while arbitration was ongoing), Scorsese sought to both acknowledge Schrader's contribution in interviews, while also asserting his authorship of the final product. Speaking about the heart-removal scene with *Film Comment*, Scorsese remarked:

> Actually, that scene, which was not in the Kazantzakis book, was written by Paul Schrader, a Dutch Calvinist, and it was kind of nudged to me as Catholic. He also wanted to show that the supernatural and the natural exist on the same plane. But we were doing that all along. He wanted to show the angel at the end turning into a gargoyle and slithering off a table. I leveled that all out.[56]

While it is true that Schrader wrote the false Guardian Angel revealing himself as Satan in the last temptation sequence, Scorsese slightly misrepresents the scene as Schrader only described the angel crouching on a table "like a gargoyle" and he doesn't slither away, but "floats off" the table and into the night.[57] Something about the adaptation process in both these cases seems to bring out the tensions that exist within a film production between collaborators all seeking to stake a space for their own voice to be acknowledged and praised. In his letter to the arbitration committee for *Last Temptation*, Schrader positioned his screenplay as establishing the "characters, themes, storyline, sequences and structures" that exist in the final film.[58] The arbitration committee sided with Schrader in both cases, awarding him sole writing credit.

Charged with adapting the source material for both *Last Temptation* and *The Mosquito Coast*, Schrader functions as the locus of translation, the first, and in many ways the most substantial, agent in the recapitulation of source material. Schrader's ability to assert his own voice derives from his selection and amplification of thematic elements in the novels that allow him to explore his interest in self-destructive men beset by conflicts both internal and external. However, as this chapter has demonstrated, the process of adaptation is neither completely linear nor does it exist in a single format. Charting the multiple drafts, outlines and research is crucial to understanding the fluid nature of adaptation as a network of agents that can and do coexist (though not always peacefully).

Moreover, Schrader's 1982 draft of *The Last Temptation of Christ* may not be the exact version of the story that ended up on the screen, but its influence on the production was still felt in many ways. Most notably, after Universal acquired the distribution rights to the film in 1987 and hired an outreach coordinator to liaise with the Christian community, they found that the script being circulated that was causing the uproar was in fact Schrader's first draft and not the carefully guarded shooting script. Representatives at Universal dubbed Schrader's script "a bootleg" and assuaged fears by insisting the "'new' scenes were not in the final shooting script."[59] This repudiation of Schrader's contribution underscores the difficulty of revealing the fractious process of film adaptation and screenwriting/development more generally within Hollywood's industrial system. Interestingly, Schrader's script was identified by the epigraph he included on the first page, which was not from Kazantzakis's novel, but from another of his works titled *The Saviors of God* (1927). This short message was meant as a spiritual affirmation, which Schrader seems to have taken as a personal and creative imperative in writing the script. It reads, "It is not God who will save us—it is we who will save God, by battling, by creating and transmuting matter into spirit."[60] Schrader not only included these words on his draft for *Last Temptation*, he wrote them onto his outline, perhaps as a reminder to himself to faithfully represent Kazantzakis's split portrait of Christ in his script. The phrase also seems an apt characterization of Schrader's attitude toward adaptation—in both *Last Temptation* and *The Mosquito Coast*, and in his later adaptations, Schrader extricated stories and characters from the novels and reformed them with his characteristic use of voiceover and arresting imagery to accord with his unique creative spirit.

NOTES

1. Paul Schrader and Martin Scorsese, "From 'Interview with Paul Schrader,'" in *Cahiers du Cinéma* (Paris), April 1982. Reprinted with permission." In *Martin Scorsese: Interviews, Revised and Updated*, edited by Robert Ribera (Jackson: University Press of Mississippi, 2017), 110.
2. Kevin Jackson, ed., *Schrader on Schrader* (London: Faber and Faber, 1992), 128.
3. For an overview of the debates and history surrounding "fidelity" and film adaptation, see David T. Johnson, "Adaptation and Fidelity," *The Oxford Handbook of Adaptation Studies*, edited by Thomas Leitch (New York: Oxford University Press, 2017), 87–100.
4. Robert Stam, *Literature Through Film: Realism, Magic, and the Art of Adaptation*, 1st edition (Malden, MA: Wiley-Blackwell, 2004), 18.
5. Linda Hutcheon and Siobhan O'Flynn, *A Theory of Adaptation*, 2nd edition (Abingdon and New York: Routledge, 2013), 176.
6. Hutcheon, 22, 34–46.
7. Brian McFarlane, *Novel to Film: An Introduction to the Theory of Adaptation* (Oxford and New York: Clarendon Press, 1996), 26.
8. Macfarlane, 26.
9. There are more recent scholarly works that take a closer look at the role of the screenwriter and their process of adapting fiction into the screenplay format. For more,

see Jack Boozer, ed., *Authorship in Film Adaptation* (Austin, TX: University of Texas Press), 2008. See also Simone Murray, "Best Adapted Screenwriter?: The Intermedial Figure of the Screenwriter in the Contemporary Adaptation Industry," *The Adaptation Industry: The Cultural Economy of Contemporary Literary Adaptation* (New York and London: Routledge, 2012), 131–55. Adaptation scholars Deborah Cartmell and Imelda Whelehan conducted an interview with frequent adaptor Andrew Davies in "A practical understanding of literature on screen: two conversations with Andrew Davies," *The Cambridge Companion to Literature on Screen* (Cambridge: Cambridge University Press, 2007), 239–51.

10. George Kouvaros, *Paul Schrader* (Urbana and Chicago: University of Illinois Press, 2008), 35.
11. Jackson, *Schrader on Schrader*, 128.
12. *American Film.* "Paul Schrader" *(Archive: 1975–1992); New York.* 1989, 19.
13. Boozer, "Introduction," 24.
14. Martin Scorsese and Richard Corliss, 1988. "Body . . . And Blood," *Film Comment* 24 (5), 43.
15. Nikos Kazantzakis, *The Last Temptation of Christ* (New York and London: Simon and Schuster, 1960), 1.
16. Graham Holderness, "'Half God, Half Man': Kazantzakis, Scorsese, and The Last Temptation," *Harvard Theological Review* 100, No. 1 (January 2007), 73. Other notable scholarly works on Kazantzakis's novel and Scorsese's film include Richard Snee, "The Spirit and the Flesh: The Rhetorical Nature of *The Last Temptation of Christ*," *Journal of Media and Religion* 4 (1),45–61.
17. Holderness, 74.
18. Michael Bliss and Paul Schrader, 2000. "Affliction and Forgiveness: An Interview with Paul Schrader," *Film Quarterly* 54 (1), 3.
19. Jackson, *Schrader on Schrader*, 136.
20. Paul Schrader, "Outlines, undated, for *The Last Temptation of Christ*," Container 55, Folder 7, Paul Schrader Papers, Harry Ransom Center, University of Texas-Austin, Austin, TX.
    Paul Schrader, "Bound volume with underlined passages of Nikos Kazantzakis's *The Last Temptation of Christ* (1960)," undated, Container 56, Folder 2, Paul Schrader Papers, Harry Ransom Center, University of Texas-Austin, Austin, TX.
21. "Outlines," Paul Schrader Papers.
22. David Itzkoff. "It Ain't Pretty No More: See Paul Schrader's Outline for 'Raging Bull,'" *ArtsBeat* (blog), March 15, 2010.
23. Kazantzakis, 150.
24. Paul Schrader, "Screenplay of *The Last Temptation of Christ*, 'first draft,'" March 25, 1982, Container 55, Folder 4, Paul Schrader Papers, Harry Ransom Center, University of Texas-Austin, Austin, TX, 16.
25. Screenplay of *Last Temptation*, "first draft," 16.
26. Ibid., 17.
27. Bruce Babington and Peter W. Evans, *Biblical Epics: Sacred Narratives in the Hollywood Cinema* (Manchester: Manchester University Press, 1993), 152.
28. Paul Schrader, Martin Scorsese, and Jay Cocks, "Screenplay of *The Last Temptation of Christ*, 'third revision,'" August 12, 1983, Container 55, Folder 5, Paul Schrader Papers, Harry Ransom Center, University of Texas-Austin, Austin, TX, 21.
29. Kazantzakis, 146.
30. Screenplay of *Last Temptation*, "third revision," 22.
31. Ibid., 23.

32. Paul Schrader, Martin Scorsese, and Jay Cocks, "Screenplay of *The Last Temptation of Christ*, 'seventh draft,'" August 5, 1987, Container 55, Folder 6, Paul Schrader Papers, Harry Ransom Center, University of Texas-Austin, Austin, TX, 25.
33. Screenplay of *Last Temptation*, "first draft," 17. For another inventory of the changes made to Schrader's script by Scorsese and Cocks, see Thomas R. Lindlof, *Hollywood under Siege: Martin Scorsese, the Religious Right, and the Culture Wars* (Lexington, KY: University Press of Kentucky, 2008), 52–5.
34. Kazantzakis, 249.
35. Screenplay of *Last Temptation*, "First draft," 41; "Third draft," 47–8; "Seventh Revision," 50.
36. "First draft," 45.
37. "Seventh revision," 58. Cocks and Scorsese's "third draft" has Jesus proclaiming, "We'll turn an ax against the Devil's kingdom, against the world," 54.
38. "London Cool to 'Temptation'," *New York Times (1923–Current File)*, September 10, 1988; "Film Reviews: The Last Temptation of Christ," *Monthly Film Bulletin* 57, No. 4 (Autumn 1988), 281; Janet Maslin, "Review/Film; 'Last Temptation,' Scorsese's View Of Jesus' Sacrifice," *The New York Times*, August 12, 1988, Late City Final Edition, sec. Weekend Desk; C.
39. Paul Schrader, "Screenplay of *The Mosquito Coast*, 'second draft revised,'" September 20, 1983, Container 68, Folder 8, Paul Schrader Papers, Harry Ransom Center, University of Texas-Austin, Austin, TX, 6.
Paul Schrader, "Inscribed and bound volume with underlined passages and notes, Paul Theroux's *The Mosquito Coast*," 1982, Container 69, Folder 3, Paul Schrader Papers, Harry Ransom Center, University of Texas-Austin, Austin, TX, 11.
40. Screenplay of *The Mosquito Coast*, "second draft," 6.
41. Jonathan Rayner, *The Films of Peter Weir*, 2nd edition (New York and London: Continuum, 2003), 175.
42. Screenplay of *The Mosquito Coast*, "second draft," 83.
43. "Second draft," 85.
44. Paul Schrader, "Outlines and notes for *The Mosquito Coast*," undated, Container 69, Folder 1, Paul Schrader Papers, Harry Ransom Center, University of Texas-Austin, Austin, TX.
45. Paul Schrader, "'Arbitration,' 'correspondence,' publicity clippings, photograph, and WGA Registration," 1982–7, Container 69, Folder 2, Paul Schrader Papers, Harry Ransom Center, University of Texas-Austin, Austin, TX, 16.
46. Serena Formica, *Peter Weir: A Creative Journey from Australia to Hollywood* (Intellect Books, 2012), 119.
47. In his review, Vincent Canby articulates this exact sentiment, writing that "without Charlie to intercede, Allie finally becomes something much worse than a relentless if brilliant bully. He becomes a monumental bore, someone whose social criticism would scarcely surprise or offend a 'Tonight Show' audience." "Film: 'Mosquito Coast,' with Harrison Ford," *The New York Times*, November 26, 1986, sec. Movies. https://www.nytimes.com/1986/11/26/movies/film-mosquito-coast-with-harrison-ford.html.
48. Paul Schrader and Peter Weir, "Screenplay of *The Mosquito Coast*, 'revised by Peter Weir,'" November–December 1985, Container 68, Folder 9, Paul Schrader Papers, Harry Ransom Center, University of Texas-Austin, Austin, TX, 2.
49. "Second draft," 110.
50. Ibid., 116.
51. "Revised by Peter Weir," 104.

52. Don Shiach, *The Films of Peter Weir: Visions of Alternative Realities* (London: C. Letts, 1993), 153.
53. *The Mosquito Coast*. Film. Directed by Peter Weir. Screenplay by Paul Schrader. Warner Bros., 1986.
54. Paul Schrader, "'Arbitration,' 'correspondence,' publicity clippings, photograph, and WGA Registration," 16.
55. "Arbitration," 2.
56. Corliss and Scorsese, *Film Comment*, 36.
57. Screenplay for *Last Temptation*, "first draft," 98.
58. Paul Schrader, "Letter to Arbitration Committee," in "Production materials, 'arbitration,' and 'correspondence,' for *Last Temptation*," 1981–8, Container 55, Folder 8, Paul Schrader Papers, Harry Ransom Center, University of Texas-Austin, Austin, TX, 2.
59. Thomas R. Lindlof, *Hollywood under Siege: Martin Scorsese, the Religious Right, and the Culture Wars* (Lexington, KY: University Press of Kentucky, 2008), 153.
60. Screenplay for *Last Temptation*, "first draft," 1.

CHAPTER 6

"So I Found Another Form of Expression": Art and Life/Art in Life in Paul Schrader's *Mishima: A Life in Four Chapters*

Thomas Prasch

In a voiceover near the outset of Paul Schrader's *Mishima: A Life in Four Chapters* (1985), Yukio Mishima intones what amounts to his suicide note, but what also comprises a testament to his form of art, and the artful form of his final act: "Recently I've sensed an accumulation of many things which cannot be expressed by an objective form like the novel. Words are insufficient. So I found another form of expression." The assertion introduces a key theme throughout the film: the tension between world and word, between action and representation. In Schrader's film, Mishima finds his new "form of expression" in that act for which he was most widely known: the failed military coup (seeking to reinstall the emperor's glorified place and to remake the military as "soul" of the Japanese) and the *seppuku* or ritual suicide he enacted to end it in an outburst of retro-nationalistic fervor in 1970.

That search for "another form of expression" fits as well Schrader's own aims for the film, an ambitious remaking of normative rules for the biopic as a genre, rejecting the linear structure typical of the biopic (and, for that matter, most Hollywood cinema) in favor of a complex nested structure imbedding an account of the day of Mishima's final act, retrospective flashbacks heavily employing voiceover to sketch a selective account of his life leading to that point, and anti-naturalistically staged excerpts from Mishima's fiction. There is a sense, too, that Schrader's film also amounts to an act of ritual suicide, at least in terms of career prospects: *Mishima* was a project from its inception doomed to failure.

Schrader, after all, in the wake of the commercial and personal disaster of his previous picture,[1] presented American audiences with a complexly structured film, much of it experimental in form, heavily reliant on voiceover for narrative connections, that declared itself in its title a biopic but then deconstructed the premises of the biopic genre. Its central figure was a Japanese writer little known to the broad public—few of his works had at that point been translated, fewer still were in print—who, if known at all, was remembered mostly for his manner of death, a gory end unlikely to resonate with an American public largely unacquainted with its historical and political contexts. Schrader worked with an all-Japanese cast. The screenplay—co-authored by Schrader and his brother Leonard Schrader, but then translated by his brother's Japanese wife Chieko Schrader—is almost entirely in Japanese with English subtitles; the one brief bit in English comes late in the film, when, at a press conference presenting the new uniforms of his Shield Society, Mishima addresses "our foreign guests in English," and his brief words to them are so heavily accented one wishes they too were subtitled.[2] It seemed an unlikely recipe for success in American markets. Meanwhile, the film was banned for distribution in the market that seemed its most obvious one: Japan. As Schrader told Glenn Rechler, "*Mishima* was a Japanese language film made for the Japanese market. The fact that it was never shown there was rather crippling to it."[3] But Schrader knew the topic of Mishima "is a very controversial subject for the Japanese,"[4] and he had alienated not just elements in the Japanese government and right-wing groups for whom Mishima still mattered, but the writer's estate-controlling widow as well.[5] His Japanese financing was, by Schrader's own account, a "con job."[6] So the ban could come as no great surprise.

And indeed, Schrader clearly never intended the film even to break even. Roger Ebert recalled a meeting with the director before the film was screened at Cannes: "But Paul knew better than anyone that its chances at the American box office were slim. We met at a backstreet Japanese restaurant, where he observed that his co-producers, Francis Coppola and George Lucas, had raised $10 million 'with no hope of getting it back.'"[7] He similarly told Kevin Jackson: "I prevailed on Lucas and Coppola, who were very flush at the time in their power and their reputation, to induce Warners to put up the other half, but I don't think anybody who invested money in that film ever expected to get it back." This put Schrader in a unique position: "So while making the movie I had a very peculiar luxury, which was that of making a film that no one ever expected to make a dime. On the other hand, that entailed enormous pressure and responsibility . . . The only criterion I could hold the film up to was that of excellence."[8] By that standard, Schrader, even well after the film flopped, stood by it.[9]

Its failure at the box office was doubtless set up by a harsh critical reception. While it did have defenders—notably Roger Ebert, who called it "a rather glorious project, in these days of pragmatic commercialism and rank cynicism in the movie industry"[10]—critics mostly ranged from confused to hostile in their response to the film. Vincent Canby in the *New York Times* called the film "as crazy and doomed an endeavor as Mishima's attempt to save modern Japan . . . That it doesn't succeed is almost a foregone conclusion." He also asserted that

"*Mishima* isn't likely to make much sense to anyone who hasn't read some of the novels or who doesn't have the film's production notes at hand to use as a guide," and further challenges the filmmakers' understanding of their chosen ground: "The Schraders probably have a better understanding of Japanese culture than do most Americans, but they are still outsiders in an alien world."[11] Paul Attanasio in the *Washington Post* starts out dismissive—"*Mishima* tries to make sense of both its subject's life and his work, and ends up illuminating neither"—and ends with a full-throated attack on Schrader's personal obsessions: "Whatever his subject, whatever his story, it ends up Schraderized. While this treatment may be unfair to Mishima—he's virtually been made into Travis Bickle—there's something sort of charming about such bizarre single-mindedness."[12] One suspects he does not really find it charming.

John Simon savaged the film in *National Review*: "*Mishima* was a total misconception ... What the Schraders have concocted is more self-contradictory than Mishima's life, more inept than his worst fiction, and rather more senseless than his death."[13] Ian Buruma trashed it in the *New York Review of Books*, accusing Schrader first of failing to penetrate Mishima's own masks:

> The film shows Mishima as he presented himself. The myths are not debunked, analyzed, or explained, but dramatized ... Mishima's "real life," as shown in the film, is his carefully stage-managed public life. And the film makers further oblige the great poseur by adding a heavy-breathing score by Philip Glass to make his actions seem even more portentous.

Buruma then suggested an appropriation-minded exoticism underpins Schrader's project: "It is hard to imagine a modern American director making a completely serious film about Hemingway as the great white hunter, Philip Glass music pounding away in the background: Perhaps the only way for the modern Western Romantic to escape ridicule is to seek heroes in more exotic places."[14] Audiences liked the film no better; the film netted less than a tenth of its budget.[15]

In response, Schrader lashed out at critics: "Well, critics are always crying, 'Give me something new. We never see anything innovative.' Then you do something they've never seen the likes of before, and they howl 'What is it?' They refuse to take the time to understand."[16] He decried his own isolation: "I did not know that by taking such an aggressively intellectual stance, I would cut myself off from a large part of the critical community."[17] He laid blame, as we have seen, on the Japanese ban of the film, and on the hostility of Mishima's estate. But, in the end, this was also the outcome he anticipated. "This may have been my last film," he told Ebert before its premiere.[18] We know now that it was not, that the failure of *Mishima* at the box office was far less a final note for Schrader than Mishima's *seppuku* was for him. The key to understanding the film, then, lies not in the realm of box-office receipts, but rather in terms of auterist intentions: what purpose the character of Mishima served Schrader, how he re-engineered the biopic to serve his ends, and to what extent that accomplishes the sort of transcendence Schrader himself, in his early work of critical theory, defined as the "transcendent style" in cinema.[19]

SCHRADER'S HEROES, "SUICIDAL GLORY," AND IDENTIFICATION

A range of critics have noticed the ways Mishima, even in small gestures, echoes other Schrader characters (especially Travis Bickle from *Taxi Driver* [1976], who almost every critic compares to Mishima). Michicko Kakutani notes: "Like Travis, Mishima projected his internal conflicts and private fantasies onto the world at large, using a final purgative bloodbath to give definition to his life. Like Julian Kay in *American Gigolo,* he invented a life and identity, constantly trying on and discarding roles to hide an interior emptiness. And like the strict Calvinist in *Hardcore* . . . [he is] nostalgic for an impossible past and unable to cope with what he saw as the fallen world around him."[20] Ebert notes that "Schrader has throughout his life as a screenwriter and director been fascinated by the starting-point of a 'man in a room,' as he describes it: a man dressing and preparing himself to go out and do battle for his goals," mentioning *Taxi Driver, Raging Bull* (1980), *American Gigolo* (1980), and *The Walker* (2007) as examples paralleling the trope in *Mishima*.[21] Similarly, Kevin Jackson notes how "the typical Schrader hero . . . was obsessed with preparing himself for some unusual mission or some fatal role," a pattern he sees in *Taxi Driver, American Gigolo,* and *Mishima*.[22] Kouvaros groups *Mishima, Patty Hearst* (1986), and *Auto-Focus* (2002) as films that take on "the challenge of telling the life story of protagonists whose personal histories are constructed around a series of irreconcilable performances and masks;[23] Bryant Frazer connects *Mishima* to *Taxi Driver* and *First Reformed* (2017) as Schrader's "meditations on troubled masculinity that characterize his greater body of work."[24] John R. Hamilton writes about the "profound spiritual hunger" in the "losers or those on the edge of society" seen in Schrader's *Taxi Driver, American Gigolo, Hardcore* (1978), *Last Temptation of Christ* (Scorsese, 1988), *Bringing Out the Dead* (Scorsese, 1999), and *Mishima*.[25] Similarly, Brian Eggert connects Schrader's attraction to Mishima in his interest "throughout his career . . . [with] characters prone to the philosophical, psychological, and sexual confusion that is resolved through purification and redemption, often by physical violence or self-destructive behavior," finding evidence in *Taxi Driver, American Gigolo,* and "Even the monsters of *Cat People* [1982]."[26] The pattern is clear.

Schrader himself recognized the pattern, discussing it with Michael Bliss in relation to *Taxi Driver*, an abandoned Hank Williams biopic, and *Mishima*: "*Mishima* is as far away from *Taxi Driver* as I can get on the same line. It has a completely different style. But they're both about suicidal glory. I was myself in the grips of this fantasy for about a decade." He also claimed he had given it up: "But during the making of *Mishima* my daughter was born, and that event sort of put an end to it. I will not make a film about suicidal glory again."[27] But such compulsive repetition of tropes suggests a form of double bind for Schrader: that, on the one hand, he is projecting his own psychological concerns onto Mishima; that, on the other hand, carrying out such plots requires his own close identification with the character, with all the dangers such identification entails (see *Cat People*). As Schrader put it:

> I came to Mishima because his story is part of my fantasy world . . . If I'm going to do a film about my own death-wishes, my own homo-erotic, narcissistic feelings, my own over-calculation of life and my own inability to *feel*, well, here's a man who has repeatedly stated those identical problems. I believe that this is the only way to do a biography which also has the force of a personal statement: two psyches have to be in sufficient synch.[28]

The identification reflects even more clearly when Schrader explains how his choice of Mishima, a character obsessed with his own aging, corresponds to his own point in life: "I'd been writing about younger characters, but I was getting older myself, and I was fishing about in my mind for a fictional character . . . who was a little older; and then it occurred to me that that character already existed, and that character was Mishima."[29] Brian Eggert sees this as a central strength in the film: "the film's thematic integrity lies in Schrader's identification with his subject's world-view."[30] But it simultaneously imposes limitations.

Buruma, too, notes: "Schrader sees both himself and Mishima as artists trapped in the plastic cages of modern ennui and spiritual emptiness; men who must act ever more violently, in fantasy and/or real life, to feel real." But Buruma also insists on a difference: "while the Calvinist [Schrader] may try desperately to jettison his religion . . . Mishima did the opposite: he tried to find his way back to religion. He wanted to believe in a mythical Japanese past where spirits were pure and values unsullied."[31] And for Buruma, this is also what opens Schrader up to critique for his fundamental failure, that Mishima's self-created "myths are not debunked, analyzed, or examined." As Nick Pinkerton notes: "Schrader's *Mishima* collaborates with Mishima, symphonizing a life conceptualized as a total work of art—the infamous narcissist would approve (though he would've preferred to play himself). The author's last moment is uncritically staged just as Mishima visualized it: as his masterpiece."³² But the dangers of Schrader's identification with his protagonist go beyond merely problematic narcissistic tendencies and the difficulty that a highly selective biographical account will produce an extremely reductive psychological portrait.³³ They obliterate a range of interpretive possibilities as well.

Most obviously, what Schrader's approach does is push his account toward a spiritualized psychobiography at the expense of social, political, or historical understanding. In *Mishima*, Schrader shows strikingly little interest in the historical backdrop to Mishima's performance of himself. When Mishima meets with radical students occupying a building, no background on those students or their aims is provided; when Mishima, in his final speech, pleads for a return to Japan's "spiritual foundation" and closes with a prayer to the Emperor, no context is provided for such a position.³⁴ For Schrader, Eggert notes, Mishima's "devotion to the samurai code . . . relates to the body, not as a political ideology,"³⁵ but that reading, placing his samurai discipline into the same box as his obsessive body-building regime, obviates any necessity to deal with Mishima's late-career militarism or attraction to fascist-tainted nationalistic ideas.³⁶

Indeed, Schrader rejects any view of Mishima that takes his political/military views seriously, telling Jaehne: "Mishima was not really a militarist. I consider him a soldier *manqué*."³⁷ Similarly arguing against the apparent evidence, he says about Mishima's play *My Friend Hitler* (1968): "he must have known he would be lambasted for it. And when he designed those uniforms, he must have known that people would misconstrue this as a form of Third Reichism . . . But that still doesn't detract from the fact that his politics were a mass of balderdash. You can't make any sense of them, but they have no relationship to fascism."³⁸ To Kevin Jackson, he insisted that Mishima "did have a fixation of the Emperor and he did have a very strong sexual fixation on militarism, but his interests were primarily ritualistic and artistic. When it came down to hard-core politics he wasn't really that interested. It was all dressing up, D'Annunzio style."³⁹ But this might get D'Annunzio wrong, and it certainly lets Mishima (and Schrader) off the hook.

Schrader's approach has one other clear limitation. It insists upon the seamlessness of Mishima's life project, as well as of his life and art (the literature taken as exemplifying the life), but that necessarily elides gaps and contradictions. Schrader recognized the problem from the outset: "Mishima was infuriatingly contradictory. By the time he could understand anything he was interested in, he had already written or said the opposite, so his entire work and his life remain a conundrum."⁴⁰ But that became a problem to be fixed, a knot to be untied. As Eggert puts it: "Schrader believes that everything about Yukio Mishima belonged to his performative existence, a life-styled art project that extended from his earliest" attempts at art "and ultimately, to his suicide."[41] This requires leaving a great deal out: some thirty novels, all Mishima's plays, his acting in Japanese gangster films. Yet this conception of Mishima's life as a performative whole governs Schrader's organization of the film. It inflects Leonard Schrader's understanding of Mishima: "By the time Mishima was 18 or so, he had begun writing his life, as well as his books . . . Very few random things happened in his life. And you can view the last day of his life as a performance drama that had been planned for years—he'd written the script, designed the costumes, prepared the publicity and then put it all in a real life situation. The whole thing . . . was an artistic creation."[42] The constructed life as work of art echoes not just aestheticist life-as-art ideas but also late-nineteenth-century notions of the totalizing, all-absorbing work of art, the *Gesamtkunstwerk*, as developed in the operatic practice of Richard Wagner and to some extent (until his break with Wagner) the philosophical writings of Friedrich Nietzsche.[43] By imbedding the fictions within that life, *Mishima* takes this one step further, arguing an internal coherence between the life and the fictions (even if, filming them in different modes, the elements cannot appear entirely unified). But Leonard Schrader's summary begs the question: what if Mishima's (and *Mishima*'s) Wagnerian *Gesamtkunstwerk* was not quite so *gesamt*?

RETHINKING AND RESTRUCTURING THE BIOPIC

In approaching the biopic, Schrader was clear about one thing: he had no interest in the conventional norms of the genre. Asked by Jaehne, "Did you ever think it was possible to make a straight bio-pic?," his answer was unequivocal: "No. Such a film would be uninteresting. The bio-pic is now in the province of television. You have to have an original approach if you try to do a biography."[44] Kouvaros summarizes the effect of Schrader's alternative structuring of the biopic: "Instead of simply telling the story of Mishima's life, Schrader's film approximates a form that embodies its contradictions. The relationship between the film and its subject is not simply imitative but also performative: it is defined by an explicit exchange between the body of the film and the body it seeks to represent."[45] The film project thus also recreates the structure it imposes on Mishima's life, as coherent performance. As Schrader told Jackson: "I have problems with conventional biographical films; I just can't bear to see movies about real events that falsify them."[46] Jackson notes elsewhere: "More routine biopics about writers and artists . . . tend to play a fairly simple game of cause and effects . . . But when your biographical subject so consistently obscured those neat boundaries between art and life, and when his imagination may have shaped his life significantly more than vice versa, more ambitious methods are required."[47] When your process entails as well close identification between the filmmaker and his subject, and the insistent aim of the filmmaker to create a coherent and single-minded life out of a contradictory mass of biographical details, that further complicates the process. Schrader's solution, Jackson writes, was "a tripartite approach to Mishima's life and art, designed to interweave reality, memory, and imagination,"[48] with the dramatized excerpts from the novels figuring as the imagination.

Schrader's solution is thus the carefully balanced structure of *Mishima*. The film's "four chapters" lay out a general progression, from "Beauty" to "Art" to "Action" to "The Harmony of Pen and Sword," which in part map out Mishima's life, from youth to young writer to political/military ambitions to final action. The movie opens with a table of contents laying out the arrangement, and title cards mark the transitions. Within each chapter, however, the treatment shuffles between three different frames: the "present" (November 25, 1970, the day of the attempted coup and suicide), Mishima's past (told chronologically from childhood forward to the formation of his private militia, the Shield Society[49]), and his fictions (represented by staged excerpts from three of his novels, one for each of the first three chapters, again chronological: *The Temple of the Golden Pavilion* [1956], *Kyoko's House* [1959], and *Runaway Horses* [1969]).[50] Though the fourth chapter includes no corresponding novel, it does, in its final moments, return to each of the three presented earlier.

Figure 6.1 Scene from the *Kyoko's House* segment.

The three frames are differentiated by different colors and styles: the present shot in somewhat bleached naturalistic color, often with handheld cameras (recalling the quasi-documentary style of Costa-Gavras[51]); the past shot in black and white, with particular heavy use of voiceover to carry the narrative (the black-and-white film recalling Ozu,[52] the voiceover echoing Bresson, thus suggesting two of the filmmakers Schrader singled out in his account of the "transcendental style"[53]); and the novel excerpts performed in deliberately theatrical sets, developed by Eiko Ishioka, and featuring richly saturated, almost glowing colors, with a different color scheme for each of the novels. As Schrader notes: "Each of the three novel sections is colour-coded to make the film a little more comprehensible, because it is such a jigsaw of a film. The first novel is gold and green; the second novel is pink and grey; and the third one is *shu*—a kind of orange that they use in temples—*shu* and black."[54] The effect is something like a surrealist Noh stage.

The film opens in the present, as Mishima dons his uniform on the day of the coup (the "man in a room" Schrader and Ebert both talk about, and a regular gesture in Schrader's cinema); the naturalism is interrupted only briefly by visions of Mishima masked, a motif that recurs near the film's end. The transition to memory is signaled by a boy in the window behind Mishima as he leaves his house; the perspective then shifts to behind the boy, and the film stock to black and white, to recall young Mishima's care for his grandmother, segueing into his first experience of theater. The shift to the first novel excerpt is marked by a close shot of the mouths of two stutterers: one the young Mishima, the next the character in his novel. In these "exchanges," as Kouvaros calls them, "Schrader draws attention to its [the film's] operation," and the effect is that "the moment of exchange enacts a type of formal disturbance whereby, for a brief moment, past and present are unsettled."[55] The shift in palette and style, however, anchor each moment in its proper frame.

Within each "chapter," the present frame moves steadily toward the coup attempt, while there is also a broad coherence correspondence between the memory and fictional frames. The young boy of the memory frame in "Beauty" anchors Mishima's self-accounting in his suicide note (starting, as it were, with his own beginnings), and the Zen acolyte of the novel shares the stutter of the boy but also moves us forward to his youth (enacted through sexual initiation). In the second chapter, the preoccupations of Mishima—we see him backstage, in the weight room, in the gay bar and with a male lover in an alley, in the film's one explicit allusion to Mishima's homosexuality—correspond with those of the actor protagonist Osamu in *Kyoko's House*: he also takes up weight training and begins an illicit love affair (his heterosexual, but violently sadomasochistic). The military emphasis in "Action" occurs in both the memory frame, with Mishima putting together his Shield Society, and in the selection from *Runaway Horses*. The excerpt from the novel, about a failed coup in 1876 against the Meiji regime's abolition of swords, also looks forward to Mishima's final act (as does the ritual suicide of *Patriotism*, which we see Mishima filming in the memory frame). The final act focuses on the present frame, with one brief memory segment showing him training with his militia, although the three novels are all invoked in the film's finale.

The action of all thee novel excerpts culminates in violence: the Golden Temple is set ablaze; the lovers enact a suicide pact; the young rebel kills his target and prepares his own *seppuku* on the beach at dawn. The "memory" frame tracks Mishima's growing obsession with his own mortality, fighting his aging and decay through rigorous exercise, and his growing concern with recovering Japanese "spiritual purity" through a rejection of Western influence, ironic as that must be for so deeply Westernized a figure, and via his private militia, with their sworn adherence to the Emperor recalling a Japanese imperial past. Meanwhile, the events of November 25 steadily advance toward their conclusion. Everything converges in Mishima's coup attempt, the vortex that concentrates all three of the film's narrative strands.

CONVERGENCE AND (FAILED) TRANSCENDENCE

The problem at the outset of *Mishima* centers on the gap between word and world, as the narrator relates it: "I realized life consisted of two contradictory elements. One was words, which could change the world. The other was the world itself, which had nothing to do with words." As one critic notes: "*Mishima* is a phantasmagoria of Cartesian dissociation, following Mishima's tortured observation that 'words' and 'reality' exist in irreconcilable universes. Mishima, obsessed with a transcendental notion of 'beauty,' is perpetually haunted by the gulf between his ideals, his body, and the masks (metaphorical and literal) he dons for the world."[56] Yet the film works, with increasing pace as it moves to its climax, to bridge those divides. Alex Lindstrom summarizes the way in which all the elements in *Mishima* converge on its climax and finale:

> The three aforementioned streams within *A Life in Four Chapters*—the present (reality), the past (memories), and the fiction (imagination)—progressively "mold into" and "catch up" to one another until they quite literally converge into the moment of his death: the past leads straight to "reality'" and the vivid dreamworld of Mishima's writing comes to precisely mirror the moment of his self-destruction. It ends right there with nothing left to say, because for both Schrader and Mishima, there *is* nothing left to say.[57]

The movie speeds up as it moves inexorably toward the conclusion we all know is coming. The conclusion, after all, Mishima's suicide, is the one thing we all know about Mishima's life.[58]

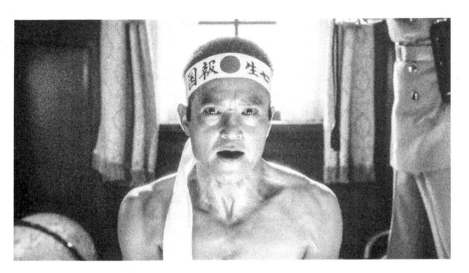

Figure 6.2 Mishima's *seppuku* (ritual suicide).

As a young film student, Schrader sought to define a "transcendental style" in film, which he saw exemplified across national traditions, and especially in the work of Japanese director Yasujiro Ozu and French director Robert Bresson (with Carl Dreyer a close third). According to Schrader, "Transcendental style seeks to maximize the mystery of existence; it eschews all conventional interpretations of reality: realism, naturalism, psychologism, romanticism, expressionism, impressionism, and finally, rationalism. To the transcendental artist rationalism is only one of many approaches to life, not an imperative."[59] In developing a transcendental style, Ozu had a distinct advantage in being Japanese: "In his films this style is natural, indigenous, and commercially successful, largely because of the Japanese culture itself. The concept of transcendental experience is so intrinsic to Japanese (and Oriental) culture, that Ozu was able both to develop the transcendental style and to stay within the popular conventions of Japanese art."[60] Further: "Oriental art in general and Zen art in particular aspire to the Transcendent. Like primitive art, traditional Oriental art makes no distinctions between the sacred and the secular . . . For thirteen hundred years Zen has cultivated the transcendental experience, and the Transcendent has found expression not only in religion and the arts, but also in a wide variety of 'commonplace' activities."[61] We can perhaps (but only barely) forgive Schrader his ethnocentric views of Asian culture—Edward Said would not publish *Orientalism* for another six years, although Schrader's broad-brush handling of ethnic difference surely must have already seemed pretty dated in 1972—but we should notice here what anchors Schrader's understanding of transcendence: its rejection of realistic and rationalistic modes of artistic representation.

And we should note that, within Schrader's understanding, Mishima, too, should have an advantage in reaching that plane. That seems borne out in

Jackson's Schrader-influenced take on Mishima's life project and the idea of "self-fashioning":

> Yet no one, not even Oscar Wilde, has so rigorously pursued the grail as Yukio Mishima. Wilde may have quipped about living up to his blue china, but he let his once graceful body grow slack and bloated ... Mishima spent countless hours at the gym, turning himself ... to a powerful muscleman. Wilde talked subversively, but allowed his subversion to seem like a mere game of naughty jokes ... Mishima turned his strange political ideals into action ... Wilde ultimately allowed the forces of intolerance to catch and ruin him; Mishima composed the final act of his life in his head, and then wrote it in his own blood with a samurai sword.[62]

But his coup also failed, his final speech was laughed at by the troops forced to gather to listen to it. Can that still be a source of transcendence?

Schrader insisted, after *Mishima*, that his own films were not transcendental: "The reason why I don't make transcendental films, the reason I don't have transcendental style, is that I believe in something that is anathema or contrary to the whole notion of transcendental cinema. I have my roots in psychological realism and audience identification with character, whereas the whole notion of transcendental style is based on repudiating psychological realism."[63] And yet in *Mishima*, however much its explanatory mode seems rooted in the psychological (and it certainly is: mother issues linked to homosexuality, narcissism to death compulsion, all crudely psychoanalytic, armchair Freudian), something else seems at work as well. Audience identification in *Mishima* is partially blocked by linguistic divide and cultural unfamiliarity. Realism, psychological or otherwise, hardly seems to describe the staged excerpts from the novels. The heavy borrowings from Ozu and Bresson in the memory frame also seem to allude to a transcendental style, even if Schrader claims to be doing something else.

Further, the language of the film's climax flirts openly with transcendental ideals. As Mishima declaims his final speech, drowned out by the jeering soldiers below, the film seems to lose interest in tracking his words, even though, as final words, they would seem significant. The voiceover asserts: "Never in physical action had I discovered the chilling satisfaction of words. Never in words had I experienced the hot darkness of action. Somewhere there must be a higher principle which reconciles art and action. That principle, it occurred to me, was death." The film stock shifts to black and white, to a moment of memory: Mishima in the cockpit of a high-flying jet. The voiceover continues: "The vast upper atmosphere, where there is no oxygen, is surrounded with death. To survive in this atmosphere, man, like an actor, must wear a mask." The film shifts back to Mishima's final address, now shot from above, still unheard, as the voiceover continues: "My mind was at ease, my thought process lively." We jump back to black and white, to the cockpit: "No movement, no sound, no memories. The closed cockpit and outer space were like the spirit and body of the same thing. Here I saw the final outcome of my final action. In this stillness was a beauty beyond words. No more body or spirit, pen or sword, male or female." And here, as the sun appears over the clouds, the screen fades to color; we are still in the cockpit, still in memory, but the color violates the code. The voiceover concludes: "Then I saw a giant circle coiled around the earth, a ring that resolved all contradictions, a ring vaster than death, more fragrant than any scent I have ever known. Here was the moment I had always been seeking." And the screen shifts back to the address, which we hear now, Mishima demanding of the inattentive crowd, "Are you men? Are you bushi?"

Returning inside, Mishima laments: "I don't even think they heard me." He proceeds with his *seppuku*, the film closing in the final moments on his straining face, caught finally in freeze-frame.[64] But this is not quite the end. Three brief tableaux bring back the three novels' endings: the acolyte in the burning temple, doomed to burn with it; the dead couple, Osamu's body scarred and bruised, his hands bound; and the young cadet, cutting open his own stomach on the beach at dawn, gets the film's last words, offering a quotation about a similar act: "The instant the blade tore open his flesh, the bright disk of the sun soared up behind his eyelids and exploded, lighting the sky for an instant." That moment takes us back to Mishima in the cockpit, the "beauty beyond words," that transcendent suddenly-coloring view of clouds and sky.

All this suggests transcendence. And yet not quite: the coups (both in 1876 and 1970) fail; the lovers die; the temple burns. The film flops. As a model for a radical revision of the form of the biopic, *Mishima* must be seen as something of a dead end. Schrader may borrow elements of the multi-part structure evident as traces in later works, even specific shots (like the "Mishima shot" in *Patty Hearst*), but nothing in his subsequent filmmaking suggests that it becomes a foundational model, nor do others follow this lead. As for transcendence, it is as if Schrader, the Westerner telling these Japanese stories, is creating space for their transcendence while not quite making his own. Or perhaps, more simply, he is trying to have his transcendental cake and eat it too.

NOTES

1. *Cat People* (1982) had been both a critical/commercial disappointment and, between a failed affair with Nastassja Kinski and way too much cocaine, a personal trial for Schrader. For the fullest (if only partly substantiated) story, see Peter Biskind, *Easy Riders, Raging Bulls: How the Rock 'n' Roll Generation Saved Hollywood* (New York: Simon and Schuster, 1988), 410–12.

2. John Simon makes this idea of the foreigner working abroad part of his critique: "It was no help . . . that the director, Paul Schrader, does not speak Japanese; that the actors and other personnel did not speak English; that the film was written by the brothers Paul and Leonard Schrader in English, but shot from a Japanese translation by Chieko, Leonard's Japanese wife." John Simon, "Mishmashima," *National Review*, 68–9. For a more sympathetic account, see George Kouvaros, *Paul Schrader* (Urbana: University of Illinois Press, 2008), 54.
3. Glenn Rechler, "*Patty Hearst*: An Interview with Paul Schrader," *Cinéaste*, Vol. 17, No. 1 (1989), 31.
4. Ibid.
5. "The problems with Mishima's widow boil down to her conception of him as a kind of Japanese Visconti . . . She clings to this idea of the enshrined poet," Schrader told Karen Jaehne. See "*Mishima*: An Interview," *Film Quarterly*, Vol. 39, No. 3 (Spring 1986), 14. She was especially averse to any overt reference to Mishima's homosexuality, and forbade use of his most openly homosexual book, *Forbidden Colours* (1951–3); see Kevin Jackson, *Schrader on Schrader*, Revised Edition (Urbana: University of Illinois Press, 2008), 177. This again anchors Simon's critique: "You do not make a film about the life of the novelist Yukio Mishima if his widow forbids you to deal explicitly with his death and at all with his homosexuality . . . Other members of the family, which looms large in Mishima's life, did not co-operate" in the filming. Simon, "Mishmashima," 68. That Schrader found a way around those prohibitions doubtless ensured Mishima's widow's and the estate's hostility to the project.
6. Jackson, *Schrader on Schrader*, 178. Kouvaros writes that $2.5 million of the film's budget came from Japanese investors, Fuji Television and Toho-Towa Distribution, both of whom "refused to acknowledge their involvement" due to Mishima's controversial status; the remainder, $3.25 million, was Warners's contribution, or really George Lucas and Francis Ford Coppola's, both of them with deep pockets full of blockbuster money at the time. Kouvaros, *Paul Schrader*, 54.
7. Roger Ebert, "Great Movies: *Mishima: A Life in Four Chapters*," December 15, 2007, at https://www.rogerebert.com/reviews/great-movie-mishima-a-life-in-four-chapters-1985. Judging from other accounts, that $10 million figure is almost double the actual budget. See, for example, Kouvaros, *Paul Schrader*, 54.
8. Jackson, *Schrader on Schrader*, 180.
9. Schrader told Kevin Jackson: "it's the film I'd stand by; as a writer it's *Taxi Driver*, but as a director it's *Mishima* . . . though I don't generally look at my films again, I can still watch the end of *Mishima*, and when he becomes one with his three creations I still get chilled." Jackson, *Schrader on Schrader*, 182.
10. Roger Ebert, "*Mishima: A Life in Four Chapters*," October 11, 1985, at https://www.rogerebert.com/reviews/mishima-a-life-in-four-chapters-1985. Ebert's later praise was even stronger: "Paul Schrader's *Mishima: A Life in Four Chapters* (1985) is the most unconventional biopic I've ever seen, and one of the best." Ebert, "Great Movies: *Mishima*." In general, more recent criticism (after the DVD release in 2008) has been more positive; Rotten Tomatoes gives it a critical assessment of 89% (https://www.rottentomatoes.com/m/mishima_a_life_in_four_chapters). But that was not true at the time of its release.
11. Vincent Canby, "*Mishima*, A Life of the Japanese Writer," *New York Times*, September 20, 1985, at https://www.nytimes.com/1985/09/20/movies/mishima-a-life-of-the-japanese-writer.html?searchResultPosition=1.
12. Paul Attanasio, "*Mishima* Impossible," *Washington Post*, October 15, 1985, at https://www.washingtonpost.com/archive/lifestyle/1985/10/15/mishima-impossible/84e5f1a6-a2d4-4785-94ff-1d60eb7fbf91/?noredirect=on&utm_term=.45c8f9e4549a.

13. John Simon, "Film: *Mishima*," *National Review*, Vol. 37, No. 21 (November 1, 1985), 68, 69.
14. Ian Buruma, "Rambo-san," *New York Review of Books*, October 10, 1985, at https://www.nybooks.com/articles/1985/10/10/rambo-san/. For a fuller survey of criticism, see John Howard Wilson, "The Empire Strikes Back: The Critical Reception of *Gandhi* and *Mishima*," *Reception: Texts, Readers, Audiences, History*, Vol. 2, No. 2 (Summer 2010), 102–5.
15. Wilson lists box office as $450,000; "Empire Strikes Back," 104.
16. Jaehne, "Schrader's *Mishima*," 12.
17. Ibid.
18. Ebert, "Great Films: *Mishima*."
19. Paul Schrader, *Transcendental Style in Film: Ozu, Bresson, Dreyer* (1972; Reprint, New York: Da Capo Press, 1988). More on this below.
20. Michiko Kakutani, "*Mishima*: Film Examines an Affair with Death," *New York Times*, September 15, 1985, at https://www.nytimes.com/1985/09/15/arts/mishima-film-examines-an-affair-with-death.html.
21. Ebert, "Great Films: *Mishima*" (borrowing Schrader's own term "man in the room"). Kouvaros notes the examples of Travis and Julian, suggesting the "meticulous manner" of their preparation suggests "heightened self-consciousness but also a desire to re-create the self through the perfecting of certain roles." *Paul Schrader*, 2.
22. Kevin Jackson, "*Mishima*: Pen and Sword," June 30, 2008, online in Criterion's On Film/Essays at https://www.criterion.com/current/posts/516-mishima-pen-and-sword/.
23. Kouvaros, *Paul Schrader*, 9; see also 117.
24. Bryant Frazer, "*Mishima: A Life in Four Chapters*," online at Film Freak Central, September 4, 2018, at https://www.filmfreakcentral.net/ffc/2018/09/mishima-a-life-in-four-chapters-criterion.html.
25. John R. Hamilton, "Schrader, Paul," online in *Senses of Cinema* 56 (October 2010) at http://sensesofcinema.com/2010/great-directors/paul-schrader/. Musing later in the essay about Mishima's "strong drama of conviction, belief in a cause, and personal honor, all undercut by the apparent folly of everything as one fails to communicate with one's contemporaries. Why, one wonders, is Schrader drawn to this sort of material?," Hamilton quotes from the Warner Brothers press release for *Mishima* that he "is the type of character I might have invented if he had not existed." Schrader repeats that would-have-invented-him claim to Kakutani in "*Mishima*: Film Examines an Affair with Death."
26. Brian Eggert, "*Mishima: A Life in Four Chapters*," online at *Deep Focus Review*, June 3, 2018, at https://deepfocusreview.com/definitives/mishima-a-life-in-four-chapters/.
27. Michael Bliss, "Affliction and Forgiveness: An Interview with Paul Schrader," *Film Quarterly*, Vol. 54, No. 1 (Autumn 2000), 8. See also Jackson, *Schrader on Schrader*, 175; Jaehne, "Schrader's *Mishima*," 12. As *First Reformed* shows, however, he was not quite done with the trope.
28. Quoted in Kouvaros, *Paul Schrader*, 55.
29. Kakutani, "*Mishima*: Film Examines an Affair with Death."
30. Eggert, "*Mishima*."
31. Buruma, "Rambo-san."
32. Nick Pinkerton, "Yukio Mishima, A Life in Four Chapters, and Countless Contradictions," *Village Voice*, December 17, 2008, online at https://www.villagevoice.com/2008/12/17/yukio-mishima-a-life-in-four-chapters-and-countless-contradictions/.
33. Bryant Frazer notes that the film's tight structure disguises this reductive tendency: "This business is unavoidably reductive, Rosebud-level analysis, but it feels like a complete psychological study; every scene either responds to something we've seen previously, or anticipates an episode yet to come." Frazer, "*Mishima*."

34. It can be noted that such contexts might not be as necessary for Japanese audiences, but recall that the ban on the film in Japan meant that his primary audience was American, and thus likely deeply unaware of currents in Japanese politics on either the left or the right.
35. Eggert, "*Mishima*."
36. Schrader's refusal to directly engage Mishima's politics becomes especially problematic given critical responses to the politics of his own works. Most notably, Robin Wood, analyzing the reactionary overtones of *Taxi Driver*, lets director Martin Scorsese off the hook (he is firmly within the "liberal humanist tradition"), while "The politics implicit in Schrader's work . . . can be simply characterized as quasi-fascist," not just in *Taxi Driver*, but also in *Blue Collar, Old Boyfriends* (1979), *Hardcore, American Gigolo*, and *Rolling Thunder* (1977). Robin Wood, *Hollywood from Vietnam to Reagan—and Beyond*, Revised Edition (New York: Columbia University Press, 2003), 45. We might give Schrader a break on *Rolling Thunder*; he has complained about the treatment of his original script: "Instead of a film about fascism, they simply made a fascist film" (quoted in n.a., "'Rolling Thunder': Another Shattering Experience from the Writer of 'Taxi Driver," *Cinephilia & Beyond* at https://cinephiliabeyond.org/rolling-thunder-another-shattering-experience-from-the-author-of-taxi-driver/; see also Jackson, *Schrader on Schrader*, 125–6). But the problem of *Taxi Driver* remains. James Naremore blames both Schrader and Scorsese for the conservative tilt of the film: "The Calvinist Schrader and the Catholic Scorsese have created a deeply conservative film about original sin and the absolute evil of modernity." See James Naremore, *More Than Night: Film Noir and Its Contexts*, Revised Edition (Berkeley: University of California Press, 2008), 35. But Marc Raymond notes of the critical consensus about the film's politics that "the blame for the film's reactionary elements was shifted almost exclusively to Schrader." See *Hollywood's New Yorker: The Making of Martin Scorsese* (Albany, NY: SUNY Press, 2013), 74–5. And the pattern in his films of the period also remains an issue. H. N. Lukes notes "His films' almost prurient attention to the failures of American liberalism," even if concluding that the work is "not strictly reactionary." See H. N. Lukes, "*American Gigolos*" in Mandy Merck, ed., *America First: Naming the Nation in US Film* (New York: Routledge, 2007), 186. Given that record, and Schrader's stated identification with Mishima, the failure to examine Mishima's politics seems an evasion.
37. Jaehne, "Schrader's *Mishima*," 12.
38. Ibid., 15.
39. Jackson, *Schrader on Schrader*, 182.
40. Jaehne, "Schrader's *Mishima*," 14.
41. Eggert, "*Mishima*." This approach entails, it should be noted, the somewhat problematic premise that Mishima's novels can be taken as illustrative of his life.
42. Quoted in Kakutani, *Mishima*.
43. Buruma notes that Mishima "freely borrowed from . . . Nietzsche, Wagner, even Hitlerism," before partially undercutting the claim: "Although much of this is name-dropping kitsch, it is also a genuine search for synthesis between Japanese aesthetics and Western modernism." Buruma, "Rambo-San." The trajectory from Nietzsche and Wagner toward Hitler might also say something about both Mishima's and Schrader's political affiliations.
44. Jaehne, "Schrader's *Mishima*," 13.
45. Kouvaros, *Paul Schrader*, 61.
46. Jackson, *Schrader on Schrader*, 127.
47. Jackson, "*Mishima*: Pen and Sword."
48. Ibid.

49. Much of the voiceover narration, Kevin Jackson notes, is drawn from Mishima's autobiographical *Sun and Steel* (1968). Jackson, "*Mishima*: Pen and Sword."
50. The end of the third chapter also features another recreation, the filming of Mishima's short film *Patriotism* (1966; not identified by name in the film), his half-hour silent film in which a Japanese officer commits *seppuku*. Technically, however, this occurs within the frame of "memory" and is thus in black and white (although so was *Patriotism*).
51. Jackson, "*Mishima*: Pen and Sword."
52. Ibid.
53. Schrader, *Transcendental Style in Film*; more still to come.
54. Jackson, *Schrader on Schrader*, 177. The last two novel re-enactments also feature striking compositions shot from above over roofless rooms, an effect he would use again: "In fact, when we were shooting *Patty Hearst* we used to refer to that as the *Mishima* shot. The reason I did it in *Mishima* was that I wanted to create a sense of the author's eye and of these events existing in limbo. Those little glowing rooms simulate the writer's vision." Ibid., 196.
55. Kouvaros, *Paul Schrader*, 62.
56. Eli, F., "*Mishima: A Life in Four Chapters*: Paul Schrader's Phantasmagoria of Cartesian Dissociation," June 11, 2018 for *Film Stage*, online at https://thefilmstage.com/features/mishima-a-life-in-four-chapters-paul-schraders-phantasmagoria-of-cartesian-dissociation/.
57. Alex Lindstrom, "On Mishima, and Feeling That One Exists," November 12, 2018, online at *PopMatters* at https://www.popmatters.com/mishima-life-in-four-chapters-2612214742.html.
58. It is also what drew Schrader to the project, as he tells Jackson: "I had heard a little bit about Mishima before . . . But the suicide captured the world's attention, and it certainly captured mine." Jackson, *Schrader on Schrader*, 172.
59. Schrader, *Transcendental Style in Film*, 11–12.
60. Ibid., 17.
61. Ibid., 17.
62. Jackson, "*Mishima*: Pen and Sword."
63. Bliss, "Affliction and Forgiveness," 9.
64. Of this frequently used device at the close of Schrader films, Kouvaros observes (of *Cat People*): "Schrader's use of the freeze frame suggests something irreconcilable about the drama that has just concluded. It is not an ending to the story as such but a literal fixing in place of a dilemma." *Paul Schrader*, 53.

CHAPTER 7

Schrader's Women: *Cat People* and *Patty Hearst*

Brian Brems

> SCHRADER: Does the void come from within or does the void come from without?
> BRESSON: Both. The void around you makes the void within you.¹

In this conversation between filmmaker Paul Schrader and one of his cinematic heroes, French director Robert Bresson, each illuminates a central struggle that defines their shared obsession, what Schrader will call in a number of other places "the existential hero."² Before his much-discussed slide into depression and obsession with guns and pornography yielded the fury of the screenplay for *Taxi Driver* (1976, Scorsese), Schrader began his work in the film industry as a critic, stumping in the press for films like *Pickpocket* (1959, Bresson), which he wrote about for two consecutive weeks in 1969 upon seeing the film in Los Angeles. In his column, he spoke unflinchingly of his admiration for Bresson who, in Schrader's effusive estimation, "attempts and achieves the highest function of art; he elevates the spirit, not only of his characters and viewers, but somehow of the system which has entrapped us all."³ Rhetorically adopting Bresson's thematic preoccupation with confinement, Schrader describes his own relationship to *Pickpocket* as though he were its prisoner: "as long as *Pickpocket* is showing in town I don't have the desire to talk about any other picture."⁴ He pursued this idea in what will remain his most impactful contribution to cinema history, the isolated cabbie at the center of *Taxi Driver*, Travis Bickle (Robert De Niro). Travis is the first of Schrader's "men and their rooms,"⁵ created in the image of Bresson's films, especially *Pickpocket*.

Schrader has long credited his own filmmaking career to the inspirational example of *Pickpocket*, but Bresson's films likewise inspired his further work in criticism; Bresson was one of the trio of filmmakers Schrader studied at length in his 1972 book, *Transcendental Style in Film: Ozu, Bresson, Dreyer*. Though Schrader's chapters on Ozu and Dreyer are illuminating, his passion for Bresson in the book's middle section stands apart; Schrader the critic clearly sees Bresson as the ultimate practitioner of transcendental style, which Schrader the filmmaker demonstrates through his continued referential and reverential attitude toward Bresson. His intellectual fascination with Bresson's work matches his instinctual draw to it. Bresson himself was a diarist; his *Notes on the Cinematograph* yields such confessional, poetic insights as "My movie is born first in my head, dies on paper; is resuscitated by the living persons and real objects I use, which are killed on film but, placed in a certain order and projected on to a screen, come to life again like flowers in water."[6] On-screen, a number of Schrader's existential heroes confess in the pages of their journals: Travis Bickle was the first, but was followed by John LeTour (Willem Dafoe) in *Light Sleeper* (1992) and Reverend Ernst Toller (Ethan Hawke) in *First Reformed* (2017). These are Bresson's pickpockets and country priests, reimagined in an American context, but plagued by the same sense of dislocation and alienation that causes them to withdraw, men beaten back into the contradictory comfort and pain of their rooms. These characters, who populate Schrader's cinema (by way of Bresson's), are inextricably bound up in the critical and popular perception of Schrader as a filmmaker.

Schrader's cinematic reputation is inextricably tied to his male creations—Bickle, LeTour, and now Toller, but also Jake Van Dorn (George C. Scott) of *Hardcore* (1979), Julian Kay (Richard Gere) of *American Gigolo* (1980), and Wade Whitehouse (Nick Nolte) of *Affliction* (1997), among others—to such a degree that he has been a target for criticism for his perceived misogyny, a charge of which a number of his existential heroes are guilty. Schrader is not without self-awareness on this subject; like Bickle's racism, the character's sexism earns its share of criticism from Schrader's screenplay, in tandem with Scorsese's direction and De Niro's performance, none of which let Bickle off the hook. While Schrader has admittedly long been preoccupied with "men and their rooms," as *Taxi Driver* and *First Reformed* demonstrate, his representation of those existential heroes has not valorized them. The conceit of *Taxi Driver*, according to Schrader, is that "gradually you're made aware that you have identified with someone you don't want to identify with, but now it's too late."[7] Throughout a number of his films, Schrader has invited the spectator to enter the troubled psychologies of his male characters, each of whom earns varying degrees of sympathy, but all of whom struggle with existential crises brought on by loneliness, aging, addiction, obsession, persecution by the law, environmental catastrophe, theological dilemmas, paranoia, or intersections of these themes, nearly all of which stem from *Pickpocket*. Schrader has nearly always been associated with how he localizes these themes in male characters;

I will demonstrate how Schrader relies on Bressonian types in *Cat People* (1982) and *Patty Hearst* (1988) in female characters, as well.

But first, there is Schrader's relationship to Bresson himself, who offers a kind of how-to manual for his own style in *Notes on the Cinematograph*. While its pages are full of useful observations that one can apply to study of his films, they might be summarized in this rather efficient note: "Someone who can work with the minimum can work with the most. One who can with the most cannot, inevitably, with the minimum."[8] Much of the scholarship on Bresson's cinema has been devoted to one degree or another with "the minimum," which characterizes his style for the duration of his career. According to Tony Pipolo, his films are exercises designed to "intensify the means by which interiorization can be achieved through the external, and to reduce these means as much as possible to the essential, eliminating redundancy and minimizing the usual accouterments of the *cinema* in favor of the *cinematographic*."[9] In an influential essay, Susan Sontag calls Bresson's approach "reflective," and elaborates on it in the context of commentary about art in general: "Great reflective art is not frigid. It can exalt the spectator, it can present images that appall, it can make him weep. But its emotional power is mediated. The pull toward emotional involvement is counterbalanced by elements in the work that promote distance, disinterestedness, impartiality. Emotional involvement is always, to a greater or lesser degree, postponed."[10] Bresson achieves this postponement through a variety of cinematic strategies, which have been well catalogued and need only quick reference: blank or uninflected acting (he famously referred to actors as "models"), largely static camera shots, judicious use of musical score, voiceover narration that matches the on-screen action rather than expanding characters' inner lives, and languid editing that disrupts conventional handling of pace. There are other techniques in Bresson's toolkit, but each works to unify form and content.

Thematically, Bresson's films fit together. In Sontag's estimation, "All of Bresson's films have a common theme: the meaning of confinement and liberty. The imagery of the religious vocation and of crime are used jointly. Both lead to 'the cell.'"[11] The cell is often literal, represented in the repeated reliance on the prison as a crucial setting. In 1956, Bresson's *A Man Escaped* chronicles the efforts of a man named Fontaine to break out of the jail in which he is imprisoned. The climactic moments of *Pickpocket* take place in Michel's jail cell, as he and his love interest, Jeanne, come to a moment of grace through the bars that separate them. Preceding both of these films, 1951's *Diary of A Country Priest* makes the title character's private rooms a kind of prison; the same is true of Michel's bare apartment in *Pickpocket*. In Bresson, "we are always dealing with privileged areas, cut off from the rest of the world, as monasteries or prisons can be."[12] The isolation of these spaces mirrors the exiled protagonists who inhabit them. These settings lend Bresson appropriate ground for his characters' interior focus. According to Bresson himself, "There's no apparent drama in a prison: you hear people being shot, but you don't react visibly to it. All the drama is interior."[13] Sontag agrees with the filmmaker: "The nature of drama being conflict, the real drama of Bresson's stories is interior conflict: the fight against oneself. And all the static and formal qualities of his films work to that end."[14]

If Bresson's films are unified by common themes, settings, and stylistic approaches, it follows that he crafts similar protagonists who share "the inner force of their personalities, their spiritual struggles, and the balance they strike between pride and passionate conviction."[15] From the perspective of narrative structure, "The central character's consciousness dominates most of Bresson's narratives."[16] Such narrowly focused point of view comes with narrative risks, which are intensified by Bresson's radical commitment to stylistic austerity. Far from traditional characters with whom audiences can easily empathize, Bresson's protagonists "emanate a sort of discomfort which means that they can never be truly sympathetic."[17] Throughout the narrative, characters' "fundamental traits—even in women—are not compassion or imagination, but will-power and lucidity, energy and obstinacy."[18] As we will see, a number of these descriptors are also applicable to Schrader's protagonists, especially his Bressonian "existential heroes" and "heroines."

Upon receiving the opportunity to interview Bresson in Cannes in 1976 while attending the festival for the premiere of *Taxi Driver*, Schrader expressed his passion for Bresson's work in effusive terms. One imagines the normally laid-back, detached Schrader leaning forward in his chair excitedly to communicate just how important Bresson's work has been to him:

> When I first saw your films, I felt I understood them immediately. No one needed to explain them to me. When Jost comes into the cell in *A Man Escaped* and Fontaine decides not to kill him, I immediately knew that the film was about grace and redemption. That was the way I was educated. I saw it as a phenomenology of grace, that is: we must choose grace as it appears to us, and, therefore, we will escape, even though we are predestined to escape.[19]

Elsewhere in his work, Schrader has been more investigative and theoretical in his treatment of Bresson. His 1969 pair of essays on *Pickpocket* identify Bresson's preoccupation with the dichotomy between prison and liberty, a theme that his own work would eventually explore deeply, by drawing parallels between *Pickpocket* and Bresson's other work: "*Pickpocket*, like all of Bresson's films, concerns the progression of a soul from confinement to freedom."[20] But these essays also contain the nascent ideas that would become Schrader's *Transcendental Style in Film*, pointing the way toward his theory of "decisive action" and "stasis," terms which mark the final two stages in films made in transcendental style, observing that "when Bresson arrives at the final station, the sepulcher of the old self, whether that be death, physical freedom or incarceration, the film abruptly ends."[21] He is likewise theorizing about Bresson's systemic approach to the totality of his cinema's style when he notices that "Bresson is cutting short of a superficial run-off of emotion, trying to keep it together submerged, intact, so that in one final moment he can make the viewer bring forth all of his emotions on a higher level."[22] This is the much-vaunted moment of transcendence, which Schrader would lift for his own films, copping to "my perhaps problematic decision to attach the ending of *Pickpocket* to *American Gigolo* and *Light Sleeper*, films which otherwise bore no evidence of transcendental style."[23]

It is worth taking a moment, before turning to a more in-depth recapitulation of Schrader's transcendental style discussion of Bresson, to acknowledge that this conflict has been the site of a number of disagreements between Schrader's critics and the filmmaker himself. Having written the book in 1972 before stepping behind the camera, *Transcendental Style in Film* became an easy road map for critics looking to apply Schrader's analysis of Ozu, Bresson, and Dreyer to his own filmmaking practice (after all, the one-to-one matchup works well with Bresson). Schrader has long resisted this pairing, insisting that the first film he has made in the transcendental style he theorized is 2017's *First Reformed*. In a number of the interviews he gave around the release of that film, Schrader took pains to distance his earlier work from transcendental style, but he would likely admit that restaging the *Pickpocket* ending twice probably encouraged the comparison. In the interview that appends this volume, he dismisses those critics who saw transcendental style in his films as "lazy" in making a connection between his academic work and his film work, despite what he saw as obvious stylistic differences between the films he wrote about and the films he wrote/directed.

And yet, despite Schrader's resolute commitment to the non-transcendental aspects of his films' style (*First Reformed* excluded), the films themselves demonstrate that Bresson is never far from his mind. Most of Schrader's films, if not fully committing to transcendental style, are at least "transcendental-curious," picking up Bressonian techniques and discarding them at will. In *Transcendental Style*, Schrader argues that Bresson "may be the prototypical director of inaction. Before Bresson, I can think of no director who proposed inaction as cinematic tool. Bresson made 'waiting' a verb."[24] The inaction Schrader references owes to Bresson's approach to cinematic style, marked by austere framing and other withholding techniques, but also to the protagonists of Bresson's films. Here he is at length on the shared characteristics he finds in Bresson's protagonists:

> Bresson's protagonists, like the country priest, cannot find metaphors capable of expressing their agony. They are condemned to estrangement: nothing on earth will placate their inner passion, because their passion does not come from earth. Therefore they do not respond to their environment, but instead to that sense of the Other which seems much more immediate. Hence the disparity; the Bresson protagonist lives in an all-inclusive cold, factual environment, yet rather than adapting to that environment, he responds to something totally separate from it.[25]

Characters who wait, who are acted upon, who react, who are alienated but unsure how to respond to that alienation—these are fundamentally passive characters that give Schrader the model for his "existential heroes."

It is not difficult to see the link between Schrader's analysis of Bresson's protagonists and *Taxi Driver*'s Travis Bickle, who has "perverse singularity of vision" and "can't see that he is the one making himself lonely."[26] Following the reincarnation of the character through his own directorial work, especially *American Gigolo, Light Sleeper*, and *The Walker* (2007), Schrader argues that the protagonists are joined by their foundational identity as watchers rather than doers. In each case, "The main character is passive; he lets the movie roll over him like waves on the beach. The waves will always come, but he will always be there."[27] Again, Schrader at length on his "existential heroes":

> These characters are not so much people as souls, they drift around and things happen to them, they watch and they are acted upon. I don't really see this group of films as a trilogy, I just think that as I get older my views about this character and these themes change. So that when the character and myself were in our twenties, he was very hostile and paranoid and felt oppressed by the world, and was a cab driver. When he was in his thirties he was very narcissistic and self-involved, and he was a gigolo. Now he's forty and he's anxious and uncertain, and he delivers drugs. He hasn't made anything of his life, and he doesn't know what will become of him.[28]

The language Schrader uses to describe his own creations parallels that which he uses to describe what he sees in Bresson's protagonists. Take Schrader at his word—or, failing that, apply the rigorous transcendental style analysis to the films themselves—and acknowledge that *American Gigolo, Light Sleeper*, and other films may not be full-throated exercises in transcendental style. However, the films still show the unmistakable influence of Bresson, not simply in their final moments, but in their structure, design, and, crucially, in Schrader's description of why he finds Bresson's work meaningful.

Schrader's women are fewer in number, but closer application of his career-long engagement with Bresson reveals that the "existential hero" can also be an "existential heroine." The first of his most dynamic female characters, Irena (Nastassja Kinski) of *Cat People* (1982), is the real protagonist of the film, despite Schrader's own admitted identification with the male zookeeper who loves her, Oliver (John Heard). Schrader's *Cat People* is a remake of Jacques Tourneur's 1942 classic by the same name, which is about a young woman's sexual awakening, with the horror-inspired twist that as she becomes aroused, she transforms into a bloodthirsty black leopard. Though Tourneur chafed against the strictures of the Hollywood Production Code and his own micro-budget, Schrader's film revels in special effects that liken it to a werewolf film, along with explicit sex and nudity. Never one to mince words, Schrader openly confesses that "during the actual shooting of the film I became involved with Nastassja Kinski and became obsessed with her,"[29] which lends the film's repeated images of Irena's nude body a decidedly "Mulveyan" valence.[30] Perhaps uncomfortable with his directorial choices in retrospect, Schrader dismisses Irena as "a male creation."[31] While Schrader undoubtedly means this as self-critique, his label also reveals the degree to which Irena comes from similar roots as Schrader's existential men. In the run-up to *Cat People*, Schrader began the film identifying with "the character of the zookeeper played by John Heard as a sort of pursuer of a Beatrice figure. He's a man who lives with animals because he doesn't like humans very much. And then his Beatrice appears and his greatest fantasy has come true, because Beatrice is an animal. Well, as we developed the character he evolved more and more along the lines of myself."[32]

However, structurally, the film is Irena's. She enters the narrative when her plane lands in New Orleans, having come to meet her long-lost brother, Paul (Malcolm McDowell). Even more so than in the 71-minute original film, Schrader's remake foregrounds Irena's sexual awakening as she begins a romance with Oliver and discovers the animal within. Paul, who is like Irena, explains that they become leopards when sexually aroused, and in order to become human again, they must kill. Irena initially resists the urges she feels, but eventually succumbs to them and embraces her sexuality and the violence that releases her from its grip. After Paul (while a leopard) is killed, Irena stalks Oliver's sometime-girlfriend Alice (Annette O'Toole) but spares her. Struggling to reconcile the competing passions inside her, she asks Oliver to make love to her ("free me," she says), knowing that she will become a leopard. The film concludes with Oliver visiting the transformed Irena, now in a cage at the big cat exhibit in his zoo, having made her choice.

Schrader calls *Cat People* "existential horror,"[33] which evokes the "existential heroes" of his other films. Irena's crisis mirrors those that afflict Schrader's men—she is a stranger in a world that does not accommodate her, torn between concerns of the body and the soul. Paul and his monstrous alter ego, the leopard, destabilize her sense of self. She is further distressed by the violence; he has, right before Irena's eyes, while in leopard form, murdered a young zookeeper, Joe (Ed Begley, Jr.), in order to facilitate his transformation back into a man and his escape from the zoo. She likewise feels the pull of the spiritual; though not Judeo-Christian, Schrader shoots scenes of the history of the cat people in lush, red-streaked sequences bordering on surrealism, complete with Giorgio Moroder's haunting electronic musical theme (paired with harmonizing by the song's lyricist, David Bowie), that evoke religious ceremony. The film's wordless prologue, set in an unfamiliar desert at the base of an ominous bare tree, luxuriates in religious imagery. A wide shot of a hovering cloud of dust dwarfs the tree and the members of the tribe who will become Irena's forebears, anticipating some of the images to which Schrader will return in his other horror film, *Dominion: A Prequel to the Exorcist* (2005). He emphasizes the dynastic relationship with a cross-fade from a tribal woman, who has entered the cave of a threatening black leopard, to a matching close-up of Irena, her first appearance in the film. In drawing these two women together—one a figure from an uncertain, provincial past and the other a modern woman in a New Orleans airport—Schrader comments upon the primacy of belief. Shared mythology has the power to unify cultures separated by time and geography. Schrader further emphasizes this spiritual connection when Paul, while a leopard, is trapped inside a low-rent hotel room after attempting to kill a prostitute there. When the zookeepers come to apprehend him and Oliver shoots him with a tranquilizer dart, the Paul leopard slams into the iron bars over the window; Schrader cuts to Irena in bed, snapping awake as if jarred by the metallic clang of the impact, and then cuts back to the Paul leopard throwing its head back in confused agony. They are linked through their shared heritage (though Irena does not know it yet), and for the first of many times, framed against prison bars, Schrader's adoption of a crucial Bressonian image that evokes the unclear boundaries between freedom and imprisonment.

Irena is the film's primary inheritor of that legacy of belief; the story, a conversion narrative, is hers. At the film's outset, Irena is a naïve woman who does not know herself, awkward around others and tentative in expressing her desires. Paul is a hedonist who seems to enjoy the sexual act at least as much, if not more than, the violent murders that free him from his felinity. When Paul is killed two-thirds of the way through the film, Irena adopts his attraction to violence, stalking Alice at the swimming pool for seemingly no other reason than pure pleasure, but pulls back from fully embracing his bloodlust. She spares Alice instead of killing her, though she surely could have. Irena's childlike wonder at the zoo in the film's first half, before the stirrings of sexual interest in Oliver begin to manifest, aligns her with male Schrader protagonists like Travis Bickle, whose pornographic curiosity is almost entirely without sexuality, complicating traditional understanding of how the male gaze views cinematic female bodies. In Schrader's own directorial hands, Jake Van Dorn in *Hardcore*, the conservative Calvinist father searching for his missing daughter in the California pornography underworld, experiences a similar sexual awakening; he outwardly disdains his deepening entry into the unfamiliar world of sex workers and peep shows but feels simultaneous attraction. Irena enacts similar ambivalence, but without the self-loathing that fuels Van Dorn. Her first conversation with Oliver in the zoo, when he finds her sketching a leopard after hours, is contrasted with a cutaway to a tracking shot that cranes in to the caged Paul leopard, growling menacingly. Moroder's ominous music creeps in, suggesting the violence that lurks beneath Irena's sexuality, but visually, Schrader again emphasizes sexual excitement as a kind of prison. The cage's bars separate Paul the leopard from the camera, and presumably from Oliver, Paul's rival for Irena, who stands in the way of his consummation of his incestuous desire for his cat-sister.

In the first half of the film, Irena exhibits virginal qualities. In their first meal together, Oliver teaches her how to eat oysters and suggests she wash it down with a sip of beer. He is surprised at her naiveté when she reaches instead for her Coke. When he secures a job for her at the zoo, she works in the gift shop amid novelties for children and stuffed animals that both emphasize her childishness but also prefigure her animal desire. Oliver spies her through barred windows that cage Irena, foreshadowing her chosen fate. Irena confesses her sexual virginity to Alice while the two are out for a drink, telling her about an attempt at sex that ultimately went unfulfilled, which she stopped after becoming frightened by the size of her partner's penis. Though the film has not yet articulated the exact nature of the leopard-sex-violence mythology (Paul will helpfully explain it in an expository scene a bit further on), Irena's discomfort with sexuality coincides with her overall innocence. One might call the scene where Paul the leopard kills Joe the zookeeper a kind of rite of passage; in an image that recalls the menstrual horror of Brian De Palma's *Carrie* (1975), a wave of Joe's blood splashes in slow motion on the tiled white floor at Irena's feet. Paul, human again, furthers the comparison when he finds Irena at home, distraught over witnessing Joe's death, and tells her, "I didn't think you were ready, but you are. I knew it when I saw you with him." The "him" is Oliver, who has already awakened Irena's desire; Paul watched them from his cage at the zoo. While stalking around the room, he confronts Irena with sexuality: "You want to fuck him. You dream about fucking him. Your whole body burns, burns all along your nerves. Your mouth, your breasts, and you go wet between your legs." Irena shouts, "Stop it!', looking directly into the camera, breaking the fourth wall in what becomes a subjective shot from Paul's point of view. At this moment, when Irena can no longer ignore the rising tide of sexuality within her, the stylistic integrity preserved by the separation between narrative subject and cinematic apparatus breaks down.

Paul articulates the contradictory, Bressonian interrogation of freedom (which can often feel like prison) and imprisonment (which can often feel like freedom) when he tells her, "You can't escape the nightmare without me, and I can't escape without you." Here, he charts Irena's struggle to reconcile the opposition between confining sexuality and liberating violence that defines her existence as a leopard woman. She rejects Paul's sexual advances, unwilling to engage in incest ("I'm not like you!" she shouts), but wishes to explore her sexuality on her own terms with Oliver, a chosen partner rather than one pre-destined by biology. Spirited away to a bayou cabin by Oliver, Irena initially finds valuable restoration in nature. Together, they fish for crabs in the river and share a romantically lit, quiet dinner, which Oliver disrupts by pushing Irena sexually; he playfully says that they have to make love to keep the alligators away, and then kisses and grabs her before she pushes away apologetically, saying "I can't." Later that night, Irena, sleeping alone in the bedroom, awakens and wanders outside as if compelled by something deep and undefinable. She stares at Oliver, asleep on the couch, and rubs her body, while framed by Schrader's camera through a window between the house and the porch (bars again). Sexually aroused, she steps outside and strips off her nightgown, walking naked through the forest. Ominous Moroder cues that resemble a synthesized heartbeat lead into subjective shots from Irena's point of view, now made strange by the infusion of dynamic blues and purples that suggest an animal's instinctual sight. She hunts and kills a rabbit, which Schrader obscures with a smash cut to black. When she returns, Oliver awakens to the sound of the porch door creaking open. Puzzled, he turns on the light, which Irena, covered in blood, smashes while screaming, "Don't look at me!" The blood immediately recalls the menstrual image that closed the scene where Joe was killed, and Irena's shameful command associates sexuality with embarrassment, fears often expressed by Schrader's men.

Schrader's application of these themes and contradictions to a female character, as opposed to the men who dominate a number of his other, more famous works, grants them access to the existential struggles often reserved for male characters on-screen. Schrader's men struggle with these same competing impulses, and often their release is violent. Travis Bickle's sexual naiveté and loneliness, exacerbated by his curiously chaste relationship with pornography, lead to his violent assassination of the pimps; in *First Reformed*, Reverend Toller refuses to reignite a sexual relationship with a former flame who works at the nearby megachurch, but also cannot consummate his obviously burgeoning feelings for the pregnant Mary (Amanda Seyfried), a parishioner whose husband Toller counseled before his suicide. Toller imagines relieving his pain first through a catastrophic act of terror, blowing up the church as an act of protest against those who ignore the realities of climate change, before turning his rage inward and (maybe) drinking drain cleaner in a suicidal flourish of his own. Schrader contrasts the violence at the heart of his film with a transcendent finale in which a swirling camera captures Toller kissing Mary passionately; the film is ambiguous—either she has really interrupted his suicide attempt and saved his life or he has envisioned this act of love after going through with it. Bickle and Toller typify Schrader's narrative instincts, which place male characters at the nexus of a critical choice between carnality and brutality; in Schrader's vision, it is never clear which offers redemption and which offers damnation.

In Irena's case, both may be possible. Having rejected the opportunity to kill the defenseless Alice, she does in fact murder the watchman who looks in on Oliver's cabin so that she may become human again after she and Oliver have sex for the first time. At this point, after killing the innocent fellow, Irena asks Oliver to "free me," while standing nude beneath a shadowed pattern of latticed window screen that emphasizes prison imagery. Oliver wordlessly agrees, ironically binding her to the bedposts with ropes in a gesture that once again foregrounds the contradiction between imprisonment and freedom while also adopting sadomasochistic imagery, before having sex with her. Irena deliberately chooses confinement through which she will be liberated. The film's closing zoo scene is another of Schrader's repurposed *Pickpocket*-endings, though he has never acknowledged it as he has for both *American Gigolo* and *Light Sleeper*. This time, it is the woman-as-leopard who has found freedom behind bars. Oliver's loving gestures, nuzzling Irena-the-leopard's face, echo the final moments of *Pickpocket* when Michel leans his head against the bars of his cell, while Jeanne places her hand against them. The placidity of the final scene suggests that Irena has found a kind of peace; she has chosen to love Oliver as a leopard from behind the bars of her cage, while he also remains in a kind of confinement, separated from Irena by the same bars, as the framing repeatedly emphasizes, with Schrader's camera jumping both into and outside of the cage but always using the cell's bars as pivot point, in a stable but passionless relationship with Alice, who does not know that the cat is Irena. Initially, the ending freeze-frame, a possible manifestation of the "stasis" Schrader marks as the final stage of transcendental style, which he frequently uses to end his films, suggests Irena's mastery of her sexual domain, having found a neutral site between sexuality and violence. However, the film suddenly unfreezes and the cat roars before freezing again. The credits roll against the leopard's teeth, frighteningly bared in an expression of its violent power ("vagina dentata," anyone?). Like Schrader's men, Irena remains trapped between imprisonment and freedom, confined physically but spiritually free, both the leopard and the woman.

Schrader was more charitable to his shaping of the central character of his 1988 film *Patty Hearst*, based on the real experiences of the heiress kidnapped

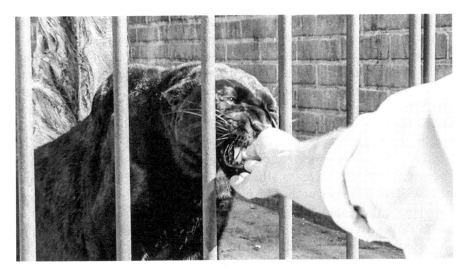

Figure 7.1 At the conclusion of *Cat People* (1982), Schrader restages the end of Bresson's *Pickpocket* (1959), with his female character, now transformed into a leopard, finding connection with the man she loves, a zookeeper who reaches through the bars to touch her.

by the Symbionese Liberation Army in 1974, before she joined the cell and participated (to conflicting accounts) in their robberies and other acts of terror. In discussing the film and the character, played in the film by Natasha Richardson, Schrader still exhibits some discomfort with the authorship of the female role at its center. Though he allows that his representation of Hearst "was really a female creation," he says "that's entirely down to [Richardson]—credit where credit's due."[34] Here too, Schrader diminishes his own role in shaping the existential heroine; Hearst's kidnapping and subsequent spiritual drift make her one of the frequently male searchers who populate Schrader's other films. The particulars of cinematic authorship have long been debated, and we can never know to a certainty whose contributions are whose when they finally end up on-screen, but Schrader opens the door to analysis when he explicitly draws a parallel between Patty and his iconic Travis Bickle: "In a way Patty Hearst is sort of the reverse of Travis Bickle because Travis is an underdog who militates against the world and Patty is an overdog against whom the world militates."[35] His instincts for telling the story also align with his male-dominated narratives, which proceed with laser-like focus from the isolated points of view of his troubled protagonists, very rarely if ever offering a look at the world outside of their blinkered perspectives. In the case of *Patty Hearst*, "The script as presented to me was entirely from Patty's point of view, and I just said, 'OK, that's valid. Let's look at the world through this person's eyes. Let's not wink at the audience; let's just follow it through and let it take us someplace interesting.'"[36]

Like *Cat People* (not to mention *American Gigolo* and *First Reformed*), *Patty Hearst* is a conversion narrative that traces the existential heroine's journey from everyday arrested development to self-realization. Schrader relies on voiceover narration to offer subjective access to Patty. In the opening moments of the film, Patty describes her sheltered existence which, knowing the character's lived history, will be shockingly disrupted; the film acknowledges this fact through its disruption of the fourth wall, when Patty looks into the camera and, in freeze-frame, says in voiceover, "Of course, there is little one can do to prepare for the unknown." Schrader's reuse of the fourth-wall break which characterized Irena's moment of destabilization does the same to Patty. She will spend the first third of the film in the captivity of the Symbionese Liberation Army (SLA), speaking in voiceover while confined to a closet. Schrader makes Patty's experience in the closet into a wildly expressionistic nightmare characterized by extremes; she is at turns in total darkness and blinded by sudden bright light when the door opens, which increases the subjective relationship between spectators and Patty. Schrader elides time by collapsing episodes that mark her captivity; the door opens, Cinque (Ving Rhames) shouts propaganda at her, and then it closes. Seconds later, it opens again, and time has passed, though it is unclear how much; the sequence continues, alternating between Cinque's propaganda and Patty's own existential nightmares.

As Irena was caught between sexuality and violence, Patty is pulled between her privilege and wealth and the radical politics of the SLA. While confined in the closet, Patty's only escape comes through her ability to imagine, fantasies that Schrader stages with expressionistic adventurousness that also illustrate the divisions within her. In one, she imagines herself in a garish living room with her family, surrounded by luxury and gold-adorned furniture, but she wears a black blindfold. Schrader introduces these contradictory visuals into a number of the fantasy sequences, memories now corrupted by new experience. In another moment, Patty remembers a family dinner—played by a younger actress, Patty is identified only by the black blindfold. The intrusion of captivity into this space, which Patty can no longer imagine as sacrosanct, inspires her growing political radicalism, reframing her wealth as a kind of captivity in itself. These contradictions invite Bressonian readings; Patty's existential awakening comes from realizing that her SLA imprisonment has shown her how confining her previous life was. Cinque asks her to imagine that "the price of freedom is daring to struggle," recasting the class privilege she formerly enjoyed as more confining than her present situation. This disruption echoes the "disparity" Schrader saw in Bresson's transcendental narratives, as Patty's everyday assumptions are knocked off their axis permanently.

Cinque and the SLA are not much of a terrorist organization, and much of their rhetoric is warmed-over nonsense that papers over a militaristic desire to wave guns around and, eventually, start robbing banks. Despite the SLA's clownishness, their abduction of Patty sets the stage for her very real existential crisis, which is Schrader's preferred territory. His cinema is not exactly apolitical, but less concerned with the ramifications of social issues than with their impact on his protagonists' inner lives. Patty's existential rut is best exemplified by her reminder to herself in voiceover: "Don't examine your feelings. Never examine your feelings. They're no help at all." Schrader pairs this testament to her unwillingness to reflect with a slow dolly-back from the outside of Patty's closet door, which aligns the symbol of her imprisonment with the expression of intellectual confinement through her narration. When Cinque offers her the opportunity to join the SLA or be set free, she imagines herself in a grave, dirt being shoveled onto the camera (her point of view) on the word "free," which visualizes the redefinition of her previous life brought about by her captivity. As a result, Patty finds no real solace in the SLA's ideological mission; they shatter her sense of self, but their efforts to piece her together in their image eventually fail.

Newly free to choose her own captivity, Patty is rechristened "Tonya" by the SLA, and she builds a new identity with shorter hair and military costumes. When she records a message for her parents, she says, "I have chosen to stay and fight." A sideways glance after she presses the stop button on the tape recorder suggests discomfort and represents her continued between-ness. She performatively rejects her old life as a rich heiress, and plays make-believe at accepting her new one as a terrorist firebrand, but neither fits. Here again, Schrader brushes against his own articulation of transcendental style. Though the film's expressionism flies in the face of Bressonian austerity, Schrader's comfort in the stage he calls "disparity," a disruption of the "everyday," exactly captures Patty's journey throughout her captivity. She waffles between the everyday realities of privilege represented in flashback and the everyday realities of her confinement, but neither feels right to her. In the SLA's first bank robbery, when Cinque boasts that his female companion is Patty Hearst to the customers and tellers, she stammers out, "This is Patty Hearst . . . Tonya . . . SLA." She has no sense of who she is supposed to be. Later, she will underline her self-doubt when she barely manages enough self-confidence to tell another visiting radical that Patty is "dead. I'm Tonya."

Her break intensifies when she participates in a violent crime with two of the more extreme radicals, Tico (William Forsythe) and Yolanda (Frances Fisher), shooting off a machine gun to save them from an interaction with a police officer. She withers when the three watch on television as the FBI stages a violent raid on Cinque's house. She slips into the bathroom and crumples between the toilet and the bathtub, and Schrader points the camera down at her to echo her time in the closet. The realization that law enforcement burned Cinque's house without offering them a chance to escape isolates Patty from her rich, privileged world. After this incident, she embraces her role with the remaining members of the SLA with renewed vigor; any ambivalence she previously experienced is temporarily wrung out. Before long, though, she confesses in voiceover, "I go deeper and deeper inside myself," losing interest in political struggle. Patty's existential dilemma cannot be resolved because she is arrested and her time with the SLA comes to an abrupt end. When being booked, she is asked to provide an occupation; is she an heiress? A bank robber? She laughs and says "Urban guerilla," with the self-awareness of how ridiculous that sounds. She is no more an urban guerilla than she is any longer an heiress, divorced from both as a result of her experience. Embracing her sisters in the prison's visiting room, she immediately flashes back to a childhood bedroom, once again surrounded by her sisters but also wearing the black blindfold. Freedom from the SLA has led to literal confinement within the legal system, but also the spiritual and intellectual imprisonment represented by her family.

Patty reaches similar existential territory as Julian Kay in *American Gigolo*, who likewise suffers disorientation when the stability of his life is undermined. Julian struggles to understand the absurdity of the legal system when he is accused of a murder he did not commit, thinking that it should protect him because he is innocent. Julian is a gigolo who cannot experience love, but simulates the experience for his clients, especially Michelle (Lauren Hutton), with whom he will consummate a loving bond through the prison glass in the film's final moments. As he does in *American Gigolo*, Schrader once again repurposes the final scene of *Pickpocket* for *Patty Hearst* (though, as with *Cat People*, he has not acknowledged doing so). In prison after being apprehended, Patty finds similar liberation behind bars. Though she is confined, she knows who she is.

Figure 7.2 Schrader's *Patty Hearst* (1988) also ends with a gloss on *Pickpocket*, as Patty (Natasha Richardson) finds herself behind bars and expresses defiant self-realization in a conversation with her wealthy father.

As Irena made her choice to live in prison as a leopard, apparently reconciling the competing tensions between sex and violence within her, Patty achieves self-definition in owning her choices. In a defiant conversation with her father after she is incarcerated, Patty expresses mastery over her appeal process in a single medium shot that minimizes the contributions of her scene partner, who largely speaks off camera. Schrader slowly pushes the camera in on Patty as she delivers a monologue about her relationship to the press, the public, and those who have prejudged her. She tells him, "No one wants to accept that their mental state is so fragile. To be turned into a totally different person. Not me! I'm too strong for that. Just don't lock me in that closet." The experience of captivity has shattered Patty's definition of self, but has also liberated her. Her defiant refusal to be returned to captivity ("that closet") contradicts her present state: incarceration. And yet, she is spiritually and intellectually free, expressed with Schrader's typical clashing aplomb: "Pardon my French, Dad, but fuck them. Fuck them all." Her body is imprisoned, but her mind and soul are free; this is a clear representation of what Schrader calls, in an interview tied to the release of *Light Sleeper*, "finding freedom behind bars, which is a very Bressonian idea."[37]

Though Schrader did not write the screenplays for either of these films, they each bear his unmistakable signature, mostly in their references to Bressonian ideas, themes, and scenes. The evidence even bears out curiosity about the transcendental structure he sketches out in his book, even though neither film adheres to the formal austerity Schrader requires. Critical study of Schrader's work has understandably focused on his male characters—he is one of the cinema's essential artists for whom masculinity is a prime subject—but there is much to be learned about Schrader's foundational filmmaking instincts from his female characters. The diaries written by Bickle, LeTour, and Toller, and Schrader's consistent use of voiceover narration throughout his many films, create close identification, which forces the cinematic experience inside the souls of his characters. Schrader's "men and their rooms" struggle in interior spaces to resolve interior conflicts. Schrader aligns these women with their male counterparts through the implementation of narrative, thematic, and formal choices lifted from Bresson. Because they share similar existential malaise that drives them to self-actualization, Schrader's women adopt the Bressonian model he uses for his men. They are "women in their rooms," a prospect made literal by their final incarcerated moments both trapped and free inside the cells where they have found themselves.

NOTES

1. Robert Bresson, "Robert Bresson, Possibly," interview by Paul Schrader, May 17, 1976, in *Robert Bresson (Revised)*, edited by James Quandt (Toronto: Toronto International Film Festival Cinematheque, 2011), 698.

2. *Schrader on Schrader*, Revised Edition, edited by Kevin Jackson (New York: Faber and Faber, 2004), 163.
3. Paul Schrader, "Pickpocket I," in *Schrader on Schrader*, Revised Edition, edited by Kevin Jackson (New York: Faber and Faber, 2004), 38.
4. Ibid., 38.
5. "It's the existential hero—what I like to call 'a man and his room' stories. You have these two characters, the man and his room—I love the movies that are about those two." Ibid., 163.
6. Robert Bresson, *Notes on the Cinematograph* (New York: New York Review of Books, 1975), 12.
7. *Schrader on Schrader*, 119.
8. Bresson, *Notes on the Cinematograph*, 23.
9. Tony Pipolo, *Robert Bresson: A Passion for Film* (New York: Oxford University Press, 2010), 79.
10. Susan Sontag, "Spiritual Style in the Films of Robert Bresson," in *Robert Bresson (Revised)*, edited by James Quandt (Toronto: Toronto International Film Festival Cinematheque, 2011), 55.
11. Ibid., 61.
12. Amedee Ayfre, "The Universe of Robert Bresson," in *Robert Bresson (Revised)*, edited by James Quandt (Toronto: Toronto International Film Festival Cinematheque, 2011), 47.
13. Robert Bresson, "The Wind Blows Where It Wants To," interview by *Cahiers Du Cinéma*, May 15, 1957, in *Bresson on Bresson, Interviews 1943–1983*, edited by Mylene Bresson (New York: New York Review of Books, 2013), 52.
14. Sontag, 62.
15. Pipolo, 26.
16. Ibid., 79.
17. Ayfre, 44.
18. Ibid., 43.
19. Bresson, interview by Schrader, 694.
20. Schrader, "Pickpocket I," 38.
21. Ibid., 38.
22. Ibid., 42.
23. Paul Schrader, *Transcendental Style in Film: Ozu, Bresson, Dreyer*, Revised Edition (Oakland, CA: University of California Press, 2018), 22.
24. Ibid., 30.
25. Ibid., 102.
26. *Schrader on Schrader*, 119.
27. Ibid., 238.
29. Ibid., 167.
30. Laura Mulvey's "Visual Pleasure and Narrative Cinema" hardly needs explanation at this point. If you made it here, you've likely been there before.
31. *Schrader on Schrader*, 194.
32. Schrader on Schrader, 166.
33. Ibid., 167.
34. Ibid., 194.
35. Ibid., 191.
36. Ibid., 191.
37. Paul Schrader, "Scott Macaulay interviews Paul Schrader about *Light Sleeper*," interview by Scott Macaulay, *Filmmaker Magazine* (Fall 1992), https://filmmakermagazine.com/archives/issues/fall1992/movie_high.php.

CHAPTER 8

Paul Schrader's Experiment in Italian Neo-decadence: *The Comfort of Strangers* and the Sadean System

Robert Dassanowsky

I

The singular attempt at translating the mostly Italian school of period neo-decadence of the 1970s into a more contemporary era resulted in a film that seethes with the condemnation of a reactionary *Weltanschauung* that made the best of the original genre so worthwhile, even with its excesses. *The Comfort of Strangers* (UK/Italy 1990), directed by Paul Schrader, is adapted from Ian McEwan's novel by Harold Pinter, who had supplied the 1960s with its first parable on power, decadence, and repressed sexuality in *The Servant* (UK 1963). Schrader's film was hardly understood by critics of the time as the type of allegory on fascism that arrived with Visconti, Cavani, Bertolucci, Wertmüller, and Pasolini. Here, in a 1990s setting, Venice underscores a monumentalized past in which two couples play out the metaphors of liberalism being sacrificed to the sinister desires of fascism. The very notion of Thomas Mann's *Death in Venice* novella and Visconti's film *Morte a Venezia/Death in Venice* (Italy/France/USA 1971), the total liberation of the senses, which results in self-destruction, is also at the heart of *Strangers*. Like Mann's character of the aging German historian (a Gustav Mahler-like composer in Visconti's film) Gustav von Aschenbach and his obsession with the Polish boy Tadzio vacationing with his mother and siblings on the Lido, the Italian aristocrat Robert's desire for handsome British tourist Colin shifts uncomfortably between aesthetic appreciation and outright homosexual desire. Is this an intentional mime of Visconti's vision of a sexually aware Tadzio from Mann's *Death in Venice*? Only the trappings of his tradition-based life—his reputation as an important man based in heritage and inheritance, his repressed but faithful wife, and the grandeur of his palazzo surroundings—allows him the thin veneer of being the connoisseur rather than the sexual predator. His self-definition is based in the static values of his "history," the phallocratic dominance of the fathers, which is at once a bourgeois defense of racial and cultural supremacy that fueled fascism in Europe.

The construction of a glorious past that can elevate the present while at the same time freezing middle-class values against the perceived threats of the Left, is one of the hallmarks of both Italian and German fascism. The phallocracy of the ideology is supported in law and culture, while its homoeroticism is denied by the figure of the "wife" (woman in a secondary if not tertiary social role as mother). This was first metaphorically stated by Visconti in the first and most imitated example of neo-decadence, *La caduta degli dei/ The Damned* (Italy/West Germany 1969). In *Strangers*, Robert's bar is filled with attractive males, who convey homoerotic interest in one another and in the British visitor. The casting of the handsome Rupert Everett as Colin, as a self-absorbed, body-conscious man, intentionally implies that his straight character shares some understanding of gay socio-cultural and aesthetic self-comprehension as a liberated but often passive man who has a female partner rather than a wife. His ultimate sexualized murder-sacrifice then, becomes, according to his hunter/ executioner Robert, one he attracted.

Steeped in the homoerotic atmosphere of his personal and cultural definition, but unable to accept his homosexual desire for Colin, Robert uses his wife as proxy (she undoes his trousers for no apparent purpose beyond humiliation, as he is being held at knifepoint by Robert) in the bondage/torture that results in Colin's execution. His sexual repression has sublimated itself into the only physical contact he can have with another man, the cutting of his throat. In Rainer Werner Fassbinder's heavily stylized cinematic version of Genet's *Querelle* (West Germany/France 1982), whorehouse madam Lysiane (Jeanne Moreau) sings knowingly how "every man kills the thing he loves ..." and Kriss Ravetto clarifies this in a discussion on the Sadean system in Pasolini's *Salò, or the 120 Days of Sodom* (Italy/France 1975): "sexual contact in the age of neo-capitalism does not produce any intimate relationships; in fact it radically deconstructs sentimental relationships, unhinging cultural illusions that mask a sadistic sexual economy."[1]

A fresh look at what is certainly one of Paul Schrader's less critically discussed examples of cinematic virtuosity is timely given the recent global tendency toward political populism and reactionary response to social, sexual, and racial diversity. Given Schrader's fascination with Italian and French cinema, sexual politics, politicized sexuality, and general human frailty in such diverse films as *Taxi Driver* (as screenwriter), *Hardcore*, *Mishima*, *American Gigolo*, *Auto Focus*, *Adam Resurrected*, *The Walker*, *The Canyons*, and *First Reformed*, among others, one can understand how he developed his approach to neo-decadent film. As a film theorist, Schrader's pivotal 1972 study, *Transcendental Style in Film*, had addressed religious symbolism, the boundaries of love, as well as an aesthetics of reflection that framed transgression and the lure of eroticism with violence.² During the planning of *American Gigolo*, Schrader hired Ferdinando Scarfiotti, "who had designed the productions of Visconti's *Death in Venice*, and Bertolucci's *The Conformist* . . . Schrader 'sat at [Scarfiotti's] knee' to learn the maestro's manner of visual thinking. The director set out to create an all-out art-film."³ Olga A. Dzhumaylo finds the adaptation of this "Venetian text" to be a valid carrier of the aesthetics of the director's transcendental style. Moreover, [Schrader] "leads the viewer to a meta-reflection about the instability and transgression of any look, and in this case a look at the beauty to be destroyed."⁴

The entrapment quality of *The Servant*, which informs so much of the 1970s neo-decadent genre, would provide the central metaphor of sadistic control in the "Venetian text," this time not servant over master, but reaction over liberalism; male over female; and with pseudo-heroic and elitist history, beauty, and innocence as pure fetish. The very opening of the film plays with symbols of imprisonment and freedom and with the gender associated to these spaces of being. The inventory camera surveys the dusky, tradition-laden interiors of Robert (Christopher Walken) and Caroline's (Helen Mirren) apartment in the Venice palazzo. The patterned ceilings of crosses that both oppress and suggest the maze of this realm echo the ceiling-tracking of *L'année dernière à Marienbad/Last Year at Marienbad* (France/Italy 1961) and its attempt to disorient the viewer in this "mythical" world. We see framed ancient maps of the city; Pre-Raphaelite paintings and crumbling wall murals; the outdated kitchen; a large canopy bed; tables with *objets d'art*; and one captive, Caroline, who enters the central salon and moves to the interior open terrace draped in silks and cushions and completes it with her presence as if it were an artistic tableau. Her husband enters as a disembodied, prophetic voice, explaining as if from scripture a Freudian drama of symbols and symbolists that are constructed to seem mythic: "My father was a very big man. All his life he wore a black moustache. When it turned grey he used a little brush to keep it black, such as ladies use for their eyes. Mascara . . ."⁵ He is at once the impersonation of monumental Paterfamilias, but with a brutal vanity which is aimed at retaining the heroics of an uncritical past. Robert continues his story, explaining that he was the only boy in a family of girls who resented the father's favoring of him by playing cruel jokes that would result in his punishment, but also protection from his gentle mother.

Countering this is the modern world at the Hotel Gabrielli, where we find Colin (Rupert Everett) dreamily observing the canals from his room's balcony. Mary (Natasha Richardson), his partner, paces with business-like impatience across the room attempting to call England on the telephone. The passive (Caroline) and active (Mary) women are both attracted to the relaxed, male-model image of Colin and oppressed by Caroline's husband, Robert, who dominates her world through the "living" history of the palazzo and its many

Figure 8.1 Robert (Christopher Walken) entertains a lost Colin (Rupert Everett) and Mary (Natasha Richardson) at his bar.

items that belonged to his father, which are laid out reverentially as a shrine to the patriarch. Caroline is an unwavering defender of Robert's culture; Mary is disturbed and offended by Robert's sexism. Caroline and her self-mythic husband represent an elitism based in a fascistic view of social control and cultural superiority; Mary and Colin are liberal representatives of a post-colonial, democratic system transitioning from elitism to egalitarianism. The starting points are strong socio-cultural oppositions that generate a dualism of allure and rejection in both parties.

II

The pattern that allows Robert and Caroline their control over Colin and Mary from the outset is their presence, their roots in Venice, and the belief in tradition as permanence—they use the city and it serves them like a cloak of elitism. Colin and Mary are confused as to their own lives and come to Venice to decide if marriage is possible, or if their relationship has run the course. They get lost in their discussions as they continuously get lost in the maze of Venice. All the while, Robert utilizes their wildness as a hunter would, shooting—albeit with a camera—from every vantage point as if to capture particularly Colin. The two couples are at odds in their communication style: Robert continues the recitative of his family saga while rubbing Caroline's shoulders and not expecting an answer in the darkening interior alcove of the terrace, while in the exterior, sitting at a restaurant, it is Mary that leads this couple's communication in a crowded restaurant, as she asks Colin if he likes children, or even if he still likes her. He is evasive, and as an opposite reflection of the Robert and Caroline dyad, it is Mary that tells a story to Colin about the past, one in which she had to comprehend bigotry, elitism, and undemocratic behavior as a child, when she agreed that one of the members was "not good enough to be in the gang." She enthusiastically insisted the person be thrown out and is surprised and disturbed at her actions even now. The film cuts to Robert and Caroline's palazzo apartment, where no one questions the past and there are no choices to be made. Robert continues the telling of the family saga as a monologue, while re-examining books in his library, a seemingly ritualistic practice done to contextualize their lives in mythic, paternalistic stability, as a silent Caroline dutifully makes tea in the kitchen.

The contrasting opposition is apparent the following day. Colin and Mary take a speedboat together and enjoy the Murano glass factory, then sleep carelessly into the evening. Robert's voiceover interrupts this "escapist" sequence which leads to vague, even misleading instructions from the porter as to where a restaurant might still be functioning (one gets the impression Robert had something to do with it), and their excursion turns into a confused trek through dark streets and alleyways. Are they travelling back into time? The scene recalls white-suited Gustav von Aschenbach following Tadzio, his sisters and their nursemaid attempting to return to the hotel through the dark streets of cholera-ridden Venice, lit by bonfires of infected clothing and blankets. He ultimately loses his way, collapsing by a sealed water well, and laughing in the dirt at the realization he may have contracted the illness. Just as Aschenbach reaches an awareness that will ultimately kill him, Colin and Mary suddenly meet Robert, dressed in his white summer suit standing amid the pale classical columns, and like the inevitability that fascism has always understood itself to be, takes control of the confused and vulnerable couple, with the brief "Good Evening. Do you need help?" and promising them "beautiful Venetian food," as he escorts them to his bar, where there is no food, only drink, breadsticks, and men.

Pointedly, Robert and Mary's socio-political beliefs immediately collide. She points out the posters on the walls from the Colletivo Feminista Venezia, which demands castration for convicted rapists. She expresses her distance from their very "radical" attitudes. Robert's response, however, is expectedly sexist and reactionary: "These are women who cannot find a man. They want to destroy everything that is beautiful between men and women." But neither Mary nor Colin respond to his obvious support for male sexual dominance and violence against women as a tradition and a patriarchal right. Moreover, when he asks if the couple live together in sin, he guesses the answer with more than a hint of disgust that "there are no standards today." He speaks of his wife, a Canadian, but to explain how he met her he would need to discuss his sisters and his father, and once again he begins with the prologue of the patriarch's moustache, as if it were biblical verse. This merges into a sadistic tale about humiliation brought on by his sisters giving him medicine after tempting him with cakes, so that he would defecate in his father's office. Not having forgiven his sisters and catching the permanent ire of his father, he found himself sleeping in his mother's bed when his father was away. The daughter of a visiting Canadian diplomat was told he sleeps in his mother's bed and remarked that it was "sweet." She eventually became his wife.

This tale of power through sadism instructs the viewer as to the roots of Robert's reactionary, even crypto-fascist beliefs and his domineering and repressive attitude toward women and sexuality. He does not trust women who are active and self-reliant as his sisters were (and Mary), but only protective and passive as his mother and his wife Caroline, who understood Robert's condition. Robert locates his masculinity in a mythology of the powerful man or leader—his father—who suggests a sadist in the satisfaction he garners in punishing Robert as a young boy. Robert reacts to this by surrounding himself with young and attractive men who frequent his bar and seemingly worship him and his favors. His specific homoerotic obsession with the "free" and undisciplined "beauty" of Colin is something he shares with his abused wife who often is in great pain from what seems to have been physical assaults from Robert. She cramps whenever she recounts something about their marriage or Robert's behavior.

Abandoned by Robert after the restaurant, the couple wander through the dark, weakened and insecure. Mary is ill and vomits, cursing Robert as a terrible man and essentially mirroring Robert's story about his poisoning at the hands of his sisters. Is this intended retribution against the sisters and the strong female? They sleep in the street and the next morning, in a state of dehydration, make their way to Piazza San Marco and collapse at a café where they wonder why they came to Venice. Mary tells Colin he will have to take care of her today. Colin's response is a startling one of resentment and selfishness: "Why, did you take care of me yesterday?" Robert's treatment has made them resentful and petty. But it is Colin's petulant child that provides a key to his destruction by Robert.

III

Charles Forceville's study of the nature of conceptual and structural metaphors and whether they can be "rendered pictorially and mixed-medially"[6] utilizes both Ian McEwan's original novel as well as Harold Pinter's and Paul Schrader's filmic *Comfort of Strangers* as his test case, tracing the concept that "Colin is a Child." This aspect was originally the central metaphor in both the novel and in Pinter's original script. McEwan gives Robert several dialogues and monologues with and about Colin, among them noting that Colin looks like an "angel" (in this case the foreshadowing of a dead child) and the accusation that "[now] women treat men like children."[7] Forceville believes Pinter wanted to strengthen this aspect in the script by creating continuous albeit indirect references to Colin as a child—notably Colin discovering he has a pimple while shaving (suggesting puberty), and Mary's response about girls not loving him anymore (e.g. "girls" signify that Colin is a "boy"). Additionally, in the scene in which Colin and Mary buy souvenir t-shirts for Mary's children, Colin draws childlike images of them on the packages. Mary shows photographs of her children to Robert, which prompts him to verify with Colin that they are clearly not his. This possession of children through photographs is mirrored with Robert's continual photos of Colin throughout the film, and the strange collection of them on his bedroom wall. The author indicates this offers a clear equation regarding parent and child relationships: Robert is to Colin as Mary is to her children.[8] Caroline later supports this by admitting to Colin that she spied on the couple sleeping after Robert invited them to rest at their apartment following the scene at the Piazza San Marco café. She tells Colin that he looked "like a baby," and that he must "always sleep sweetly."

Schrader apparently considered that the basic direction of the novel suggests that "no amount of civilization can paper over the animosity between men and women" and credited Pinter for "upgrading the childhood tension" along with the "elevation" of the character of Robert to strengthen the idea that childhood experiences are at the root of adult characteristics.[9] Schrader emphasizes the direction of Pinter's screenplay with specific body language of the actors and the mise-en-scène: Colin has his hands in his pockets; he skips steps; he allows Mary to speak for them both; he always wears an article of white clothing, suggesting innocence. We see a baby boy bouncing on his mother's knee at the Piazza San Marco, which cuts to a shot of Mary sitting with Colin, mirroring this mother–son relationship. Ultimately the parental figures are influenced by painful memories from their childhood past: Robert's sadomasochistic experiences with his older sisters and his father; Mary's story of being in a children's "gang" and having insisted on the expulsion of one of the children that turned out to be her. Finally, at the climax of the film, as Mary is incapacitated by a drugged drink and as Colin attempts to escape Robert and Caroline's grasp, Robert drags him to the wall of the apartment where the killing takes place, as a father would grasp and move an unruly, disrespectful child.

Schrader indicates that his choice of Rupert Everett to play Colin was based on his handsome, boyish, narcissistic, cinema image, as he would "essentially be the battleground over which the drama takes place."[10] What is even more compelling in this examination of the pattern of parents and children in the film, and particularly the mother–son reflected by the mother–son metaphor of Colin and Mary, are the queer signals of Colin throughout the film, and his continued difficulty in considering marriage to Mary and becoming a stepfather to her children. His character is quite at odds with the heteronormative lifestyle that he would be asked to undertake. Although this role came before Everett openly announced his homosexuality in his autobiography, it mirrors the key neo-decadent films that set the standard for the genre, not only the seminal homoerotic power play in Pinter's *The Servant*, but that of Visconti's aforementioned Nazi period piece, *The Damned*, in which the young, decadent dandy, Martin von Essenbeck (Helmut Berger), heir to the aristocratic Krupp-like dynasty's steel industry desired by the Nazi regime, is an infantile mother-son, mother-rapist, and pederast whose homosexuality is more of an associative quality (his notorious performance in Marlene Dietrich *Blue Angel* drag at a respectful family gathering; his flamboyant mannerisms) than actual activity. Visconti selected the young Austrian actor for his boyish beauty and the ability to display narcissism and self-absorption, which, as for Colin in *Strangers*, make him essentially the battleground over which the drama takes place. It all allowed critic Pauline Kael, no friend of the work, to accuse Visconti that he is "not using decadence as a metaphor for Nazism but the reverse: he's using Nazism as a metaphor for decadence and Homosexuality . . ."[11] Kael misjudges Visconti and the genre because she avoids dealing with the homoeroticism culturally implied and socially denied by fascism, which is represented by the supposedly heterosexual predator character of Martin, as it would also be represented by the character of Robert in Schrader's film.

IV

In Liliana Cavani's *Il portiere di notte/ The Night Porter* (Italy 1974) we return to meet former SS man, Max (played by Dirk Bogarde, who was the failed bourgeois and stepfather figure in Visconti's *The Damned*), and are presented with a host of former SS "father figures" who conspire to rid themselves of him because of sudden amorous actions that occur while serving as a night porter in an elegant Vienna hotel in the 1950s. Max's past returns to haunt him when his concentration camp victim/lover suddenly appears at the hotel as the wife of an American opera conductor. Max has been caring for a dissolute Countess and for another former SS officer who is also a ballet dancer, unable to practice his art publicly due to his hidden identity. He has all of the homoerotic body awareness, narcissism, and insecurities that are found in Schrader's man-child Colin. The perversion of the parental relationship for the desire of sex or destruction of threatening beauty arises, however, in the flashback to his camp relationship with Lucia (Charlotte Rampling), whom he favors with special attention, after he forces her into a passive, childlike target of his sadistic pleasure: oppressively photographing her, placing her in a swinging carousel ride in which children are used as target practice, and finally shooting at her as she cowers naked in a camp shower. With her emaciated adult's body now dressed in a young girl's sheer pink party dress and with her shorn head, she becomes the helpless child Max can dominate. Cavani thus builds the central metaphor of the masses under fascism as subservient and punished children. One of the most notorious scenes of the film shows Lucia topless, wearing the trousers, suspenders, and cap of an SS uniform and black leather opera gloves as she performs in Dietrich style for the guards and their favored prisoners in a sinister carnival atmosphere that echoes Helmut Berger's Dietrich drag show and the debauched orgy of the Storm Troopers in Visconti's *The Damned*. In reward for this entertaining behavior, Max surprises her with a box that contains the head of a prisoner who had abused her. In childlike, wordless shock, Lucia is both horrorstruck at the grotesque magnitude of Max's attentions to her and the role she must accept to survive.

This parody on the biblical relationship between Herod Antipas and his stepdaughter Salome, daughter of Herod II, who in the treatments by Oscar Wilde and Richard Strauss seduces her stepfather with an erotic dance and is rewarded with the head of John the Baptist, also seasons Schrader's *Strangers* as Colin and Mary are titillated by each other's nakedness as they awake in Robert's bedroom and admire themselves in the white and gold caftan that is left for them. Mary tells Colin "You look like a god!" As she wanders out of the bedroom to the terrace where Caroline, also in a caftan, is awaiting her, the room and their figures take on a mythological if not to say biblical quality. Caroline tells Mary she embroidered the caftans they are wearing, as if this were a gathering of ancient females enjoying their limited roles in a harem-like setting. Caroline asks Mary to stay for dinner and informs her that Robert is at his bar, admitting she has never been there. As she suggests ignorance of Robert's life and the sexuality that the audience is aware of, she is suddenly gripped by a painful back spasm, which suggests that this topic has come up between the couple in the past and she has been physically abused by Robert for exceeding her limited position. She immediately changes the subject to one that is from her own point of view to one that is supported by Robert. She admits to Mary that they watched her and Colin sleeping, and that "Colin is very beautiful—Robert said so too." Caroline immediately corrects herself and tells Mary, "Oh, you are too!"

Caroline's appreciation of Colin's body reveals itself as one directed by Robert's male gaze. In what seems to be true curiosity by a woman who apparently has no female friends, Caroline asks Mary if she and Colin are in love, sharing her own definition of love from the sadomasochistic relationship with Robert, as "letting someone do anything to you." Surprised at this female passivity, Mary questions this, as Colin enters the room wearing only a towel, which adds to the eroticism of the atmosphere that is based in male dominance and female vulnerability or even sexual subservience. Caroline underscores this by responding to Colin's request for their clothing by insisting that Mary tell him what she did (watch them sleeping), and begs them both to stay for dinner: "if you don't he'll blame me." Her handmaiden-like behavior continues as she asks Mary what she does, and Mary's response that she worked in a women's theater group surprises Caroline, who asks: "All women? How can you do a play with only women? What could happen? Nothing could happen." Mary's attempt to enlighten her by suggesting their conversation on the terrace is a good example, elicits laughter from Caroline, who insists they are probably waiting for a man "and then something will happen!" The result of this independent attitude sends her into back pain once again, which occurs whenever she thinks for herself beyond some proscribed dogma, or allows herself an unbridled emotion: "It hurts when I laugh," she explains.

Robert's entrance sparks his usual narrative of the past, this time about his grandfather who owned the apartment. He insists that the view from the terrace is particularly important, not because of any beautiful architecture, but because one can see Cemetery Island, where both his father and grandfather are buried. Life and status are venerated through death, beauty is transformed into erotic mythology, and reality is set in the selected memory of the past: Robert tells Colin he looks like an angel, and informs the couple that the books in the room represent the "favorite literature" of his father and grandfather, and their varied items collected on the table shrine as religious artifacts belonged to them as well. Independent thought is taken as lack of respect and acknowledgment of this patriarchal order, and is responded to with violence. Colin derides Robert's collection as "a museum dedicated to the good old days" and is punched in the stomach by Robert, who then winks at him, suggesting that punishment is always an option, and that there is an understood sadomasochistic relationship between men and above women.

Figure 8.2 Colin (Rupert Everett) and Mary (Natasha Richardson) enter Caroline's (Helen Mirren) timeless world.

During dinner, Robert asks how it is in England: "beautiful old traditions?" Mary responds that they are not so beautiful and emphasizes the word freedom, to which Robert questions the concept, and insists that "a few rules are not a bad thing. Society needs to be protected from perverts. Put them up against a wall and shoot them. The English government is going in the right direction." Robert's extremist views, not only in his actions which display male superiority over women, but in not recognizing his own sinister faults and creating scapegoats for the ills of society. His approval of the English government during the era of the film is meant to underscore the policies of Margaret Thatcher as an arch-conservative positioned against the welfare state, nationalized industry, post-war consensus and the EU. Robert's uninformed praise of Thatcherism, however, does not represent any true knowledge regarding political opposition to the Labour Party in Britain, and therefore suggests the extremist generalization of political and social targets, which are reduced to racist, sexist, and simplistic ideological formulae. To Colin's retort—that for him as an English man "what you say is shit"—Robert resorts to name-calling, which again centers on the supposed superiority of the right-wing nationalist and is without any sense of personal irony: "I respect you as an English man, but not if you are a Communist poof!"

At this point in the film, the audience clearly sees the oppositions in the two sets of partners. There appears to be no physical sex between Robert and Caroline, aside from perhaps the sadomasochistic play that they engage in. Not only does Caroline's back pain suggest physical violence by Robert, she is apparently held prisoner in the apartment because of this condition. When Colin and Mary want to leave the dinner, Caroline all but begs Colin to come back as she cannot get out. She is a willing prisoner of her keeper, as Lucia is of Max in Cavani's *The Night Porter*, once she has moved from the hotel to his small apartment where she abandons her new life. They play at sadomasochistic games, as they begin to fear the outside world and literally starve, fearing their murder by Max's Nazi comrades. Max and Lucia are far more equal in their second sadomasochistic relationship than Caroline can be with Robert, but both couples hide from contemporary reality (1957 Vienna and 1990 Venice) to act out transgressive relationships. Colin and Mary, on the other hand, are now clearly defined as modern, liberal, and diverse. They live together out of wedlock; Mary has children from a previous husband and is often the more dominant figure in the coupling with the man-child Colin; they have diverse opinions and deal with their differences openly. The dinner at the palazzo apartment seals the segment of the film dealing with the liberal couple's seduction through Robert and Caroline's carefully staged performance that transcends even the hostility at the table.

V

Psychologist Neil Maizels utilizes *Strangers* as an example of the defenses the infant mind must struggle with in the face of the emotional impact of the mother's beauty, particularly when there is no absolute guarantee of this being reciprocated. In a section he titles "Dangerous Beauty," he lays out the "center of gravity" of the film, which is the not the aggression of Robert and Caroline, who literally hunt the British couple, but that of the "exploration" of Colin and Mary's fascination with their perverse hosts. Maizels points out that they become entangled physically and through projective identification with "a malicious, psychotic, and sadomasochistic couple who masquerade as good Samaritans—but who, in fact, are their enthralling executioners." Maizel's view is that the liberal couple's fascination with the "perverse couple" is both "aphrodisiacal and terrifying." Beauty is the prey of this hunting and stalking, particularly by Robert, who contextualizes all that he does as maintenance of the world of his father and grandfather, his own lessons of subservience to them, and continuation of their control through misogyny, humiliation, threat, violence, and mistrust. Here the transgressive relationship and violence of the older couple is understood to stimulate a younger couple who harbor "quite similar, if not more cruel, and fascistic fantasies about each other's beauty."[12]

Colin and Mary's own sexual torture fantasies begin after they comprehend the value of their bodies to the leering older couple, as they sleep in their hosts' bed, are unable to access their clothing, and as they become aware of each other's beauty trying on the single caftan left for them. They return to their hotel to a night of joyous lovemaking and stay in bed the entire day until dinner. Sitting at a restaurant they suddenly become self-consciously but also narcissistically aware that others are looking at them and desire their bodies. Their insecurity and their hesitation regarding the marriage commitment they have come to Venice to consider is thus revealed as being charged by the fear of losing the other sexually or being "tortured by each other's beauty." This leads to grotesque sadomasochistic fantasies of punishment for their "beauty" in which Mary plays with the idea of having Colin's arms and legs amputated so that he would remain her passive sex slave, and Colin would imprison Mary in an escapeless sex machine which would operate continuously and for years until her death.

"They spend three days in the room intoxicated by Robert and Caroline's vibrations,"[13] is how Schrader explains Colin and Mary's enslavement to the desires of the older couple that occurs in this Dionysian phase, which breaks their instinctive will to flee what they both sense is a threat—as in Visconti's *Death in Venice* critique of the sudden overwhelming Dionysian spirit of Gustav von Aschenbach, which forces him to stay in cholera-infested Venice and to die there all for the impossible obsession with Tadzio's idealistic youthful beauty, which inspired him to compose new work. In *Strangers* there is similar self-destructive paralysis. Mary wakes from a nightmare about a photo of Colin she spied at Robert's apartment. She is troubled by the photograph, but does nothing. Colin also questions why she said nothing when Robert hit him in the stomach. Are they both becoming seduced by a sexualized dominance that plays to their vanity of desirability and their loss of rationality? The segment also underscores in a metafilmic way the critique of the neo-decadent films as attracting audiences to the fetishized, sexualized politics in the same manner that fascism seduced and controlled the masses. This sparked not only Pauline Kael's aforementioned diatribe against Visconti's *The Damned*, but also the 1974 Susan Sontag essay "Fascinating Fascism," exploring the aesthetics of Leni Riefenstahl's photography and films, which supposedly connects the "glamour" of the SS to neo-decadent cinema which eroticizes Nazism as sadomasochistic theater.[14]

Schrader admits that "beauty is itself dangerous" in this film and perhaps in much of his oeuvre. But he also suggests the importance of audience seduction: "Design became a huge factor. Originally Robert was a hustler in a bad apartment. He [Schrader] had to polish it like a delicious apple for the audience to want to bite in only to discover the maggots in it."[15] And like the Italian neo-decadent films of the 1970s that were set in the period of the 1930s through 1950s, the director uses a voyeuristically wandering camera from the establishing scene of the palazzo apartment to the tragic ending in the police station. To make the apartment even more mysterious and Venice more darkly exciting, Schrader exploited the city's Moorish roots and "made it Istanbul."[16] Most of the exterior shots select architecture of Moorish or Arabic flavor rather than the usual tourist monuments and spaces, the one exception being the Piazza San Marco. There also, we do not see the architectural icons, but instead a sea of tourists and patrons in the sunlight, a seemingly safe place for the couple adrift in the masses, before Robert comes to collect them. The diegetic and non-diegetic music of the film underscores the exoticism with Turkish and Middle Eastern melodies, which underscores the harem quality of the scene between Caroline and Mary in their caftans discussing the presence of men without men being present. Puccini also is heard sporadically in the film for more accessible romantic opulence, but certainly also as a tribute to the operatic drama of the neo-decadent films by Visconti, Cavani, and Bertolucci.

Schrader points to the "neo-*Conformist* style," referring to Bertolucci's film on Mussolini's seductive/deadly Italy, his fluid camera, and dolly-to-dolly edits that he uses not only in *Strangers*, but in such other films of eroticized danger as *American Gigolo* and *Cat People*.[17] The literary/musical references of the Italian neo-decadent films also influence Schrader's redux. Visconti's *The Damned* suggests *Macbeth* and Wagner's *Götterdämmerung* [Twilight of the Gods], and later for *Death in Venice* there is Thomas Mann and Gustav

Mahler; Cavani's *The Night Porter* features Salome and John the Baptist along with Mozart; and ultimately there is the notorious overlay of the Marquis de Sade's *120 Days of Sodom* onto Mussolini's brutal last stand, in Pasolini's *Salò*. For Schrader, Puccini in sound and opera in general are intended for visual reference, while the narrative one is found in classical literature—"going into the Underworld"—and as Colin and Mary allow themselves to return to the palazzo apartment, they are "being drawn back there by Caroline on the River Styx at the end of the film."[18]

VI

What makes Schrader's fable of a crypto-fascism that intends to protect the patriarchy from female empowerment, liberalism, and the perversions it harbors itself so potent is that it also plays with the original problem of the neo-decadent genre, which in its critique often enforces the eroticism or titillation that underpinned fascism's psychosexual lure in the first place. However, the contemporary setting, even with its romantic Venetian qualities, manages to underscore without ambiguity the attractiveness of the liberal British couple, and show the fascist couple to be unhealthy, parasitical, and grotesque. Robert's grandiose enshrinement of a "heroic" past offers little to conquer the freedoms of the present.

Andrew Hewitt suggests that the very basis of the original genre lies in the fascination with the "erotics of power," and fascism's "psychosexual manifestations of homosexual narcissism."[19] Ravetto also sees these films exposing fascist economies "that extend beyond historical fascism—reaching into discourses of victimization, gender difference, capitalism and bourgeois moralism."[20] But in Schrader's update, the battle may be lost but the war is won: there are no truly "fascinating fascists" here. The climax of the film provides a sadomasochistic tableau that emphasizes the self-indulgent qualities of the liberal democratic Western world and not the dire, unstable problems of inter-war Europe. The drugging of Mary is to literally silence and disempower the woman who can now only witness. The pathetic childlike plea by the film's object of beauty, Colin, that he would to do anything their captors want in order to help Mary, and who does nothing extraordinary to free himself from the weaker grasp of an older man, is less the symbolic marching of victims into Nazi death camps without resistance and far more a conclusion of Robert's hunt in which Colin would narcissistically "sacrifice" himself to some sexual game concocted by the couple. He only realizes Robert and Caroline's unyielding cruelty of objectification as they slash his throat. Yet both the passive victims of the death camps and Colin's passive murder are naïve miscalculations, born of resignation or even trust, by these targets regarding the actual intentions of fascism.

The killing of Colin "the child" by the Venetian would-be patriarch reflects the same theme on a more reductive level as the destruction of the youths though humiliation, torture, and murder in Pasolini's *Salò*. And while it is also dictated by four grotesque and ugly men representing the remains of the fascist government, there are also the young guards and the constant suggestion that anything sexual (but also murderous) might occur for the sake of demonstrating Hewitt's "erotics of power." The POV in *Salò* is often that of a torturer or the debauched older perpetrators. Other times it is not, and instead suggests the POV of the camera, representing the unspoken voyeur, or the audience spectator. As Forceville indicates about *Strangers*, "many shots can be neither unequivocally attributed to the external narrator, nor to the spying Robert."[21] "Since the context makes it clear that it is not Robert who is watching—in some of these shots he is himself in the frame—these are not POV shots, but shots for which the self-conscious external narrator is responsible, and which stress the viewer's voyeurism."[22]

Despite *Salò*'s orgy of depravity, it is Schrader's *The Comfort of Strangers* that is the more socio-politically powerful film in retrospect and the more effective in allegorizing the destruction of personal freedom by totalitarian fascism, given that *The Damned*, *The Night Porter*, *The Conformist*, *Salò*, etc. are period pieces that provide cinematic glamour and nostalgia of the era tied to its horror show. Schrader's film is as much of a warning as the films of the 1970s, but his takes place in contemporary Europe, with images of contemporary life identifiable to the audience of the day and beyond. Fascists are not in leading power, and much of what was considered sexually taboo in the narratives of the period neo-decadent films is part of everyday life in the 1990s. Here Colin and Mary are the audience's titillation, not the fascists, and we feel pity for the couple and their sense of freedom and security. Robert and Caroline represent potent warnings of what even yet exists and manipulates, and can too easily return out of the shadows even in a new century and ask, "Do you need help?"

NOTES

1. Kriss Ravetto, *The Unmaking of Fascist Aesthetics* (Minneapolis: University of Minnesota Press, 2001), 135.
2. Paul Schrader, *Transcendental Style in Film: Ozu, Bresson, Dreyer* (Berkeley: University of California Press, 1972; reprinted, New York: Da Capo Press, 1988).
3. Andersch, Brecht, "Hardcore: Paul Schrader in the 1970s-4," *Open Space/SFMOMA*, September 3, 2010, https://openspace.sfmoma.org/2010/09/hardcore-paul-schrader-in-the-70s-4/
4. See English translation from the Russian of annotation and excerpts of Olga A. Dzhumaylo, "'Venetian Text' and the Aesthetics of Reflections in Paul Schrader's *The Comfort of Strangers* based on the novel by Ian McEwan." Bulletin of Perm University. Russian and Foreign Philology, 10:4 (2018).

5. Paul Schrader, *The Comfort of Strangers*, Italy/USA: Erre Produzioni/Sovereign Pictures, 1990.
6. Charles Forceville, "The Metaphor 'COLIN IS A CHILD' in Ian McEwan's, Harold Pinter's, and Paul Schrader's *The Comfort of Strangers*", *Metaphor and Symbol*, 14:3 (1999), 179.
7. Ibid., 186.
8. Ibid., 187.
9. Ibid., 188.
10. Kevin Jackson, ed., *Schrader on Schrader & Other Writings* (London: Faber and Faber, 1990), 200.
11. Martin Stiglegger, "Karneval des Todes. Luchino Viscontis *La cauduta degli dei*," in *Film Konzepte Heft 48: Luchino Visconti*, edited by Jörn Glasenapp (Munich: edition text+kritik, 2017), 78.
12. Neil Maizels, "Narcissus Rejects—the Surrender to Beauty vs Aesthetical Anguish," *Aesthetic Conflict and its Clinical Relevance*, edited by Meg Harris Williams (Harris Meltzer Trust, 2018), 133–5.
13. Paul Schrader et al., "Audio Commentary," *The Comfort of Strangers*, special edition. Directed by Paul Schrader (Twentieth Century Fox Home Entertainment International UK, 2018), DVD.
14. Sontag, Susan, "Fascinating Fascism," *Under the Sign of Saturn* (New York: Farrar, Straus, Giroux, 1980), 84.
15. Schrader, "Audio Commentary."
16. Ibid.
17. Ibid.
18. Ibid. Beyond these classical references, Schrader's filmic version of the killing of the "innocent" man-child Colin by Robert, the elitist and sadistic Venetian, can also carry the subtext of the killing of Christians by the Romans, if it is filtered through the experiences of Schrader's "strict Calvinist upbringing [which] has played a critical role in shaping Schrader's filmmaking . . . Biblical characters serve as prototypes for his own creations; his films are peppered with Christian iconography and theological debates . . ." Deborah Allison, "Paul Schrader," *The Comfort of Strangers, Directed by Paul Schrader* (DVD/Blu-ray special edition booklet) (London: BFI, 2018), 18.
19. Andrew Hewitt, *Political Inversions: Homosexuality, Fascism, and the Modernist Imaginary* (Stanford: Stanford University, 1996), 38–9.
20. Ravetto, 12.
21. Charles Forceville, "The Conspiracy in *The Comfort of Strangers*—Narration in the Novel and the Film," *Language and Literature*, 11:2 (2014), 13.
22. Ibid., 15.

CHAPTER 9

"Just Being Transparent Baby": Surveillance Culture, Digitization, and Self-regulation in Paul Schrader's *The Canyons*

James Slaymaker

Upon its release in 2013, *The Canyons* was unanimously dismissed as a crass erotic thriller with little ambition other than to turn a quick profit, and although a small handful of critics have acknowledged its virtues in the intervening years, the feature is still largely considered the low point of Schrader's body of work. Stephen Rodrick of *The New York Times* writes that the film "drag[s] endlessly," and that the prevailing atmosphere is one of "monotony" and "deadness."[1] Writing for the same publication, Manohla Dargis writes that "*Sunset Boulevard* is narrated by a corpse; *The Canyons* is overrun with them," while Christy Lemire of RogerEbert.com complains of the "flatness and tedium," before declaring it a "micro-budget train wreck."[2] The reputation of *The Canyons* is so poor that Chris Knight of the *National Post* goes as far as to describe 2017's *First Reformed* as Schrader's "directorial redemption" for his earlier failure.[3] This chapter will work against the grain of the hostility which has dominated the discourse surrounding *The Canyons* and argue that it is, in fact, an ambitious, nuanced film worthy of deeper consideration. Curiously, the aesthetic strategy of affective disconnect which the majority of critics have bemoaned is key to understanding the themes that Schrader is tackling in the film. *The Canyons* is a brazen formal experiment which explores alienation in the age of digital surveillance. Its protagonist, Christian (James Deen), is an utterly isolated individual who internalizes the inhuman gaze of the CCTV camera to the extent that he is not only alienated from his peers, but also from his own emotional and phenomenological experience.

Interpreted from this angle, *The Canyons* reveals itself to be in alignment with Schrader's other, far more esteemed, cinematic portraits of lonely men, such as *Taxi Driver* (1976, Scorsese), *Bringing Out the Dead* (1999, Scorsese),

Light Sleeper (1992, Schrader), *Hardcore* (1979, Schrader), *American Gigolo* (1980, Schrader) and *First Reformed*. What distinguishes *The Canyons* from these character studies is that it pointedly denies any sense of transcendence; while Schrader's lonely men typically take a course of action which enables them to ultimately break through their isolation and achieve a higher level of consciousness, Christian lacks any sense of higher purpose and remains stubbornly tethered to a materialistic, secular environment. The question of why Schrader decided to construct a feature around such a vapid, irredeemable character is one which plagued many of the critical responses to the film, and it is worth asking in the context of exploring what *The Canyons* says about consumerism and solipsism within contemporary American society. *The Canyons* is undoubtedly a satire of the twenty-first-century yuppie, but it is also a study of new forms of subjectivity engendered by radical paradigms of digital surveillance which encourage a mentality of paranoia, emotional indifference, and perpetual performance.

Few American filmmakers have produced such a large and esteemed catalogue of film criticism as Paul Schrader, which makes the act of writing about his directorial work a peculiar challenge. Before embarking on a career in Hollywood, Schrader had already established himself as a major force in film academia with his published MA thesis *Transcendental Style in Film*. In this work, Schrader, inspired by the theological framework developed by the French phenomenologists Henri Agel and Amédée Ayfre, works against the grain of the dogmatic materialism of the formalist and semiotic scholarly approaches which dominated American cinema scholarship during the late 1960s and focuses on the potential of film form to express a metaphysical spiritual reality. Schrader finds commonalities in the approaches of three filmmakers he describes as being exemplary practitioners of spiritual film form: Ozu, Bresson, and Dreyer. He argues that all three directors exemplify an approach to filmmaking he terms the "Transcendental Style." This style allows for the expression of the divine by first denying the traditional pleasures of conventional film form through a strict adherence to austerity, before finally unleashing a cathartic outpouring of feeling in the final moment. This climax creates the sensation that the material world has been transcended and the artwork has achieved a direct connection with the ephemeral essence that exists beyond lived experience. Although Schrader's work as a critic is deeply informed by his Calvinist upbringing, it is important to note that his conception of the spiritual in film is not necessarily tied to any particular religious denomination. Rather, in his definition: "The Transcendent is beyond normal sense experience and that which it transcends is, by definition, the immanent."[4] As Hamilton observes, although Schrader's own films do not wholly adhere to the transcendental style as outlined in his thesis (they are far too concerned with psychological realism, traditional emotional involvement, and the conventions of narrative), his work is deeply informed by his conception of a "transcendental universe."[5]

This is most clearly expressed in Schrader's portraits of masculine alienation, in which a protagonist disconnected from his immediate environment "strives toward the ineffable and invisible," and their struggle is ultimately rewarding in a "moment of redemption, when ordinary reality is transcended."[6] These works may not function as a direct expression of the transcendental, but they dramatize man's relationship *with* the transcendental. Schrader's conception of alienation is rooted in Ayfre's concept of "disparity," a dialectical clash between the realm of the carnal and the realm of the sacred which lies at the centre of human experience, a result of the "insertion of 'human density' into the cold context of the everyday."[7] Protagonists such as Travis Bickle, Reverend Toller, Frank Pierce, Jake Van Dorn, and Yukio Mishima are suspended between the degraded secular world and the immaterial realm of the sacred which lies beyond it. Schrader's description of the existential hero of Bresson's *Diary of a Country Priest* (1951, Bresson) is revealing: "What seems to be a rejection by the environment is more accurately a rejection by the priest—and not because he wishes to estrange himself, but because he is the unwilling instrument of an overwhelming and self-mortifying passion."[8]

In a similar manner, Schrader's troubled characters feel uncomfortable within a social environment they find morally repellent and, through their dedication to some moral purpose, demonstrate a virtue—justice, courage, temperance, self-sacrifice—which elevates them to that upward plane of transcendence in a moment which liberates them from the shackles of their earthly malaise. At first blush, then, *The Canyons*' Christian may seem dissimilar from the aforementioned existential heroes. He is not a wilfully isolated outsider, but a stylish society player with a bottomless trust fund, a glamorous girlfriend, and lucrative career. His home is a chintzy McMansion complete with pool, Jacuzzi, and private bar, and filled to the brim with state-of-the-art luxury items. His mind is free of the lofty spiritual concerns of the typical Schrader protagonist and is concerned solely with shallow and materialistic desires. Yet Christian registers a profound disaffection with his life. He has no real friends to discuss his feelings with, no true sense of connection in his romantic partnership, and no trust in psychoanalysis (he only visits his therapist because his father threatened to cut his access to his spending account if he refused). He gathers no fulfillment from his career as a producer of low-budget B-movies, or the material wealth it affords. He drifts through the sphere of high-end consumerism with disinterest, his life a never-ending cycle of dinner dates at luxury restaurants, gym sessions, and orgies.

The Schrader character which Christian most closely resembles, then, is *American Gigolo*'s Julian Kaye (Richard Gere). With *American Gigolo*, Schrader introduced moviegoers to the new yuppie archetype which, as John Potvin notes, was the product of a:

> Consumer-driven typology propelled largely by savvy marketing agents unabashedly flirting with generating desire amongst a growing male consumer base no longer afraid to display pleasure and desire through their clothing in a period of rapid economic prosperity and expansion.[9]

The film portrays 1980s Los Angeles as a modern-day Gomorrah, a land characterized by unchecked consumer spending, amoral indulgence, and the selfish pursuit of sensual pleasure. Julian is the consummate consumer, a high-earning callboy who defines himself purely through his fashionable physical appearance and arsenal of luxury commodities. Schrader's film, however, locates the spiritual emptiness at the core of this seemingly joyous character. Trapped in a series of meaningless, transitory sexual flings with the bored housewives of the elite class, Julian is a solitary, aimless figure. His copious consumption and obsession with maintaining an external image of glamour cannot disguise the fact that there is an essential void at his core. His misguided belief that self-determination may be achieved purely through consumer spending, through building a lifestyle based on standardized images of material success propagandized by advertisements, results in a destabilization of the self.

Three decades later, the yuppie remains in full force, economic inequality is more egregious than ever, and the twin poles of predatory capitalism and consumer culture remain fixed as the all-encompassing Gods of post-Fordist America. Christian is marred by a malaise that is similar to Julian's, though Schrader's vision of the American consumer has grown considerably more pessimistic in the intervening years. While Julian's narcissism is expressed through his excessive vanity and ostentatious behavior, Christian is an egomaniacal predator whose chief characteristic is his sociopathic sense of entitlement. Furthermore, Julian gleans a genuine glee from buying and displaying possessions, while Christian only demonstrates an intense dissatisfaction. The difference in attitude is expressed formally. Julian is introduced speeding down the Los Angeles highway in a convertible Mercedes, sporting designer sunglasses and an Armani suit. Set to the fast-paced rhythms of Blondie's *Call Me* and drawing from the visual language of television advertisements and music videos, Schrader seduces the viewer into the decadence of Julian's lifestyle, even though the emphasis on commodities rather than the body of the human protagonist immediately hints at the film's major theme, the loss of the self within the culture of consumerism. No such sense of seduction is registered during Christian's introduction. Where the visual scheme of *American Gigolo* emphasises speed, both on the diegetic level (Julian speeds through the LA freeway) and on the formal level (the fast-paced, fragmented cutting and rapid camera movement), *The Canyons* emphasises stasis. All four lead characters—Christian, his live-in girlfriend Tara (Lindsay Lohan), his assistant Gina (Amanda Brooks), and Gina's boyfriend Ryan (Nolan Funk)—are seated finishing a dull dinner at the Chateau Marmont. Tara, Gina, and Ryan are introduced in a series of flat, frontal one-shots, each character's eyeline angled toward the camera. The neutral lighting, flat angles, and sluggish pacing de-glamorizes the opulent environment and the expensive commodities on display. Although the location is crowded, the ambient sound is dialed down to near-silence, giving the scene an eerie sense of somnolent unreality. An awkward, stilted conversation plays out on the soundtrack, but the speaking voice is unrelated to the character that is shown on-screen. The non-synchronic sound creates an immediate sense of cognitive and perceptual confusion. In the classical style, the close-up is the filmmaking technique which invites the viewer into a closer engagement with the character and their emotional state through shot-reverse-shot patterns which clearly orientate us in relation to clearly delineated narrative rhythms and character relationships. In the opening scene of *The Canyons*, however, the viewer is uncertain how the characters relate to each other spatially, and this upsets our desire to determine how they relate to each other on an emotional and narrative level. The wilful obscuration of spatial relations purposefully upsets the identification process, immediately establishing the theme of interpersonal estrangement and foregrounding Christian's disconnect from the social world. That we are denied easy identification with any of these faces plunges us into Christian's alienated subjectivity. We are unable to empathize with the film's supporting characters just as Christian is unable to forge genuine connections with any of his peers. The sound and image only become synchronized when we cut to Christian for the first time, who is absent-mindedly playing on his smartphone instead of focusing on the discussion at hand.

"I like the idea of somebody looking at something they can't have," Christian tells Tara later that evening, explaining his fetish for inviting over other men to watch them have sex but denying them the act of penetration. "It's a guy thing," he continues. "Power and control." Their partner Reed (Christopher Zeischegg) arrives, dressed down in cheap distressed jeans and adolescent frosted tips, and clearly of a lower social standing. Christian takes pleasure in Reed's awe at the grandeur of his abode, and cockily parades Tara in front of him as if she was part of the furniture. "She's hot right?" Christian patronizingly asks. Reed awkwardly concurs "way hotter than the photos you showed me." Following Christian's instructions, Tara then leads Reed to the couch, briefly kisses him. Christian follows close behind, recording the pair on his phone. Schrader's camera tracks from over his shoulder, so the viewer perceives the tryst through the mediation of the camera phone, framed in the centre of the composition. Once Reed has been aroused, Christian pulls Tara away and tells him to undress. Christian's casual disdain for others, his inflated sense of self-regard, and his view of Tara as an instrument to demonstrate his superiority establishes him as a character who embodies the "phantasies of power, omnipotence, mastery, and control" that Steve Neale identifies as being central to the narcissistic condition that besets the prototypical Schrader protagonist.[10] But what is most fascinating about this scene is the role of the electronic recording device within it. After pulling Reed away from Tara, Christian places the phone on the couch, positioned so that its camera can capture the entire room, and engages in relations with Tara, energized by the twin gazes of the masturbating Reed and the iPhone lens. Schrader cuts away from the characters and tracks in on the iPhone, as it impassively captures the action, divorced from any grounding human element. At this point, Schrader cuts to a reverse angle, taken from the perspective of the iPhone camera. The image is positioned at a slanted angle so that the heads of the characters are cropped off by the top of the frame. What is highlighted in this moment is the disinterested, subjectless gaze of the digital iPhone camera as well as the splintered subjectivity of Christian, who is focused not on his own phenomenological experience but on the gaze of an imagined audience. As Christian is unable to focus on the moment as it is lived but instead imagines it through the camera lens, sex is rendered a performative act rather than a moment of intimacy. Christian has internalized the gaze of the disinterested surveillance camera which saturates his landscape, and the resulting self-regulation he demonstrates renders him an emotionally numb, isolated figure. The purposefully affectless, distancing aesthetic style of *The Canyons* thus enables the viewer to enter Christian's own self-alienated subjectivity. Not only does Schrader encourage the viewer to view the diegetic world from an icy remove which aligns their vision with Christian's disconnected perspective, but he employs a number of formal strategies to alienate the viewer from Christian himself, framing him as a small figure within a dwarfing architectural space, positioning him behind planes of glass, or filtering his image through the lens of a diegetic camera. As such, it is difficult to feel close to him as a subject. This aesthetic alienation is a purposeful technique which foregrounds Christian's estrangement from his *own* interiority.

Figure 9.1 Christian is obscured behind a pane of glass in his Malibu mansion.

Ian Murphy perceptively argues that Schrader's portraits of modern alienation frame the spiritual crisis of each protagonist as "a crisis of the body," and hence intertwine "inextricable issues of personal identity and embodied experience."[11] Like the films that Murphy uses as case studies, *The Canyons* is constructed around the theme of the body functioning as a "metaphysical prison in which the protagonists are helplessly trapped," but what distinguishes the film is that it tackles this issue through an engagement with ideas regarding the nature of bodily discipline and self-regulation in the era of digital surveillance.[12] In this sense, *The Canyons* offers a variation on Foucault's concept of *panopticisme* within the context of a more advanced, dispersed regime of digital surveillance. In 1787, Jeremy Bentham proposed that the ideal prison would be a circular structure in which blocks of individual cells face a tall watchtower at the centre, in which a single guard is housed. Because the structure of the prison allows for the guard to monitor the prisoners without them being able to return his gaze, the prisoners will internalize the oppressive eye of the onlooker and effectively police their own behavior.[13] Foucault draws on Bentham's panopticon to sketch his own model of power relations within modern "disciplinary societies." For Foucault, the dominance of monitoring mechanisms in public spaces creates the impression of omniscient surveillance.[14] As the human subject feels that they are being watched at all times, they feel pressured to conduct their behavior according to the expectations of the dominant authority. Within a "society," individual agency is thus circumscribed, giving rise to ideal citizens who live according to the socially conditioned expectations of obedience and normality. Modes of surveillance therefore instil a perpetual sense of paranoia within all citizens, which leads to a visual economy of self-regulation (*panopticisme*). In *Postscript on the Societies of Control*, Gilles Deleuze builds on Foucault's theory to argue that the "disciplinary society" has evolved into a "society of control." Whereas an individual in a disciplinary society is constantly moving through varied closed institutions, each one marked by a different form of surveillance (the school, the workplace, the military, etc.), these boundaries dissolve in a society of control, wherein "one is never finished with anything—the corporation, the educational system, the armed services being metastable states coexisting in one and the same modulation."[15] Control societies therefore "no longer operate by confining people but through continuous control and instant communication."[16] *The Canyons* investigates both Deleuze and Foucault's models of social control while simultaneously expanding upon them, by considering elements of synoptic surveillance alongside the traditional panoptical modes.

Randall Poster observes that the rapid proliferation of consumer-grade electronic surveillance over the early years of the twenty-first century has given rise to a "superpanopticon"; advances in digital technologies have filled contemporary society with computerized eyes which submit human activity to an unprecedented level of monitoring.[17] As a result of this, the panoptical mode of a small group observing a large swath of people is augmented by synoptic methods of surveillance which, per Mathiesen, allow "the many to see and contemplate the few."[18] For Jamais Cascio, these two modes have fused into a new regime of "participatory surveillance," which has become the primary organizational principle of power relations in contemporary society. While in the panoptical model, citizens have surveillance devices forced upon them against their will, in the participatory model they willingly subject themselves to their mechanical gaze, as well as using these technologies to keep track of their peers:

> This constant surveillance is done by the citizens themselves, and is done by choice. It's not imposed on us by a malevolent bureaucracy or faceless corporations. The participatory panopticon will be the emergent result of myriad independent rational decisions, a bottom-up version of the constantly watched society.[19]

This concept of the participatory panopticon, based upon the fusion of the digital and physical realms in contemporary control societies, is manifest in *The Canyons*. The social environment of the film is built upon a combination of panoptic and synoptic surveillance strategies, as the characters compulsively mediate their experiences through iPhones, webcams, and handheld digital cameras, while also monitoring the behavior of others. *The Canyons* begins with a montage of abandoned movie theatres, ranging from giant multiplexes, to mall theatres, to small independent arthouses. The soundtrack is filled with heavy, discordant, electronic beats which set an immediate apocalyptic atmosphere. Schrader's decision to open the feature with images of closed cineplexes positions *The Canyons* at a bifurcation point, the moment of rupture in the genealogy of cinematic history at which classical paradigms of cinematic production and spectatorship is being overwhelmingly replaced by the language of digital imaging and new media. Laura Mulvey writes of this turn in the dominant visual regime: "cinema's centenary coincided with the arrival of a technology that created a divide between the 'old' and the 'new' media [. . .] the fact that all forms of information and communication can now be translated into binary coding with a single system signals more precisely the end of an era."[20]

This shift in the ontological basis of society is reflected in *The Canyons*, as digital technologies give rise to a radical paradigm of participatory surveillance which shapes subjectivity and fosters a mentality of perpetual performativity. Rather than internalizing the authoritarian gaze of Foucault's guard, Christian internalizes the detached gaze of consumer-grade surveillance devices as the lens through which he experiences life. The digital surveillance camera is marked by detachment and alienation from human emotion. By internalizing this gaze, Christian becomes self-alienated; he is unable to fully engage with lived experience and can only perceive of the outside world through an emotional disconnect. Trapped within the isolating sphere of his own self-surveillance and suspended between the digital and physical realms, Christian embodies the new mode of selfhood which Sherry Turkle outlines in her study *Alone Together*: "[D]evices provide space for the emergence of a new state of the self, itself, split between the screen and the physical real, wired into existence through technology."²¹

Unlike films such as *The Conversation* (1974, Coppola) and *Blow Out* (1981, De Palma), the surveillance network here is not a hidden entity subjecting citizens to an authoritarian gaze against their will but instead is open and participatory; characters happily forfeit their right to privacy and submit themselves to the data stream. Christian is not the only character who is addicted to the camera eye; the Los Angeles of *The Canyons* is packed with young hopefuls who exist in a state of semi-fame. Their longing to break into the realm of the instant celebrity reflects a cultural mentality which Caroline Hamilton identifies as being the result of "the ubiquity of mobile telephones, the rise of reality TV, along with internet 'narrowcasting' via blogs and YouTube," and relies on the constant "documentation and exhibition of everyday life."²² An early scene lingers on the body of Ryan as he poses in his underwear for a photoshoot. Ryan is positioned in middle-ground, while in the foreground a digital camera is placed next to a computer image which displays a static image of his body in a photo-editing program. For the purpose of amassing social and monetary capital, Ryan willingly allows for his body to be transformed into pure spectacle.

Christian's inability to feel present is a symptom of the self-displacement that is the common type of existence within this landscape of perpetual self-surveillance. "Nobody has a private life anymore," he authoritatively tells Tara at one point, as both characters sit in the living room of his mansion, a cold, oversized interior with huge windows collapsing the boundary between inside and outside. Dominated by curtain walls, marble floors, and septic designs, and coded with a near-monochromatic color palette of muted blues, greys and whites, and metallic silvers, Christian's minimalistic home is a cold, antiseptic environment, clearly designed for decorative effect rather than for practical purposes. It is so free of individualized touches, in fact, that it resembles a public space such as a showroom or a chic hotel lobby rather than an actual living space with a personal history. It is a reflection of the "architectural uniformity" which Manuel Castells identifies as being the dominant mode of postmodern urban spaces, as "architecture escapes from the history and culture of each society and becomes captured into the new imaginary."²³ In order to illuminate the intangibility of postmodern architecture, much of *The Canyons* unfolds within places of spatial liminality, such as balconies, patios, windows, and doors, to create moments of imbrication which complicate the boundary between internal and external space.

Figure 9.2 Christian and Tara enclosed in their prison-like living space.

In *American Gigolo*, Julian's apartment functions as his sole space of solitude, a personalized place which offers him brief respites from the relentless world of performative appearances which he is forced to engage with socially. Christian, however, feels no more at home in his own mansion than he does in any other building in the city. The fluid, unstable relations between inside and outside within the visual environments of *The Canyons* therefore add an extra layer to the film's formal concern with the dissolving boundaries between private and public. Solitude can never truly be attained within the LA of *The Canyons*, just as real feeling can never pierce through the interplay of artificial appearances which defines social life in the film.

Schrader's experimentation with the formal properties of the digital image, viewer identification, and sound design informs its exploration of individual alienation in the context of the digital era. The low-fi visual language of *The Canyons* approximates the appearance of the very kind of footage that the consumer-grade video-making devices that permeate the diegetic world of the film capture. The viewer is thus constantly reminded that they are viewing the events of the film through the same devices that the characters are slaves to. Furthermore, there are several scenes in which the layers of the image are multiplied, as characters are shown rewatching or manipulating footage captured in earlier parts of the narrative. As such, *The Canyons* constantly reminds the viewer that digital machines are so central to modern sociality that they do not merely record the real, they play an active role in shaping real events. This combination of the disparate modes of classical narrative immersion and modernist reflexivity results in a pronounced tension between the viewer's investment in the diegetic proceedings and their knowledge that the artwork is a manufactured construct.

The friction between authenticity and fabrication parallels the nature of Christian's lived experience. For Christian, life is not something to be simply lived, but something to be self-consciously moulded for an imagined audience; as such, he lacks a stable sense of self, and instead takes on the external properties of whatever he feels the social situation demands. "We're all actors, aren't we?", he muses at a low moment, reflecting on the societal pressure he feels to engage in performative behavior. "We all act differently, depending on the situation we're in. Who we're around. I don't act the same way with you as I do when I'm with Tara." Christian feels like an "actor" in the social world, forced to cycle through a series of shallow personas rather than being able to embody a stable and fully integrated identity. The film's formal interconnection between performative behavior and a low-fi digital aesthetic calls to mind the mechanisms of reality television. As Christopher Lasch observes in *The Culture of Narcissism*, the trend of reality television that came to dominate airwaves over the late twentieth century contained the formerly ominous mode of surveillance within a safe, inviting form. The popularity of such programs naturalized the notion of the omnipresent camera eye, by encouraging the mentality that being recorded is desirable, and public visibility is something to aspire to rather than avoid:

> We live in a world of images and echoes that arrest experience and play it back in slow motion. Cameras and recording machines not only transcribe experience but alter its quality, giving to much modern life the character of an enormous echo chamber, a hall of mirrors.[24]

The culture of narcissism has only intensified in the intervening years, buttressed by intertwined developments in digital media visibility, instant celebrity, and social media. An environment based on the fusion of panoptic and synoptic surveillance, in which media visibility is easier to obtain than ever, results in, as Thomas De Zengotita describes, "lives composed of an unprecedented fusion of the real and the represented, lives shaped by a culture of performance," resulting in a new form of consciousness that he terms "the mediated person."[25]

This culture of performance is the basis of *The Canyons*, a film in which there is no clear distinction between authenticity and performance, exhibitionism and voyeurism, directors and actors. Christian's fascination with constructing different identities according to his social situation, in his life suspended between the realm of the physical and the realm of the virtual, is symptomatic of what Sherry Turkle describes as the new societal condition in which "many more people experience identity as a set of roles that can be mixed and matched whose diverse demands need to be negotiated."[26] Therefore, although it is not incorrect to describe Christian as a depthless character, it is more accurate to describe *The Canyons* as a film which visualizes the loss of individual personality in a landscape saturated with media images and luxury commodities. And therein lies the major difference between *American Gigolo* and *The Canyons*: Julian may construct an identity through advertising images in an attempt to distract from the essential void at his center, but there remains an essential self which may be reached, and is glimpsed in the moments when he is alone. Christian, in contrast, shows no such sign of humanity. Behind his artificial façade lies only a void; he is a solitary and obscure figure who remains as distant to the viewer as he does to the people around him.

Christian's sense of emptiness is rooted in what Patrick McHugh, in an analysis of *Gravity's Rainbow*, calls "the affect particular to white male postmodernism," which involves staking out a sense of self which exists in opposition to "the forces of capitalism, patriarchy, and colonialism" which have constructed and protected that white male selfhood.[27] As the white postmodern male is only able to construct his identity in relation to marginalized others, he has no essential, stable identity, and he works through these anxieties regarding his own lack of selfhood by projecting them onto the cultural Other. Christian is undeniably a product of all three of these cultural forces, and though he does not register this conflict consciously, his fundamental distrust of bodies which differ from the recognizable mode of the cis white heterosexual male subject reveals a fear of his identity being destabilized by alterity. The film's primary narrative through-line revolves around Christian's fear that Tara is cheating on him with Ryan. Discovering that Tara used to be romantically involved with Ryan instils within him an intense feeling of paranoia, and he responds by enforcing invasive methods of surveillance to track her every movement, including paying men to follow her, encouraging her friends to make regular phone calls to him to keep him up to date with her actions, and interrogating her at length regarding the content of her day. Christian's obsessive watch over her is primarily facilitated through his monitoring of her online posts, texts, and email exchanges—the digital trace created by her constant use of social-media feeds is hacked and used against her. Christian's overwhelming fear that the woman he views as his subordinate plaything may assert herself and express her sexuality with another man reflects his unfortunate tendency to displace his own insecurities onto the Other, and his actions are primarily motivated by a desire to defend himself against usurpation from that Other. Christian is therefore a prisoner of his own design, projecting a falsified persona of white male success which he feels completely disconnected from yet is desperate to defend at all costs.

It is notable, then, that the major turning point of the narrative occurs when Christian's identity as a heterosexual male is most violently threatened, and his intertwined sexual and social anxieties reach a peak. In the second group-sex scene of the film, the power dynamic which structured the first one is aggressively upended. Christian's control over the situation is wrestled away from him by Tara as she forces him to perform fellatio on another man, while teasingly commenting: "That's what I want to see." This is the one scene in the film which deviates from the established, distanced visual language. The room is darkened, with the only source of lighting being a luminescent red-and-green disco ball which throws abstract shapes around the walls. The camera is no longer static, but rapidly captures fragments of bodies in a series of quick cuts. As the scene breaks down into an impressionistic blur of colour and motion, the image becomes increasingly difficult to decipher. This shift in the film's visual scheme marks the first time that Christian falls out of control of his tightly controlled world of pristine appearances, being forced to submit to the gaze of another rather than imposing his own. This illustrates Bruzzi's thesis that, in male-oriented cinema, "doubts concerning masculine authority often come to be expressed as a loss of control over the mise en scène."[28]

Christian reflects on this loss of power in the following scene, during which he is uncharacteristically open with his psychiatrist (Gus Van Sant). He tellingly voices his concerns through the metaphors of acting and directing: "I didn't feel like I was in control. I felt objectified. The way the two of them watched and told me what to do. It doesn't usually go down like that. Usually I'm the one directing the scene. It made me feel like an actor. Which is kind of how I feel when I'm here." Christian is comfortable with performance and self-objectification, as it occurs on his own terms. However, being forced to submit his body to the female gaze in a homosexual act risks destabilizing his carefully cultivated identity in a way that he considers unbearable.

Like so many Schrader features, *The Canyons* ends in bloodshed. Schrader's lonely men are often driven toward extreme acts of violence as a means of escaping their current situation, exemplifying the theme of "regeneration through violence" which Richard Slotkin identifies as being a central motif in American literature.[29] Travis Bickle's climactic shoot-up of a local brothel is committed in an attempt to lift him from his earthly shackles into the realm of the great men; Yukoi Mishima's self-immolation is a protest against the unjust forces of capitalism overtaking post-war Japan; Reverend Toller's final gesture to explode the center of his neighboring parish is an act of martyrdom intended to shake his colleagues out of their apathy regarding climate change. What differentiates the climactic act of violence in *The Canyons* from these cases, however, is that it does not elevate Christian to a new level of consciousness or relieve him from his alienation. Instead, Christian merely dispatches the threat to his masculine identity and hence re-establishes the status quo. Threatened by Tara's sexual agency and the duplicity of his mistress Cynthia (Tenille Houston), who has fabricated a rumor about his sexual mistreatment of her in the hopes of breaking the couple up, Christian methodically hatches a plan to murder Cynthia and frame Ryan for the crime. The act is cold and calculated, more driven by opportunism than passion or revenge. The moment of impact itself is pointedly kept off-screen, so as to deny any sense of catharsis for either Christian or the viewer. The artificially constructed social persona is not pierced through but rather reclaimed, and Christian is able to regain narrative control.

Schrader underlines Christian's inability to ascend to the transcendental in the film's closing moments. The ending of *American Gigolo* infamously transposes the finale of *Pickpocket* (Bresson, 1959) into the gaudy landscape of late-capitalist LA, seemingly a strange place to search for the transcendent. In the introduction to a collection of his screenplays, Schrader explains this unusual choice which many critics interpreted as being willfully perverse: "At the end of *American Gigolo*, I wanted to perversely plunge my lizardy protagonist into icy Bressonian waters, so I lifted the ending of *Pickpocket* and gave it to Julian Kaye. A grace note as unwarranted as Christ's promise to the thief on the cross."[30] Although Schrader describes this 'grace note' as being 'unwarranted' there is nothing ironic about its depiction within *American Gigolo*. It registers as an act of empathy, a final outpouring of emotion which breaks through the deliberate reserve of Gere's performance up until that moment. Although this intertextual weaving may stress the gulf between Bressonian asceticism and Schrader's hyper-seductive aesthetic language, it enables Julian to break through his disconnect. As often in Schrader, the assuaging force takes the shape of a woman, who grants him an unconditional, perhaps irrational love, an earthly expression of spirituality which redeems Julian and pulls him out of the mercenary, inhuman environment of late capitalism.

Christian's final meeting with Tara plays out nearly as a dark parody of Julian's final meeting with Michelle. Instead of using her empathy to break through her lover's façade, Tara merely becomes aware of the depth of his sociopathy. Christian proudly tells Tara of his violence with no sense of hesitation, guilt, or regret, and agrees to allow her to move out of the house as long as she serves as his alibi. The fact that Christian has no qualms with letting Tara leave as long as it happens on his terms illustrates the lack of true feeling in their relationship: "If you ever see [Ryan] again. If he ever contacts you. If you're even in the same room together. I will kill him. Look at me. I will kill him, and I will get away with it." Christian's delusion that he does not need to be accountable for his actions, either ethically or legally, is a symptom of his monstrous narcissism. Any sense of a clearly demarcated beginning or end is brutally dashed by a static structure of constancy.

Interpreted as such, *The Canyons* is revealed to be an undeniably pessimistic film. As Schrader does not envision a way to puncture the inertia of Christian's disconnected, self-alienating perspective, he remains trapped within the dehumanizing effects of the late-capitalist surveillance state. For the uncharitable critic, this may be perceived as a major ideological failure on Schrader's part, but I believe that, when considered within the context of his larger body of work, this lack of progression is more reflective of the total apathy of his characters than it is of the filmmaker's worldview. A few years following the release of *The Canyons*, Schrader would revisit similar thematic material in *First Reformed*, a far more esteemed study of a male body in crisis within a neo-liberal society driving itself toward ruin. But Pastor Toller is a figure of resistance rather than conformity, and his character arc follows a far more traditionally Schrader-esque transcendental trajectory. *First Reformed* is an internalized film rather than an externalized one, and Toller's rich and conflicted inner life contrasts with Christian's inhumanity. This goes some way to explaining why the latter film was so enthusiastically embraced while *The Canyons* was largely treated with disdain. Nevertheless, this chapter has made the case for *The Canyons* as a major work in its own right, a formally rigorous anti-spectacle which gazes into the abyss of dehumanization as engendered by late-capitalist excess.

NOTES

1. Stephen Rodrick, "This is what happens when you Cast Lindsay Lohan in Your Movie," *The New York Times*, January 10, 2013, https://www.nytimes.com/2013/01/13/magazine/here-is-what-happens-when-you-cast-lindsay-lohan-in-your-movie.html.
2. Manohla Dargis, "The Cell Phone Gets its Close-Up," *The New York Times*, August 1, 2013, https://www.nytimes.com/2013/08/02/movies/the-canyons-is-an-erotic-thriller-with-lindsay-lohan.html; Christy Lemire, "The Canyons," Rogerebert.com, August 2, 2013. https://www.rogerebert.com/reviews/the-canyons-2013.
3. Chris Knight, "*First Reformed* is Paul Schrader's Directorial Redemption," *National Post*, May 31, 2018, https://nationalpost.com/entertainment/movies/first-reformed-is-paul-schraders-directorial-redemption.
4. Paul Schrader, *Transcendental style in film: Ozu, Bresson, Dreyer* (Berkeley: University of California Press, 1972), 5.
5. John R. Hamilton, "Great Directors: Schrader, Paul," *Senses of Cinema*, 56 (2010), http://sensesofcinema.com/2010/great-directors/paul-schrader/.
6. Schrader, *Transcendental Style*, 42.
7. Ibid., 42.
8. Ibid., 74.
9. John Potvin, "From Gigolo to New Man: Armani, America, and the Textures of Narrative," *Fashion Theory: The Journal of Dress, Body and Culture*, Vol. 15, No. 3 (2015), 291.
10. Steve Neale, "Masculinity as Spectacle: Reflections on Men and Mainstream Cinema," in *Screening the Male: Exploring Masculinities in Hollywood Cinema*, edited by Steven Cohan and Ina Rae Hark (New York: Routledge, 1993), 11.
11. Ian Murphy, "Corporeal prisons: dynamics of body and mise-en-scène in three films by Paul Schrader," PhD dissertation (University College Cork, 2015), 9.
12. Ibid., 25.
13. Jeremy Bentham, *A Bentham Reader*, edited Mary Peter Mack (New York: Pegasus, 1969).
14. Michel Foucault, *Discipline and Punish: The Birth of the Prison*, translated by Alan Sheridan, New Edition (Westminster: Penguin, 1991).
15. Gilles Deleuze, "Postscript on the Societies of Control," *October*, 59 (1992), 5.
16. Gilles Deleuze, *Negotiations 1972-1990*, translated by Martin Joughin (New York: Columbia University Press, 1995), 174.

17. Mark Poster, *The Mode of Information, Post-Structuralism and Social Context* (Chicago: University of Chicago Press, 1990), 93.
18. Thomas Mathiesen, "The Viewer Society: Foucault's 'Panopticon' Revisited," *Theoretical Criminology: An International Journal*, Vol. 1, No. 2 (1997), 219.
19. Jamais Cascio, "The Rise of the Participatory Panopticon," *Open the Future* (blog), WorldChanging Archive, May 4, 2005, http://www.openthefuture.com/wcarchive/2005/05/the_rise_of_the_participatory.html.
20. Laura Mulvey, *Death 24× a Second: Stillness and the Moving Image* (London: Reaktion, 2006), 1.
21. Sherry Turkle, *Alone Together: Why We Expect More From Technology and Less From Each Other*, 3rd Edition (New York: Basic Books, 2017), 16.
22. Caroline Hamilton, "Blank Looks: Reality TV And Memoir In *A Heartbreaking Work Of Staggering Genius*," *Australian Journal of American Studies*, 28:2 (2009), 33.
23. Manuel Castells, *The Rise of the Network Society. 2nd Edition. Vol. 1. The Information Age: Economy, Society, and Culture* (Cambridge: Blackwell, 2000), 448.
24. Christopher Lasch, *The Culture of Narcissism: American Life in an Age of Diminishing Expectations* (New York: W. W. Norton, 1978), 47.
25. Thomas de Zengotita, *Mediated: How the Media Shape Your World* (London: Bloomsbury, 2005), 6.
26. Sherry Turkle, *Life on Screen: Identity in the Age of the Internet* (New York: Simon and Schuster, 1995), 248.
27. Patrick McHugh, "Cultural Politics, Postmodernism, and White Guys: Affect in *Gravity's Rainbow*," *College Literature*, Vol. 28, No. 2 (2001), 2.
28. Stella Bruzzi, *Men's Cinema: Masculinity and Mise-en-Scène in Hollywood* (Edinburgh: Edinburgh University Press, 2013), 30.
29. Richard Slotkin, *Regeneration Through Violence: The Mythology of the American Frontier, 1600–1860* (Middletown, CT: Wesleyan University Press, 1973).
30. Paul Schrader, *Paul Schrader: Collected Screenplays Volume 1: Taxi Driver, American Gigolo, Light Sleeper* (London: Faber and Faber, 2002), viii.

CHAPTER 10

"Every Act of Preservation is an Act of Creation": Paul Schrader's Eco-theology in *First Reformed*

Tatiana Prorokova

INTRODUCTION

Humanity's relations with nature and the environment, as well as the very existence of all living species, humans included, have been greatly challenged in the shadow of the looming threat of climate change. While "apocalyptic stories are as old as narrative itself,"[1] they seem to have revived with a new potency today, when climate change and the general ecological decline force us to reconsider our treatment of the environment, as well as to imagine the new world that we all will inevitably live in (if surviving climate change is possible), transformed as a result of irrevocable changes that take place today. Particularly interesting are the explorations of the relationship between humans and the environment through the prism of science and religion, two perhaps radically different perspectives that, this notwithstanding, are both helpful in approaching the issue. Paul Schrader's recent film *First Reformed* (2017) uses scientific rationality and religious morality as tools to tackle the problem of environmental and human degradation to comment on a number of profound questions.

This chapter focuses on *First Reformed* to examine Schrader's stance on one of the most serious problems that humanity is currently facing: climate change. Analyzing the issue of ecological decline through the prism of religion, Schrader outlines the ideology that presumably might help humanity survive in the age of global warming. Through complex discussions of such issues as despair, anxiety, and hope, Schrader deduces the formula of survival in which preservation is the key component. *First Reformed* is certainly a primal scream about humanity's inaction on climate change and ecological degradation in general, and the nervous, almost hysterical desire to radically and immediately change the situation by the main character actively supports this view. Yet, even more importantly, it is the film that forces the viewer to meditate upon the issue of survival in this ecologically precarious time, suggesting that survival as such, in the form as one might picture it, continuing to exist in the world as it is, is *not* possible. Schrader does not sketch out a simplistic scenario of apocalypse when everything disappears within a second—painlessly and remorselessly, instead, he uses death as a tool through which to communicate ecological and environmental degradation, as well as illustrate decay and disappearance. Once the Earth is gone, it can never return. And if humanity cannot understand this plain rule by example of dying nature, then it perhaps can better picture it observing the death of the representatives of its own species. Action is a key to survival; yet *First Reformed* does not offer eco-terrorism as an appropriate response. Human death that the viewer can witness against the background of much more horrifying images of already dead nature is an inevitable ramification of environmental degradation. After all, we are part of nature, part of the environment. Schrader intertwines the concepts of survival, preservation, and death to frame climate change as the problem that affects *everyone* and *everything* on this planet. The film is both a political story and a human story that plays out against a political context. It calls for action and uses individual stories to reinforce the sense of despair and fright that neglecting climate change should indeed provoke in everyone.

Equating humans to God, Schrader, on the one hand, censures those actions that led to progress but destroyed the environment. On the other hand, he foregrounds the fact that humans can also *save* the planet today. Schrader portrays both humans and the Earth as living organisms created by God. He draws explicit parallels between the current state of our planet and the problems that we experience, from the political, including war, to the personal, like health issues. Schrader thus not only makes the viewer think about the planet as a being that needs help, but also invites his audience to look at political, social, and environmental problems as destructive to humanity. Climate change for Schrader is not only the result of human actions that have been destroying our planet, but it is also a metaphor for degradation that sheds light on current problems that cause our fears and despair. Employing degradation as another crucial concept, Schrader not only effectively accentuates the essence of climate change, but he also forces the viewer to take a closer look at what is happening in the world we live in: a world of personal, spiritual, societal, as well as environmental degradation. This chapter scrutinizes the complex relationship between climate change and theology, as represented in *First Reformed*, as well as Schrader's understanding of humanity's major problems today.

CLIMATE CHANGE

First Reformed tells a story of Reverend Ernst Toller (Ethan Hawke) of the First Reformed Church in Snowbridge, New York. The complexity of Toller's character is developed through him writing a journal and reading various religious and mystic writings, but also negotiating the death of his son Joseph in the Iraq War, his alcoholism, and, in the end, stomach cancer. The church seems to serve primarily as a tourist attraction, as Toller shows a group of visitors around it, or later, when he explains to a group of younger schoolchildren that the church used to be part of the Underground Railroad. Toller soon meets pregnant Mary (Amanda Seyfried), whose husband, Michael (Philip Ettinger), adhering to the ideology of radical environmentalism, wants her to abort the baby, for he fears of bringing it into the world that will soon be destroyed by climate change. Mary asks Toller to talk to her husband, which Toller does, as it seems, in vain. Having soon discovered a suicide vest in a garage, both Toller and Mary suspect that Michael can harm himself, and soon Toller finds Michael's dead body in a park—the man shot himself. Michael's ashes, according to his will, are scattered over a local toxic-waste dump. In the end, Toller decides to blow up the church during its reconsecration ceremony, wearing Michael's suicide vest. When Mary arrives despite his warning her not to attend, he removes the vest and wraps his torso in barbed wire instead. As he is ready to drink a glass of drain cleaner, Mary comes in, and Toller drops the glass. The film ends depicting Toller and Mary kissing—a moment in swirling camera shot, overwhelmed with *Everlasting Arms* on the soundtrack, that is the culmination of the film's transcendental structure which also preserves narrative ambiguity.

Paul Schrader has long been interested in religious ideas and has used them to one degree or another throughout his career as a screenwriter, director, and critic. His book, *Transcendental Style in Film: Ozu, Bresson, Dreyer*, which has recently gone into a new edition, coinciding with the release of *First Reformed*, is an essential text for understanding Schrader's use of the visual and auditory techniques in the film's design. Transcendentalism, that the filmmaker both employs as a tool as well as seeks to better understand, offers profound knowledge through which to interpret societal and environmental havoc that one can witness today. Schrader writes:

> Transcendental style seeks to maximize the mystery of existence; it eschews all conventional interpretations of reality: realism, naturalism, psychologism, romanticism, expressionism, impressionism, and, finally, rationalism. To the transcendental artist rationalism is only one of many approaches to life, not an imperative ... The enemy of transcendence is immanence, whether it is external (realism, rationalism) or internal

(psychologism, expressionism). To the transcendental artist these conventional interpretations of reality are emotional and rational constructs devised by man to dilute or explain away the transcendental.[2]

It is thus crucial for Schrader to speak about existence as a phenomenon that is beyond traditional understandings and explanations, as a phenomenon that indeed *transcends* the reality and is, in principle, outside of human knowledge. Moreover, Schrader continues:

> Transcendental style *stylizes* reality by eliminating (or nearly eliminating) those elements which are primarily expressive of human experience, thereby robbing the conventional interpretations of reality of their relevance and power. Transcendental style, like the mass, transforms experience into a repeatable ritual which can be repeatedly transcended.[3]

Schrader's transcendentalism is thus both unique and unattainable; it is a phenomenon on its own, but it is also a means through which explorations of reality can be most precise and effective. *First Reformed*'s focus on societal and environmental degradation through the prism of transcendentalism is not only in itself an ambitious approach to the existing problems, but it is effective in communicating these problems in the most powerful and thus alarming ways to the audience.

To understand the portrayals of the environment and climate change in *First Reformed*, one needs to understand Schrader's vision of transcendentalism as well as the reason why the filmmaker chooses to use the transcendental style to explore the current crises. Schrader's politics of transcendentalism foreground the importance of exploring and trying to achieve something that can, in principle, never be achieved or fully grasped. To borrow from William Mai, "Schrader's mystery, in his writing and directorial efforts, is determined to sort through this unknown, while never expecting to solve what is unsolvable."[4] Two terms surface as key here: "experience" and "expression." And Schrader's vision of transcendentalism unmistakably suggests that transcendentalism might have started with the exploration of the experience, yet its primary and ultimate goal is to celebrate the expression.[5] Finding ways to verbalize and visualize the unattainable, which in the case of *First Reformed* are multiple crises that humanity faces today, climate change being one of the problems, simultaneously realizing that both tasks cannot really be fulfilled, is Schrader's primary concern. The prototype of Schrader's transcendentalism was arguably probed in Ingmar Bergman's drama *Winter Light* (1963), where the filmmaker "equates a transcendental style to the hardship, and revelation, of God's silence."[6] With the release of *First Reformed*, Schrader seems to provide the fullest, deepest, and richest interpretation of his vision of transcendentalism and the style's power to explore and express existential issues. *First Reformed* sends the following message:

> The body can only take so much, and the mind is frequently let down by what we do not know or cannot comprehend, but the fact that we can push through our Earthly pain by committing to Earthly duties, and in a sense, rise past the realities of the everyday, is Schrader's ultimate breakthrough, both as a writer and an artist. The world still looks the same at the end of the day, and yet, the way you perceive the fabric of the known existence is fresh and anew.[7]

The dynamics of *First Reformed* largely define Schrader's understanding of the transcendental style. The filmmaker elucidates the major characteristic of a transcendental film as follows: "If you come to expect action, you're not going to get it."[8] Instead, Schrader forces the viewer to see the so-called "dead time."[9] Schrader's "dead time" constructs much of *First Reformed*, which does not have a twisted or complex plot; instead, it rather steadily, monotonously, and in a very detailed manner narrates the everyday reality, lending complexity to simplicity. As his directing career reveals, Schrader is particularly keen on exploring the issues of "obsession, guilt, repression, catharsis and psychosis often culminating in acts of anti-social psychosexual violence."[10] All these themes are implicitly or explicitly raised in *First Reformed*. *First Reformed* is the film that has brought together a number of Schrader's disparate career threads, including his filmmaking work and his academic writing; it is the film that represents fusion between Schrader's theoretical ideas about cinema and his execution of those ideas on screen. Through *First Reformed*, Schrader skillfully transfers his theoretical understanding of the transcendental style into practice, revealing through the issues of guilt, despair, moral collapse, individual and collective responsibility, and, of course, existence that such problems as environmental degradation and climate change align with transcendental style. Existence in ecologically and environmentally precarious times interests Schrader in *First Reformed*.

In his inaugural address in 2013, President Obama stated: "Some may still deny the overwhelming judgment of science, but none can avoid the devastating impact of raging fires and crippling drought and more powerful storms."[11] Obama drew attention to the problem of climate change, but he also acknowledged the role of science. Science provides us with important data to understand the scale of the environmental degradation; yet, as *First Reformed* demonstrates, it can become much more powerful when juxtaposed and ultimately merged with religious thinking. For the first, and perhaps most potent time in the film, the clash of scientific and religious views can be perceived through the dialogue between Toller and Michael. Toller comes to explain to Michael that having an abortion is not a way out for the couple, suggesting that no matter what, human life is precious. Michael strongly disagrees with the Reverend, citing data regarding rising temperatures, refugees, and our transforming planet in general. The viewer senses that Toller does not support Michael's radical thinking; more than that, he experiences discomfort listening to Michael's speech about the inevitable end. Yet soon Toller shares his personal story with Michael, telling that he lost his own son in the Iraq War, which he encouraged him to fight in. Slowly, the Reverend tries to persuade Michael that radicalism in his attitudes will not help him find ways to continue living on the planet that is indeed affected by humanity's reckless actions. And while minimizing the effects of climate change is usually described as being possible only through radical changes, consider, for example, the way Martin J. Tracey puts it: "Human activity is degrading our planet in ways that gravely threaten life on earth. Communications media have failed to convey the true nature of the environmental threats we face. Radical changes are urgently needed to redress them."[12] It is evident that Michael's radicalism is aimed not at sustaining life but rather it outlines the ideology of apocalypse, thus suggesting that no actions are any longer needed, for we *are* already at the end of our road.

Michael's radicalism helps reinforce Schrader's use of the transcendental style and its implementation in the film. In *Transcendental Style in Film*, Schrader discusses what he calls "withholding techniques."[13] These he evidently uses in *First Reformed*, too, to achieve the transcendental effect. These are hard and fast rules, which, if the filmmaker is going to remain in the transcendental style, he/she must not violate, until the moment of transcendence, of course. In *First Reformed*, that is at the end of the film in the scene with the swirling camera. From a stylistic vantage point, this is a kind of dogmatic radicalism, not dissimilar from Michael's and eventually Toller's. Thus, the film's own radical commitment to its own stylistic integrity is meant to mirror the environmental radicalism of the characters. According to Schrader, "withholding techniques" help to "retard time" and "withhold the expected," ultimately providing less.[14] Similarly, Michael's, and later Toller's, radicalism is manifested through their decisions to commit suicide, to kill, and essentially to destroy.

Michael's funeral is another scene when scientific truth about climate change is represented in the film. While the moment seems to be deeply religious, for Reverend Toller gives a sermon, a church choir sings a song, and Mary is depicted crying over the urn of her husband, the scene is by no means reduced to an act of a funeral ceremony held for one human being but instead is an explicit portrayal of the environment's funeral. The viewer hardly pays attention to the rather modest group of people, but instead ponders the surroundings, which display the devastating effects of human activity on the environment.

"EVERY ACT OF PRESERVATION IS AN ACT OF CREATION" 177

Figure 10.1 At Michael's funeral, the viewer is forced to face the death of the environment.

Thus, radical environmentalism preached by Michael finds an extension in the scene, where the attendees at the funeral are crying for both Michael and the vast landscapes of destroyed nature and ecology. Part of the visual design of the funeral scene from both a narrative and filmmaking perspective is to directly align Michael with the environment because of the staging of the scene itself. Michael's wishes are to have the funeral at the superfund site to explicitly draw a parallel between his own situation and that of the environment, a provocation that is meant to force humanity to confront its ecological sins. The scene makes its audience step out of its comfort zone—our individual worlds where everything seems fine—and look around us, see how much our planet has changed. The ideology of radical environmentalism is verbalized through the song chosen by Michael and performed by the local church choir. This song is an appeal to humanity to essentially protect the planet, the diversity of animal and plant species that inhabit it, and to stop the violence and destruction that manifests itself in a variety of ways—from the exploitation of nature to the use of fossil fuels and beyond—that have been conducted for centuries because of "the greed of man."[15] The lyrics claim that this is a necessary action to preserve life on the planet and thus guarantee a future to the next generations, and call for the action of every human: "This all starts with you and me."[16] As the scene ends, Mary scatters the ashes into polluted water, thus only adding to the already existing grave.

Figure 10.2 The mass grave: Michael's ashes are scattered over nature's grave.

Through these two scenes that provide a scientific interpretation of climate change, the film not only foregrounds the idea that "humans are a force, maybe *the* force, shaping the planet,"[17] but it also challenges the very notion of progress. It is not a secret that climate change largely reinforced the already-existing world inequality. Racial subjugation of multiple peoples during colonial times only intensified further with the emergence of industrial progress. Lisa Vox claims that after the Civil War, by the end of the nineteenth century, "most white Americans agreed with Europeans that Western nations were spiritually, culturally, and racially better suited to lead the rest of the world."[18] This leadership carried out by the industrially advanced Western countries since the Industrial Revolution led to the degradation of world ecology. *First Reformed* criticizes humanity's reliance on various comforts of civilization and the capitalist world in general, which offer abundance while degrading the state of the environment—the approach that has turned our planet into a dangerous, polluted zone, and that illustrates the concept of "Apocalyptic Narcissism" which "relates to insatiable overconsumption from greed"[19] so characteristic of humanity today.

First Reformed explicitly discusses climate change as an environmental issue. But the film also uses climate change as a powerful metaphor to talk about degradation in general—degradation that takes place not only on the levels of nature and ecology, but also on cultural, social, and political levels. Evan Berry provides an interesting interpretation of climate change:

> Climate change can be understood as a ubiquitous trope through which the material, psychological and cultural agency of the idea of climate is performed in today's world. In this context, climate change should not be understood as a decisive break from the past nor as a unique outcome of modernity. It should be seen as the latest stage in the cultural evolution of the idea of climate, an idea which enables humans to live with their weather through a widening and changing range of cultural resources, practices, artefacts and rituals.[20]

First Reformed, in that sense, adds another intriguing component to the issue of climate change, suggesting that it is not only about weather, the environment, and climate in general, but it is also about destruction, degradation, and change on different levels that is negative in any way. The death of nature is frequently juxtaposed with the death of humans—consider, for example, the death of Toller's son in Iraq, or Michael's suicide, or the thoughts about aborting Mary's baby. Yet not only do these images of death compound, but there are smaller, more subtle ways through which Schrader communicates this theme. The clogged toilet in the church's living quarters, the broken organ, the erosion of interest in church services at First Reformed compared to the corporatized mega-church Abundant Life—all of these contribute to the cultural degradation. Through the church that gradually but steadily turns into an architectural ruin, Schrader develops a larger narrative of degradation, stretching it out to the spiritual degradation that is both the reason for and the result of social and environmental degradation. *First Reformed* is thus a film about degradation in its many forms, and the climate acts as the film's chief representation of it. This is so because climate change is not *just* another problem, as Schrader makes it evident, it is the reality that surrounds us, yet we either remain blindfolded and refuse to face it or simply underestimate the extent to which it has transformed. This narrative backdrop manifests itself in individual scenes, moments, and ground-level metaphors that contribute to a collective pattern of meaning, making *First Reformed* a transcendental meditation about the *reality* of climate change.

RELIGION

Christianity provides an interesting interpretation of the relationship between humanity and nature and of the overt dominance of the former over the latter. *First Reformed* adopts an eco-theological stance on climate change to demonstrate how, along with science, religion can effectively explain the problem of environmental degradation and provide answers regarding humanity's future.

Science and religion are often considered oppositional to one another: "Religion serves non-cognitive functions missing in science, such as eliciting attitudes, personal involvement, and transformation. It also contains elements not found in science, including story, ritual, and historical revelation. Lower-level laws are not found in religion as they are in science, and the emergence of consensus in religion seems an unrealizable goal."[21] This is vividly illustrated in the dialogue between Toller and Michael: while Michael persuasively explains why the world might come to end, Toller's comments only vaguely outline why it is important to continue living, no matter what humanity has already done to the planet. Schrader's visual approach to shooting the scene also places these two characters and their ideologies in tension. An extended section of the scene takes place in a two-shot where each character is framed in profile, opposing one another. Otherwise, Schrader uses isolating close-ups, not over-the-shoulder shots, to keep Toller and Michael separated from one another. Schrader's directorial choices, characteristic of transcendental style, which is influenced heavily by religious thinking, underline his approach to the debate between science and theology. Science provides facts, while religion teaches one how to remain spiritually strong even in such apocalyptic situations as climate change. Yet *First Reformed* does not reduce religion to such a level, introducing religion itself in crisis.

The church is barely attended, and when it is, these are mostly tourists. But Toller himself carries a crisis of faith within him; while the man opposes abortion and explains to Michael that living, even in such a destructed world, is essential, he himself embodies a strong contradiction to his own views. He evidently blames himself for encouraging his son to enlist in the army and ultimately for his death in Iraq. His role as a church servant is largely undermined as we see him working as a tour guide. But along with the degradation of the spiritual, Toller also experiences degradation of the physical. Toller is an alcoholic, and alcohol literally becomes his food; in a private breakfast, he pours alcohol into a bowl to dip his bread in. The destruction of Toller's body becomes explicit through the blood urinating and vomiting scenes, designating serious health issues, which turn out to be symptoms of stomach cancer.

Crucially, after the death of Michael, Toller gradually turns into Michael himself. First, he researches climate and realizes that Michael's despair regarding the state of our planet and humanity's role in this destruction was well-earned. He even finds out that the church receives considerable financial support from one of such industries that pollute the environment—the next morning Toller changes the church's message board to read "Will God Forgive Us?"[22] Toller also becomes close friends with Mary. One evening he even performs Michael's role in the couple's non-sexual physical intimacy, in which

Mary lies on top of Toller on the floor. Suddenly, their bodies are lifted in the air, the room transforms into cosmos, and the two fly, first, over snowy mountaintops, next, over majestic green rocks, then over clear water, and after that over forests. At that moment, the surroundings change first to roads overfilled with cars, then large quantities of old car tires, and finally the two disappear from the picture, and the viewer observes industries exhaling smoke into the environment, then acts of deforestation, a dried-out river polluted with plastic and other trash, fires destroying vast spaces, and finally old ships left in a sea of trash. This chain of images effectively communicates the problem of human involvement in environmental degradation, the impact of industrialization on nature, and the radical transformation of the planet. Schrader takes a global perspective, distorting the frames and proportions in which we perceive the world, thus allowing us to see the whole picture. The transformation from the landscape's wilderness and virginity, rendered through bright colors, to the images of environmental destruction, represented though dull grey, brown, and black, and nature's death is not only made visually explicit here, but it forces one to rethink the reality that we are part of.

Christianity positions humanity's exploitation of nature as an acceptable phenomenon. Consider, for example, the words from Genesis: "Be fruitful and multiply, and fill the earth and subdue it; and have dominion over the fish of the sea and the birds of the air and over every living thing that moves upon the earth."[23] Laurel Kearns claims that these words "sum up the religious roots of a destructive, anti-ecological, Western world-view."[24] Friedrich Lohman makes a similar argument, observing the following: "Some of today's ecotheologians—as well as many non-Christian environmentalists—claim that the traditional idea of human superiority over the rest of nature is the main reason for the long history of human exploitation and destruction of nature; others maintain anthropocentrism and reject the idea of an intrinsic value of nature altogether."[25] Kearns himself claims that "from a Christian perspective, it is adequate to ascribe an intrinsic value to nature while, at the same time, preserving the notion of dignity as proper only to humans."[26] Yet, would not it be more correct to state, like Andy Bell does, that "nothing within the is-ness, seen or unseen belongs to human beings"?[27] I think this is exactly the idea that *First Reformed* tries to convey, mostly through two characters, Edward Balq (Michael Gaston)—one of the key financial backers of Abundant Life—and Reverend Joel Jeffers (Cedric Antonio Kyles). Their relationship is one of mutual benefit, wherein Jeffers's church is supported by Balq's charitable donations, and Balq receives a kind of spiritual absolution for his environmental sins. Toller threatens to disrupt that status quo through his fulfillment of Michael's funeral wishes, and further intends to do so through the suicide vest. Through his representation of the characters, Schrader engages with this theological justification for a laissez-faire approach to the environment, foregrounding spiritual corruption. The church is ready to justify any crimes against nature as long as it receives sufficient financial support, whereas those who are directly involved in these crimes believe in atonement that can be bought. The environment becomes a casualty of complex moral, religious, and political rationalizations that justify its destruction on the one hand and mourn such treatment on the other. In the film's representation of Toller's crisis of faith, however, it does not offer religion as an answer to climate-induced despair. Scholars recognize the potency of religion in helping tackle the problem of climate change: "Religions affect societies at every level, from the individual to the transnational. What they say and do about climate change—whether they encourage concern or help their adherents recognize and cope with the challenge—could, therefore, make a decisive difference."[28] However, this is not what *First Reformed* tries to achieve. Instead, the film uses religion to intensify the atmosphere of crisis and hopelessness.

Schrader calls *First Reformed* a "transcendental" film.[29] I argue that Schrader's transcendentalism emerges as a response to radical environmentalism, providing a softer and more humane approach to the existing problems. It doubtless does not belittle the scale of these problems, nor does it suggest inaction. *First Reformed* not merely makes us recognize the problem of climate change, it teaches us *how* to do that through its slow pace and quiet mood. There are numerous silent scenes in the film where the audience simply observes the characters walking, sitting, eating. It is exactly through these scenes that *First Reformed* most effectively communicates the ritual of the everyday, creating space for the film's larger ideas. It is curious that providing his own understanding of religion, Schrader states: "Religion is about the how, it's not about the what. It's not what you believe, it's about how you believe, so ritual becomes highly important."[30] Schrader seems to adopt a similar understanding dealing with climate change. First Michael, then Toller, both men represent the minority of those who do something to influence the problem of environmental degradation, while the majority do not see, or continue to pretend not to see, literally *living* in this transformed world. Schrader's film, however, turns into a form of activism by finding a way to make everyone watching it *stop* and *think*.

Yet the question of sacrifice that emerges with regard to climate change as an act of redemption that humanity can commit is largely questioned in the film. Sacrifice is committed in the film at least twice: Michael's suicide, and Toller's actions at the end. If the film ended (as Schrader considered at one point) with the bomb going off and everyone inside the church being killed, one might be able to make the case that the film argues for the value of sacrifice. But because Michael's sacrifice is rendered pointless by the relative insignificance of his funeral in the shadow of a monument to environmental destruction, and Toller's own ends up aborted, one can conclude that Schrader views sacrifice as useless. Toller, like Michael, recedes into the personal decision to end his life (whether he succeeds or not is another matter). When his act of martyrdom is frustrated by Mary's arrival at the church, he decides that his personal pain is too much to endure, seemingly abandoning all hope of giving meaning to his death. Schrader thus sees sacrifice as a meaningless, selfish, and, importantly, unwanted act. Sacrifice that is essentially death is viewed as another form of degradation, for it destroys both the physical body and the spiritual essence, it contributes to havoc as well as causing it. From an eco-critical perspective, there is no difference between the death of a human and, for example, the waters polluted with toxic waste. Both are the manifestations of degradation and the sites of destruction. Largely backgrounding Michael's suicide and Toller's (attempted) suicide, Schrader foregrounds that it is indeed *preservation* but not destruction that are the tools for improvement.

At the end of the film, Toller decides to blow up the church during its reconsecration ceremony, which will be attended by some representatives from the government and industry who adhere to anti-environmental policies. One can also argue that Toller protests against this specific church, recognizing it as a disgrace to religion in general, for the church accepts financial support from polluting industries. Toller puts on Michael's suicide vest under his clothing, yet soon he has to take it off when he sees Mary entering the church. He then decides to wrap his naked torso in barbed wire, and soon the viewer witnesses the body in pain, bleeding, suffering. Toller puts on his clothes, blood soaking through, pours a glass of drain cleaner, yet Mary enters the house and the audience never sees him drinking the liquid.

Schrader himself comments on the problem of sacrifice as follows:

> It's built into the DNA of Christianity . . . We used to need animals to be sacrificed and then one man came along and sacrificed himself for us, and if we participate in his sacrifice—if we are washed in his blood—we can be redeemed. So it's not surprising that when Christian young men and women start to go off the rails they go off in this kind of pathology, which is "If I myself suffer as my Lord did, he will respect my suffering and I will be redeemed." In effect, it's a kind of heresy of selfishness. It's saying: "God's suffering isn't enough and I've got to help out." It's exactly the same message that happens in Jihadism. They are both heresies and very potent heresies. Every Easter we see people on the news flagellating themselves or crucifying themselves in Jesus's name, but in fact Jesus would want no part of that.[31]

The Christian sacrifice committed by Toller—the barbed wire round Toller's body is so reminiscent of Christ's crown of thorns—is juxtaposed with the act of fanatic martyrdom that he attempts to commit earlier. The film indeed sees any form of murder/suicide as perverse in itself. Suicide in particular is, in a sense, a weakness demonstrated by Michael and Toller, who are incapable of living in a world where humanity sinned so much against nature and now has to find ways to compensate for such deeds, if not to change its lifestyle completely.

The character of Mary, her name obviously evoking the Virgin, considering this religious subplot, is rather ambiguous and is arguably much more than just a neighbor girl. She is pregnant with a child that will eventually be brought into the world of sin, just like Jesus Christ was. The only difference is that in the context of *First Reformed* it is the eco-sin that is central. When Mary, despite Toller's begging her not to do so, enters the church, she thus symbolically protects it from the physical destruction that would happen as a result of explosion, but also from the sin of suicide. Her appearance in Toller's house, however, is much more equivocal. One can speculate that Mary, indeed, saves Toller by her timely coming, preventing him from drinking the drain cleaner. If that is so, then the film dramatizes the idea of preservation on the verge of death. Toller's example illustrates that salvation and survival are possible, with Mary functioning as an angelic savior, while Toller stands for the havoc that humanity finds itself in. Yet it is also possible to argue that Toller has indeed drunk the portion of drain cleaner and died. The moment when the glass is falling out of his hand symbolizes his physical weakness and actual death. He then sees not the neighbor girl Mary, but the Virgin Mary, who welcomes him in her embrace, forgiving him for what he has done. If that is what the film's ambiguous ending is about, then the film does not necessarily undermine the idea of preservation but rather demonstrates how close we are to death, emphasizing the necessity to act right now, without any delays, to save the planet. The fact that the film abruptly ends, never clarifying what has really happened to Toller, make both theories plausible.

Interpreting the character of Toller and the actions he commits in the course of the film, A. O. Scott claims: "There are several ways to describe what happens to him [Toller]—as a midlife crisis, a psychological breakdown, a political awakening or a religious reckoning. Mr Schrader doesn't suggest that these are mutually exclusive choices, but rather shows how the strands of Toller's experience twist into a rope that binds and scourges him, until extreme actions start to feel logical and inevitable."[32] The film is an attempt to "organize something that is by its very nature an unholy mess: one person's life."[33] Such an effort, however, is made not only integrally throughout the film, but also through selected scenes where Schrader most overtly articulates the tension between the sacred and the profane. Consider, for example, the scene when Toller is unclogging the toilet while he says, in voiceover, "Discernment intersects with Christian life at every moment. Discernment. Listening and waiting for God's wish what action must be taken."[34] In this image, Schrader creates a clash of sacred and profane. After all, what could be less characteristic of the sublimity of God's grace than unclogging a toilet? Through such details, however, Schrader skillfully constructs a larger picture that illuminates the opposition between the sacred and the profane in today's world, reinforcing the issue of environmentalism, the sacred nature of the environment, and the ungodly actions of us, humans, toward it, leading to destruction, and thus challenging our very existence. In doing so, Schrader not only explores the complexity of climate change but also foregrounds the transcendental style as an apt approach to visualization and expression of today's environmental degradation as a subject matter.

The deaths of Michael and Toller—in the case of the latter, if not a physical then a spiritual one—symbolize the futility of individual, random fights against environmental degradation, and call for a collective action. The film might see transcendentalism as a "form of surrogate religion," suggesting everyone, like transcendentalism did in the United States in the nineteenth century, "pursu[e] self-transcendence . . . leading nature devotees into the continent's own forests, fields, river valleys, and mountains."[35] Transcendentalism preached by *First Reformed* is, however, based not on mere contemplation but, indeed, on preservation. From preservation of human lives—the accents made on the saved Mary's baby and the lost lives of Michael and Toller—to the preservation of the environment, the film sees godliness in acts of preservation, for it speaks through Toller: "Every act of preservation is an act of creation. Everything preserved renews creation. It's how we participate in creation."[36]

CONCLUSION

The sense of helplessness, indeed, entwines *First Reformed*. Yet in Schrader's film humanity's survival is not doomed, despite Michael's physical death and Toller's spiritual crash—on the contrary, the film suggests that hope is always possible. *First Reformed* does not portray climate change as such as apocalypse; rather, the spiritual apocalypse is already here. In that sense, *First Reformed* is doubtless not the first film to use the apocalypse metaphor to talk about social, cultural, political, and environmental degradation in the twenty-first century. Vox emphasizes that "the twenty-first-century national obsession with apocalypticism is as revelatory of American turmoil over its national identity as it is of American beliefs in science, technology, and religion."[37] One should therefore observe a much more complex subtext in apocalyptic narratives as well as consider apocalypse a much more versatile concept. Twenty-first-century narratives, *First Reformed* included, teach us that apocalypse is not limited to the biblical imagery that depicts humanity being obliterated for its sins. It is also illustrative that *First Reformed* rejects the primitive understanding of apocalypse but uses many other issues as some of its manifestations. Climate change becomes the most powerful visual representation of human sins with regard to our living environment; the Iraq War as well as the references to governments, industries, and various institutions that make money but pollute the planet are used to reflect political wrongdoings.

But it is most fascinating how Schrader plays with the issues of the physical and the spiritual, introducing the character of Toller, a church servant who is no longer sure that the church truly serves God as well as that humans will ever be forgiven for the sins that they commit, but who is also depicted as being slowly destroyed physically, due to his various illnesses. Degradation becomes the central issue in *First Reformed*, whether it is physical degradation of the environment, the death and extinction of various plant and animal species, the destruction of natural habitats, or spiritual degradation, manifested through the absence of strong will, moral loss, suicide, as well as numerous human vices and unredeemed sins. The main message of the film, which it so persistently and firmly conveys employing various cinematic techniques, among which narrating at a slow pace is perhaps the most significant one, is that humanity has enough potency to overcome these grave situations by slowing down, stopping to destroy in order to satisfy its insatiable greed, and starting to *preserve*. I would like to cite one more time what I consider the key lines in *First Reformed* to emphasize the film's message: "Every act of preservation is an act of creation. Everything preserved renews creation. It's how we participate in creation."[38] It can be tempting to read the film in a didactic way and interpret its message as follows: Once we reconsider consumption and turn to recycling and preservation, we will start participating in individual, sacred acts of creation that have a strong religious subtext but are, as evident from *First Reformed*, not exclusive to God or any other supernatural forces, but are in our own power, too. Yet the ending complicates this interpretation mightily, and resists simplistic readings. Whether Toller dies or not, Schrader's directorial choice to end the film with the ambiguous images of death helps reinforce the deadly nature of the world we live in. The (near-to-)suicidal mood that the scene sets effectively sums up social, cultural, and environmental degradation, leaving the viewer unaware of possible ways out, and if such ways out generally exist. Certainly preservation is the concept that surfaces in the film, to both blame humanity for its anti-environmental actions and suggest rather obviously what should be done to keep the planet alive. Yet because *First Reformed* concludes with the scene that is completely opposed to "preservation," it seems more correct to argue that Schrader's primary interest is to render the current state of things and thus picture the world as is: desperate, dark, and dying. This is by no means a pessimistic approach; this is a realistic view that Schrader skillfully sketches, making *First Reformed* an effective example of eco-cinema through which to explore degradation as a larger and complex concept and the state of our world today.

NOTES

1. Andrew Tate, *Apocalyptic Fiction* (London: Bloomsbury, 2017), 2.
2. Paul Schrader, *Transcendental Style in Film: Ozu, Bresson, Dreyer* (Oakland, CA: University of California Press, 2018), 42.
3. Ibid.; italics in original.
4. William Mai, "A Beginner's Guide to Transcendental Style," *Talk Film Society*, May 29, 2019, https://talkfilmsociety.com/articles/a-beginners-guide-to-transcendental-style.
5. Ibid.
6. Ibid.
7. Ibid.
8. Schrader, quoted in Julia Teti, "Director Paul Schrader Talks Transcendental Style in Film," May 6, 2018, https://theplaylist.net/paul-schrader-transcendental-style-20180506/.
9. Ibid.
10. The Playlist Staff, "The Essentials: The Directorial Career of Paul Schrader," *The Playlist*, August 5, 2013, https://theplaylist.net/retrospective-the-directorial-career-of-paul-schrader-20130805/#cb-content.
11. Barack Obama, quoted in "Climate-Change Religion," *Oil & Gas Journal*, January 28, 2013, 16.
12. Martin J. Tracey, "Pope Francis on the Ecological Crisis: Its Nature, Causes, and Urgency," in *Interdisciplinary Essays on Environment and Culture: One Planet, One Humanity, and the Media*, edited by Luigi Manca and Jean-Marie Kauth (Lanham: Lexington Books, 2016), 207.
13. Schrader, *Transcendental Style in Film*, 11.
14. Ibid.
15. Paul Schrader, *First Reformed* (New York: A24, 2017), DVD.
16. Ibid.
17. Jedediah Purdy, *After Nature: A Politics for the Anthropocene* (Cambridge: Harvard University Press, 2015), 2; italics in original.
18. Lisa Vox, *Existential Threats: American Apocalyptic Beliefs in the Technological Era* (Philadelphia: University of Pennsylvania Press, 2017), xiv.
19. Andy Bell, "An Eco-Theology," *Crosscurrents* (2013), 387.
20. Evan Berry, "Social Science Perspectives on Religion and Climate Change," *Religious Studies Review*, Vol. 42, No. 2 (2016), 78.
21. Robert John Russell and Kirk Wegter-McNelly, "Science," in *The Blackwell Companion to Modern Theology*, edited by Gareth Jones (Hoboken: Blackwell, 2004), 514.
22. Schrader, *First Reformed*.
23. Quoted in Laurel Kearns, "The Context of Eco-theology," in *The Blackwell Companion to Modern Theology*, edited by Gareth Jones (Hoboken: Blackwell, 2004), 467.
24. Laurel Kearns, "The Context of Eco-theology," in *The Blackwell Companion to Modern Theology*, edited by Gareth Jones (Hoboken: Blackwell, 2004), 467.
25. Friedrich Lohmann, "Climate Justice and the Intrinsic Value of Creation: The Christian Understanding of Creation and its Holistic Implications," in *Religion in Environmental and Climate Change: Suffering, Values, Lifestyles*, edited by Dieter Gerten and Sigurd Bergmann (London: Continuum, 2012), 85.
26. Ibid.
27. Bell, "An Eco-Theology," 386.
28. Robin Globus Veldman, Andrew Szasz, and Randolph Haluza-DeLay, "Introduction: Climate Change and Religion—A Review of Existing Research," *Journal for the Study of Religion, Nature and Culture*, Vol. 6, No. 3 (2012), 255.

29. Schrader, quoted in Philip Concannon, "Faithful Servant," *Sight & Sound*, August 2018, 40.
30. Schrader, quoted in Sean Nam, "Hungering and Thirsting for Righteousness: An Interview with Paul Schrader," *Cineaste*, Summer 2018, 21.
31. Schrader, quoted in Concannon, "Faithful Servant," 43.
32. A. O. Scott, "Review: 'First Reformed' Is an Epiphany. Ethan Hawke Is, Too," *The New York Times*, May 17, 2018, https://www.nytimes.com/2018/05/17/movies/first-reformed-review-paul-schrader-ethan-hawke.html.
33. Ibid.
34. Schrader, *First Reformed*.
35. John Gatta, *Making Nature Sacred: Literature, Religion, and Environment in America from the Puritans to the Present* (Oxford: Oxford University Press, 2004), 3.
36. Schrader, *First Reformed*.
37. Vox, *Existential Threats*, 193.
38. Schrader, *First Reformed*.

CHAPTER II

Leaning on the Everlasting Arms: Love and Silence in *First Reformed*

Robert Ribera

They were once more delivered from questions and uncertainties and could see their road straight ahead. In this case it is not even a question of seeing a road. It is simpler than that. For as soon as you stop traveling you have arrived.

—Thomas Merton, *The Sign of Jonas*[1]

Cries of silence rage
Now our lives collide
Where's this magic place
Where sorrow dies?

—Michael Been, *Fate*

All meditative cinema shares an end point. It is silence.

—Paul Schrader

On the walk home after presenting *Ida* director Pawel Pawlikowski the Best Foreign Language Film award at the New York Film Critics Circle in 2014, Paul Schrader decided it was time to write the film he had refused to write his entire career. After becoming both a celebrated screenwriter in the years after his graduation from UCLA, critics and scholars have found ways to connect his work as a screenwriter and director with the book that came from his master's thesis, *Transcendental Style in Cinema*. And although there are bountiful connections with the films he examined as well as the aesthetic considerations of Ozu, Bresson, and Dreyer, Schrader never fully embraced the style himself. Talking with the writer and director about *First Reformed*

(2017), Nicolas Cage mused to Schrader that the film serves as a culmination of his career. "I couldn't help but thinking all roads must have led to this moment."[2] These roads—nearly fifty years as a critic, scholar, screenwriter, and director—lead to the slow dolly shot toward the doorway of First Reformed that begins the film. The austere images that follow are an embrace both of Schrader's influences and of the transcendental style, withholding from the audience simple answers and emotional guidance. *First Reformed* leans away so that the audience may lean in.

In an interview with David Poland, when asked if his career held some consistencies, Schrader conceded that, indeed, his work as a filmmaker has a through line and that "At this particular moment, it's uniquely gratifying to see that through line come to some sort of culmination."[3] Some of this connective tissue is immediately apparent. His characters have known isolation and the quest for redemption. His films oftentimes demonstrate a sense of restraint punctuated by violent action. These qualities have dominated Schrader's career, no matter the genre. As George Kouvaros has argued, what ties these varied styles and genres together is an overall "concern with the possibilities of self-realization."[4] From the righteousness of Travis Bickle in *Taxi Driver* (1976) to Jake Van Dorn in *Hardcore* (1979), both seek redemption through saving others. Likewise, the struggles of life and death in *Bringing Out the Dead* (1999), or even in *Dominion* (2005), his prequel to *The Exorcist*, religion and righteousness, discernment, hope, and despair provide some of the contrasting forces at work in his characters. This chapter will read *First Reformed* as an embodiment and fulfillment of Schrader's career, a film that fully embraces the transcendental style, serving as a meditation on, in the crushing silence of a higher power, our responsibility toward each other and our Earth, and spiritual discernment. Moving toward the transcendent, I argue that it is love that becomes a final comfort to Reverend Ernst Toller (Ethan Hawke) and Mary (Amanda Seyfried), and perhaps to the audience. As the Curé d'Ambricourt remarks about God in *Diary of a Country Priest* (1951), "He is not the master of love. He is love itself. If you would love, don't place yourself beyond love's reach." *First Reformed* challenges us, in the emptiness and solitude of God's silence, to go on this journey ourselves.

A PROBLEM LOOKING FOR AN ANSWER: TRANSCENDENTAL STYLE

As a young graduate student at UCLA film school, Paul Schrader began writing *Transcendental Style in Film: Ozu, Bresson, Dreyer*. It was, as he writes in the updated introduction to the volume, a way of working out the answer to a problem. At Christian Reformed Church, a Calvinist denomination in Grand

Rapids, Michigan where Schrader was brought up, film had been prohibited. He attended Calvin College, but was drawn to the forbidden. After graduation, he made his way from the Midwest to Los Angeles, leaving behind the sacred of the church for the profane of the screen. With his "full blown love" of cinema overtaking the knowledge of theological aesthetics still in his mind, he sought the bridge between these two worlds. As he would explain years later, "That old environment never goes away. It doesn't matter how far or fast you run, you don't outrun that childhood. Those spiritual issues continue to nag until you find different ways to deal with them or not deal with them. And you just keep circling around it."[5] Could cinema provide a similar path toward the spiritual that had originally been provided by organized religion and thought? "I wanted to square my love of movies with my religious upbringing."[6] Ozu, Bresson, and Dreyer provided that bridge.

He found that it was not through *content* that these films were able to approach deeper spiritual meaning, but through *style*. To "express the Holy," these artists did not need to produce films about religious subjects, but rather films that approached the transcendent. Their films were meditative, spiritual, leading toward the experience of God. This is different than religious films, or the contemporary "faith based" films. To Schrader, these are religious in plot but not spiritually transcendent, as they use the same devices to engage with the audience and lead them. To create a truly meditative film is to use withholding devices, rather than guiding the audience; it is a style defined by an embrace of the everyday, minimal camera movement, a lack of underscoring, long takes, with edits that linger on spaces rather than cutting away, and performances that give away little of the emotion the audience desires. Watching the film is a *journey*. As Schrader says about Bresson: "He lays out a way, almost like a path through a garden. And if you walk this path, and see what he shows you, you will eventually reach a point where your eyes will be lifted toward a deeper, more spiritual meaning. And this is a transcendental style."[7] The style also fits with Schrader's upbringing in the Calvinist faith. He speaks about John Calvin's own goal to "reduce the window of faith to as small an aperture as possible" in his writing, with "the tinier the aperture, then the more blinding the light of faith becomes in its brilliance," and then links this work directly to the transcendental style: "strip away conventional emotional associations and then you're left with this tiny little pinpoint that hits you at the end and freezes you into stasis."[8] Similar to Bresson's own claim from *Notes on the Cinematograph*, the transcendental style follows a "Production of emotion determined by a resistance to emotion."[9] In one of Bresson's few interviews in the later part of his career, he tells the young Schrader, "There is a presence of something which I call God, but I don't want to show it too much. I want people to feel it."[10] In *First Reformed*, Toller acknowledges this struggle, when he writes in his journal, "How often we ask for genuine experience when all we really want is emotion."

Schrader sets up a difficult task in analyzing the transcendental film, or rather, how the audience reaches stasis. The transcendent, he notes, "is beyond normal sense experience."[11] It is indescribable, an out-of-body experience, a connection with the Holy that can only be achieved in cinema through the various withholding techniques leaning away from the viewer, from realism and rationalism. He explains: "Transcendental style seeks to maximize the mystery of existence; it eschews all conventional interpretations of reality: realism, naturalism, psychologism, romanticism, expressionism, impressionism, and finally, rationalism."[12] How can we analyze such work? It is essential to understand that, in a way, we cannot. According to Schrader, criticism of these films is "a self-destructive process," because of the precise nature of transcendental art.[13] The task is "futile" for the very fact that "transcendental expression in religion and art attempts to bring man as close to the ineffable, invisible, and unknowable as words, images, and ideas can take him."[14] There is a mysticism to this work, a path to the spiritual that makes the endpoint a highly personal experience unable to be described, because even the critic's "most eloquent statements can only lead to silence."[15] The critic "can recognize the Transcendent, he can study those methods which brought him to that realization, but that actual 'why' of that realization is a mystery."[16]

This does not mean, however, that these films completely deflect critical engagement or are inscrutable. Certainly, Schrader wrote a book on the subject, and is able to discover the way these films present the immanent as they lead toward the transcendent. Like Bresson's pathway through the garden, we can describe the elements of the film—its connections to Schrader's own influences and preoccupations—to "describe the immanent and the manner in which it is transcended. He can discover how the immanent is expressive of the Transcendent."[17]

Although critics would ask him about using the style in his own work, Schrader often denied it, going so far as to tell one interviewer that he could never make a transcendental film. "They're the product of the type of artist that I can never be," he remarked, "That's the pure soul."[18] Over the course of his career, however, Schrader occasionally used the transcendental style, or at least stylistic choices that seemed incongruent with the studio product in which they appeared. We might consider Mishima's suicide in *Mishima: A Life in Four Chapters* (1985) or the final image of John LeTour's hand in *Light Sleeper* (1992) as examples. But these moments, while powerful, were isolated, as Schrader admits, the balance between his use of austere and abundant means created both interest in his work and criticism. "If you are going to fool around with spiritual issues, not propaganda—then you have to be really tricky."[19] He even worried about the effectiveness of film as a spiritual medium. "I don't really see film as a very useful tool for someone who wants to create religious, transcendental, or spiritual art," Schrader once explained, arguing that films are "probably inherently anti spiritual."²⁰ Talking to Sofia Coppola about *First Reformed* and the difficulties of guiding an audience toward the transcendental, he again advocates for the sparse means of storytelling. "You can't really push anybody into the mystery. All you can do is earn and guide them, but those steps they take." Like Bresson, a pathway is set through the garden, but it is restricted: "When you decide to touch the mystery, it's because you've been put in a kind of a tight spot by the artist, and one of the ways you can go is to jump forward."²¹

First Reformed is unique because it filters Toller's discernment through the transcendental style so that the audience no longer gets an invitation to identify with a character who, although righteous, later commits to a violent act of martyrdom. The plot, simply put, follows a pastor as he councils a young man against despair due to the implications of catastrophic climate change and then takes up his cause after he fails to keep him from suicide. In a variety of ways, Schrader uses *style* to keep easy answers or identification at a distance. The film's muted color palette dulls the emotional response and the use of 1:33:1 aspect ratio even denies the audience the standard theatrical perspective while eliminating over-the-shoulder shots during conversations. The camera rarely moves, and the editing leaves us in empty rooms for extra beats after characters leave, the lingering frame left free for our wandering eye. Lustmord's score acts more as sound design, bubbling underneath the surface along with Toller's internal struggle. These stylistic choices make for an austere, meditative film, stripping away at almost every corner the temptation to lead the audience rather than let them fall into the frame. Even while Schrader's earlier films are marked with similarly motivated characters, and glimpses of the transcendent, the formal qualities of his work were guided by the action, empathy, and violence that interested him. The film contains echoes of Schrader's influences—the character and journey of Toller is an amalgam of the men of the cloth in Ingmar Bergman's *Winter Light* (1963) and Robert Bresson's *Diary of a Country Priest*, with some of the environmental concerns in *The Devil, Probably* (1977) and the self-destructive journey taken in *Taxi Driver*—but the austere formalism of *First Reformed* makes it both a culmination of Schrader's thematic interests and an entirely new type of work for the director. Travis Bickle may keep a journal like the country priest, but *Taxi Driver* is not a transcendental work. *First Reformed* is a journey into stasis. The audience is left to read those near-inscrutable shadows of Toller's face, what Schrader calls the "certain physiognomy of a suffering man of the cloth."²² If Schrader is, as Kouvaros argues, always in search of an intellectual form to guide his work, it is doubly frustrating and fulfilling to situate Toller's journey in the transcendental style. The withholding devices—the lack of music, how the camera lingers, how the performances do not allow for easy interpretation, all make for an intimate response.

In a significant change, Toller is not only a man in search of community, but called to lead one. However, the dwindling flock and his inability to cause change leaves him feeling isolated and empty. Into this vacuum of God's silence pours the infection of martyrdom. Rather than lead, Toller eventually wants to destroy. He pours out his every thought on paper, as does Bresson's country priest. He is, as another pastor complains, "always in the garden," struggling while attending to his sparse flock. He asks unanswered questions, hearing only the silence of Bergman's God. And there is an explosive vigilantism in him, a righteousness not unlike that of Schrader's earlier creations. The film examines Toller's despair: despair about God's silence, despair about the inability of human beings to connect with one another, and eventually, his despair about the sense of impending destruction brought on by global warming. Will God forgive us for destroying His creation? Like all questions of faith, it is unanswerable, and will ultimately only be met with silence, but it does not mean that these characters can go on the journey toward their own understanding in this cloud of unknowing. Unfortunately for Toller, this journey leads toward destruction.

Toller surrounds himself with the guidance of the mystical theologians. On his bedside table are a stack of books that give further hints at his state of mind. Wedged between *The Cloud of Unknowing*, G. K. Chesterton's *Heretics*, and

Figure 11.1 Reverend Toller's bedside reading: the mystical theologians as well as Schrader's own childhood Bible.

Figure 11.2 "This journal is a form of speaking. Of communication, from one to the other. Communication which can be achieved simply, and in repose without prostration or abnegation. It is a form of prayer."

Thomas Merton: A Life in Letters is Schrader's own Bible from his childhood, the gift of his parents.[23] Along with the journal and his bottle of liquor on his desk, Toller also has an image of an outstretched hand holding a hazelnut. It is a reference from Julian of Norwich's *Revelations of Divine Love*. In one of the mystic's visions, she finds in the smallest object the recognition of the mysteries of the divine, and the power of God's love. These influences guide Toller, and give us a fuller understanding of both his struggle and his eventual humility.

Thomas Merton figures into the story in other ways. In his autobiography *The Seven Story Mountain*, he writes of a fateful summer during his childhood at Zion Episcopal church. While his mother was sick, he spent Sundays in Douglaston with his father, who played the organ during services. He describes the grounds as having a deep connection to community and history. "The old Zion church was a white wooden building, with a squat, square little belfry, standing on a hill, surrounded by high trees and a large graveyard," he writes, "and in a crypt underneath it were buried the original Douglas family, who had settled there on the short of the Sound some hundred years before." To the young boy, a stained-glass anchor behind the altar reveals contradictory desires. Rather than "stability in Hope: the theological virtue of Hope, dependence on God," he sees adventure and heroism at sea. A "strange interpretation," he concedes. And yet, the community teaches him the value of finding purpose in life as well as acknowledging a dependence on God. "One came out of the church with a kind of comfortable and satisfied feeling that something had been done that needed to be done, and that was all I knew about it." It is in our "very essence," he argues, that we "stand together with other men in order to acknowledge their common dependence on God, their Father and Creator."[24] In this formative time, he is already examining the value of community and the dependence on God. Later that year, Merton's mother died of stomach cancer, and they moved away, his life forever changed.[25] Although *First Reformed* is set in upstate New York, in the fictional town of Snowbridge outside Albany, it was filmed on the very same grounds of Merton's childhood stay in Douglaston.

In an early scene of the film, while walking through the cemetery of First Reformed, Reverend Ernst Toller finds an overturned grave. Toller, described in the screenplay as having a "face like a half rubbed away engraving on those tombstones, revealed in degrees of shadow," stands before the tombstone, leans over, and lifts it back into place. It is the everyday task of maintenance, tending the grounds of which he is the steward. Like so many of his cinematic predecessors, he longs to understand his place in the world. He thinks about the role of a pastor. "Some," his voiceover intones, "are called for their gregariousness. Some are called for their suffering. Some are called for their loneliness." Paul Schrader's protagonists have long been called for their loneliness, and like *Taxi Driver*'s Travis Bickle before him, Toller reminds us of Thomas Wolfe's lines from *God's Lonely Man*: "The whole conviction of my life now rests upon the belief that loneliness, far from being a rare and curious phenomenon, is the central and inevitable fact of human existence." Of those lonely men called to the priesthood, Toller finds some comfort in his understanding of the true depths of isolation and emptiness: "They are called by God because through the vessel of communication they can reach out and hold beating hearts in their hands. They are called because of their all-consuming knowledge of the emptiness of all things, that can only be filled by the presence of our savior." Throughout the film, he struggles with this emptiness.

"Discernment intersects with Christian life at every moment," he says later in the film. "Discernment. Listening and waiting for God's wish what action must be taken." In *First Reformed*, Toller dwells on this question of action, a continual meditation on the fundamental questions of who he is to be in this world, how he can connect to the people around him, and the role of God in the process. Toller struggles with prayer, but longs to communicate. He struggles with the fellowship of his community and his role in their lives. His body is failing him as he refuses to seek treatment beyond the bottle, and in his small, upstate New York church, he wrestles with hope and despair.

Merton, as a young seminarian, writes about his experiences of discernment. "My intention is to give myself entirely and without compromise to whatever work God wants to perform in me and through me," he writes in an early journal. "He has signified a certain path, a certain goal to be mine. That is why I am to keep in view, because that is His will."[26] Discernment remains this balance of understanding God's will and one's own path through and toward that place. Over the course of the film, Toller is confronted by his own place in the trajectory of his life and the church. A former military chaplain, he joined the service in the tradition of his father, and his father before him. He convinced his son to do the same and fight in Iraq, against the wishes of his wife, and their son died six months later in the desert. Convincing his son to fight in a war that had "no moral justification," all for the sake of tradition, tears a hole in his family, and leaves Toller with a lingering sense of guilt and shame. At First Reformed, he finds himself the latest in a long line of shepherds to a dwindling flock. "All those mighty men of God," he calls them, who have given years of service to the building and community he now leads. He gives tours about the long history of the church, complete with mentions of a bullet hole left from a Revolutionary War battle, and a secret hiding place once used in the Underground Railroad. But there remain just a handful of members of Toller's community. The biggest draw is a tidy gift shop where he sells one-size-fits-all hats to curious tourists. Dangling on the threads of history and tradition, Toller is lost. He wants to lead, to help, to be needed.

Two conversations between a pastor and a man despairing with similar questions provide the framework for *First Reformed*. The questions asked—"Will God forgive us?" and "Why must we go on living?"—get to the heart of both our possible destruction and the despair that follows once the characters realize these questions will not be answered—at least not by God. In *First Reformed*, Toller is confronted by a member of the community, Michael (Philip Ettinger), about the destruction of the Earth due to global warming. In the film's spiritual predecessor, Ingmar Bergman's *Winter Light*, Tomas must console Jonas, overcome with fear of the atomic bomb. The Earth is on the path to destruction. In *Winter Light*, it is the Chinese who leave Jonas in fear. An article he reads about the atom bomb in the hands of those "who have nothing to lose" leaves him without hope. In *First Reformed*, the stakes are similarly high, a new destructive, collective force to fear. To Tomas and Toller, Jonas and Michael, these questions lead them to question their worth, their very lives. In both films, the pastors are challenged to rise to the occasion, providing comfort and guidance to members of their community.

GOD'S SILENCE

In *Winter Light*, Tomas reassures Jonas that "Everyone feels this dread to some extent. We must trust God." But as Jonas looks up, Tomas cannot meet his gaze and withdraws. His hand wavers as he draws it across his desk. How to proceed? He moves over to Jonas. "We live our simple daily lives. And atrocities shatter the security of our world. It's so overwhelming, and God seems so very remote. I feel so helpless. I don't know what to say. I understand your anguish," he turns to Jonas, "but life goes on." "Why do we have to go on living?" Jonas replies, before begging off the conversation. "Besides, we're powerless to do anything." Tomas's conversation with Jonas reveals the depths of his own despair. Afterward, he reflects on their conversation. What could he have done differently? What combination of words might lead Jonas to hope, to go on living rather than continue to slip into despair. He feels abandoned by God, echoing Jesus's lament on the cross, "Why hath thou forsaken me?"

Thomas Merton, writing at the same time Jonas is despairing about the Cold War fears of nuclear annihilation in *Winter Light*, considers the implications of this threat on the individual. As Ronald E. Powaski notes, the "relatively trivial political issue" dangled over the heads of millions of individual citizens with everything to lose but without a say in the matter. These civilian populations were left with the feeling of powerlessness while the issue remained "the greatest and most agonizing moral issue of our time."[27] The fear and sense of powerlessness in the face of destruction threatens to lead humanity directly down the path of inevitability. As Merton remarks:

> If we continue to yield to theoretically irresistible determinism and to vague 'historic forces' without striving to resist and control them, if we let these forces drive us to demonic activism in the realm of politics and technology, we face something more than the material evil of universal destruction. We face moral responsibility for global suicide. Much more than that, we are going to find ourselves gradually moving into a situation in which we are practically compelled by the 'logic of circumstances' deliberately to choose the course that leads to destruction.[28]

What could the individual accomplish in this situation? Merton feared the resignation of the masses to the inevitability of such annihilation. "Every free man," he argued, needed to "refuse his consent and deny his cooperation to this greatest of crimes." Just as Toller cautions against the imbalance between hope and despair, calling for wisdom, Merton fears that we may be "rendered physically helpless by the consequences of judgments made in high places over which we have no control." We must, he argues, "develop moral, spiritual, and political wisdom" to combat what is immoral.[29] Furthermore, he argues, this is a Christian duty. Faced with the possibility of destruction, Christians "are most gravely and seriously bound" to "try at all costs to avoid so enormous a disaster."[30] Although Merton is writing in the years of the Cold War, reflecting some of the fears of Jonas, his words are easily applied to the struggles of Michael and Toller in *First Reformed*. Courage, Toller suggests, is the solution to despair. In the face of the unknown, we must embrace the will of God. Reconciling these forces remains "life itself." Toller's engagement with Michael is, on the surface, more of a challenge he is willing to meet than Tomas. They both wrestle over the possibilities of the conversation, but while Tomas only offers his own fear, Toller provides at least a call for courage in the light of these fears. And yet neither is able to deter them from committing suicide. Both Jonas and Michael, counseled by struggling, lonely men of God, succumb to their despair and take their own lives.

Tomas and Toller are left to deal with the consequences of their perceived failures. For Tomas, his despair eventually leads him back to the church, to those who continue to desire the routine of communion. Writing about his preparation for *Winter Light* and the search for how to resolve Tomas's despair, Bergman recalls his process and the inspiration for the ending. Travelling to different churches in the spring, he would sit inside and watch the light change, trying to figure out how to end the film. During a visit from his father, they also attend a service. The pastor comes in, says he is sick and will conduct an abbreviated service without communion. Bergman's father, himself a pastor, rises from the pew. "I must speak to that creature," he says, and goes back to the sacristy to scold him. "A short and agitated conversation ensued," Bergman remembers, and, "A few minutes later, the churchwarden appeared. He smiled in embarrassment and explained that there would be a communion service."

Bergman declares:

Thus I was given the end of *Winter Light* and the codification of a rule I have always followed and was to follow from then on: irrespective of everything, you will hold your communion. It is important to the churchgoer, but even more important to you. We shall have to see if it is important to God. If there is no other god than your hope as such, it is important to that god too.[31]

Winter Light ends as it begins, with a return to the ceremony, a reliance on the power of community and a reliance on God, a continued balance between hope and despair.

First Reformed uses a similar framework. After the opening service, Toller is approached by Mary, the pregnant wife of Michael, a climate activist recently returned from a stint in jail. Michael now questions the ethics of bringing their child into the world in the face of the near-certain destruction of our planet due to climate change. Toller agrees to meet with him the next day, and the conversation follows similar lines as in *Winter Light*, but with the sparse means of the transcendental style that refuses to tell us how to feel. Instead, we watch what Toller will later call an exhilarating conversation, like Jacob wrestling the angel, "every response a mortal struggle." Michael's despair is palpable when the conversation begins. Standing up from his seat, he leads Toller through a litany of facts about the effects of global warming. Temperatures are rising at an alarming rate. We are approaching a threshold of no return. He points out martyrs to the cause. José Cláudio Ribeiro da Silva and his wife, Maria do Espírito Santo, who were assassinated in the fields of Brazil after protesting deforestation and fighting for rural farmers. And there is Dorothy Stang, a Roman Catholic nun in the order of the Sisters of Notre Dame, assassinated in 2005 for her outspoken opposition of the loggers and landowners of Brazil. "She was a nun," he tells Toller, his voice faltering, connecting climate activism directly to religious and moral responsibility. "And what was the reason for their deaths?" he asks. "If nothing was done," he pleads, then what is the value of their sacrifice? Throughout the scene, we watch as Toller's face remains inscrutable. Other than a slight dolly toward his face, we see little of the exhilaration. What we do not see, however, continues to invite the viewer to participate in his struggle. "Who can know the mind of God?" Toller responds. And the audience must sit with that question. Instead of an answer, Toller and the film submit that "life itself" is living in the shadow of these unanswerable questions. "Hope and Despair. Holding these two ideas in our head at the same time is life itself," he tells Michael. But for Toller, Michael's death leads him toward a darker end, his misguided path toward destruction and martyrdom.

Schrader has commented at length about Michael's real-life concerns. Whereas the eventual path toward martyrdom is understood as the troubling response by a sick man, the cause is seen as just. "We have chosen, more or less, not to sacrifice our present lifestyle for the lives of our children. There's not much we can do about that," Schrader laments about the destruction of the planet. Through greed and selfishness, it seems that nothing will be left behind for future generations. The response to this crisis, transferred from Michael to Toller, is what drives the narrative of despair:

> What I found interesting in doing this film is, you have a man, Reverend Toller, who is sick—he has what Kierkegaard called "the sickness unto death," which is despair. And he's trying to fix it somehow, either through the rituals of the church or through alcohol or keeping a journal. And then he comes across this boy, who is also in despair, and he fails to help the boy, but then he catches the boy's "virus," which I found so interesting. Was he an environmentalist all along, or was he just looking for an excuse to enable his death trip?[32]

The death trip is initiated by Michael's suicide and Toller's investigation into Balq Industries. Toller, taking up Michael's cause, spends the dark hours of the night searching the Internet for facts about the company's history of pollution, while also watching videos of suicide bombers.

But when he challenges Balq (Michael Gaston) and Jeffers (Cedric Kyles) to simply discuss the matter, Toller is met with resistance. The president of Balq Industries, both the fiscal sponsor of his church's improvements and the mouthpiece for a company that pollutes the local water and soil, scoffs at the performance of Neil Young's *Who's Gonna Stand Up?* at the memorial for Michael. He requests that "there won't be anything political" at the 250th anniversary reconsecration of First Reformed, which he is underwriting, and, if it were not for his donations, would have seen the church become a "parking lot." In Balq's hypocrisy, we see the destructive possibilities of humanity. He questions Toller's knowledge of God's intentions while he pollutes the Earth. What is a man of God to do in the face of such ignorance? Toller wonders what Michael's death was for. What his own life is for. If he cannot fight back against Balq, who helps fund his own church's restoration, then what can he do? Toller falls deeper into despair, the twisted response to what he has learned about Balq, climate change, and Michael's death. In his journal, Toller laments, "Despair is a development of pride so great that it chooses someone's certitude rather than admit that God is more creative than we are." This echoes Merton's own words in *New Seeds of Contemplation*, where he writes of despair as a result of pride. "Despair is the ultimate development of a pride so great and so stiff-necked that it selects the absolute misery of damnation rather than accept happiness from the hands of God and thereby acknowledge that God is above us and that we are not capable of fulfilling our destiny by ourselves."[33] Toller's intended suicide bombing is the unfortunate end of the road for a man who can no longer stand the silence of those around him, and misunderstands the need for bloodshed in light of such inaction. It is all he has to give, for he too despairs in God's silence.

But his path also leads him toward the possibility of life and love. Ultimately, Toller and Mary find comfort and community with each other. Her embrace of hope and life shows the wisdom that Toller hoped to instill in Michael even as he himself despaired. "I share Michael's beliefs, but not his despair," she tells him. "I wanna live. I want to be a mother. I want to have this child." Their shared concern about Michael and grief over his loss slowly transforms into a different kind of dependence. They try to find happiness in the ordinary. They go on a bike ride—yet another nod to *Diary of a Country Priest*. He helps her pack up Michael's belongings. And he helps dispose of his suicide vest—or so she thinks.

One night, in distress, Mary visits Toller at home. She is restless and anxious, but tells him about the Magical Mystery Tour—something she and Michael would do in order to focus themselves and connect. After an awkward beat, he asks if she would like him to try, and she agrees. Toller and Mary lie face to face, leaning on each other, slowly breathing and clasping hands. As they make this intimate connection, the world slips away, and they begin to float, similar to the mother in Tarkovsky's *Mirror* (1975). After the stylistic sparseness of the film, this is the first hint that these characters will transcend beyond the formally austere frame. The room slips away as they float in air. Their breathing in rhythm transforms the world around them to a vast field of stars, then into the beautiful landscapes of the Earth. However, the peaceful images slip away as Toller can't help but think about the waste and destruction. Instead his vision transforms into a wasteland of tires and factories. It is seemingly too late. Toller glides past the site of Michael's memorial service. The dead man stands on the deck of a rusting ship, haunting him.

LEANING, LEAN IN

Discernment and despair. Toller's despair in *First Reformed*, rooted in isolation, disconnection, and his failure to guide the church, leads him astray. His "new form of prayer" is martyrdom, and in the last reel of the film he makes Michael's vest his own. He begins to twist the words of scripture to his own means, such as Ephesians 6:12: "For our struggle is not against flesh and blood, but against the rulers, against the authorities, against the powers of this dark world." He tours a Balq Industries warehouse and paces at the edge of the Hanstown Kill where Michael's ashes have been spread. He speaks with passion to Jeffers about the government's inaction on climate issues and the silence of the church. But their debate is fruitless, as they trade competing lines from scripture that both criticize the destruction of the Earth and embrace the possibility of a new biblical flood.

For Toller, this despair culminates in the final moments of the film, in his "new form of prayer." After painstakingly keeping the audience at a distance, Schrader pulls us in and we reach the ineffable. A crowd gathers for First Reformed's reconsecration ceremony, but Toller is nowhere to be found. While members of the community enter the church, including the governor, Toller remains in his room. Radicalized by Michael's work and his own investigation into Balq Industries, he dons the suicide vest. Rebuked by both Jeffers and Balq for his attempts to even discuss environmental policy he is left, he believes, with no other choice but martyrdom. With his choice, the screen erupts with the decisive action, and, if Schrader has succeeded, the audience now falls into the screen.

Similar to Bresson's work, music becomes a defining aspect of shattering the transcendental style.[34] In *First Reformed*, as Schrader prepares his intended martyrdom, the congregation waits inside the church. Esther climbs the steps of the altar and faces them. She begins to sing Anthony J. Showalter and Elisha Hoffman's *Leaning on the Everlasting Arms*: "What a fellowship, what a joy divine, Leaning on the everlasting arms; What a blessedness, what a peace is mine, Leaning on the everlasting arms." It is a fitting song that brings emotion and empathy to the screen, the lyrics celebrating both human connection and a reliance on the embrace of the unknown. While the crowd waits, Toller writes a final journal entry, connects the wires of the vest, and prepares to enter the church for the last time. But just as we fear Toller will go through with his plan, he sees Mary enter the building and he immediately wavers, his once-relaxed face now twisting into a grimace as he changes his plans. He bends over and screams into his garments, removes the vest and leaves the frame. The song continues to build.

In a nod to Hazel Motes in Flannery O'Connor's *Wise Blood*, Toller re-emerges from his room and begins to wrap barbed wire, which until recently was set up to catch rabbits on the grounds of the church, around his torso.[35] We watch as each length of flesh-tearing wire is strung around his body, his own flesh replacing the destruction of the communal body. After his crown of thorns is complete, he wraps himself in white, his blood marking his wounds through the fabric. In another break from the austere style, we see Toller empty his glass, the liquid hitting the floorboards in slow motion. On the table where Toller has poured out his thoughts, he places the glass into which he now pours drain cleaner.

It is in this moment that the story very well may be over, as it is unclear if the final images are of life or death. Mary appears in the room. No footsteps have been heard, the door never opened. For the first time in the film, we hear Toller called by his name. "Ernst," she says from the doorway, a simple recognition of Toller not as a man of the cloth, but simply as a man.

Ernst and Mary rush toward each other and embrace. As the camera swirls around them, the song continues. It is into Mary's arms that he falls, as she into his. Inside the church, Esther continues to sing while the congregation remains oblivious to how close they have come to death. *Leaning, lea*—the film cuts to black as the song is cut short. We are jarringly reminded that "All meditative cinema shares an end point. It is silence."[36]

The lingering question of God's forgiveness is never answered, but, as Thomas Merton writes, "But there is greater comfort in the substance of silence than in the answer to a question. Eternity is in the present. Eternity is in the palm of the hand. Eternity is a seed of fire, whose sudden roots break barriers that keep my heart from being an abyss."[37] Perhaps it is as Julian of Norwich writes of the hazelnut that adorns Toller's desk:

> And he showed me more, a little thing, the size of a hazelnut, on the palm of my hand, round like a ball. I looked at it thoughtfully and wondered, "What is this?" And the answer came, "It is all that is made." I marvelled that it continued to exist and did not suddenly disintegrate; it was so small. And again my mind supplied the answer, "It exists, both now and for ever, because God loves it." In short, everything owes its existence to the love of God.[38]

During the press tour for the film, Schrader remarked on various occasions how the ending is meant to be ambiguous. Does Toller die, having drunk the drain cleaner he used earlier in the film to unclog the toilet as he thought about Christian discernment? Is Mary a vision from God, a miracle to behold as Toller ends his life, a misbegotten attempt at martyrdom as a way to equate his own toil with that of Christ's suffering? Or does Mary's entrance and utterance of his name provide him with that last-second glimmer of hope to keep on living?

While Schrader provides no answer to the narrative question, he is clear about the issues of climate change. "His cause is just," Toller says of Michael's activism. And yet, there is much room for despair. "The universe will be well rid of us," Schrader says of the impending destruction that awaits. Claiming that "we have more or less soiled our nest," with our prioritization of comfort rather than future generations, he says, "Anyone who is hopeful is simply not paying attention."[39] Between hope and despair, even believing that we will be shaken from the bonds of a soiled planet, hope, suggests Schrader, is the only choice we have. In light of the apparent destruction of the environment, with seemingly little room for a course correction, there remains only the *choice*. "We have entered a time in human history where you must choose hope, even if you have no reason to," he explained. Accepting the possibility that human beings have squandered their time on Earth, there is still the decision to make. "You have to choose, because there isn't much reason to hope."[40]

In the end, *First Reformed* raises more questions than answers. It provides an avenue for both hope and despair. It does not answer the central question of whether or not God will forgive us for what we have done to the planet, or if there will be a response to our queries at all. Just as Algot recognizes in the final moments of Bergman's *Winter Light*, the physical suffering of Christ through the passion and crucifixion were not the worst part of his final hours. Instead, it was the absence of the voice of God. We, too, must acknowledge this absence and choose between hope and despair, "life itself," as Toller explains to Michael. *First Reformed* becomes intensely personal, with Schrader only guiding us through the garden. Where we go from there is our choice, whether it is toward contemplation or action. As Neil Young's lyrics remind us, "This all starts with you and me."

NOTES

1. Thomas Merton, *The Sign of Jonas* (New York: Octagon Books, 1983), 28.
2. Nicolas Cage, "Paul Schrader," *Interview*, April/May 2018, 115.
3. David Poland, "DP/30: Paul Schrader, First Reformed," YouTube video, 26:48, May 15, 2018, https://www.youtube.com/watch?v=7yOZB2MJOLM.

4. George Kouvaros, *Paul Schrader* (Urbana: University of Illinois Press, 2008), 5.
5. Jennifer L. Holberg, *Shouts and Whispers: Twenty-One Writers Speak about their Writing and their Faith* (Grand Rapids, MI: Eerdmans, 2006), 113.
6. Paul Schrader, *Transcendental Style in Film: Ozu, Bresson, Dreyer* (Oakland, CA: University of California Press, 2018), 2.
7. *The Road to Bresson*, DVD, directed by Leo De Boer and Jurriën Rood, 1984, New York: Criterion, 2003.
8. Kevin Jackson, *Schrader on Schrader* (London: Faber and Faber, 2004), 29.
9. Robert Bresson and Jonathan Griffin, *Notes on the Cinematographer* (New York: New York Review Books, 2016), 116.
10. Paul Schrader, "Robert Bresson, Possibly," *Film Comment*, September–October 1977, 27.
11. Ibid., 37.
12. Ibid., 42.
13. Ibid., 39.
14. Ibid., 39.
15. Ibid., 39.
16. Ibid., 111.
17. Ibid., 39.
18. Michael Bliss, "Affliction and Forgiveness: An Interview with Paul Schrader," *Film Quarterly*, Autumn 2000, 9.
19. Holberg, 114.
20. Holberg, 114.
21. Sofia Coppola, "This Is How It Should End with Paul Schrader & Sofia Coppola," A24 Films, May 30, 2018, https://a24films.com/notes/2018/05/episode-04-this-is-how-it-should-end-with-paul-schrader-sofia-coppola.
22. Ibid.
23. Schrader reveals this in the DVD commentary for the film.
24. Thomas Merton, *Seven Story Mountain* (New York: Harcourt, Brace, 1948), 13.
25. I do not wish to make the connection here to the country priest and Toller's stomach ailments, but the coincidence remains.
26. Merton, *The Sign of Jonas*, 30.
27. Ronald E. Powaski, *Thomas Merton on Nuclear Weapons* (Chicago: Loyola University Press, 1988), 27.
28. Ibid., 27. Although I found this quote in my research on Merton's responses to the Cold War and nuclear disarmament, Gillian Horvat has also made this connection in an insightful article about Schrader's *Exorcist* prequel, *Exorcist: Dominion*. See Gillian Horvat, "Paul Schrader's Priests and Transcendental Style: From *Dominion* to *First Reformed*," *Sight and Sound*, December 12, 2018, https://www.bfi.org.uk/news-opinion/sight-sound-magazine/features/paul-schrader-first-reformed-dominion-exorcist-priests-transcendental-style.
29. Powaski, 28.
30. Ibid., 77.
31. Ingmar Bergman and Joan Tate, *The Magic Lantern: An Autobiography* (New York: Penguin Books, 1944), 272.
32. Nicolas Cage, "Paul Schrader," *Interview*, April/May 2018, 115.
33. Thomas Merton, *New Seeds of Contemplation* (New York: New Directions, 1972), 180.
34. The ending of *Light Sleeper* has a similar moment that prefigures both the path the film has taken as well as Mary's sudden appearance in Toller's room. The lyrics of Michael Been's song *Fate* play over the final moments: "The beast is at the door/the book is open wide/Now to seal my fate/now to step inside."

35. When asked why he puts stones and glass in his shoes, and wraps barbed wire around his chest, Motes tells the landlady, "to pay," for he is "not clean."
36. Schrader, 31.
37. Merton, *The Sign of Jonas*, 361.
38. Julian of Norwich and Clifton Wolters, *Revelations of Divine Love* (Harmondsworth: Penguin, 1990), 68.
39. Brent Lang, "Paul Schrader: The Human Race is Ending," *Variety*, September 15, 2017, https://variety.com/2017/film/news/paul-schrader-first-reformed-toronto-film-festival-1202560593.
40. Michael Ewins, "In Conversation: Paul Schrader," *Clash Music*, July 30, 2018, https://www.clashmusic.com/features/in-conversation-paul-schrader.

PART III

Interview

CHAPTER 12

Interview with Paul Schrader conducted by Michelle E. Moore and Brian Brems on 9/27/2018 at the Rail Line Diner, NYC

MEM: Now that the jaunt for *First Reformed* is over, how are you spending your time?

Schrader: Well, I've got to, now, go back on that road again because award season is coming. And so they have a few things planned for me. A24 [the distributors] is going to make a push for both Ethan and myself. And so it's starting up again. But mostly I've been writing and done a number of scripts. But to be honest I'm not in any great hurry. There was something I was going to do in April that I wrote but that fell apart half an hour ago on the West Side Highway.

BB: Wow. What was that?

Schrader: The thing I was doing with Willem and Ethan. But maybe we could put it back together.

BB: So we want to look both kind of back and forward a little bit. You've had a very different career from a lot of your contemporaries: [Martin] Scorsese and [Steven] Spielberg and [George] Lucas and [Brian] DePalma and [Francis Ford] Coppola, and those people. What do you think your place is among that generation of filmmakers?

Schrader: Well, I never really was drawn to the big toys. And they all are on—the big toys is the big budgets, the long shooting schedules, all of that, which means that you have to really play in the systems. And because my interest in film began with European cinema in the '60s, if I could make films like those, that was enough. If I could do my [Ingmar] Bergman or my [Jean-Luc] Godard films, it was still hard, but I had no real desire to do a big-budget thing. And so for me to do *First Reformed* at three and a half million is just—I mean, *Pickpocket* is seventy-five minutes long.

MEM: Now that you've been a director for some time, what do you think about auteur theory, now in 2018?

Schrader: I think they're valid. But they're valid to the extent that the director in most films is the nozzle through which everything must move. And you're making decisions very, very fast. Now, making decisions about whether you should put that top button up or whether we want to swap that tie out and whether we want to throw a little light over here and whether we want—anyway, I'm making decisions that fast. A lot of them are instinctual. And so you get in the editing room after, and you have all this footage. And you say, well, I guess that's who I am. And so even if you are not an auteur, an author in terms of theme, you are in terms of what is put together. And Ridley Scott put together a film this year, just like he did thirty and forty years ago. And now for me, an auteur is not just the guy in charge of the crews because that's all a director really is. To me, an auteur is also someone who has a mobilizing vision and so I would have a much narrower view of what a film auteur is.

Figure 12.1 Interview with Paul Schrader. Photo credit: © 2018 by Mark Weissburg.

BB: Speaking to that, many of your films feature alienated men who often turn to crime or violence as an outlet for their frustrations, so what keeps you returning to that characterization?

Schrader: Well, you don't have that many stories to tell. I think it was [Jean] Renoir who said, "Every director has one movie to make, and he just makes it in different ways." And for me, the defining moment is when I realized I needed to get out of an insular community, one which was not only trying to dictate what you did but also what you thought. And you'll have to do that with a certain amount of propulsion and a certain amount of cruelty. And so when you take that urge and then you mix it with the Christian dogma which is a lot about the dark night of the soul and the need for redemptive blood, and you start mixing those two together, and in an adolescent way it comes out as *Taxi Driver* and in old man's way it comes out in *First Reformed*. It's not really that different. Now, clearly, a film that has such a strong signature as those films, you can't do every single time. And so I have made other kinds of films. They are united. I see the linkages. Some people do, some people don't, but they're all united by a certain intelligence, which is: Wouldn't it be interesting to do something a little different? And some lean a little heavier on issues of morality than others do.

BB: What frustrates you about filmmaking in the last ten years?

Schrader: Well, it's so obvious. It's about raising money enough, very frustrating. Now, with the new technology, there's a good and bad side to that. The good side is that almost anybody can make a movie, the bad side is almost no one can make money at it. So it used to take five million dollars to make a movie, and if somebody gave you five million dollars, there was a good chance they thought they'd get their money back. Now, you can make a film for—a friend of mine showed me his film yesterday—made for thirty thousand dollars. He'll lose all thirty of it. And in the past, if you made a film, you got paid. The director got paid. The writer got paid. Today, it's much more like painting and music. You can actually do the work and not get paid. You can do twenty paintings in your basement and not earn a dime. So the democratization of the technology has made film much more like the other arts. It had an exceptional relationship with capitalism for a hundred years, but that special relationship is over.

MEM: You've had your share of run-ins with executives and producers over the years about exactly what you've been just talking about. And your films seem to be about frustration to some extent, so how do these run-ins play out in the depiction of frustrated characters?

Schrader: Not more than normal. I've had two bad cases, and both of those is because money was coming into the industry that wasn't really movie money. And so, the first three or four films I did it at the studios and then the independent route, and I never thought I needed final cut because they would have their notes and you would have your notes and you'd talk a lot and that sometimes the film would get a little better and sometimes it wouldn't, but it was pretty much what you wanted. Then you add in this new crop of people who not only don't like movies much, don't even see movies much and have just sort of formulas. And so, that's when I really got caught on—well, at first I caught on *The Exorcist* because that was a producer that I knew other directors wouldn't work for because he was Harry Scissorhands. But I thought I would be all right and I wasn't. And then, I had another situation when I thought I'd be all right and I wasn't. And that's why I did *Dog Eat Dog*, to get final cut. But I would have—I didn't feel the need to ask for final cut in the past. I mean, I did some things I shouldn't have done, but I did them of my own volition. If you miscast a film, it's not their fault.

MEM: So your work continually blurs the line between pornography and Hollywood filmmaking, especially with your repeated emphasis on full-frontal male nudity.

Schrader: Well, I wouldn't say that. I mean, I had that shot in *Gigolo*, which is the first of its kind. And our thinking at that time was they have full-frontal female but not male, with a few exceptions like *Women in Love*. And I said if you're going to make a film about a male sex object, you've got to do the same thing you would do if it was a female sex object. And so, I talked to Richard about it and we decided to do it, but I think that's my only instance all the films that—

MEM: No, not all the films. *Canyons* has one. [Note: And *Dog Eat Dog* and *Cat People*.]

Schrader: Oh yeah, yeah, yeah. But that's Bret [Easton Ellis].

[Laughter.]

Schrader: But I would have liked to do it in *Auto Focus*. But Willem is well-endowed by nature. And Greg is normal by nature. And the characters they played were the flip. So Greg came to me and said, "I've seen Willem on-screen, and I'm supposed to be the one with the—who did the operation to get the bigger dick. I don't know if you've seen the two of us together. That's going to be a plot point." [Laughter.] And so we couldn't do that.

BB: So on that, you've received a lot of attention for your male characterizations. But what about the women in your films? Why did they receive less

Figure 12.2 Interview with Paul Schrader. Photo credit: © 2018 by Mark Weissburg.

attention? Do you approach the female-driven films differently? *Cat People*, *Patty Hearst*—

Schrader: Yeah, those are the two. *Patty Hearst*, in a way, is a story of survival. But in both those cases, that was material developed by someone else and I was approached. I don't think I have ever developed anything on my own for anything other than a male character.

BB: Why not?

Schrader: You do what you're comfortable with. There's plenty of other people who can do female characters. I can do a certain kind of male character in a way that is mine. Why should I try to compete with Nancy Meyers or what's-her-name, from *Detroit*?

BB: Bigelow. Kathryn Bigelow.

Schrader: Yeah. I have a feeling that if I went into that arena, I would just make an inferior version of what I do. And why do that just to make a political point that I can? And the same thing's true about other authors. Some authors write great female characters even though they're men, and their male characters aren't as good as their female characters. But you do what you're good at.

MEM: So you brought up Willem Dafoe in your last answer. So why do you continue to collaborate with him?

Schrader: Well, I know him. That has a lot to do with it. We're friends. Very few actors and directors are friends because the care and maintenance of an actor's ego is usually something you can kind of tolerate while you're working. But once you're not working together, they've got other people to take care and maintain their egos. You don't have to do it anymore. But Willem is a friend, and I also—I was first attracted to him because he can go small, he can go big. And people were having him go big—the whole Bobby Peru thing. And thinking about *Light Sleeper*, I thought it would be interesting to see him play small. But in the case of *Light Sleeper*, you had a movie that was hard to finance, was getting made in the middle of a strike. I knew Willem because of *Last Temptation* [*of Christ*]. And I could get it made with him. And if that had been a mistake, if I had felt I made a mistake, obviously, I wouldn't be working with him again. If it had been like Woody [Harrelson] and *The Walker* where I made that mistake to get it made and we both knew it—but so yeah, no. It's not like this new one I was going to do with Willem and Ethan [Hawke]. But I went to them because I had sent them both the script and I knew they'd give me an answer in a few days. You go the other route, you wait four months before they even read, another four months before you get an answer. You could spend forever waiting. I've got a script that we're going to Plan B [Entertainment Company] and Brad Pitt on. I said, "Well, when are you going to answer?" We'll wait a couple months, and then if we don't hear, then we'll move on. And I don't have that many more films left in me, and I don't want to wait two years to get an answer.

BB: You tend to cast well-known actors in your roles, so Ethan Hawke, Lindsay Lohan in *The Canyons*, Nicolas Cage, even De Niro—I know that Scorsese cast De Niro in *Taxi Driver*, but why those particular actors in those roles?

Schrader: Well, you've got to justify your budget, so you need to put some people in there. So I go to Ethan on *First Reformed*. Then the financiers say, "For the girl, here's ten names." And you look at the ten names. You go through them all and say, "Amanda [Seyfried], she's interesting. I think she might do this." Then you go to her, but you don't go to her in a vacuum. You go to her because she's on that list [laughter]. And so you have to have a—you have to package your film. I mean, one of the nice things about *Canyons* was that we didn't need anything. We didn't need stylists. We didn't need insurance. We just made it ourselves. And I didn't think I would cast Lindsay. She came to us because she couldn't work. And so she was willing to do it for a hundred dollars a day. So then all of a sudden, we had a name. But we didn't need a name. Everybody else in the film was cast online through YouCastIt. But that was an interesting experiment and I'm really glad I did it. I wouldn't do it again!

MEM: And yet these actors you're choosing off the list always offer such amazingly compelling performances.

Schrader: I mean, I think that has to do with the writing. Most actors, if they're working, are pretty good. And if they have good material, they're going to give good performances. And if they have bad material—the directing of actors is primarily casting. You get the right actor in the right role. Right time of his life, the mindset. He or she is going to give a terrific performance, and you put Ethan in *First Reformed*, he's going to give a great performance. I haven't seen the film, but I could put him in something like *Stockholm Syndrome*, I assume he'd give a bad performance, or you put him in that *Valerian* thing, he's going to give a bad performance. Nobody could make that work.

MEM: For so many of your films, we're watching because we're watching the actors perform their lines. And we're not in close-up, but we are in shots where all we're doing is watching these actors perform. And it makes me wonder about Cinema of the Face [Georges Méliès], and I'm wondering if that informs the filming for you as you direct these actors?

Schrader: Yeah. I mean obviously, you take a situation like *Affliction*, I had planned to have a very mobile camera. Going to rehearsal, I looked up to the cinematographer and said, "Paul [Sarossy], all those shots we were talking about, we ain't going to do it. I just saw Nick rehearsing, and the most interesting thing is him. No need to dance around the room. He's there." Whereas other films, you move a lot. *Comfort of Strangers* is very, very fluid, and almost always on the move except in a few situations. And that's a very dialogue-driven movie because it's Harold Pinter, but something about the sensuousness of always moving and I like it in that film. Whereas in *First Reformed*, I didn't move at all. So it's horses for courses.

MEM: So how does that—does it—connect to the idea of transcendental filmmaking?

Schrader: Well, I've only tried to do that in one film. Use the withholding devices. As I said in that essay, there's about ten of them. And everybody who works on the contemplative side goes back to those devices, but they don't use them all in the same proportion. Like a buffet, some people get the dim sum and other people get the corned beef. But you do come back to these ten or so devices if you are going to withhold. And you can't have transcendental style without withholding. There is no such thing as active-transcendental style any more than there is such a thing as fast meditation [laughter].

BB: So you've been very clear that you don't think you've used transcendental until *First Reformed*, so why do you think critics make the case that some of your other films do? What are they seeing in those movies that move them to make those connections?

Schrader: They're just being lazy.

BB: Okay.

Schrader: I mean. Here's the book. Here's the film. And let's make some connection. And I've been saying for decades. You'll know when I'm trying to make transcendental films. You don't have to read it in there. I'm smart enough to know the rules. And one of the reasons I've been doing it in the past was also budgetary because that kind of film is a very esoteric, limited audience kind of film. And if you go out and raise eight or ten million dollars to make that film, it's going to be a debacle, and your reputation will be permanently hurt, and your ability to make more films will be hurt. But now when the price point comes down to under four, you're saying, okay. This is not an irresponsible investment anymore. And anybody who invests in this film has a pretty good chance of getting their money back. So that was also a consideration. If I had tried early on in my life to emulate Bresson or Bergman, I would have failed not only creatively, but also financially. And that would have been that.

BB: Would you say you've made use of those withholding techniques from time to time, even in a non-transcendental-style film?

Schrader: Well, sometimes the tableaus, like the pillow shots in *American Gigolo*, which is a little bit of that. But I'm always using music. And music is numero uno withholding device. I've always liked to move the camera. And I've always liked depth-of-field. So you start to use planimetric compositions. There are no over-the-shoulders in *First Reformed*. And over-the-shoulders is a basic bread and butter of storytelling. But over-the-shoulder is a depth and creates a sense of relationship between the characters. Whereas frontality doesn't. So you're asking the viewer to supply something that you're not supplying. What is the depth in here?

MEM: The new introduction to your book sets up the book as a problem looking for an answer, which is the academic question. Do you conceive of filmmaking the same way? Is there a problem that filmmaking is trying to solve?

Schrader: Well, I mean, individual films are always based on a problem. That's how I started out with *Taxi Driver*. The problem, the metaphor, the story. And when I taught it was always about problems. We wouldn't get into writing for maybe four, five weeks. The first four or five weeks were essentially extended therapy sessions with everybody because I believe, and I've said this often, that filmmaking—art's rather, quite practical that way, as practical as any other tool, that you can actually use it to address problems. But you asked a slightly different question. I don't understand—were you talking about the problem with filmmaking?

MEM: Well, I'm asking how—because in the introduction—there's this academic formulation with the theory that you have the problem—you pose the problem and then you write it to answer the problem that's posed. So I'm wondering if that formulation is—

Schrader: The problem being, how do you address the immaterial with the material medium?

MEM: Yes. In the book, it's just to think in those terms. To set things up as a problem, a question, then to search for the answers. It's very academic, and I'm seeing in your films, there's a problem and then the search for the answers in the film, and sometimes the characters are even searching for answers to the problems, and I'm wondering how you see those two disciplines informing each other.

Schrader: Well, I mean, obviously, critical discipline and the creative discipline are very different, and I'm sure you've read, I've given this analogy about the pregnant woman versus the corpse. And you have to leave room for the mystery in there, and so how does that manifest itself? In the case of *First Reformed*—you make a rule. Rule is, no camera movement, no pan, no tilt, so that if a character is sitting down and he stands up, he's going to stand out of frame because you're not going to adjust, and he walks—film art's filled with all those little adjustments—because you don't make pan or tilts, people walk out of frame. But then the beauty, the intuitive beauty of making a rule is that when you break it, and you have to break it to remind the viewer that you made it in the first place or they'll forget. And so one day, you're on location and you say to the DP—I said, "You have some track in the truck?" And he said, "Of course." "Let's lay some rail." "We weren't going to move the camera on this film."

"I know, but just looking at this scene right now, I think we have to—today's the day we break the rule. Then we'll go back." And why was it that day? That's instinctual. That is not academic. There is no academic answer to why at a particular moment that I'd choose to put on a red hat. That's instinctual. I mean, academics can posit all the reasons in the world, but I don't know how they can have the right answer if what you're doing is totally instinctual.

BB: So what's kept you writing criticism throughout your filmmaking career, then?

Schrader: Well, I mean, I had to stop reviewing, of course, because you can't get actors if you review. There's no praise sufficient, so I moved out of the reviewing realm into the more theoretical realm, but I still like to do it. That's why I'm on Facebook, in a way, because a lot of the people I know who are on Facebook are critics or filmmakers, whatever, and it's a way of being able to essentially write many reviews without the burden of it being an official review, and also with the surfeit of film product out there now, you need this neuro system in order to become aware what is out there that I should watch. People start saying, "Watch *Collateral*." Yeah. Another person, "I saw *Collateral*. It's terrific." Well, maybe I will, because there's so much out there that in fact when you watch the first episode of an episodic series and it doesn't hit, doesn't have any traction, in fact, you're relieved. You say, "Whew. I don't have to watch all of that." [laughter] And I saw the first couple episodes of *Maniac* and I said, "Boy, I dodged one there." [laughter]

BB: So it acts as curation.

Schrader: Yeah.

MEM: In the introduction to your book, you repeat [Fredric] Jameson's assertion that Tarkovsky likes to gorge the spectator's eyes whereas Bresson prefers to starve them. What do you do to the spectator's eyes?

Schrader: I'm certainly not in either camp, really. I'm not a Malickian kind of imagistic poet and I'm not austere either, so I wouldn't put myself in either of those categories.

MEM: What category would you put yourself in?

Schrader: Well, I mean, in the different fields, different categories, but I'm much more narrative-driven than either of those men, so when all of a sudden you're telling a story and you've got a plot and you've got a theme and that, now you're creating a film style that's good for this particular story, a palette that works for this story, and it often means that you do something you've never done before. I mean, I've always admired Kubrick because every time he did something he wanted to do it for the first time. Let's make a low-light British historical film or let's make this pop Anthony Burgess novel, and my ambitions are not as grand as his but every time you like to think: "There's got to be something new here. Something to keep me interested. But even with *Canyons*, is can I make a film this way? Is this even possible?" I would say to Bret, "I think the economics are such that we could just do this ourselves, and let's just do it. See if we can pull it off." And that was part of the fun was just pulling the damn thing off.

BB: How would you articulate the influence of Bela Tarr?

Schrader: Not much. Those incremental, lateral dollys and that and, obviously, it was that shot from—what's the name of the film? But the one that long-shot when they're in the prison or mental home and they go in crashing in all the rooms. Which film is that? Not *Satantango*?

MEM: It's not the new one. It's—

Schrader: No, it's one of the older ones.

[Crosstalk]

Schrader: It's not *Elective Affinities* because that's Goethe, but it sounds like *Elective Affinities* [most likely *Werckmeister Harmonies*]. But occasionally there's just kinds of terrific shots, but I remember when I went to see *The Turin Horse*, and I had to make myself stay. I mean, I think films could be slow, but I have a problem when they're slow and they're long. *Pickpocket* is a slow film, but it's seventy-five minutes long. You could do that without testing people's patience. You can use boredom as a scalpel without actually making somebody stay in a room for three or four hours. You just have to be pretty good at it. But, on the other hand, I think the new version of *Tree of Life* is better than the old because the theatrical version from ten years ago was almost a slow film. The one that's an hour longer actually is a slow film. And because [Malick] didn't have any more music, he had to keep repeating those cues, and because he didn't have any more narration, things just got attenuated and it felt like the new *Tree of Life* really feels like a slow film. The first one was sort of one.

BB: Do you think slow cinema is uniquely suited to tackle these larger questions of life and death and the beginning of life and the apocalypse?

Schrader: Well, good things happen while you wait, and when you put people in that kind—if you can keep them in the room in that kind of contemplative way, their minds will start to work, and they'll start doing interesting things. And like I said, they'll start making their own movie, and that's going to be a pretty good movie. But, yeah, I mean, obviously, any of the heavy subjects takes some time, some patience. If you're going to deal with existential issues, you're going to do it at a certain pace. Sartre and Camus write at a certain pace. It is not the pace of the kind of plot-driven stories. But that's probably a good example because they're very, very readable, but then you get to some of these other authors who are using the languors of languages and you say, "Why? Well, why does this book have to be a hundred pages long?'

MEM: What is your connection to Gus Van Sant?

Schrader: Not much. When we were doing that, a good producer Braxton Pope was friends with Gus. And I was looking for an interesting guy to play the psychiatrist [in *The Canyons*]. And I asked a few actors and directors I know and Braxton said, "Let me ask Gus." So that was the beginning and end of it.

MEM: In the film, he plays a character named Dr Campbell and right behind him in the shot is a book that very prominently spells out "mythology." [Schrader laughs] If a character's named "Christian" who's seeing "Dr Campbell" with the book with mythology behind him, it must be significant, right? So is there a relationship between Jung's deep dive into the human archives, transcendental film-making and Christian. What are we supposed to be seeing here?

Schrader: Some of it is just eye-winking. I'm just winking at you. Like Chris Walken in *The Comfort of Strangers*. I'm just playing with you, having a little fun, nothing more than that. And just to keep myself interested and how to do the décor for that room and put all the objects on the desk like Freud had and stuff like that. But that's play. I mean, that's not real, just the kind of references. And there's, like in *First Reformed*, a reference to Flannery O'Connor. Is that really serious? No, Flannery O'Connor is a quite different kind of artist, but it's a kind of nice little resonance for people who know *Wise Blood* to say: "Yeah, yeah, that was in *Wise Blood*", but you're not saying I'm making a film like Flannery O'Connor.

BB: Would you say that *Dog Eat Dog* is a movie that's kind of existing in this crime genre space? As paying homage to or referencing say somebody like David Lynch with some of the shots? And there's the presence of Nicolas Cage and Willem Dafoe who are back together after *Wild At Heart*?

Schrader: I wouldn't venture to compete with Lynch. I was at AFI with both David and Terry Malick and I wouldn't try to imitate either one of them and I like Lynch's stuff a lot. I just don't know how he does it. I don't think I could pull it off. What I was doing was just having fun with excess, doing things too much. Obviously, there's a Tarantino kind of influence in there, too. Actually, this was the table we sat at when we were doing *Dog Eat Dog*, my team, and it wasn't really just—we would meet every week here, and I just said, "Come up with stuff. Come up with stuff." And I said, "I have Final Cut. I can do anything. And you can suggest anything. Just don't make it boring." And so every week, they all came in with stuff, and so that was sort of the fun of making that film and having that kind of freedom. [Scrolling through images on his phone.] Waiting for this photo here.

BB: Did you see the *Twin Peaks: The Return*?

Schrader: Yeah, yeah, yeah.

BB: Would you say that it is slow cinema or slow cinema-adjacent?

Schrader: Well, if Bruce Conner is slow cinema, yeah. Episode eight is terrific. And I just thought that was terrific. But I don't think that's what Lynch is up to. Lynch is up to some kind of surrealistic effect. Here it is.

[Shows picture on phone of department heads sitting around booth]

Okay, so this was the gimmick behind *Dog Eat Dog*. These are all my department heads, and this is the same booth we're in now.

MEM: Wonderful.

Schrader: So they were all under thirty, and this was all the first credit for each of them. And I intentionally put that team together so I wouldn't be bound by any preconceptions. Let's just do anything that we want to do.

BB: Would you say that the Tarantino spirit of *Dog Eat Dog* comes from the fact that all those people are under thirty?

Schrader: Yeah, and that I realized something that had changed in film-making is the idea of the consistent style was breaking down and that you could have a pastiche style and I saw all this in the films of the Quebecois director. What's his name? He did *Mommy*. Enfant terrible, little young kid. Must be almost thirty now, the French-Canadian director. He's been at Cannes a bunch of times. Bruno? No, that's Bruno [last name unclear]. Well, I was looking at his first film, and he made that film when he was nineteen. And there would be a Godard scene and then there would be a [Bernardo] Bertolucci scene and then there'd be a [John] Cassavetes scene and he just threw them all together. And I realized that that worked now so that what—Xavier Dolan.

BB: Oh, Dolan. Okay.

Schrader: And I realized that Xavier Dolan was doing this not because he had decided to do this, because he didn't know better. He realized that you don't have to have a consistent style. You can do a Godardian scene and put it right next to the Cassavetes scene and people will take you there—will go with you. And so that was the thinking behind *Dog Eat Dog*. Let's just do a mismatch of things, different kinds of things. And so it was very liberating.

BB: What's changed in the film-making environment or the film-viewing audiences that makes a pastiche style like that okay now?

Schrader: People are raised multi-tasking. That seven-year-old sitting on the subway playing video games on his phone has a different processing mechanism than you do or I do. And he can handle so much of the—so many of the films that we made in the past seem so slow now because we're in this Tony Scott kind of rapid-fire imagery. And so in the same way, a kid can simultaneously text, play a video game, and watch the news, you can have a pastiche of styles. And if you're smart about it, audiences will put them together.

MEM: In *American Gigolo*, you used an entire sequence from Coppola's *The Conversation*.

Schrader: No.

MEM: Towards the end of it when he's going and he's tearing things apart and tearing—

Schrader: Oh. Oh. Oh. Yeah. Yeah. Yeah. Yeah. Yeah. Yeah.

MEM: Right? And of course, it's actually a fairly—you see that sequence in quite a number of films and even television shows now and you do allude to it. What is it about that film that seems to be compelling and interesting?

Schrader: You talking about *The Conversation*?

MEM: *The Conversation*, Coppola.

Schrader: You know Francis was really on to something there and it was because of Walter Murch and that stuff Walter Murch was doing. And seeing film as sound, it was a really smart film. But by the time Brian [De Palma] got around to copying it [in *Blow Out*, 1981], the air I thought, had gone out of it.

MEM: Your book lays out the role of sound in slow cinema in that it only uses diegetic sound. This is something that becomes more apparent in the last half of *The Canyons* and in *First Reformed* where you have the pre-recorded music and then *The Canyons* turns into all diegetic sound. Could you talk about the use of sound in your films?

Schrader: Well, I mean, I was going to have no music in *First Reformed*, and I don't have music. But I started introducing soundscaping. Those aren't actual instruments, that's all soundscapes. And it just starts to come in a little bit. But for the longest time I don't have music. So you have a scene where he discovers this body. And that scene is normally scored. And it's not scored, although I do use an airplane overhead. And usually, when you have a scene like that in a movie, you don't have to worry about how you're supposed to feel because the music's telling you. So here's this guy. He's walking around. He sees a body. And there's no music to tell you how to feel. The first time I was working that way. Every other film I've done, I have supported the scene musically. *First Reformed*, I didn't. *Canyons*, I supported the scenes musically. I didn't go without sound there. And once I made that intellectual decision to do a film of this nature, then it just became, can I pull it off? Can I not move the camera? Can I not have music? Can I not have dynamic compositions?

MEM: What do you think you'll be doing in the future with it?

Schrader: Several films I'm fooling around with. One I just finished the script up a couple days ago, which would be much more in the *Tree of Life* style. And then I have this other film that I was going to do, which was sort of a mix of—was a remake of a Budd Boetticher film, with a Lynchian twist at the end, where the two characters switched, also from *Obscure Object of Desire*. But I don't imagine I would ever be doing a film in this style again.

BB: What is your approach to genre? References and awareness of other films is always so important to everything you do. How do you know when you should engage with the conventions of a genre, or avoid or subvert them? How do you make those choices?

Schrader: Well, you have to give me some examples. I haven't worked much in traditional genres. I don't think *Cat People* was a horror film.

BB: For instance, I think you said on the commentary for *Cat People* about how you delivered a film that was sort of a hybrid of horror and philosophy that was heavy on philosophy and light on horror. So how do you know, I'm going to make these decisions? How do you make a film that wears genre clothes, but doesn't really conform to that dress?

Schrader: Yeah, well you're using genre as bait. You're using it in the poster and that's to get people in the room. And once they're in the room, now you've got to keep them there. But you use the genre to keep them, to get them in the room. The same thing about using a certain kind of a crime movie or a heist movie, all that. If I made a heist movie, it would be a kind of Bressonian heist. But I would use that convention to get people in the room. So just like Bresson uses the convention of a prison escape film to get people in a room. Or a petty crime film to get people in a room.

MEM: You've been very direct along with Martin Scorsese about the ending of *Taxi Driver* not being a dream sequence.

Schrader: Well, I mean, let me correct that. When we made it, it wasn't intended to be. But after people started interpreting it that way, we both realized that that was valid too. And so neither of us have a problem with people who say it is. It just wasn't meant to be. Whereas when they came around at *First Reformed*, then I said let's build it right in. So that it can be read more than one way. But that wasn't the notion when we did *Taxi Driver*. It was more of a kind of ironic epilogue. One of the things in my mind when I was writing that script was there was a woman named Sarah Moore who shot at President Gerald Ford and she was on the cover of *Newsweek*. And that was a big deal to be on the cover of *Newsweek*. And I thought to myself, here's this befuddled woman who takes a shot at the President and misses and now she's a star. Now, what kind of a—how's our culture working? And so that's where I sort of got the idea that he's going to try to [laughter], he's going to try to kill all of these people and he ends up becoming a star.

BB: So the ending of *First Reformed* you've been very much open towards, and even seemingly conceived of the ending as being read two ways, as a potential dream or as a potential reality. So what is the difference in you as not intending in your initial ending of *Taxi Driver* to be read that way and then opening up to that possibility in the ending of *First Reformed*?

Schrader: Well, I mean once people had been interpreting *Taxi Driver* that way, I thought that was interesting. And I thought maybe we should have done it that way intentionally. But I could calibrate the ending of *First Reformed*. When Amanda comes in the room, in one cut, I had her walk in and that threw perception of it as a real event too much. So then we took out the walk and she just appears, like a vision. And as we were editing, trying to keep it both ways. And when I went out with a film to the festivals, I would often ask people, is he alive or dead. And it would often break down at about half and half, which is exactly what we wanted.

MEM: There's a sequence at the end of *American Gigolo* where he's following her and then they duck into a record store, which is also in, almost shot for shot, *The Canyons*. It also resembles [a sequence] in *Taxi Driver*. What is it about that sequence that's so compelling that it keeps repeating?

Schrader: I knew, obviously, when I'd be doing that thing, that Amoeba [Music], in *Canyons*, and I had done it in Tower Records in Westwood. So I knew I was doing something I had done before. In one case I had written it. In the other case Bret had written it.

MEM: It would seem because you posit in your book that walking shot as non-narrative and because that's such the intense walking shot—we're walking one person walk and follow the other—it would seem that that motif has a significance.

Schrader: Well, I know, but it's also right at the heart and soul of cinema voyeurism. What is cinema but watching somebody who doesn't know you're watching them, whether you're watching them on a subway or going down the street. That's one of the appeals of the voyeuristic elements of cinema. So it's just really part of the basic toolkit of cinema. Just like Godard once said, every movie is a story of boys taking pictures of girls. And you could say, well, I do that too. But that doesn't mean I'm like Godard, everybody does that. The difference between the male gaze and the female gaze is an interesting one, although I don't know—I've never really read somebody who nailed down the difference. People talk about the female gaze. People talk about the male gaze. I don't really know if there is a difference. I would love to hear the difference.

MEM: Have you seen *Meek's Cutoff*?

Schrader: Yeah.

MEM: In it, she uses the bonnet view.

BB: Kelly Reichardt.

Schrader: No. I mean, I saw the film. I don't remember the bonnet view.

MEM: She changed the aspect ratio on the screen so that you were forever looking through a bonnet. And you can see slightly as the camera turns that she would block in the sides a little bit. But that was her attempt, she says, at the female gaze. There are some theories about it. But that's the female gaze.

BB: And it, like *First Reformed*, is the Academy ratio, right? It's like the 1:33.

Schrader: It is? I don't remember that.

MEM: Did you like the film?

Schrader: Well, I saw it so long ago. I liked her new one.

BB: *Certain Women*?

Schrader: Yeah. Yeah. But I saw that a long time ago, and so I don't have a clear memory of it.

MEM: Is there a film of someone else's that you watch and wished you actually made it?

Schrader: So there's certain films that I would tend to watch just because they invigorate you creatively. You can't really watch performance without getting ideas. It's just so full of ideas. Same thing is true, with *Conformist* and other films. Just like when you're in pre-production, everything starts to come alive. And if you go to a museum, virtually everything you're seeing is somehow related to the film you're working on. You see a painting, you see somebody wearing certain clothes because your mind is completely open, completely aggressive, just snatching things all over. And so there are certain films that you'd like to watch when you're in that mindset because you know that you'll be just ripping them off right and left.

BB: You've been kind of dismissive of the visual style of your first few films, *Blue Collar*, *Hardcore*. How did you get better? Are you still learning?

INTERVIEW WITH PAUL SCHRADER 227

Schrader: Well, I mean I would just kind of stay alive and tell a story because my background was rather Cromwellian and did not rely heavily on the idea of images as ideas. It took me a while to figure out that images were ideas as well as words. And I didn't really figure that out until *Gigolo*, and that was because of [visual consultant Ferdinando] Scarfiotti, who had such strong presence in that way. And he made me realize that a composition was an idea. It wasn't just a way to tell a story.

BB: Are any of those early films or films throughout your career you wish you could go back and make again with the benefit of this hindsight and visual experience?

Schrader: Well, I mean, no. Probably not. I probably wouldn't make them again. *Hardcore* is a very kind of sophomoric film. And even if I had made it the way I intended, it probably wouldn't be right. It was written with a *Chinatown* ending and then ended up with a *Searchers* ending. But I'm lucky, in a way, that they've held up, some of them, as well as they have because I was just reading an article about films of the '80s are completely collapsing because of our new MeToo culture. Films like *Animal House*. You just can't even watch them anymore.

MEM: What keeps you watching films today?

Schrader: Curiosity. And well, also now with the new technology, so many new voices are coming into films that would've been filtered out before.

MEM: Like who, for example?

Schrader: I'm just saying that the technology had not allowed all these voices—gay, Hispanic, African. All kinds of people who are filtered out of the system by the economics in the past are now in the system, and so you're seeing a lot of very original films. Much more than you would have normally.

BB: What about TV shows? Are there any episodic television shows that you are interested in that you follow regularly? Any exciting, cinematic ideas expressed in those television shows?

Schrader: Yeah. I try to only watch one at a time. [*Mr*] *Robot*, they were recomposing in post with all those odd compositions which you can do now if you're shooting in 6K because you have so much digital information that I can shoot this two shot and have enough digital information in it, we have two singles at the same time and cut them all together and you wouldn't know because I'm using 6K of information to get a 2K shot so that when you look at [*Mr*] *Robot* you're looking at a lot of compositions done in post which is why they can be so peculiar. Also, *The Revenant*, a lot of the compositions are in post-shooting in 6K wide open, wide lens, and then in post you can make the adjustments.

MEM: Would you ever do television again?

Schrader: Nah. I only have a few films left. It's too big of a commitment. To tell you the truth I don't even know if I want to make films anymore [laughter].

BB: So you've done some fairly big films throughout your career and a lot of small ones and you've done a Kickstarter project, with the films that you said you have remaining what's an experiment you'd like to run, what would those potential films be?

Schrader: I'm involved in three films, one is a kind of Malick-like introspective mosaic of memory and some thought, another is this kind of neo-Western, and the third is a noir. And hopefully I'll get to make one of them and just try to—the challenge on *Dog Eat Dog* was how do you make a gangster film in 2015? After Scorsese, and Tarantino, and Guy Ritchie, and all those people. And so that was the fun of it. How do you make a noir today? And this is a James Ellroy book—I'm not quite sure, I hope I get a chance to answer that question.

BB: We are almost to the point now where it's gone through noir, evolved into neo-noir, and now there's "neo" neo-noir that's referencing neo-noir, what do you do?

Schrader: Yeah.

MEM: Right. So what do you think of voices in the film-making community who say that cinema is dead?

Schrader: What do they mean by cinema? Do they mean theatrical cinema? Do they mean audio-visual entertainment? Audio-visual entertainment isn't dead. What kind of cinema is dead?

MEM: Theatre experience.

Schrader: Yeah. Well, that's a 20th-century phenomenon that'll fade away. It won't fade away. It'll become an adjunct just like the concert hall and the opera hall and the live music club. At one time, the only way you could hear music was to hear it live. Now we all listen to it over speaker systems. But we still go to live music from time to time. Just like you still go to the theatrical experience from time to time. We're down to about five categories for theatrical. The main category is the dramatic ones and the murder mysteries and all that. They're out of theatrical now. The only thing left for theatrical is scale, family, horror, and film club. Those are the reasons you go.

MEM: Cinema might also be dead because people don't want to concentrate on one thing for two hours.

Schrader: Yeah. And also it's—it's so much hassle, that most people at this point have better audio and visual at home than they have at the cinema. And lives are all so chock-a-block with stuff. Do I really want to schlep up to Lincoln Center to see something that's in New York Film Festival when I can wait two months and see it on my widescreen at home?

BB: Your screenplays and films are being taught in film school and classrooms as classic and canonical examples of American film. Has this changed your view of yourself as a filmmaker? What do you think of this as a phenomenon, that people teach your work?

Schrader: I mean, I think I did bring something new. I sort of stumbled into it with *Taxi Driver*. And so, as Richard Brody said, one of the formative voices of the New Cinema. And just because you teach something doesn't mean it's good. [laughter]

MEM: How has this changed your view as a filmmaker? It must be very different now knowing that the film schools are interested in your work versus when you started.

Schrader: No. I don't think much in those terms. I don't go back and look at the films myself either. So that when I do—sometimes I do a retro. And they've just shown a movie, and everybody in the audience knows more about the film than I do. I'm sort of scratching myself. [laughter] What did that character play? What did he do again?

BB: You said earlier that—you referenced a quote about how a filmmaker is just making the same film over and over again.

Schrader: That was a quote from [Jean] Renoir. Yeah.

BB: So what's your one long movie? What is the one thing you've been making throughout the duration of your career that you could say, "That's what I had to say, or what I did"?

Schrader: Well, it's this kind of introspective fellow whose looking at the world through a pane of glass and he can't quite touch it. But, on the other hand, I'm willing to try almost anything.

MEM: So what stories do you still want to tell? What's left?

Schrader: Well, the Malick thing I just finished the first draft. It's the story of me and my brother. And obviously, it's through the filter of fiction and imagination. But this whole notion of what is memory? Is memory something that once happened or is it something that we formulate? Is there such a thing as memory? Or do we design our past and tell ourselves what it is? And so this is the story of a character who, after his brother's death, starts exploring his brother's life. So it's kind of a mixture of *Citizen Kane* and *Tree of Life*. [laughs]

MEM: Does the idea of nostalgia fit into that at all?

Schrader: No. Just the fungibility of memory.

Filmography

WRITER

The Jesuit (screenplay) (*completed*)
1999 *Bringing Out the Dead* (screenplay)
1996 *City Hall* (written by)
1988 *The Last Temptation of Christ* (screenplay)
1986 *The Mosquito Coast* (screenplay)
1980 *Raging Bull* (screenplay)
1979 *Old Boyfriends* (written by)
1977 *Rolling Thunder* (original story) / (screenplay)
1976 *Obsession* (screenplay) / (story)
1976 *Taxi Driver* (written by)
1974 *The Yakuza* (screenplay, with Leonard Schrader)

DIRECTOR

2016 *Dog Eat Dog*
2013 *Venice 70: Future Reloaded* (documentary)
2013 *The Canyons*
2008 *Adam Resurrected*
2005 *Dominion: Prequel to the Exorcist*
2002 *Auto Focus*
1995 *Untitled: New Blue* (documentary short)
1994 *Witch Hunt* (TV movie)
1990 *The Comfort of Strangers*
1988 *Patty Hearst*

WRITER AND DIRECTOR

Nine Men from Now (*pre-production*)
2017 *Dark*
2017 *First Reformed* (written by)
2014 *Dying of the Light* (screenplay)
2007 *The Walker* (written by)
1999 *Forever Mine* (written by)
1997 *Affliction* (screenplay)
1997 *Touch* (screenplay)
1992 *Light Sleeper* (written by)
1987 *Light of Day* (written by)
1985 *Mishima: A Life in Four Chapters* (written by, with Leonard Schrader)
1982 *Cat People* (uncredited)
1980 *American Gigolo* (written by)
1979 *Hardcore* (written by)
1978 *Blue Collar* (written by, with Leonard Schrader)

Criticism and Selected Interviews

"Beyond the Silver Screen." *The Guardian*. June 18, 2009. https://www.theguardian.com/film/2009/jun/19/paul-schrader-reality-tv-big-brother.

"The Birth of Narrative." *Film Comment* 50, No. 4 (July 2014), 32–9.

"Budd Boetticher: A Case Study in Criticism." *Schrader on Schrader*, edited by Kevin Jackson (New York: Faber and Faber, 2004), 45–57.

"Camera Movement." *Film Comment* 51, No. 2 (March 2015), 56–61.

"Canon Fodder." *Film Comment* (September/October 2016), 33–49.

"The Close-Up." *Film Comment* 50, No. 5 (September 2014), 58–61.

"Color." *Film Comment* 51, No. 6 (November 2015), 52–6.

"Director Commentary." *Auto Focus*. DVD. Sony Pictures Classics, 2002.

"Director Commentary." *Blue Collar*. Blu-ray. With Maitland McDonagh. Kino Lorber, 2019.

"Director Commentary." *Cat People*. DVD. Universal Pictures, 1982.

"Director Commentary." *First Reformed*. Blu-ray. A24, 2018.

"Director Commentary." *Hardcore*. Blu-ray. Twilight Time, 2017.

"Director Commentary." *The Comfort of Strangers*. DVD/Blu-ray. British Film Institute, 2017.

"Easy Rider," in *Schrader on Schrader*, Revised Edition, edited by Kevin Jackson (New York: Faber and Faber, 2004), 34–7.

"Editing." *Film Comment* 50, No. 6 (November 2014), 48–53.

"'First Reformed' Director Paul Schrader on Why The Film Industry is Dying." Interview by Sarah Foulkes. *Slashfilm*. October 25, 2018. https://www.slashfilm.com/paul-schrader-interview-film-industry/.

"Interview: Paul Schrader on Making *Dog Eat Dog* His Own Way." Interview by Magdalena Maksimiuk. *Slant Magazine*. October 31, 2016. https://

www.slantmagazine.com/film/interview-paul-schrader-on-making-dog-eat-dog-on-his-own-terms/.

"Interview: Paul Schrader." Interview by Richard Thompson. *Film Comment*. March/April 1976. https://www.filmcomment.com/article/paul-schrader-richard-thompson-interview/.

"Notes on Film Noir," in *Schrader on Schrader*, Revised Edition, edited by Kevin Jackson (New York: Faber and Faber, 2004), 80–94.

"On Yasujiro Ozu." *Film Comment*. November 25, 2016. https://www.filmcomment.com/blog/paul-schrader-on-yasujiro-ozu/.

"Paul Schrader." *The Film Comment Podcast*. June 21, 2018. https://www.filmcomment.com/blog/film-comment-podcast-paul-schrader/.

"Paul Schrader: Deliberate Boredom in the Church of Cinema." Interview by Alex Ross Perry. *Cinema Scope*. Issue 74. https://cinema-scope.com/cinema-scope-magazine/paul-schrader-deliberate-boredom-in-the-church-of-cinema/.

"Paul Schrader Tells Nicolas Cage Why *First Reformed* is His Masterpiece." Interview by Nicolas Cage. *Interview Magazine*. April 6, 2018. https://www.interviewmagazine.com/film/paul-schrader-nicolas-cage-april-issue-2018-interview.

"Pickpocket I," in *Schrader on Schrader*, Revised Edition, edited by Kevin Jackson (New York: Faber and Faber, 2004), 38–42.

"Pickpocket II," in *Schrader on Schrader*, Revised Edition, edited by Kevin Jackson (New York: Faber and Faber, 2004), 42–5.

"A Postscript from Paul Schrader." *Film Quarterly* 34, No. 4 (Summer 1981), 13.

"Production Design." *Film Comment* 52, No. 2 (March 2016), 58–60.

"Robert Bresson: Robert Bresson, Possibly." *Film Comment* 13, No. 5 (1977), 26.

"Roberto Rossellini: The Rise of Louis XIV," in *Schrader on Schrader*, Revised Edition, edited by Kevin Jackson (New York: Faber and Faber, 2004), 57–67.

"Sam Peckinpah Going to Mexico," in *Schrader on Schrader*, Revised Edition, edited by Kevin Jackson (New York: Faber and Faber, 2004), 67–80.

Schrader, Paul and Martin Scorsese, "From 'Interview with Paul Schrader,' in *Cahiers du Cinéma* (Paris), April 1982. Reprinted with permission," in *Martin Scorsese: Interviews, Revised and Updated*, edited by Robert Ribera (Jackson: University Press of Mississippi, 2017), 99–111.

"Scott Macaulay interviews Paul Schrader about *Light Sleeper*." Interview by Scott Macaulay. *Filmmaker Magazine*. Fall 1992. https://filmmakermagazine.com/archives/issues/fall1992/movie_high.php.

"Shooting Stars." *Film Comment*. July/August 2013. https://www.filmcomment.com/article/shooting-stars/.

"Slow, Fast, and Reverse Motion." *Film Comment* 51, No. 4 (July 2015), 52–5.

"Sound." *Film Comment* 52, No. 1 (January 2016), 60–5.
Taxi Driver: Published Screenplay (New York: Faber and Faber, 1990).
"Top of the World." *Film Comment.* July/August 2018. https://www
  .filmcomment.com/article/top-of-the-world/.
Transcendental Style In Film: Ozu, Bresson, Dreyer (Berkeley: University of
  California Press, 1972).
Transcendental Style in Film: Ozu, Bresson, Dreyer, Revised Edition (Oakland,
  CA: University of California Press, 2018).
"Widescreen." *Film Comment* 51, No. 5 (September 2015), 62–5.

MANUSCRIPTS AND COLLECTION

Paul Schrader Papers, Harry Ransom Center, University of Texas-Austin,
  Austin, TX.

Bibliography

Allison, Deborah. "Paul Schrader." *The Comfort of Strangers, Directed by Paul Schrader* (DVD/Blu-ray special edition booklet). London: BFI, 2018.
Andersch, Brecht. "Hardcore: Paul Schrader in the 1970s-4." *Open Space/SFMOMA*. September 3, 2010. https://openspace.sfmoma.org/2010/09/hardcore-paul-schrader-in-the-70s-4/.
Attanasio, Paul. "*Mishima* Impossible." *Washington Post*. October 15, 1985. https://www.washingtonpost.com/archive/lifestyle/1985/10/15/mishima-impossible/84e5f1a6-a2d4-4785-94ff-1d60eb7fbf91/?noredirect=on&utm_term=.45c8f9e4549a.
Ayfre, Amedee. "The Universe of Robert Bresson," in *Robert Bresson (Revised)*, in James Quandt (ed.). Toronto: Toronto International Film Festival Cinematheque, 2011, 39–53.
Babbington, Bruce and Peter W. Evans. *Biblical Epics: Sacred Narratives in the Hollywood Cinema*. Manchester: Manchester University Press, 1993.
Baron, Cynthia. *Modern Acting: The Lost Chapter of American Film and Theatre*. London: Palgrave Macmillan, 2016.
Barton Fink. Directed by Joel Coen. 1991: Los Angeles, CA: Kino Lorber, 2019. Blu-ray.
Bell, Andy. "An Eco-Theology." *Crosscurrents* (2013), 386–9.
Bentham, Jeremy. *A Bentham Reader*, edited by Mary Peter Mack. New York: Pegasus, 1969.
Bergman, Ingmar and Joan Tate. *The Magic Lantern: An Autobiography*. New York: Penguin Books, 1994.
Berry, Evan. "Social Science Perspectives on Religion and Climate Change." *Religious Studies Review* 42, No. 2 (2016), 77–85.

Biskind, Peter. *Easy Riders, Raging Bulls: How the Rock 'n' Roll Generation Saved Hollywood.* New York: Simon and Schuster, 1988. Reprint New York: Touchstone Books, 1998.
Bliss, Michael and Paul Schrader, "Affliction and Forgiveness: An Interview with Paul Schrader." *Film Quarterly* 54 No. 1 (2000), 2–9.
Bloom, Harold. *The Western Canon: The Books and School of the Ages.* New York: Riverhead, 1995.
Boozer, Jack (ed.). *Authorship in Film Adaptation.* Austin, TX: University of Texas Press, 2008.
Bordwell, David. *On the History of Film Style.* Cambridge, MA: Harvard University Press, 1997.
Bordwell, David, Janet Staiger, and Kristin Thompson. *The Classical Hollywood Cinema: Film Style & Mode of Production to 1960.* London: Routledge, 1994.
Bresson, Robert. *Notes on the Cinematograph.* Translated by Jonathan Griffin. New York: New York Review of Books, 1975. Reprint 2016.
Bresson, Robert. *Notes on the Cinematographer.* London: Encounter; New York: Quartet Books, 1986.
Bresson, Robert. "Robert Bresson, Possibly." Interview by Paul Schrader, May 17, 1976, in *Robert Bresson (Revised)*, in James Quandt (ed.). Toronto: Toronto International Film Festival Cinematheque, 2011.
Bresson, Robert. "The Wind Blows Where It Wants To." Interview by *Cahiers Du Cinéma*, May 15, 1957, in *Bresson on Bresson, Interviews 1943-1983.* Edited by Mylene Bresson. New York: New York Review of Books, 2013, 47–54.
Brodsly, David. *L.A. Freeway: An Appreciative Essay.* Burbank: University of California Press, 1981.
Bruzzi, Stella. *Men's Cinema: Masculinity and Mise-en-Scène in Hollywood.* Edinburgh: Edinburgh University Press, 2013.
Burke, Kenneth. *Permanence and Change: An Anatomy of Purpose.* New York: New Republic, 1935.
Buruma, Ian. "Rambo-san." *New York Review of Books.* October 10, 1985. https://www.nybooks.com/articles/1985/10/10/rambo-san/.
Byron, Stuart. "The Keitel Method." *Film Comment* 14 No. 1 (1978), 36–41.
Cage, Nicolas. "PAUL SCHRADER." *Interview* 48, No. 2 (2018), 112.
Canby, Vincent. "Film: 'Mosquito Coast,' with Harrison Ford." *The New York Times.* November 26, 1986, sec. Movies. www.nytimes.com/1986/11/26/movies/film-mosquito-coast-with-harrison-ford.html.
Canby, Vincent. "Film: On the Auto Front: The Assembly Line." *New York Times.* February 10, 1978. https://www.nytimes.com/1978/02/10/archives/film-on-the-auto-frontthe-assembly-line.html.

Canby, Vincent. "*Mishima*, A Life of the Japanese Writer." *New York Times*. September 20, 1985. https://www.nytimes.com/1985/09/20/movies/mishima-a-life-of-the-japanese-writer.html?searchResultPosition=1.

Cartmell, Deborah and Imelda Whelehan. "A practical understanding of literature on screen: two conversations with Andrew Davies," in *The Cambridge Companion to Literature on Screen*. Cambridge: Cambridge University Press, 2007, 239–51.

Cascio, Jamais. "The Rise of the Participatory Panopticon." *Open the Future* (blog), WorldChanging Archive. May 4, 2005. http://www.openthefuture.com/wcarchive/2005/05/the_rise_of_the_participatory.html.

Castells, Manuel. *The Rise of the Network Society*. 2nd ed. Vol. 1. *The Information Age: Economy, Society, and Culture*. 2nd Revised Edition. New Jersey: Wiley-Blackwell, 2000.

Christie, Ian and David Thompson (eds). *Scorsese on Scorsese*. Revised Edition. New York: Faber and Faber, 2003.

"Climate-Change Religion." *Oil & Gas Journal*. January 28, 2013, 16.

Concannon, Philip. "Faithful Servant." *Sight & Sound*. August 2018, 40–3.

Coppola, Sofia. "This Is How It Should End with Paul Schrader & Sofia Coppola," *A24 Films*. May 30, 2018. https://a24films.com/notes/2018/05/episode-04-this-is-how-it-should-end-with-paul-schrader-sofia-coppola.

Dargis, Manohla. "The Cell Phone Gets its Close-Up." *The New York Times*. August 1, 2013. https://www.nytimes.com/2013/08/02/movies/the-canyons-is-an-erotic-thriller-with-lindsay-lohan.html.

Deleuze, Gilles. *Cinema 2: The Time-Image*. Translated by Hugh Tomlinson and Robert Galeta. Minneapolis: University of Minnesota Press, 1989.

Deleuze, Gilles. *Negotiations 1972–1990*. Translated by Martin Joughin. New York: Columbia University Press, 1995.

Deleuze, Gilles. "Postscript on the Societies of Control." *October* 59 (1992), 3–7.

de Zengotita, Thomas. *Mediated: How the Media Shape Your World*. London: Bloomsbury, 2005.

De Palma, Brian. *Body Double*. Los Angeles: Delphi II Productions, 1984.

Denson, Shane. "Crazy Cameras, Discorrelated Images and the Post-Perceptual Mediation of Post-Cinematic Affect," in *Post-Cinema*, edited by Shane Denson and Julia Leyda. Falmer: Reframe, 2016. Available at http://reframe.sussex.ac.uk/post-cinema/. Last accessed May 30, 2019.

Durgnat, Raymond. *Films and Feelings*. Cambridge, MA: MIT Press, 1967.

Dzhumaylo, Olga A. "'Venetian Text' and the Aesthetics of Reflections in Paul Schrader's *The Comfort of Strangers* based on the novel by Ian McEwan." *Bulletin of Perm University. Russian and Foreign Philology* 10, No. 4, 2018, 118–24.

Ebert, Roger. "*Mishima: A Life in Four Chapters.*" *Chicago Sun Times.* October 11, 1985. https://www.rogerebert.com/reviews/mishima-a-life-in-four-chapters-1985.

Eggert, Brian. "*Mishima: A Life in Four Chapters.*" June 3, 2018. Online at Deep Focus Review, at https://deepfocusreview.com/definitives/mishima-a-life-in-four-chapters/.

Eli, F. "*Mishima: A Life in Four Chapters*: Paul Schrader's Phantasmagoria of Cartesian Dissociation." June 11, 2018 for Film Stage, online at https://thefilmstage.com/features/mishima-a-life-in-four-chapters-paul-schraders-phantasmagoria-of-cartesian-dissociation/.

Ewins, Michael. "In Conversation: Paul Schrader." *Clash Music.* July 30, 2018. https://www.clashmusic.com/features/in-conversation-paul-schrader.

Feldman, Silvia. "Blue-collar villainy." *Human Behavior* No. 7.5, 1978, 75.

Fine, Marshall. *Harvey Keitel: The Art of Darkness.* New York: Fromm International, 1998.

Forceville, Charles. "The Conspiracy in *The Comfort of Strangers*—Narration in the Novel and the Film." *Language and Literature* 11, No. 2, 2014, 131–47.

Forceville, Charles. "The Metaphor 'COLIN IS A CHILD' in Ian McEwan's, Harold Pinter's, and Paul Schrader's *The Comfort of Strangers.*" *Metaphor and Symbol* 14, No. 3, 1999, 179–98.

Formica, Serena. *Peter Weir: A Creative Journey from Australia to Hollywood.* Bristol: Intellect Books, 2012.

Foucault, Michel. *Discipline and Punish: The Birth of the* Prison. Translated by Alan Sheridan. New Edition. Westminster: Penguin, 1991.

Frazer, Bryant. "*Mishima: A Life in Four Chapters.*" September 4, 2018. Online at Film Freak Central, at https://www.filmfreakcentral.net/ffc/2018/09/mishima-a-life-in-four-chapters-criterion.html.

Friedberg, Anne. *Window Shopping: Cinema and the Postmodern.* Burbank: University of California Press, 1992.

Gaita, Paul. "Yaphet Kotto. *TCM: Turner Classic Movies.* ND. http://www.tcm.com/tcmdb/person/104926%7C158298/Yaphet-Kotto/biography.html.

Gaskill, Nicholas. *Chromographia: American Literature and the Modernization of Color.* Minneapolis: University of Minnesota Press, 2018.

Gatta, John. *Making Nature Sacred: Literature, Religion, and Environment in America from the Puritans to the Present.* Oxford: Oxford University Press, 2004.

George, Ann. *Kenneth Burke's "Permanence and Change": A Critical Companion.* Columbia: University of South Carolina Press, 2018.

Goodman, Nelson. *Ways of Worldmaking.* Indianapolis: Hackett Publishing Company, 1978.

Hamilton, Caroline. "Blank Looks: Reality TV And Memoir In *A Heartbreaking Work Of Staggering Genius*." *Australian Journal of American Studies* 28 No.2, 2009, 31–46.

Hamilton, John R. "Paul Schrader." *Senses of Cinema* 56, October 2010. http://sensesofcinema.com/2010/great-directors/paul-schrader.

Hansen, Mark B. N. "Algorithmic Sensibility: Reflections on the Post-Perceptual Image," in *Post-Cinema*, edited by Shane Denson and Julia Leyda. Falmer: Reframe, 2016. Available at http://reframe.sussex.ac.uk/post-cinema/. Last accessed May 30, 2019.

Harris, Hunter. "How Paul Schrader Made Ethan Hawke Float in *First Reformed*." *Vulture*. February 8, 2019. www.vulture.com/2019/02/paul-schrader-first-reformed-script-ethan-hawke-levitation-scene.html.

Haun, Harry. "From 'Taxi Driver' to 'First Reformed,' an Interview with Paul Schrader." *America: The Jesuit Review*. January 5, 2019. https://www.americamagazine.org/arts-culture/2019/01/05/taxi-driver-first-reformed-interview-paul-schrader.

Haynes, Todd. "Bob Dylan Times Six: An Interview With 'I'm Not There' Director Todd Haynes." Interview by Greil Marcus. *Rolling Stone*. November 29, 2007. https://www.rollingstone.com/movies/movie-news/bob-dylan-times-six-an-interview-with-im-not-there-director-todd-haynes-67251/.

Hewitt, Andrew. *Political Inversions: Homosexuality, Fascism, and the Modernist Imaginary*. Stanford: Stanford University, 1996.

Holberg, Jennifer L. *Shouts and Whispers: Twenty-One Writers Speak about their Writing and their Faith*. Grand Rapids, MI: Eerdmans, 2006.

Holderness, Graham. "'Half God, Half Man': Kazantzakis, Scorsese, and The Last Temptation." *Harvard Theological Review* 100, No. 1, 2007, 65–96.

Horvat, Gillian. "Paul Schrader's Priests and Transcendental Style: From *Dominion* to *First Reformed*." *Sight and Sound*. December 12, 2018. https://www.bfi.org.uk/news-opinion/sight-sound-magazine/features/paul-schrader-first-reformed-dominion-exorcist-priests-transcendental-style.

Hutcheon, Linda and Siobhan O'Flynn. *A Theory of Adaptation*. Abingdon and New York: Routledge, 2013.

Itzkoff, David. "It Ain't Pretty No More: See Paul Schrader's Outline for 'Raging Bull.'" *ArtsBeat* (blog), 2010. artsbeat.blogs.nytimes.com/2010/03/15/it-aint-pretty-no-more-see-paul-schraders-outline-for-raging-bull/.

Jackson, Kevin. "*Mishima*: Pen and Sword." June 30, 2008. Online in Criterion's On Film/Essays at https://www.criterion.com/current/posts/516-mishima-pen-and-sword/.

Jackson, Kevin (ed.). *Schrader on Schrader & Other Writings*. London: Faber and Faber, 1990.
Jaehne, Karen. "*Mishima*: An Interview." *Film Quarterly* 39, No. 3, Spring 1986, 11–17.
Jameson, Fredric. *Postmodernism, or the Cultural Logic of Late Capitalism*. Durham: Duke University Press, 1992.
Johnson, David T. "Adaptation and Fidelity," in *The Oxford Handbook of Adaptation Studies*. Edited by Thomas Leitch. New York: Oxford University Press, 2017, 87–100.
Julian of Norwich, and Clifton Wolters. *Revelations of Divine Love*. Harmondsworth: Penguin, 1990.
Kakutani, Michiko. "*Mishima*: Film Examines an Affair with Death." *New York Times*. September 15, 1985. https://www.nytimes.com/1985/09/15/arts/mishima-film-examines-an-affair-with-death.html.
Kaufman, Stanley. "Stanley Kaufman on Films." *The New Republic* 178 No. 6, 1978, 25.
Kazantzakis, Nikos. *The Last Temptation of Christ*. New York and London: Simon and Schuster, 1960.
Kearns, Laurel. "The Context of Eco-theology," in *The Blackwell Companion to Modern Theology*. Edited by Gareth Jones. Hoboken: Blackwell, 2004, 466–84.
Knight, Chris. "First Reformed is Paul Schrader's Directorial Redemption." *National Post*. May 31, 2018. https://nationalpost.com/entertainment/movies/first-reformed-is-paul-schraders-directorial-redemption.
Kohn, Eric. "Paul Schrader's Secret New Movie: How The Director Resurrected a Wild Nicolas Cage Performance Without Permission." *IndieWire*. December 11, 2017. https://www.indiewire.com/2017/12/paul-schrader-dying-of-the-light-nicolas-cage-dark-new-cut-1201905124/.
Kouvaros, George. *Paul Schrader*. Urbana: University of Illinois Press, 2008.
Lang, Brent. "Paul Schrader: The Human Race is Ending," *Variety*, September 15, 2017. https://variety.com/2017/film/news/paul-schrader-first-reformed-toronto-film-festival-1202560593.
Lasch, Christopher. *The Culture of Narcissism: American Life in an Age of Diminishing Expectations*. New York: W. W. Norton, 1978.
Lemire, Christy. "The Canyons." Rogerebert.com. August 2, 2013. https://www.rogerebert.com/reviews/the-canyons-2013.
Lindlof, Thomas R. *Hollywood under Siege: Martin Scorsese, the Religious Right, and the Culture Wars*. Lexington, KY: University Press of Kentucky, 2008.
Lindstrom, Alex. "On Mishima, and Feeling That One Exists." November 12, 2018. Online at PopMatters at https://www.popmatters.com/mishima-life-in-four-chapters-2612214742.html.

Lohmann, Friedrich. "Climate Justice and the Intrinsic Value of Creation: The Christian Understanding of Creation and its Holistic Implications," in *Religion in Environmental and Climate Change: Suffering, Values, Lifestyles*. Edited by Dieter Gerten and Sigurd Bergmann. London: Continuum, 2012, 85–106.

Lukes, H. N. "*American Gigolos*," in *America First: Naming the Nation in US Film*. Edited by Mandy Merck. New York: Routledge, 2007, 177–98.

Mai, William. "A Beginner's Guide to Transcendental Style." *Talk Film Society*. May 29, 2019. https://talkfilmsociety.com/articles/a-beginners-guide-to-transcendental-style.

Maizels, Neil. "Narcissus Rejects—the Surrender to Beauty vs Aesthetical Anguish," in *Aesthetic Conflict and its Clinical Relevance*. Edited by Meg Harris Williams. Np: Harris Meltzer Trust, 2018, 124–39.

Manovich, Lev. "What is Digital Cinema?", in *Post-Cinema*. Edited by Shane Denson and Julia Leyda. Falmer: Reframe, 2016. Available at http://reframe.sussex.ac.uk/post-cinema/. Last accessed May 30, 2019.

Maslin, Janet. "Review/Film; 'Last Temptation,' Scorsese's View Of Jesus' Sacrifice." *The New York Times*. August 12, 1988. www.nytimes.com/1988/08/12/movies/review-film-last-temptation-scorsese-s-view-of-jesus-sacrifice.html.

Mathiesen, Thomas. "The Viewer Society: Foucault's 'Panopticon' Revisited." *Theoretical Criminology: An International Journal* 1, No. 2, 1997, 215–32.

McCluskey, Audrey Thomas. "Richard Pryor: Comic Genius, Tortured Soul," in *Richard Pryor: The Life and Legacy of a "Crazy" Black Man*. Edited by Audrey Thomas McCluskey. Bloomington: Indiana University Press, 2008, 1–22.

McFarlane, Brian. *Novel to Film: An Introduction to the Theory of Adaptation*. Oxford and New York: Clarendon Press, 1996.

McHugh, Patrick. "Cultural Politics, Postmodernism, and White Guys: Affect in *Gravity's Rainbow*." *College Literature* 28, No. 2, 2001, 1–28.

McPherson, James Alan. "The New Comic Style of Richard Pryor (1975)," in *Richard Pryor: The Life and Legacy of a "Crazy" Black Man*. Edited by Audrey Thomas McCluskey. Bloomington: Indiana University Press, 2008, 201–13.

Merton, Thomas. *New Seeds of Contemplation*. New York: New Directions, 1972.

Merton, Thomas. *Seven Story Mountain*. New York: Harcourt, Brace, 1948.

Merton, Thomas. *The Sign of Jonas*. New York: Octagon Books, 1983.

Monnet, Jerome. 'The Everyday Image of Space in Los Angeles,' in *Looking for Los Angeles: Architecture, Film, Photography and the Urban Landscape*.

Edited by Charles Salas and Michael Roth. Los Angeles: Getty Research Institute, 2001, 289–306.
Morris, Wesley. "Future Imperfect." *Grantland.* August 8, 2013. Available at https://grantland.com/features/the-disappointing-elysium-terrible-canyons/. Last accessed May 27, 2019.
Mulvey, Laura. *Death 24× a Second: Stillness and the Moving Image.* London: Reaktion, 2006.
Murphy, Ian. "Corporeal prisons: dynamics of body and mise-en-scène in three films by Paul Schrader." PhD dissertation. University College Cork, 2015.
Murray, Simone. "Best Adapted Screenwriter?: The Intermedial Figure of the Screenwriter in the Contemporary Adaptation Industry," in *The Adaptation Industry: The Cultural Economy of Contemporary Literary Adaptation.* New York and London: Routledge, 2012, 131–55.
Nam, Sean. "Hungering and Thirsting for Righteousness: An Interview with Paul Schrader." *Cineaste,* Summer 2018, 18–23.
Naremore, James. *More Than Night: Film Noir in Its Contexts.* Burbank: University of California Press, 1998. Revised edition 2008.
Neale, Steve. "Masculinity as Spectacle: Reflections on Men and Mainstream Cinema," in *Screening the Male: Exploring Masculinities in Hollywood Cinema.* Edited by Steven Cohan and Ina Rae Hark. New York: Routledge, 1993, 9–23.
Nichols, Bill. "*American Gigolo*: Transcendental Style and Narrative Form." *Film Quarterly* 34, No. 4, Summer 1981, 8–13.
Nystrom, Derek. *Hard Hats, Rednecks, and Macho Men: Class in 1970s American Cinema.* New York: Oxford University Press, 2009.
Omi, Michael. "Race Relations in *Blue Collar*." *Jump Cut: A Review of Contemporary Media,* No. 26, 1981, 7–8. http://www.ejumpcut.org/archive/onlinessays/JC26folder/BlueCollar.html.
"Paul Schrader." *American Film* (Archive: 1975–92). New York: 1989.
Pinkerton, Nick. "Yukio Mishima, A Life in Four Chapters, and Countless Contradictions." *Village Voice.* December 17, 2008. Online at https://www.villagevoice.com/2008/12/17/yukio-mishima-a-life-in-four-chapters-and-countless-contradictions/.
Pipolo, Tony. *Robert Bresson: A Passion for Film.* New York: Oxford University Press, 2010.
Poland, David. "DP/30: Paul Schrader, First Reformed." YouTube video, 26:48. Posted May 15, 2018. https://www.youtube.com/watch?v=7yOZB2MJOLM.
Pope, Braxton. 'In Lindsay's Stardust Orbit.' *Vanity Fair.* August 2, 2013. Available at https://www.vanityfair.com/hollywood/2013/08/the-canyons-lindsay-lohan-producer. Last accessed May 29, 2019.

Poster, Mark. *The Mode of Information, Post-Structuralism and Social Context.* Chicago: University of Chicago Press, 1990.
Potvin, John. "From Gigolo to New Man: Armani, America, and the Textures of Narrative." *Fashion Theory: The Journal of Dress, Body and Culture* 15, No. 3, 2015, 279–98.
Powaski, Ronald E. *Thomas Merton on Nuclear Weapons.* Chicago: Loyola University Press, 1988.
Purdy, Jedediah. *After Nature: A Politics for the Anthropocene.* Cambridge: Harvard University Press, 2015.
Ravetto, Kriss. *The Unmaking of Fascist Aesthetics.* Minneapolis: University of Minnesota Press, 2001.
Raymond, Marc. *Hollywood's New Yorker: The Making of Martin Scorsese.* Albany, NY: SUNY Press, 2013.
Rayner, Jonathan, *The Films of Peter Weir.* 2nd Edition. New York and London: Continuum, 2003.
Rechler, Glenn. "*Patty Hearst*: An Interview with Paul Schrader." *Cinéaste* 17, No. 1, 1989, 31.
Reich, Steven A. *A Working People: A History of African American Workers Since Emancipation.* Lanham, MD: Rowman and Littlefield Publishers, 2014.
Reilly, Sue. "Richard Pryor's Ordeal." *People* 9, No. 10, 1978. https://people.com/archive/cover-story-richard-pryors-ordeal-vol-9-no-10/.
Rodrick, Stephen. "Here Is What Happens When You Cast Lindsay Lohan in Your Movie." *The New York Times.* January 10, 2013. https://www.nytimes.com/2013/01/13/magazine/here-is-what-happens-when-you-cast-lindsay-lohan-in-your-movie.html.
"'Rolling Thunder': Another Shattering Experience from the Writer of 'Taxi Driver.'" *Cinephilia & Beyond* at https://cinephiliabeyond.org/rolling-thunder-another-shattering-experience-from-the-author-of-taxi-driver/.
Ross, Stephanie. "Style in Art," in *The Oxford Handbook of Aesthetics.* Edited by Jerrold Levinson. Oxford and New York: Oxford University Press, 2003, 228–44.
Russell, Robert John, and Kirk Wegter-McNelly. "Science," in *The Blackwell Companion to Modern Theology.* Edited by Gareth Jones. Hoboken: Blackwell, 2004, 512–56.
Sarris, Andrew. *The American Cinema: Directors and Directions 1929–1968.* Accessed on Google Books. Available at https://books.google.com.au/books?id=_NGzswEACAAJ&dq=the+american+cinema+directions+and+directors&hl=en&sa=X&ved=0ahUKEwiy7Mvo34PjAhWx4nMBHRNYCq0Q6AEIKTAA. Last accessed May 30, 2019.
Saul, Scott. *Becoming Richard Pryor.* New York: Harper, 2014.

Schrader, Paul. *Paul Schrader: Collected Screenplays Volume 1: Taxi Driver, American Gigolo, Light Sleeper.* London: Faber and Faber, 2002.
Scorsese, Martin and Richard Corliss. "Body . . . And Blood." *Film Comment* 24, No. 5, 1988, 34–43.
Scott, A. O. "Review: 'First Reformed' Is an Epiphany. Ethan Hawke Is, Too." *The New York Times.* May 17, 2018. https://www.nytimes.com/2018/05/17/movies/first-reformed-review-paul-schrader-ethan-hawke.html.
Scranton, Roy. "Film in Review." *The Yale Review* 107, No. 1, January 2019, 185–98.
Shiach, Don. *The Films of Peter Weir: Visions of Alternative Realities.* London: C. Letts, 1993.
Sharf, Zack. "Paul Schrader Criticizes Brian De Palma as 'Trite' and Artistically Weak." *IndieWire.* June 29, 2019. https://www.indiewire.com/2019/06/paul-shrader-brian-de-palma-trite-artistically-weak-1202154370/.
Shaviro, Steven. *The Cinematic Body.* Minneapolis and London: University of Minnesota Press, 1993.
Shaviro, Steven. *Post Cinematic Affect.* London: Zero Books, 2010.
Simon, Alex. "Paul Schrader: The Hollywood Interview." January 8, 2013. http://thehollywoodinterview.blogspot.co.uk/2008/01/paul-schrader-hollywood-interview.html.
Simon, John. "Mishmashima." *National Review* 37, No. 21, November 1, 1985, 68–70.
Slotkin, Richard. *Regeneration Through Violence: The Mythology of the American Frontier, 1600–1860.* New Edition. Norman, OK: University of Oklahoma Press, 2000.
Smukler, Maya Montanez. *Liberating Hollywood: Women Directors & The Feminist Reform of 1970s American Cinema.* New Brunswick, NJ: Rutgers University Press, 2019.
Snee, Richard. "The Spirit and the Flesh: The Rhetorical Nature of *The Last Temptation of Christ.*" *Journal of Media and Religion* 4, No. 1, 45–61.
Sobchack, Vivian. "The Scene of the Screen: Envisioning Photographic, Cinematic and Electronic 'Presence,'" in *Post-Cinema.* Edited by Shane Denson and Julia Leyda. Falmer: Reframe, 2016. Available at http://reframe.sussex.ac.uk/post-cinema/. Last accessed May 30, 2019.
Sontag, Susan. "Fascinating Fascism." *Under the Sign of Saturn.* New York: Farrar, Straus, Giroux, 1980.
Sontag, Susan. "Spiritual Style in the Films of Robert Bresson," in *Robert Bresson (Revised)*, James Quandt (ed.), Toronto: Toronto International Film Festival Cinematheque, 2011, 55–69.

Stam, Robert. *Literature Through Film: Realism, Magic, and the Art of Adaptation*. 1st Edition. Malden, MA: Wiley-Blackwell, 2004.

Stiglegger, Martin. "Karneval des Todes. Luchinio Viscontis *La cauduta degli dei*," in *Film Konzepte Heft 48: Luchino Visconti*. Edited by Jörn Glasenapp. Munich: edition text+kritik, 2017.

Sypher, Wylie. *Rococo to Cubism in Art and Literature*. New York: Vintage Books, 1963.

Tait, R. Colin. "When Marty Met Bobby: Collaborative Authorship in *Mean Streets* and *Taxi Driver*," in *A Companion to Martin Scorsese*. Edited by Aaron Baker. Malden, MA: Wiley-Blackwell, 2015, 292–311.

Tate, Andrew. *Apocalyptic Fiction*. London: Bloomsbury, 2017.

Teti, Julia. "Director Paul Schrader Talks Transcendental Style in Film." May 6, 2018. https://theplaylist.net/paul-schrader-transcendental-style-20180506/.

The Playlist Staff. "The Essentials: The Directorial Career of Paul Schrader." *The Playlist*. August 5, 2013. https://theplaylist.net/retrospective-the-directorial-career-of-paul-schrader-20130805/#cb-content.

The Road to Bresson. DVD, directed by Leo De Boer and Jurriën Rood, 1984. New York: Criterion, 2003.

Theroux, Paul. *The Mosquito Coast*. Boston and New York: Houghton Mifflin, 1982.

Tobias, Scott. "Dominion: Prequel to the Exorcist." *The AV Club*. May 24, 2005. https://film.avclub.com/dominion-prequel-to-the-exorcist-1798200762.

"Urban Brooder." *Horizon* 21, No. 2, 1978, 64.

Tracey, Martin J. "Pope Francis on the Ecological Crisis: Its Nature, Causes, and Urgency," in *Interdisciplinary Essays on Environment and Culture: One Planet, One Humanity, and the Media*. Edited by Luigi Manca and Jean-Marie Kauth. Lanham: Lexington Books, 2016, 207–13.

Turkle, Sherry. *Alone Together: Why We Except More From Technology and Less From Each Other*. 3rd Edition. New York: Basic Books, 2017.

Turkle, Sherry. *Life on Screen: Identity in the Age of the Internet*. New York: Simon and Schuster, 1995.

Veldman, Robin Globus, Andrew Szasz, and Randolph Haluza-DeLay. "Introduction: Climate Change and Religion—A Review of Existing Research." *Journal for the Study of Religion, Nature and Culture* 6, No. 3, 2012, 255–75.

Vox, Lisa. *Existential Threats: American Apocalyptic Beliefs in the Technological Era*. Philadelphia: University of Pennsylvania Press, 2017.

White, Hayden. *Metahistory: The Historical Imagination in Nineteenth-Century Europe*. Baltimore and London: Johns Hopkins University Press, 1975.

Wikipedia. "Westfield Century City." Available at https://en.wikipedia.org/wiki/Westfield_Century_City. Last accessed May 29, 2019.

Wilson, John Howard. "The Empire Strikes Back: The Critical Reception of *Gandhi* and *Mishima*." *Reception: Texts, Readers, Audiences, History* 2, No. 2, Summer 2010, 94–115.

Wilson, John Howard. "Sources for a Neglected Masterpiece: Paul Schrader's *Mishima*." *Biography* 20, No. 3, Summer 1997, 265–83.

Wölfflin, Heinrich. *Principles of Art History: The Problem of the Development of Style in Modern Art*. Translated by Jonathan Blower. Los Angeles: Getty Research Institute, 2015.

Wood, Robin. *Hollywood From Vietnam to Reagan*. New York: Columbia University Press, 1986. Revised Edition. New York: Columbia University Press, 2003.

Yamato, Jen. "Paul Schrader Wages Silent Protest Over Re-Edited 'Dying of the Light.'" *Deadline*. October 16, 2014. https://deadline.com/2014/10/paul-schrader-dying-of-the-light-nicolas-cage-protest-853521/.

Index

Note: italic indicates illustrations; n indicates notes

A24, 9, 209
Adam Resurrected (Schrader, 2008), 8
adaptation theory, 88–90
Adler, Stella, 76
Affliction (Schrader, 1998), 6, 123, 215
Agel, Henri, 156
alienation, 4, 157, 161, 162–3, 211
Altman, Robert, 3
American Film, 90
American Gigolo (Schrader, 1980), 34–8, *37*
  boundaries between private and public, 164
  The Canyons (Schrader, 2013), 225
  The Conversation (Coppola, 1974), 222–3
  Julian Kay (character), 89, 108, 123, 136, 157–8, 166
  love, 27
  male nudity, 212
  Pickpocket (Bresson, 1959), 126, 168

Scarfiotti, 141, 227
sexuality, 4
Steadicam, 49
"transcendental style," 18–19
voyeurism, 40, 127
"withholding techniques," 216
Anger, Kenneth, 35
Animal House (Landis, 1978), 227
L'année dernière à Marienbad (Resnais, 1961), 141
Apocalypse Now (Coppola, 1979), 78
Attanasio, Paul, 107
auteurism, 3, 10, 12, 52, 55, 210
Auto Focus (Schrader, 2002), 7, 42–5, 108, 212
Ayfre, Amédée, 156, 157

Babington, Bruce, 93
Bailey, John, 35
Banks, Russell, 6
Baron, Cynthia, 77, 86n
Barthes, Roland, 89

Barton Fink (Coen, 1991), 3
Becker, Harold, 6
Been, Michael, *Fate*, 189
Bell, Andy, 181
Bentham, Jeremy, 161
Berg, Jeff, 99–100
Bergman, Ingmar
   First Reformed (Schrader, 2017)
      influence on, 9, 45, 193
   God's silence, 197–9, 204
   "transcendental style," 174, 216
Berry, Eavan, 179
Bertolucci, Bernardo, 141, 151–2, 222
Bickle, Travis (character)
   "existential hero," 127
   influence on films, 1
   influence on *Mishima: A Life in Four Chapters* (Schrader, 1985), 108–9
   and loneliness, 196
   "man in a room," 122–3
   and pornography, 129, 131
   and redemption, 190
   as underdog, 133
Bigelow, Kathryn, 213–14
biopics, 111–14, 118n
Biskind, Peter, *Easy Riders, Raging Bulls*, 10
Bliss, Michael, 109
Bloom, Harold, 54–7
   The Western Canon, 52
Blow Out (De Palma, 1981), 163, 223
Blue Collar (Schrader, 1978), 3, 27, 71–86, *71*, *84*, 226
Body Double (De Palma, 1984), 59–60
Boetticher, Budd, 223
Bogarde, Dirk, 146
Boozer, Jack, 90
"Born in the USA," 5

Bresson, Robert
   Christianity, 19, 25
   Diary of a Country Priest (Bresson, 1949), 6, 157
   First Reformed (Schrader, 2017)
      influence on, 9, 45
   genre, 224
   inaction, 126–7
   memory frame, 116
   music, 202
   Notes on the Cinematograph, 123–4, 191
   Patty Hearst (Schrader, 1988)
      influence on, 134
   Pickpocket (Bresson, 1959), 4, *133*, *136*, 168
   Schrader's fascination with, 122–8
   spirituality, 191–3
   starves spectator's eyes, 218
   "transcendental style," 2, 21–2, 29, 115, 216
   voiceover, 113
   "women in their rooms," 137
   see also entries for individual films
Bringing Out The Dead (Scorsese, 1999), 6, 108, 190
Brodsly, David, 64
Brody, Richard, 229
Bruzzi, Stella, 167
Burke, Kenneth, *Permanence and Change: An Anatomy of Purpose*, 17, 27–9
Buruma, Ian, 107, 109, 120n

La caduta degli dei (Visconti, 1969), 140, 146–7, 151
Cage, Nicolas, 6, 8, 190, 214, 220–1
Cahiers du Cinéma, 12, 87
Calvinism, 2, 3–4, 190–1
Canby, Vincent, 79, 103n, 106–7
Cannes, 106, 125

"Canon Fodder," Schrader, Paul, 49, 52–7, 66, 67
canons of American cinema, 51–3, 61–7
The Canyons (Schrader, 2013), 57–61, *160, 164*, 219
  cast, 214–15
  Lohan in, 8
  Los Angeles, *59*, 61–7
  male nudity, 212
  slow cinema, 223
  surveillance culture, 155–70
  Taxi Driver (Scorsese, 1976) similar sequence, 225
  Van Sant, 220
Carrie (De Palma, 1975), 130
Cascio, James, 162
Cassavetes, John, 222
Cat People (Tourneur, 1942), 4, 128
Cat People (Schrader, 1982), 122–38, *133*
  alienation, 4
  Bailey, 35
  philosophical, 7, 224
  redemption, 108
  Schrader's identification with, 109
  trial for Schrader to make, 117N
Cavani, Liliana, 146–7, 149
Certain Women (Reichardt, 2016), 226
Christianity, 1–2, 19, 25–7, 32n, 154n, 179–85
Cinema of the Face, 215
City Hall (Becker, 1996), 6
Clift, Montgomery, 53
climate change, 173–9, 186
Cocks, Jay, 5, 90, 93–5, 100
Coen Brothers, 3

Columbia Pictures, 9
The Comfort of Strangers (Schrader, 1990), 38–41, *41*, 139–54, *142, 148*
  authorship, 5–6
  camera jerkiness, 43
  Colin (character) as child, 144–6, 149, 153, 154n
  mobile camera, 215
  opulent style, 38–41
  Walken in, 220
The Conformist (Bertolucci, 1970), 34–5, 141, 226
Conner, Bruce, 221
Conrad, Mark, 95
The Conversation (Coppola, 1974), 163, 222–3
Coppola, Francis Ford, 78, 106, 118n, 222–3
Coppola, Sophia, 193
Crane, Bob, 7, 42–5
"crisis of the body," 161
Cusack, John, 6

Dafoe, Willem, 6, 93–4, 212, 214, 220–1
The Damned (Visconti, 1969), 140, 146–7, 151
"Dangerous Beauty," 150, *151*
D'Annunzio, Gabriele, 110
Dargis, Manohla, 155
Dark (TV series, 2017), 8
De Niro, Robert, 3, 62, 74, 77–8, 123, 214
De Palma, Brian, 3, 17, 49, 59–60, 130, 223
De Zengotita, Thomas, 165
Death in Venice (Visconti, 1971), 139–40, *141*, 150–1
"Decisive Moment," 21, 29
Deen, James, 8, 57–8

degradation, 178–9, 186
Deleuze, Gilles, 22, 32n, 52
   Postscript on the Societies of Control, 161
The Devil, Probably (Bresson, 1977), 193
Diary of a Country Priest (Bresson, 1949), 6, 45, 124, 157, 190, 193–4, 201
"disparity," 157
Dog Eat Dog (Schrader, 2016), 8–9, 212, 220–2, 228
Dolan, Xavier, 222
Dominion: A Prequel to the Exorcist (Schrader, 2005), 7, 129, 190, 212
Dougherty, Joseph, 6
Dreyer, Carl Theodor, 2, 21, 45, 191
The Duellists (Scott, 1977), 78
The Dying of The Light (Schrader, 2014), 8
Dylan, Bob, 4
Dzhumaylo, Olga A., 141

Eames, Charles, 49
Easton Ellis, Bret, 8, 57, 212, 219, 225
Easy Rider (Hopper, 1969), 2
Ebert, Roger, 106, 107, 108, 113, 118n
eco-theology, 171–88
Eggert, Brian, 108, 109–11
"electronic presence," 61
Ellroy, James, 228
entrapment, 141
Evans, Peter W., 93
Everett, Rupert, 140, 145, 146
"existential hero," 122–3, 125, 127–9, 134, 157
"existential horror," 128–9

The Exorcist (Friedkin, 1973), 7
Exorcist: The Beginning (Harlin, 2004), 7

Facebook, 218
Fassbinder, Rainer Werner, 140
female gaze, 225–6
Film Comment, 2, 76, 100
Fingers (Toback, 1978), 78
First Reformed (Schrader, 2017), 45–8, 171–88, 177, 178, 189–207, 194, 195
  aspect ratio, 226
  budget, 210
  camera movement, 217–18
  cast, 214–15
  "dead time," 175
  "directorial redemption," 155
  dream sequence, 224–5
  looking and being looked at, 34
  male body in crisis, 169
  "man in a room," 123
  O'Connor, 220
  preservation, 182–5, 186
  redemption, 1–2, 211
  religion, 179–85
  sexuality and violence, 131–2
  slow cinema, 223
  style, 18, 29–30
  "transcendental style," 9, 126, 216
  troubled masculinity, 108
Flynn, John, 3
Forceville, Charles, 144–5, 153
Ford, Gerald, 224
Ford, Harrison, 97
Ford, John, 3
Forever Mine (Schrader, 1999), 7
Foucault, Michel, 161
Frankenheimer, John, 7
Frazer, Bryant, 108, 119n

freeze frames at the end of films, 17, 31n, 71–2, 73, 121n
French New Wave, 12
Friedberg, Anne, 61
Funk, Nolan, 58

Genet, Jean, 140
genre, 223–4
George, Ann, 28
Gere, Richard, 4, 168, 212
Gesamtkunstwerk, 111
Glee (TV series, 2009-15), 58
God, humans and, 172
Godard, Jean-Luc, 9, 49, 222, 225
God's silence, 197–202
Goldblum, Jeff, 8
Goodman, Nelson, "The Status of Style," 25–6
Gravity's Rainbow, 166

Hamilton, John R., 108, 119n, 156–7
Hansen, Mark B. N., 65
Hardcore (Schrader, 1979)
  Affliction (Schrader, 1998), 6
  Calvinism, 108, 130
  creative challenges, 3–4
  personal, 5
  redemption, 190
  Schrader as director, 27
  Schrader dismissive of, 226–7
  self-destructive male behavior, 89
Harlin, Renny, 7
Harrelson, Woody, 7–8, 214
Harry Ransom Center, University of Texas, 8, 88
Hawke, Ethan, 9, 214–15
Haynes, Todd, 4
HBO, 6
Hellman, Jerome, 88, 99–100
Hershey, Barbara, 90
Hewett, Andrew, 152, 153
Hitchcock, Alfred, 3

Hogan's Heroes (TV series, 1965-71), 42–5
Holderness, Graham, 91
Hollywood Production Code, 4, 128
homosexuality, 118n, 146
Horizon, 78
Human Behavior, 72
Hutcheon, Linda, *A Theory of Adaptation*, 88–9

ICM, 99–100
Ida (Pawlikowski, 2014), 189
I'm Not There (Haynes, 2007), 4
Ishioka, Eiko, 113
Italian neo-decadence, 139–54
Itzkoff, David, 92

Jackson, Kevin, 18, 106, 108, 110, 111–12, 116, 121n
Jaehne, Karen, 110, 111, 118n
Japan, film banned in, 106, 120n
Japanese language, 106, 115, 118n, 120n
Japanese cinema, 2–3

Kael, Pauline, 2, 146
Kakutani, Michicko, 108
Kaniuk, Yoram, 8
Kay, Julian (character)
  disoriented, 136
  identity construction, 166
  like Mishima, 108
  as loner, 89
  male creation, 123
  secular and sacred, 157–8
Kazantzakis, Nikos, 87–8, 90–5, 101
  The Saviors of God, 101
Kearns, Laurel, 181
Keitel, Harvey, 3, 71, 73–8, 80–5, 84
Kickstarter, 8, 228
Kierkegaard, Søren, 25
Kinski, Natassja, 128

Knight, Chris, 155
Kotto, Yaphet, 3, 73, 75–6, 76, 80–5
Kouvaros, George
  biopics, 111
  film canon, 51
  freeze frames at the end of films, 121n
  identity and performance, 108
  intellectual form, 193
  Mishima: A Life in Four Chapters (Schrader, 1985), 113, 118n
  Paul Schrader, 31n
  Schrader's contradictions, 19
  self-realization, 190
  style, 18
Kubrick, Stanley, 219
Kustom Kar Kommandos (Anger, 1965), 35

Lady Sings the Blues (Furie, 1972), 78
Lambert, Gavin, *The Slide Area: Scenes of Hollywood Life*, 36
Lasch, Christopher, *The Culture of Narcissism*, 165
The Last Temptation of Christ (Scorsese, 1988), 5, 87–104, 94, 108, 214
Last Year at Marienbad (Resnais, 1961), 141
leaning, lean in, 202–204
Lemire, Christy, 155
Leonard, Elmore, 6
Lewton, Val, 4
liberty, 124–5, 129, 131, 137, 141
Light of Day (Schrader, 1987), 5
Light Sleeper (Schrader, 1992), 29, 30
  Dafoe in, 214
  "existential hero," 123, 127
  music, 205n
  personal, 6

Pickpocket (Bresson, 1959), 126
prison, 137
"transcendental style," 192
Lindstrom, Alex, 114
Lohan, Lindsay, 8, 57–8, 214–15
Lohman, Friedrich, 181
loneliness, 155–6, 196
Los Angeles, 53–67, 57, 59, 158–9, 163–40, 168
love and silence, 189–207
Lucas, George, 106, 118n
Lukes, H. N., 120n
Lynch, David, 67, 220–1, 223

Mai, William, 174
Maizels, Neil, 150
male gaze, 225–6
male nudity, 66, 128, 212
Malick, Terence, 221, 228, 230
A Man Escaped (Bresson, 1956), 124
"man in a room," 108, 113, 122, 137
Mann, Thomas, *Death in Venice*, 139
Marxism, 19, 25–7
masculine authority, 166–7
McCluskey, Audrey Thomas, 78
McEwan, Ian, 5–6, 38–40, 139, 144–5
McFarlane, Brian, *Novel to Film*, 89
McHugh, Patrick, 166
McPherson, James Alvin, 77
Mean Streets (Scorsese, 1973), 77–8
mechanical gaze, 162
Meek's Cutoff, 225–6
Méliès, Georges, 215
memory frame, 113, 116, 121n
Merton, Thomas
  New Seeds of Contemplation, 201
  The Seven Story Mountain, 195–6, 197, 198
  The Sign of Jonas, 189
"Method" acting, 74, 76–8, 85, 86n
MeToo, 227

Meyers, Nancy, 213–14
Mirror (Tarkovsky, 1975), 202
mise-en-scène, 41, 77, 145, 167
Mishima, Yukio, 4, 121n
 and Hitlerism, 120n
 My Friend Hitler, 110
Mishima: A Life in Four Chapters (Schrader, 1985), 10, 105–21, *112*
 banned in Japan, 106, 120n
 and critics, 107–8
 freeze frames at the end of films, 3n
 self-destructive male behavior, 89
 suicide, 105, 108, 111–14, *115*, 117, 121n, 192
 visual invention, 4, 5
Monnet, Jerome, "The Everyday Imagery of Space in Los Angeles," 63–4
Moore, Sarah, 224
Moroder, Giorgio, 129
Morris, Wesley, 66–7
Morte a Venezia (Visconti, 1971), 139–40, 141, 150–1
The Mosquito Coast (Schrader, 1985), 5, 87–104, 97, 103n
Mother, Jugs, and Speed (Yates, 1976), 78
movement and meaning, 33–50
Mr Robot (TV series, 2015), 227–8
Mulvey, Laura, 162
Murch, Walter, 223
Murphy, Ian, 161
music, 151–2, 202–3

Naremore, James, 63, 120n
Nashville (Altman, 1975), 3
National Post, 155
National Review, 107
NBC, 79
Neale, Steve, 160
neo-noir, 228

New Cinema, 229
New Hollywood, 10
The New Republic, 72
New York Film Critics Circle, 189
New York Review of Books, 107
New York Times, 79, 92, 106–7, 155
New York Times Magazine, 77
Newsweek, 224
Nichols, Bill, 18–19, 25, 27
Nicholson, Jack, 97
Nietzsche, Friedrich, 111, 120n
The Night Porter (Cavani, 1974), 146–7, 149
Nystrom, Derek, 73

Obama, President, 175
Obscure Object of Desire (Buñuel, 1977), 223
Obsession (1976), 3
O'Connor, Flannery, 220
 Wise Blood, 203
Old Boyfriends (Tewkesbury, 1979), 3
Omi, Michael, 72–3
Ordet (Dreyer, 1955), 45
Orthodox Church of America, 91
Ozu, Jasujirō, 2, 21, 29, 113, 115–16, 191

Pacino, Al, 6
panopticisme, 161–2
Pasolini, Pier Paolo, 140, 152, 153
Patriotism (Dômoto and Mishima, 1966), 121n
Patty Hearst (Schrader, 1988), 5, 108, 121n, 122–38, *136*, 213
Pawlikowski, Pawel, 189
Peckinpah, Sam, 2
People, 79
Pesci, Joe, 3
Pickpocket (Bresson, 1959), 122–6
 budget, 210
 camera movement, 45

ending used in films, 4, 6, 132,
    136–7, 168
  review of, 2
  slow cinema, 219
piety, 27–9
Pinkerton, Nick, 109–10
Pinter, Harold, 5–6, 38, 41, 139,
    144–5, 215
  The Servant, 141, 146
Pipolo, Tony, 124
Pitt, Brad, 214
Plan B, 214
Poitier, Sidney, role of decent black
    guy, 75
Poland, David, 190
Pope, Braxton, 220
Il portiere di notte (Cavani, 1974),
    146–7, 149
Poster, Randall, 161
Powaski, Ronald E., 198
prison, 124–5, 131, 136–7, 141
Pryor, Richard, 3, 71, 73–85, *84*
Puccini, Giacomo, 152

Querelle (Fassbinder, 1982), 140

racial tension, 71–86, 178
Raging Bull (Scorsese, 1980), 3, 77,
    87, 108
Ravetto, Kriss, 140, 152
Raymond, Marc, 120n
Rayner, Jonathan, 96
Rechler, Glenn, 106
reflexivity, 7, 8, 124, 164
Reichardt, Kelly, 226
Renoir, Jean, 1, 211, 229
The Revenant (TV series), 227–8
Richard Pryor: Live in Concert
    (Margolis, 1979), 79
The Richard Pryor Show (TV series,
    1977), 79
Richardson, Natasha, 133

Riefenstahl, Leni, 151
Ritchie, Guy, 228
RKO, 4
Rodrick, Stephen, 155
RogerEbert.com, 155
Rolling Thunder (Flynn, 1977), 3,
    120n

Sadean System, 139–54
Salò, or the 120 Days of Sodom
    (Pasolini, 1975), 140, 152, 153
Sarossy, Paul, 215
Sarris, Andrew, 52
Saul, Scott, 78, *84*
Scarfiotti, Ferdinando, 4, 35, 141, 227
Schrader, Chieko, 106
Schrader, Leonard, 74, 106, 111
Schrader, Paul
  American Film, 90
  interview with, 209–30, *210, 213*
  as screenwriter/adaptor, 88–90
  style, 17–32
  teaching of films, 229
  Writing
  "Canon Fodder," 49, 52–3, 54–7,
      66, 67
  "Notes on Film Noir," 2, 18
  Schrader on Schrader, 32n
  *Transcendental Style in Film: Ozu,
      Bresson, Dreyer*; authorship, 23–4;
      Bresson, 123, 125–7; Calvinism,
      2, 190–1; canons of American
      cinema, 51–2; film criticism, 156;
      First Reformed (Schrader, 2017),
      45, 173–4, 189–90; sexuality,
      140–1; style, 18, 20–2, 25, 31–2n;
      "withholding techniques," 176
  Films and TV
  Adam Resurrected (Schrader,
      2008), 8
  Affliction (Schrader, 1998), 6,
      123, 215

Schrader, Paul (*cont.*)
   American Gigolo (Schrader, 1980), 34–8, *37*; boundaries between private and public, 164; *The Canyons* (Schrader, 2013), 225; *The Conversation* (Coppola, 1974), 222–3; Julian Kay (character), 89, 108, 123, 136, 157–8, 166; love, 27; male nudity, 212; *Pickpocket* (Bresson, 1959), 126, 168; Scarfiotti, 141, 227; sexuality, 4; Steadicam, 49; "transcendental style," 18–19; voyeurism, 40, 127; "withholding techniques," 216
   Auto Focus (Schrader, 2002), 7, 42–5, 108, 212
   Blue Collar (Schrader, 1978), 3, 27, 71–86, *71*, *84*, 226
   Bringing Out The Dead (Scorsese, 1999), 6, 108, 190
   The Canyons (Schrader, 2013), 57–61, 160, 164, 219; cast, 214–15; Lohan in, 8; Los Angeles, 59, 61–7; male nudity, 212; slow cinema, 223; surveillance culture, 155–70; *Taxi Driver* (Scorsese, 1976) similar sequence, 225; Van Sant, 220
   Cat People (Schrader, 1982), 122–38, *133*; alienation, 4; Bailey, 35; philosophical, 7, 224; redemption, 108; Schrader's identification with, 109; trial for Schrader to make, 117n
   City Hall (Becker, 1996), 6
   The Comfort of Strangers (Schrader, 1990), 38–41, *41*, 139–54, *142*, *148*; authorship, 5–6; camera jerkiness, 43; Colin (character) as child, 144–6, 149, 153, 154n; mobile camera, 215; Walken in, 220

   Dark (TV series, 2017), 8
   Dog Eat Dog (Schrader, 2016), 8–9, 212, 220–2, 228
   Dominion: A Prequel to the Exorcist (Schrader, 2005), 7, 129, 190, 212
   The Dying of The Light (Schrader, 2014), 8
   First Reformed (Schrader, 2017), 45–8, 171–88, *177*, *178*, 189–207, *194*, *195*; aspect ratio, 226 budget, 210; camera movement, 217–18; cast, 214–15; "dead time," 175; "directorial redemption," 155; dream sequence, 224–5; looking and being looked at, 34; male body in crisis, 169; "man in a room," 123; O'Connor, 220; preservation, 182–5, 186; redemption, 1–2, 211; religion, 179–85; sexuality and violence, 131–2; slow cinema, 223; style, 18, 29–30; "transcendental style," 9, 126, 216; troubled masculinity, 108
   Forever Mine (Schrader, 1999), 7
   Hardcore (Schrader, 1979); *Affliction* (Schrader, 1998), 6; Calvinism, 108, 130; creative challenges, 3–4; personal, 5; redemption, 190; Schrader as director, 27; Schrader dismissive of, 226–7; self-destructive male behavior, 89
   The Last Temptation of Christ (Scorsese, 1988), 5, 87–104, *94*, 108, 214
   Light of Day (Schrader, 1987), 5
   Light Sleeper (Schrader, 1992), 29, 30; Dafoe in, 214; "existential hero," 123, 127; music, 205n; personal, 6; *Pickpocket* (Bresson, 1959), 126; prison, 137; "transcendental style," 192

INDEX 257

Mishima: A Life in Four Chapters (Schrader, 1985), 10, 105–21, 112; banned in Japan, 106, 120n; and critics, 107–8; freeze frames at the end of films, 31n; self-destructive male behavior, 89; suicide, 105, 108, 111–14, 115, 117, 121n, 192; visual invention, 4, 5
The Mosquito Coast (Schrader, 1985), 5, 87–104, 97, 103n
Obsession (1976), 3
Old Boyfriends (Tewkesbury, 1979), 3
Patty Hearst (Schrader, 1988), 5, 108, 121n, 122–38, 136, 213
Raging Bull (Scorsese, 1980), 3, 77, 87, 108
Rolling Thunder (Flynn, 1977), 3, 120n
Taxi Driver (Scorsese, 1976); based on a problem, 217; *Bringing Out The Dead* (Scorsese, 1999), 6; *The Canyons* (Schrader, 2013), 62; cast, 214; De Niro, 77; dream sequence, 224–5;"existential hero," 127; fascism, 120n; influence on films, 8–10, 12; "man in a room," 122–3; redemption, 190, 211; Scorsese, 87; screenwriting, 74; self-destructive male behavior, 193; teaching of films, 229; Travis Bickle (character), 1, 108–9, 129, 131, 133, 196
Touch, 6
The Walker (Schrader, 2007), 7–8, 108, 127, 214
Witch Hunt (TV movie, Schrader, 1994), 6
The Yakuza (Pollack, 1974), 2–3
Scorpio Rising (Anger, 1963), 35
Scorsese, Martin

Bringing Out The Dead (Scorsese, 1999), 6
casting, 214
gangster films, 228
Keitel, Harvey, 76–8
The Last Temptation of Christ (Scorsese, 1988), 5, 17, 87, 90–5, 100
music, 17
Raging Bull (Scorsese, 1980) rewrite, 3
seen as more important than Schrader, 10
Steadicam, 49
Taxi Driver (Scorsese, 1976), 74, 120n, 123, 224
visual approach, 1
see also entries for individual films
Scott, A. O., 184
Scott, George C., 3–4
Scott, Ridley, 78, 210
Scranton, Roy, 18
The Searchers (Ford, 1956), 3
self-destructive male behavior, 7, 8, 89, 95, 100, 108, 151, 193
sexuality, 4, 7, 129–32, 139–40
Shaviro, Steven, 22, 54
Post Cinematic Affect, 56
Siegel, Don, 74
Silver Streak (Hiller, 1976), 78
Simon, John, 107, 118n
Sir Crazy (Poitier, 1980), 79
Slotkin, Richard, 167
slow cinema, 219–20, 221
sound in, 223
Sobchak, Vivian, 61
Sontag, Susan, 124–5
"Fascinating Fascism," 151
Spinotti, Dante, 39
spirituality, 7, 19, 26, 27, 45, 129, 168
Springsteen, Bruce, 5

Stam, Robert, *Literature Through Film*, 88–9
Stanislavski system, 76
"stasis," 21, 29, 67, 126, 132, 158–9, 192–3
Steadicam, 49
Stein, Gertrude, 24
Strasberg, Lee, 76
"superpanopticon," 161–2
surveillance culture, 155–70
Sypher, Wylie, *Rococo to Cubism in Art and Literature*, 31–2n

Tait, R. Colin, 74
Tarantino, Quentin, 221, 228
Tarkovsky, Andrei, 202, 218
Tarr, Bela, 219
Taxi Driver (Scorsese, 1976)
  based on a problem, 217
  Bringing Out The Dead (Scorsese, 1999), 6
  The Canyons (Schrader, 2013), 62
  cast, 214
  De Niro, 77
  dream sequence, 224–5
  "existential hero," 127
  fascism, 120n
  influence on films, 8–10, 12
  "man in a room," 122–3
  redemption, 190, 211
  Scorsese, 87
  screenwriting, 74
  self-destructive male behavior, 193
  teaching of films, 229
  Travis Bickle (character), 1, 108–9, 129, 131, 133, 196
Taylor, Elizabeth, 67
television, 227–8
Tender Buttons, 24
Tewkesbury, Joan, 3
theatre experience, 228–9

Theroux, Paul, 88, 95–9
Thieves Like Us (Altman, 1973), 3
time-image, 22, 32n, 52
Toback, James, 78
Touch, 6
Tourneur, Jacques, 4, 128
"transcendental style," 2, 18–24, 29–30, 156–7, 190–7
  Bresson, 134
  First Reformed (Schrader, 2017), 173–5, 176, 180, 182, 215–16
  Mishima: A Life in Four Chapters (Schrader, 1985), 114–16
Transcendental Style in Film: Ozu, Bresson, Dreyer
  authorship, 23–4
  Bresson, 123, 125–7
  Calvinism, 2, 190–1
  canons of American cinema, 51–2
  film criticism, 156
  First Reformed (Schrader, 2017), 45, 173–4, 189–90
  sexuality, 140–1
  style, 18, 20–2, 25, 31–2n
  "withholding techniques," 176
Tree of Life (Malick, 2011), 219, 223
The Turin Horse (Tarr and Hranitsky, 2011), 219
Turkle, Sherry, *Alone Together*, 163, 165
Twin Peaks: The Return (video), 221
2 or 3 Things I Know About Her (Godard, 1967), 9

Universal Pictures, 79, 101
"unmotivated" camera, 33–50
Uptown Saturday Night (Poitier, 1974), 78

Van Sant, Gus, 220
Vertigo (Hitchcock, 1957), 3

Visconti, Luchino, 139–40, 141, 150–1
 The Damned (Visconti, 1969), 140, 146–7, 151
Vox, Lisa, 178, 185
voyeurism, 38–43, 151, 153, 165, 225–6

Wagner, Richard, 111, 120n
Walken, Christopher, 220
The Walker (Schrader, 2007), 7–8, 108, 127, 214
Warner Brothers, 7, 106, 118n, 119n
Washington Post, 107
Weir, Peter, 5, 90, 95, 97–100
Welles, Orson, 52
White, Hayden, 24
Who's That Knocking at My Door (Scorsese, 1967), 77–8
Wild At Heart (Lynch, 1990), 220–1
Wilder, Gene, 78, 79
Winter Light (Bergman, 1963), 9, 45, 174, 193, 197–9, 204

Wise Blood (Huston, 1979), 220
Witch Hunt (TV movie, Schrader, 1994), 6
"withholding techniques," 126, 176, 190–3, 215–16
Witness (Weir, 1985), 97
Wolfe, Thomas, *God's Lonely Man*, 196
Wölfflin, Heinrich, 20, 22
 Principles of Art History, 22–3
women, 122–38, 212–13
Wood, Robin, 120n
 Hollywood From Vietnam to Reagan, 10
Writers Guild of America (WGA), 90, 99–100

The Yakuza (Pollack, 1974), 2–3
Yates, Peter, 78
Yelchin, Anton, 8
YouCastIt, 215